JavaScript Frameworks for Modern Web Dev

Tim Ambler

Nicholas Cloud

Apress®

JavaScript Frameworks for Modern Web Dev

ISBN-13 (pbk): 978-1-4842-0663-8

ISBN-13 (electronic): 978-1-4842-0662-1

Managing Director: Welmoed Spahr
Lead Editor: Louise Corrigan
Technical Reviewer: Robin Hawkes
Editorial Board: Steve Anglin, Mark Beckner, Gary Cornell, Louise Corrigan, James DeWolf,
    Jonathan Gennick, Robert Hutchinson, Michelle Lowman, James Markham, Matthew Moodie,
    Jeffrey Pepper, Douglas Pundick, Ben Renow-Clarke, Gwenan Spearing, Matt Wade, Steve Weiss
Coordinating Editor: Kevin Walter
Copy Editor: Bill McManus
Compositor: SPi Global
Indexer: SPi Global
Artist: SPi Global
Cover Designer: Crest

Distributed to the book trade worldwide by Springer Science+Business Media New York, 233 Spring Street, 6th Floor, New York, NY 10013. Phone 1-800-SPRINGER, fax (201) 348-4505, e-mail orders-ny@springer-sbm.com, or visit www.springeronline.com. Apress Media, LLC is a California LLC and the sole member (owner) is Springer Science + Business Media Finance Inc (SSBM Finance Inc). SSBM Finance Inc is a Delaware corporation.

For information on translations, please e-mail rights@apress.com, or visit www.apress.com.

Apress and friends of ED books may be purchased in bulk for academic, corporate, or promotional use. eBook versions and licenses are also available for most titles. For more information, reference our Special Bulk Sales–eBook Licensing web page at www.apress.com/bulk-sales.

Any source code or other supplementary material referenced by the author in this text is available to readers at www.apress.com/. For detailed information about how to locate your book's source code, go to www.apress.com/source-code/.

There was a young lady named Laura,
Who was a beautiful señora.
Her love and assurance
Was a frequent occurrence
Which allowed me to write this book for yah.

—Tim

Dedicated to Brittany who supported me and gave me space
during the long hours that writing demands.

—Nicholas

Contents at a Glance

Contents

About the Authors

Tim Ambler is a software engineer from Nashville, Tennessee. His passion for programming follows in the footsteps of his father, who introduced him to computers at a young age with a Commodore 64. Tim is the author of several popular open source projects, one of which (whenLive) has been featured by GitHub's staff. An occasional conference speaker and frequent writer, Tim has been referenced multiple times in online publications such as JavaScript Weekly and Node Weekly. He currently lives in the 12 South area with his wife, Laura, and two cats. You can follow him on Twitter at @tkambler.

Nicholas Cloud is a software developer who lives in the very humid city of St. Louis. For over a decade he has forged his skills into a successful career. He has developed web applications, web services, and desktop software on diverse platforms with JavaScript, C#, and PHP. A strong proponent of open source software, Nicholas contributes to userland projects and has written several of his own open source libraries libraries. He speaks at a variety of user groups and conferences and writes books, technical articles, and blog posts in his spare time. He opines on Twitter at @nicholascloud.

About the Technical Reviewer

Robin Hawkes lives to learn and thrives on combining design and code to solve problems. He's the author of *Foundation HTML5 Canvas* (Apress, 2011), which is all about making games with JavaScript. He's also the one-man band behind ViziCities, a WebGL-powered 3D city visualization platform. In a previous life Robin worked in worldwide developer relations at both Mozilla and Pusher.

Acknowledgments

This book would not have been possible without the encouragement and support of a number of people:

Nicholas Cloud, my friend and co-author, without whom this book would be much more limited in scope and depth. His knowledge, experience, and steadfast dedication to this project have been immeasurably helpful. Thank you.

Louise Corrigan, Kevin Walter, Christine Ricketts, Melissa Maldonado, and the rest of the staff at Apress who supported us throughout the course of this project. I am grateful for the invitation that was extended to embark upon this journey and for the ongoing support that you have provided.

Robin Hawkes, our technical reviewer. The examples and source code included with this book have greatly benefited from his keen insight and sharp eye.

James Coglan, the creator of Faye. Thank you for taking the time to share your technical expertise and feedback.

My friends and colleagues Greg Jones, Jeff Crump, Seth Steele, Jon Zumbrun, and Brian Hiatt. I am grateful for your feedback and encouragement.

—Tim

Acknowledgements are slippery things. I have so many debts, and so little space to repay.

First, the debt to my co-author Tim who reached out and invited me on this journey. We've never met in person but worked remotely as co-workers for about half a year—enough time for each of us to leave an impression on each other across the miles. For his trust, encouragement, and constant effort I am grateful.

Second, my debt to the staff at Apress who guided us through the publishing process: Kevin, Louise, Christine, and Melissa. Their patience and careful guidance spared you, the reader, from no small amount of cringes, and kept me on my toes during the entire writing process. They are all sharp professionals with whom I hope to work again some day.

Third, I am indebted to Robin for his excellent technical reviews; for reading and executing more code samples than a developer should ever be tasked with groking.

Finally, I cannot repay the subject-matter expertise I gleaned from Michael Jackson (@mjackson) while researching Mach, and Ryan Niemeyer (@RPNiemeyer) while researching Knockout—I can only pay it forward to you, the reader.

—Nicholas

Introduction

They tell me we're living in an information age, but none of it seems to be the information I need or brings me closer to what I want to know. In fact (I'm becoming more and more convinced) all this electronic wizardry only adds to our confusion, delivering inside scoops and verdicts about events that have hardly begun: a torrent of chatter moving at the speed of light, making it nearly impossible for any of the important things to be heard.

—Matthew Flaming, *The Kingdom of Ohio*

The notion that "technology moves quickly" is a well-worn aphorism, and with good reason: technology does move quickly. But at this moment, JavaScript in particular is moving very quickly indeed—much like that "torrent of chatter moving at the speed of light" that Matthew Flaming refers to in *The Kingdom of Ohio*. The language is in the midst of what many have called a renaissance, brought about by the rapidly increasing sophistication of browser-based applications and the rising popularity of JavaScript on the server, thanks to Node.js.

An almost feverish pace of innovation is occurring within the JavaScript community that, while endlessly fascinating to follow, also presents some unique challenges of its own. JavaScript's ecosystem of libraries, frameworks, and utilities has grown dramatically. Where once a small number of solutions for any given problem existed, many can now be found... and the options continue to grow by the day. As a result, developers find themselves faced with the increasingly difficult task of choosing the appropriate tools from among many seemingly good options.

If you've ever found yourself wondering why JavaScript seems to be attracting so much attention lately, as we have, it's worth stopping for a moment to consider the fact that JavaScript, a language that was created by one person in ten days, now serves as the foundation upon which much of the Web as we know it sits. A language that was originally created to solve relatively simple problems is now being applied in new and innovative ways that were not originally foreseen. What's more, JavaScript is a beautifully expressive language, but it's not without its share of rough edges and potential pitfalls. While flexible, efficient, and ubiquitous, JavaScript concepts such as the event loop and prototypal inheritance can prove particularly challenging for those coming to the language for the first time.

For these and many other reasons, the development community at large is still coming to terms with how best to apply the unique features that JavaScript brings to the table. We've no doubt only scratched the surface of what the language and the community behind it are capable of. For those with an insatiable appetite for knowledge and a desire to create, now is the perfect time to be a JavaScript developer.

We have written *Pro JavaScript Frameworks for Modern Web Dev* to serve as your guide to a wide range of popular JavaScript tools that solve difficult problems at both ends of the development stack: in the browser and on the server. The tutorials and downloadable code examples contained within this book illustrate the usage of tools that manage dependencies, structure code in a modular fashion, automate repetitive build tasks, create specialized servers, structure client side applications, facilitate horizontal scaling, perform event logging, and interacting with disparate data stores.

The libraries and frameworks covered include Bower, Grunt, Yeoman, PM2, RequireJS, Browserify, Knockout, AngularJS, Kraken, Mach, Mongoose, Knex, Bookshelf, Faye, Q, Async.js, Underscore, and Lodash.

In writing *Pro JavaScript Frameworks for Modern Web Dev*, our goal was to create a filter for the "torrent of chatter" that often seems to surround JavaScript, and in so doing, to allow what we believe are some important things to be heard. We hope the information contained within these pages proves as useful to you as it has to us.

Who This Book Is For

This book is intended for web developers who are already confident with JavaScript, but also frustrated with the sheer number of solutions that exist for seemingly every problem. This book helps lift the fog, providing the reader with an in-depth guide to specific libraries and frameworks that well-known organizations are using right now with great success. Topics pertaining to both client-side and server-side development are covered. As a result, readers will gain the most benefit from this book if they already have at least an intermediate familiarity with both the web browser Document Object Model (DOM), common client-side libraries like jQuery, and Node.js.

How This Book Is Structured

This book covers a wide selection of JavaScript tools that are applicable throughout the entire development process, from a project's first commit to its first release and beyond. To that end, the chapters have been grouped into the following parts.

Part 1: Development Tools

Bower

Dependency management is hardly a new idea - well-known examples include Node's npm, Python's pip, and PHP's composer. A practice that has only recently begun to see widespread adoption, however, is the application of this concept to the management of front-end web assets - the JavaScript libraries, stylesheets, fonts, icons, and images that serve as the building blocks of modern web applications. In this chapter, we'll discover several ways in which Bower - a popular tool within this field - can improve your development process by providing you with a mechanism for organizing these dependencies within your application.

Grunt

Larry Wall, the creator of Perl, describes the three virtues of a great programmer as: laziness, impatience, and hubris. In this chapter, we'll focus on a tool that will help you strengthen the virtue of laziness - Grunt. This popular task runner provides developers with a framework for creating command-line utilities that automative repetitive build tasks such as running tests, concatenating files, compiling SASS / LESS stylesheets, checking for JavaScript errors, and more. After reading this chapter, you'll know how to use several popular Grunt plugins, as well as how to go about creating and sharing your own plugins with the community.

Yeoman

Yeoman provides JavaScript developers with a mechanism for creating reusable templates ("generators") that describe the overall structure of a project (initially required dependencies, Grunt tasks, etc...) in a way that can be easily re-used over and over. Broad community support also allows you to take advantage of a wide variety of pre-existing templates. In this chapter, we'll walk through the process of installing Yeoman and using several popular pre-existing generators. Finally, we'll take a look at how we can create and share our own templates with the community.

PM2

In this chapter, we will close out our discussion of development tools by taking a look at PM2, a command-line utility that simplifies many of the tasks associated with running Node applications, monitoring their status, and efficiently scaling them to meet increasing demand.

Part 2: Module Loaders
RequireJS and Browserify

JavaScript's lacks a native method for loading external dependencies in the browser—a frustrating oversight for developers. Fortunately, the community has stepped in to fill this gap with two very different and competing standards: the Asynchronous Module Definition (AMD) API and CommonJS. We'll dive into the details of both and take a look at widely-used implementations of each: RequireJS and Browserify. Each have their merits, which we'll discuss in detail, but both can have a profoundly positive impact on the way in which you go about structuring your applications.

Part 3: Client-Side Frameworks
Knockout and AngularJS

In recent years, web developers have witnessed a sharp rise in popularity of so-called "single-page apps." Such applications exhibit behavior once available only on the desktop, but at the expense of increased code complexity within the browser. In this section, we'll dive into two widely-used front-end frameworks that help minimize that complexity by providing proven patterns for solving frequently-encountered problems: Knockout and AngularJS. Knockout focuses on the relationship between view and data, but otherwise leaves the application architecture and plumbing to the developer's discretion. AngularJS takes a more prescriptive approach, covering the view, application routing, data transfer, and module design.

Part 4: Server-Side Frameworks
Kraken and Mach

Client-side applications aren't very useful without a server with which to interact. In this section, we'll take a look at two popular frameworks that support developers in the creation of back-end applications: Kraken and Mach.

Mach is more than just a simple web server: it is HTTP for the web. Mach can both serve and retrieve content via an intuitive, extensible HTTP stack. The Mach interface remains the same whether servicing web page requests in a Node.js application, fetching JSON data with a Mach AJAX request in the browser, or rewriting and proxying requests to another web stack entirely. In many ways Mach is the Swiss army knife of HTTP.

Part 5: Managing Database Interaction

Mongoose, Knex, and Bookshelf

At the core of every application lies the most important component of any development stack - the data that our users seek. In this section, we'll become familiar with two libraries that help simplify some of the complexity that's often experienced when interacting with popular storage platforms such as MongoDB, MySQL, PostgreSQL, and SQLite. After reading this section, you'll be comfortable defining schemas, associations, lifecycle "hooks", and more.

Part 6: Communication

Faye

In this section, you'll be introduced to Faye, a Node.js library that provides developers with a robust and easy-to-use platform for building products that rely on real-time communication between servers and all major browsers.Much of Faye's popularity stems from the project's goal of working everywhere the Web works. Faye accomplishes this by providing seamless fallback support for a number of communication protocols.

Part 7: Managing Control Flow

Q and Async.js

The asynchronous nature of JavaScript provides developers with a significant degree of flexibility - as opposed to forcing developers to execute their code in a linear fashion, JavaScript allows developers to orchestrate multiple actions simultaneously. Unfortunately, along with this flexibility comes a significant degree of additional complexity - what many developers refer to as "callback hell" or the "pyramid of doom." In this section, we'll examine two popular libraries that will aid you in taming the complexities of asynchronous control flow: Q and Async.js.

Part 8: Further Useful Libraries

A number of wonderfully useful libraries exist that this book would be remiss not to cover, but for which additional parts are not necessarily warranted. This part will cover such libraries.

Underscore and Lo-Dash

Underscore (and its successor, Lo-Dash) is an incredibly useful collection of functions that simplifies many frequently used patterns that can be tedious to implement otherwise. This brief chapter will bring these libraries to your attention, along with some of the more popular extensions that can also be included to enhance their usefulness even further. Examples are included that that highlight some of the most frequently used portions of these libraries.

Downloading the Code

Each chapter in this book contains many examples, the source code for which may be downloaded from http://www.apress.com/9781484206638 in zipped form.

Subdirectories within each chapter's zip file contain source code (often executable) that corresponds to specific example listings in each chapter. The first line in each chapter listing will be a source code comment identifying the specific file path where the source code lives. If you were to encounter Listing 0-1 in Chapter 10 (covering Mach), for example, the actual source code file would be located in mach/example-000/no-such-file.js, relative to where the mach.zip file was extracted.

Listing 0-1. Not a Real Example

```
// example-000/no-such-file.js
console.log('this is not a real example');
```

Most examples are run with the Node.js runtime, which may be obtained from https://nodejs.org. Chapters with additional prerequisites will explain the necessary procedures for downloading and installing the examples. (For example, MongoDB is necessary to run examples in Chapter 11, which covers Mongoose.)

Any additional steps necessary for running code examples (e.g., executing curl requests) or interacting with a running example (e.g., opening a web browser and navigating to a specific URL) are explained alongside each listing.

CHAPTER 1

■ ■ ■

Bower

Great things are done by a series of small things brought together.

—Vincent Van Gogh

The concept of *package management*, also known as *dependency management*, is not new. Utilities within this category provide developers with a mechanism for managing the various third-party libraries that a project relies on. Widely used examples include

- *npm*: The package manager for Node.js

- *Composer*: A tool for dependency management in PHP

- *pip*: The PyPA recommended tool for installing Python packages

- *NuGet*: The package manager for the Microsoft development platform including .NET

While package management is hardly a new idea, a practice that has only recently begun to see widespread adoption is the application of this concept to the management of front-end web assets—the JavaScript libraries, stylesheets, fonts, icons, and images that serve as the building blocks of modern web applications. The need for such structure has become evident as the foundations on which modern web applications are built have grown in complexity. Web applications that once relied on a small selection of broadly defined, "one size fits all" third-party libraries (e.g., jQuery) now find themselves using the work of many more smaller libraries, each with a tightly defined purpose. Benefits of this approach include smaller modules that are easier to test, as well as an enhanced degree of flexibility on the part of the parent application, which can more easily extend third-party libraries or replace them altogether when necessary.

This chapter is designed to get you up and running quickly with Bower, the front-end package manager whose roots lie in open source initiatives at Twitter. Topics covered include

- Installing and configuring Bower

- Adding Bower to a project

- Finding, adding, and removing packages

- Semantic Versioning

- Managing the dependency chain

- Creating Bower packages

1

Getting Started

All interaction with Bower occurs through a command-line utility that can be installed via npm. If you do not already have Bower installed, you should install it before you continue, as shown in Listing 1-1.

Listing 1-1. Installing the bower Command-Line Utility via npm

```
$ npm install -g bower
$ bower --version
1.3.12
```

■ **Note**   Node's package manager (npm) allows users to install packages in one of two contexts: locally or globally. In this example, bower is installed within the global context, which is typically reserved for command-line utilities.

Configuring Bower

Bower is configured on a per-project basis through a single (optional) JSON file that exists in your project's root folder, .bowerrc. For the purposes of this introduction, we'll only look at the most frequently changed setting within this file (see Listing 1-2).

Listing 1-2. The .bowerrc File from This Chapter's Sample Project

```
// example-bootstrap/.bowerrc

{
    "directory": "./public/bower_components"
}
```

By default, Bower will store your project's dependencies in the bower_components folder. You will likely want to change this location, and the directory setting allows you to do so.

The Manifest

Bower provides developers with a single point of entry from which third-party libraries can be found, added, upgraded, and removed. As these actions occur, Bower updates a JSON file referred to as the "manifest" with an up-to-date list of the project's dependencies. The Bower manifest for this chapter's sample project is shown in Listing 1-3. In this example, Bower is aware of a single dependency, the Bootstrap CSS framework.

Listing 1-3. Bower Manifest for This Chapter's Sample Project

```
// example-bootstrap/bower.json

{
    "name": "example-bootstrap",
    "version": "1.0.0",
    "homepage": "https://github.com/username/project",
```

```
    "authors": [
        "John Doe <john.doe@gmail.com>"
    ],
    "dependencies": {
        "bootstrap": "3.2.0"
    }
}
```

If we were to accidentally delete all of our project's dependencies by removing the `public/bower_components` folder, we could easily restore our project to its previous state by issuing a single command, as shown next. Doing so would cause Bower to compare its manifest with our project's current file structure, determine what dependencies are missing, and restore them.

```
$ bower install
```

As a result of this behavior, we have the option of ignoring our project's `/public/bower_components` folder within version control. By committing only Bower's manifest, and not the dependencies themselves, our project's source code can be kept in a cleaner state, containing only files that pertain directly to our own work.

■ **Note**   Opinions differ as to whether or not keeping your project's dependencies out of version control is a good idea. On the one hand, doing so results in a cleaner repository. On the other hand, this also opens the door to potential problems should you (or the Bower registry, or GitHub, etc.) encounter connection issues. The general consensus seems to be that if you are working on a "deployable" project (i.e., an application, not a module), committing your dependencies is the preferred approach. Otherwise, keeping your project's dependencies out of version control is probably a good idea.

Creating a New Manifest

When you begin to use Bower within a project for the first time, it's typically best to allow Bower to create a new manifest for you, as shown next. Afterward, you can modify it further if necessary.

```
$ bower init
```

Finding, Adding, and Removing Bower Packages

Bower's command-line utility provides a number of useful commands for locating, installing, and removing packages. Let's take a look at how these commands can help simplify the process of managing a project's external dependencies.

Finding Packages

One of the primary ways in which Bower can improve your development workflow is by providing you with a centralized registry from which third-party libraries can be found. To search the Bower registry, simply pass the `search` argument to Bower, followed by a keyword to search for, as shown in Listing 1-4. In this example, only a short excerpt from the returned list of search results is shown.

Listing 1-4. Searching Bower for jQuery

```
$ bower search jquery
```

```
Search results:
```

```
    jquery git://github.com/jquery/jquery.git
    jquery-ui git://github.com/components/jqueryui
    jquery.cookie git://github.com/carhartl/jquery-cookie.git
    jquery-placeholder git://github.com/mathiasbynens/jquery-placeholder.git
```

Adding Packages

Each search result includes the name under which the package was registered, along with the URL of the GitHub repository at which it can be accessed directly. Once we have located the desired package, we can add it to our project as shown in Listing 1-5.

Listing 1-5. Adding jQuery to Our Project

```
$ bower install jquery --save
bower jquery#*              cached git://github.com/jquery/jquery.git#2.1.3
bower jquery#*            validate 2.1.3 against git://github.com/jquery/jquery.git#*
bower jquery#>= 1.9.1      cached git://github.com/jquery/jquery.git#2.1.3
bower jquery#>= 1.9.1    validate 2.1.3 against git://github.com/jquery/jquery.git#>= 1.9.1
bower jquery#>= 1.9.1      cached git://github.com/jquery/jquery.git#2.1.3
bower jquery#>= 1.9.1    validate 2.1.3 against git://github.com/jquery/jquery.git#>= 1.9.1
bower jquery#>= 1.9.1     install jquery#2.1.3

jquery#2.1.3 public/bower_components/jquery
```

■ **Note**   Bower does not host any of the files associated with the packages contained within its registry; it defers to GitHub for that responsibility. While it is possible to host packages at any URL, the majority of public packages are found on GitHub.

Take note of the fact that in Listing 1-5, we pass the --save option to Bower's install command. By default, the install command will add the requested package to a project without updating its manifest. By passing the --save option, we instruct Bower to permanently store this package within its list of dependencies.

Listing 1-6 shows the HTML from this chapter's sample project. After adding jQuery to our project via Bower, we can load it via a script tag as we would any other library.

Listing 1-6. HTML from Our Sample Project That References the jQuery Package Just Added

```
// example-jquery/public/index.html

<!DOCTYPE html>
<html lang="en">
    <head>
        <meta charset="utf-8">
        <meta http-equiv="X-UA-Compatible" content="IE=edge">
        <meta name="viewport" content="width=device-width, initial-scale=1">
        <title>Bower Example</title>
    </head>
    <body>
        <div id="container"></div>
        <script src="/bower_components/jquery/dist/jquery.min.js"></script>
        <script>
        $(document).ready(function() {
            $('#container').html('<p>Hello, world!</p>');
        });
        </script>
    </body>
</html>
```

Development Dependencies

By default, any packages that Bower installs are considered to be "production" dependencies, but this behavior can be overridden by passing the --save-dev option. Doing so will flag any installed packages as "development" dependencies. Such packages are intended for development purposes only, not for the final users of a project.

Once we are ready to deploy our application to a production environment, we can instruct Bower to install only the production dependencies, as shown next, resulting in a leaner build that does not contain extraneous files of no interest to the end user.

```
$ bower install --production
```

Removing Packages

The process of removing Bower packages is straightforward. As in previous examples, we pass the --save argument to update Bower's manifest to reflect this change:

```
$ bower uninstall jquery --save
```

Semantic Versioning

If you were to install jQuery (as shown in Listing 1-5) and then look at the contents of your project's Bower manifest, you would see something that resembles Listing 1-7.

Listing 1-7. Semantic Version (Semver) Number

```
"dependencies": {
    "jquery": "~2.1.3"
}
```

The version number 2.1.3 that we see in Listing 1-7 (ignore the ~ character for a moment) is what is known as a *semantic version* number (*semver* for short). Semantic versioning is a standard that describes a common format that developers can use to assign version numbers to their projects. The format is illustrated here:

Version X.Y.Z (Major.Minor.Patch)

The semantic versioning format dictates that developers create clearly defined (either by documentation or by clear, self-documenting code) APIs that provide users with a single point of entry into a library. New projects that are just getting off the ground typically begin at version 0.0.0 and work their way up incrementally as new releases are created. A project with a version number below 1.0.0 is considered to be under heavy development and, as such, is allowed to make sweeping changes to its API without altering its major version number. A project with a version number at or above 1.0.0, however, is guided by the following set of rules that determines how version numbers should be changed:

- A project's major version number should change when updates occur that result in breaking changes with how users have interacted with a project's API in previous versions.

- A project's minor version number should change when new features are added to a project in a way that is backward-compatible (i.e., the existing API is not broken).

- A project's patch version number should change when backward-compatible bug fixes are introduced.

These rules provide developers with insight into the extent of changes that have occurred between any two versions. Such insight will prove useful as our Bower manifest grows and we begin adding more and more dependencies to our project.

▪ **Note**   The ~ character shown in Listing 1-7 tells Bower that whenever the `install` command is run, it is allowed to automatically install future versions of jQuery that are "relatively close to" version 2.1.3. If the use of the phrases "relatively close to" and "automatically install" within the same sentence makes your skin crawl, you're not alone. Best practices *suggest* that you *avoid* the "~X.Y.Z" format when referencing dependencies *with* Bower. Instead, you are better off specifying the exact version of the dependency that you wish to include within your project. As future updates are released, you can then manually review them and make your own decisions regarding if and when to update. Subsequent examples within this chapter will follow this advice.

Managing the Dependency Chain

One of the primary benefits that developers gain as a result of using Bower is the ease with which updates to a project's entire dependency chain can be monitored and integrated. To illustrate this point, let's take a look at the list of dependencies contained within this chapter's sample project (see Listing 1-8).

Listing 1-8. Installing and Listing the Various Bower Packages Required by Our Sample Project

```
$ bower install
bower bootstrap#3.2.0      cached git://github.com/twbs/bootstrap.git#3.2.0
bower bootstrap#3.2.0     validate 3.2.0 against git://github.com/twbs/bootstrap.git#3.2.0
bower jquery#>= 1.9.0      cached git://github.com/jquery/jquery.git#2.1.3
bower jquery#>= 1.9.0     validate 2.1.3 against git://github.com/jquery/jquery.git#>= 1.9.0
bower bootstrap#3.2.0      install bootstrap#3.2.0
bower jquery#>= 1.9.0      install jquery#2.1.3

bootstrap#3.2.0 public/bower_components/bootstrap
└── jquery#2.1.3

jquery#2.1.3 public/bower_components/jquery

$ bower list
bower check-new     Checking for new versions of the project dependencies..
example-bootstrap#1.0.0 /opt/example-bootstrap
└─┬ bootstrap#3.2.0 (latest is 3.3.2)
  └── jquery#2.1.3
```

Thanks to Bower, we now have a simple graph that describes the external dependencies that our project relies on, as well as the relationships between them. We can see that we have a Bootstrap dependency, which in turn has its own dependency on jQuery. Bower also prints the specific version of each component that is currently installed.

■ **Note**   Many third-party libraries are not entirely self-contained—they have dependencies of their own. Bootstrap (with its reliance on jQuery) is one such example. When adding such a package, Bower is smart enough to recognize these additional dependencies and will proactively add them to your project if they don't already exist. It is important to note, however, that unlike more sophisticated package managers (e.g., npm), Bower stores all of its packages within a flat folder structure, which means you will occasionally run into version conflicts, if you're not careful.

In Listing 1-8, Bower has informed us that a version of Bootstrap (3.3.2) newer than the version currently relied upon by our project (3.2.0) is available. We can update this dependency by modifying our project's manifest to refer to this newer version and rerunning the install command, as shown in Listing 1-9.

Listing 1-9. Installing Bower Packages After Having Updated the Version of jQuery Our Project Relies On

```
$ bower install
bower bootstrap#3.3.2      cached git://github.com/twbs/bootstrap.git#3.3.2
bower bootstrap#3.3.2      validate 3.3.2 against git://github.com/twbs/bootstrap.git#3.3.2
bower bootstrap#3.3.2       install bootstrap#3.3.2

bootstrap#3.3.2 public/bower_components/bootstrap
└── jquery#2.1.3
```

Creating Bower Packages

Until now, our focus has been on integrating Bower into our own projects. We've initialized Bower within our project and discovered how we can go about finding, adding, and removing packages. At a certain point, however, you'll hopefully find yourself wanting to share your own packages with others. To do so, you'll need to ensure that you follow a few simple guidelines, starting with choosing a valid name.

Choose a Valid Name

You'll need to settle on a name for your package that is unique throughout Bower's public registry. Use Bower's search command to find out if your desired name is available. Additional requirements include

- The name should be in "slug" format; for example, my-unique-project.

- The name should be all lowercase.

- Only alphanumeric characters, dots, and dashes are allowed.

- The name should begin and end with an alphabetic character.

- Consecutive dots and dashes are not allowed.

- After settling on a name, update the contents of your project's bower.json file accordingly.

Use Semver Git Tags

Earlier in the chapter, we took a look at the concept of semantic versioning, a common standard for assigning meaningful version numbers to projects. You'll want to ensure that you follow this standard, as this will allow the consumers of your package to track and integrate your future changes.

If the package you want to share is just getting started, an appropriate version number would be 0.0.0. As you commit future changes and create new releases, you can increment this value as appropriate, depending on the extent of your updates. When you determine that your project has reached its first "stable" milestone, update your version number to 1.0.0 to reflect that status.

Every version number of your project should have a corresponding tag on GitHub. It is this relationship between GitHub tags and the versions of your package that allows consumers to reference specific versions within their projects.

Assuming you've already committed your code to GitHub, see Listing 1-10 for an example of how you might go about creating your first tag.

Listing 1-10. Creating Your First Semver Git Tag

```
$ git tag -a 0.0.1 -m "First release."
$ git push origin 0.0.1
```

Publish Your Package to the Registry

Now that we've chosen an appropriate name for our package and assigned a version number (along with a corresponding tag on GitHub), it's time to publish our package to the public Bower registry:

```
$ bower register my-package-name https://github.com/username/my-package-name.git
```

▨ **Note** Bear in mind that Bower is intended to serve as a centralized registry for libraries and components that other developers can use within their own projects. It is not intended to serve as a distribution mechanism for entire applications.

Summary

Bower is a simple command-line utility that eases some of the tedious tasks associated with managing front-end assets. Unlike well-known package managers from other platforms (e.g., Node's npm), Bower was not designed to handle the specific needs of any one platform or language; instead, it favors a rather generic approach to the concept of package management. The developers who created Bower intentionally set out to create a very simple tool for managing a wide variety of front-end assets—not just code, but also stylesheets, fonts, images, and other, unforeseen future dependencies.

Developers working on trivial web applications with few external dependencies may find little value in the benefits that Bower brings to the table. That said, trivial web applications have a tendency to quickly evolve into complex web applications, and as that process occurs, developers often come to appreciate Bower's benefits.

Regardless of how complex (or simple) you consider your project to be, we would encourage you to consider integrating Bower into your workflow sooner rather than later. As bitter experience has taught us—the project itself. Err on the side of too little structure, and you risk creating an ever-increasing burden of "technical debt" for which you must eventually pay a price. The process of striking a delicate balance between these undesired alternatives is as much an art as it is a science. It is also a process that is never fully learned, but must continuously be adapted as the tools of our trade change.

CHAPTER 2

Grunt

I'm lazy. But it's the lazy people who invented the wheel and the bicycle because they didn't like walking or carrying things.

—Lech Walesa, former president of Poland

In his book *Programming Perl*, Larry Wall (the well-known creator of the language) puts forth the idea that all successful programmers share three important characteristics: laziness, impatience, and hubris. At first glance, these traits all sound quite negative, but dig a little deeper, and you'll find the hidden meaning in his statement:

> *Laziness*: Lazy programmers hate to repeat themselves. As a result, they tend to put a lot of effort into creating useful tools that perform repetitive tasks for them. They also tend to document those tools well, to spare themselves the trouble of answering questions about them later.

> *Impatience*: Impatient programmers have learned to expect much from their tools. This expectation teaches them to create software that doesn't just react to the needs of its users, but that actually attempts to anticipate those needs.

> *Hubris*: Good programmers take great pride in their work. It is this pride that compels them to write software that others won't want to criticize—the type of work that we should all be striving for.

In this chapter, we'll focus on the first of these three characteristics, laziness, along with Grunt, a popular JavaScript "task runner" that supports developers in nurturing this trait by providing them with a toolkit for automating the repetitive build tasks that often accompany software development, such as:

- Script and stylesheet compilation and minification
- Testing
- Linting
- Database migrations
- Deployments

In other words, Grunt helps developers who strive to work smarter, not harder. If that idea appeals to you, read on. After you have finished this chapter, you will be well on your way toward mastering Grunt. You'll learn how to do the following in this chapter:

- Create configurable tasks that automate the repetitive aspects of software development that accompany nearly every project

- Interact with the file system using simple yet powerful abstractions provided by Grunt

- Publish Grunt plugins from which other developers can benefit and to which they can contribute

- Take advantage of Grunt's preexisting library of community-supported plugins, of which over 4,400 examples exist at the time of writing

Installing Grunt

Before continuing, you should ensure that you have installed Grunt's command-line utility. Available as an npm package, the installation process is shown in Listing 2-1.

Listing 2-1. Installing the grunt Command-Line Utility via npm

```
$ npm install -g grunt-cli
$ grunt --version
grunt-cli v0.1.13
```

How Grunt Works

Grunt provides developers with a toolkit for creating command-line utilities that perform repetitive project tasks. Examples of such tasks include the minification of JavaScript code and the compilation of Sass stylesheets, but there's no limit to how Grunt can be put to work. Grunt can be used to create simple tasks that address the specific needs of a single project—tasks that you don't intend to share or reuse—but Grunt's true power derives from its ability to package tasks as reusable plugins that can then be published, shared, used, and improved upon by others. At the time of this writing, over 4,400 such plugins exist.

Four core components make Grunt tick, which we will now cover.

Gruntfile.js

At Grunt's core lies the *Gruntfile*, a Node module saved as Gruntfile.js (see Listing 2-2) at the root of your project. It's within this file that we can load Grunt plugins, create our own custom tasks, and configure them according to the needs of our project. Each time Grunt is run, its first order of business is to retrieve its marching orders from this module.

Listing 2-2. Sample Gruntfile

```
// example-starter/Gruntfile.js

module.exports = function(grunt) {

    /**
     * Configure the various tasks and plugins that we'll be using
     */
    grunt.initConfig({
        /* Grunt's 'file' API provides developers with helpful abstractions for
        interacting  with the file system. We'll take a look at these in greater
        detail later in the chapter. */
        'pkg': grunt.file.readJSON('package.json'),
        'uglify': {
            'development': {
                'files': {
                    'build/app.min.js': ['src/app.js', 'src/lib.js']
                }
            }
        }
    });

    /**
     * Grunt plugins exist as Node packages, published via npm. Here, we load the
     * 'grunt-contrib-uglify' plugin, which provides a task for merging and minifying
     * a project's source code in preparation for deployment.
     */
    grunt.loadNpmTasks('grunt-contrib-uglify');

    /**
     * Here we create a Grunt task named 'default' that does nothing more than call
     * the 'uglify' task. In other words, this task will serve as an alias to
     * 'uglify'. Creating a task named 'default' tells Grunt what to do when it is
     * run from the command line without any arguments. In this example, our 'default'
     * task calls a single, separate task, but we could just as easily have called
     * multiple tasks (to be run in sequence) by adding multiple entries to the array
     * that is passed.
     */
    grunt.registerTask('default', ['uglify']);

    /**
     * Here we create a custom task that prints a message to the console (followed by
     * a line break) using one of Grunt's built-in methods for providing user feedback.
     * We'll look at these in greater detail later in the chapter.
     */
    grunt.registerTask('hello-world', function() {
        grunt.log.writeln('Hello, world.');
    });

};
```

Tasks

Tasks are the basic building blocks of Grunt and are nothing more than functions that are registered with assigned names via Grunt's `registerTask()` method. In Listing 2-2, a simple `hello-world` task is shown that prints a message to the console. This task can be called from the command line as shown in Listing 2-3.

Listing 2-3. Running the `hello-world` Task Shown in Listing 2-2

```
$ grunt hello-world
Running "hello-world" task
Hello, world.

Done, without errors.
```

Multiple Grunt tasks can also be run in sequence with a single command, as shown in Listing 2-4. Each task will be run in the order in which it was passed.

Listing 2-4. Running Multiple Grunt Tasks in Sequence

```
$ grunt hello-world uglify
Running "hello-world" task
Hello, world.

Running "uglify:development" (uglify) task
>> 1 file created.

Done, without errors.
```

The `hello-world` task that we've just seen serves as an example of a basic, stand-alone Grunt task. Such tasks can be used to implement simple actions specific to the needs of a single project that you don't intend to re-use or share. Most of the time, however, you will find yourself interacting not with stand-alone tasks, but instead with tasks that have been packaged as Grunt plugins and published to npm so that others can reuse them and contribute to them.

Plugins

A Grunt plugin is a collection of configurable tasks (published as an npm package) that can be reused across multiple projects. Thousands of such plugins exist. In Listing 2-2, Grunt's `loadNpmTasks()` method is used to load the `grunt-contrib-uglify` Node module, a Grunt plugin that merges a project's JavaScript code into a single, minified file that is suitable for deployment.

■ **Note**   A list of all available Grunt plugins can be found at `http://gruntjs.com/plugins`. Plugins whose names are prefixed with `contrib-` are officially maintained by the developers behind Grunt.

Configuration

Grunt is known for emphasizing "configuration over code": the creation of tasks and plugins whose functionality is tailored by configuration that is specified within each project. It is this separation of code from configuration that allows developers to create plugins that are easily reusable by others. Later in the chapter, we'll take a look at the various ways in which Grunt plugins and tasks can be configured.

Adding Grunt to Your Project

Earlier in the chapter, we installed Grunt's command-line utility by installing the grunt-cli npm package as a global module. We should now have access to the grunt utility from the command line, but we still need to add a local grunt dependency to each project we intend to use it with. The command to be called from within the root folder of your project is shown next. This example assumes that npm has already been initialized within the project and that a package.json file already exists.

```
$ npm install grunt --save-dev
```

Our project's package.json file should now contain a grunt entry similar to that shown in Listing 2-5.

Listing 2-5. Our Project's Updated package.json File

```
// example-tasks/package.json

{
    "name": "example-tasks",
    "version": "1.0.0",
    "devDependencies": {
        "grunt": "0.4.5"
    }
}
```

The final step toward integrating Grunt with our project is the creation of a Gruntfile (see Listing 2-6), which should be saved within the root folder of the project. Within our Gruntfile, a single method is called, loadTasks(), which is discussed in the upcoming section.

Listing 2-6. Contents of Our Project's Gruntfile

```
// example-tasks/Gruntfile.js

module.exports = function(grunt) {
    grunt.loadTasks('tasks');
};
```

Maintaining a Sane Grunt Structure

We hope that by the time you have finished this chapter, you will have found Grunt to be a worthwhile tool for automating many of the repetitive, tedious tasks that you encounter during the course of your daily workflow. That said, we'd be lying if we told you that our initial reaction to Grunt was positive. In fact, we were quite turned off by the tool at first. To help explain why, let's take a look at the Gruntfile that is prominently displayed within Grunt's official documentation (see Listing 2-7).

Listing 2-7. Example Gruntfile Provided by Grunt's Official Documentation

```
module.exports = function(grunt) {

    grunt.initConfig({
        pkg: grunt.file.readJSON('package.json'),
        concat: {
            options: {
                separator: ';'
            },
            dist: {
                src: ['src/**/*.js'],
                dest: 'dist/<%= pkg.name %>.js'
            }
        },
        uglify: {
            options: {
                banner: '/*! <%= grunt.template.today("dd-mm-yyyy") %> */\n'
            },
            dist: {
                files: {
                    'dist/<%= pkg.name %>.min.js': ['<%= concat.dist.dest %>']
                }
            }
        },
        qunit: {
            files: ['test/**/*.html']
        },
        jshint: {
            files: ['Gruntfile.js', 'src/**/*.js', 'test/**/*.js'],
            options: {
                // options here to override JSHint defaults
                globals: {
                    jQuery: true,
                    console: true,
                    module: true,
                    document: true
                }
            }
        },
        watch: {
            files: ['<%= jshint.files %>'],
            tasks: ['jshint', 'qunit']
        }
    });
```

```
grunt.loadNpmTasks('grunt-contrib-uglify');
grunt.loadNpmTasks('grunt-contrib-jshint');
grunt.loadNpmTasks('grunt-contrib-qunit');
grunt.loadNpmTasks('grunt-contrib-watch');
grunt.loadNpmTasks('grunt-contrib-concat');

grunt.registerTask('test', ['jshint', 'qunit']);

grunt.registerTask('default', ['jshint', 'qunit', 'concat', 'uglify']);

};
```

The Gruntfile shown in Listing 2-7 is for a relatively simple project. We already find this example to be slightly unwieldy, but within larger projects we have seen this file balloon to many times this size. The result is an unreadable and difficult-to-maintain mess. Experienced developers would never write their code in a way that combines functionality from across unrelated areas into a single, monolithic file, so why should we approach our task runner any differently?

The secret to maintaining a sane Grunt structure lies with Grunt's loadTasks() function, as shown in Listing 2-6. In this example, the tasks argument refers to a tasks folder relative to our project's Gruntfile. Once this method is called, Grunt will load and execute each Node module it finds within this folder, passing along a reference to the grunt object each time. This behavior provides us with the opportunity to organize our project's Grunt configuration as a series of separate modules, each responsible for loading and configuring a single task or plugin. An example of one of these smaller modules is shown in Listing 2-8. This task can be executed by running grunt uglify from the command line.

Listing 2-8. Example Module (uglify.js) Within Our New tasks Folder

```
// example-tasks/tasks/uglify.js

module.exports = function(grunt) {

    grunt.loadNpmTasks('grunt-contrib-uglify');

    grunt.config('uglify', {
        'options': {
            'banner': '/*! <%= grunt.template.today("dd-mm-yyyy") %> */\n'
        },
        'dist': {
            'files': {
                'dist/app.min.js': ['src/index.js']
            }
        }
    });

};
```

Working with Tasks

As previously mentioned, tasks serve as the foundation on which Grunt is built—everything begins here. A Grunt plugin, as you'll soon discover, is nothing more than one or more tasks that have been packaged into a Node module and published via npm. We've already seen a few examples that demonstrate the creation of basic Grunt tasks, so let's take a look at some additional features that can help us get the most out of them.

Managing Configuration

Grunt's config() method serves as both a "getter" and a "setter" for configuration. In Listing 2-9, we see how a basic Grunt task can access its configuration through the use of this method.

Listing 2-9. Managing Configuration Within a Basic Grunt Task

```
module.exports = function(grunt) {

    grunt.config('basic-task', {
        'message': 'Hello, world.'
    });

    grunt.registerTask('basic-task', function() {
        grunt.log.writeln(grunt.config('basic-task.message'));
    });

};
```

■ **Note** In Listing 2-9, "dot notation" is used for accessing nested configuration values. In the same way, dot notation can be used to set nested configuration values. If at any point Grunt encounters a path within the configuration object that does not exist, Grunt will create a new, empty object without throwing an error.

Task Descriptions

Over time, projects have a tendency to grow in complexity. With this additional complexity often comes new Grunt tasks. As new tasks are added, it's often easy to lose track of what tasks are available, what they do, and how they are called. Fortunately, Grunt provides us with a way to address this problem by assigning descriptions to our tasks, as shown in Listing 2-10.

Listing 2-10. Assigning a Description to a Grunt Task

```
// example-task-description/Gruntfile.js

module.exports = function(grunt) {

    grunt.config('basic-task', {
        'message': 'Hello, world.'
    });
```

```
grunt.registerTask('basic-task', 'This is an example task.', function() {
    grunt.log.writeln(grunt.config('basic-task.message'));
});

grunt.registerTask('default', 'This is the default task.', ['basic-task']);
```

```
};
```

By passing an additional argument to the registerTask() method, Grunt allows us to provide a description for the task being created. Grunt helpfully provides this information when help is requested from the command line, as shown in Listing 2-11, which includes an excerpt of the information Grunt provides.

Listing 2-11. Requesting Help from the Command Line

```
$ grunt --help
...
Available tasks
    basic-task  This is an example task.
       default  This is the default task.
...
```

Asynchronous Tasks

By default, Grunt tasks are expected to run synchronously. As soon as a task's function returns, it is considered finished. There will be times, however, when you find yourself interacting with other asynchronous methods within a task, which must first complete before your task can hand control back over to Grunt. The solution to this problem is shown in Listing 2-12. Within a task, a call to the async() method will notify Grunt that it executes asynchronously. The method will return a callback function to be called when our task has completed. Until this is done, Grunt will hold the execution of any additional tasks.

Listing 2-12. Asynchronous Grunt Task

```
// example-async/tasks/list-files.js

var glob = require('glob');

module.exports = function(grunt) {

    grunt.registerTask('list-files', function() {

        /**
         * Grunt will wait until we call the `done()` function to indicate that our
         * asynchronous task is complete.
         */
        var done = this.async();
```

```
        glob('*', function(err, files) {
            if (err) {
                grunt.fail.fatal(err);
            }
            grunt.log.writeln(files);
            done();
        });

    });

};
```

Task Dependencies

Complicated Grunt workflows are best thought of as a series of steps that work together to produce a final result. In such situations, it can often be helpful to specify that a task requires one or more separate tasks to precede it, as shown in Listing 2-13.

Listing 2-13. Declaring a Task Dependency

```
// example-task-dependency/tasks/step-two.js

module.exports = function(grunt) {
    grunt.registerTask('step-two', function() {
        grunt.task.requires('step-one');
    });
};
```

In this example, the step-two task requires that the step-one task run first before it can proceed. Any attempt to call step-two directly will result in an error, as shown in Listing 2-14.

Listing 2-14. Grunt Reporting an Error When a Task Is Called Before Any Tasks on Which It Depends Have Run

```
$ grunt step-two
Running "step-two" task
Warning: Required task "step-one" must be run first. Use --force to continue.

Aborted due to warnings.
```

Multi-Tasks

In addition to basic tasks, Grunt offers support for what it calls "multi-tasks." Multi-tasks are easily the most complicated aspect of Grunt, so if you find yourself confused at first, you're not alone. After reviewing a few examples, however, their purpose should start to come into focus—at which point you'll be well on your way toward mastering Grunt.

Before we go any further, let's take a look at a brief example (see Listing 2-15) that shows a Grunt multi-task, along with its configuration.

Listing 2-15. Grunt Multi-Task

```
// example-list-animals/tasks/list-animals.js

module.exports = function(grunt) {

    /**
     * Our multi-task's configuration object. In this example, 'mammals'
     * and 'birds' each represent what Grunt refers to as a 'target.'
     */
    grunt.config('list-animals', {
        'mammals': {
            'animals': ['Cat', 'Zebra', 'Koala', 'Kangaroo']
        },
        'birds': {
            'animals': ['Penguin', 'Sparrow', 'Eagle', 'Parrot']
        }
    });

    grunt.registerMultiTask('list-animals', function() {
        grunt.log.writeln('Target:', this.target);
        grunt.log.writeln('Data:', this.data);
    });

};
```

Multi-tasks are extremely flexible, in that they are designed to support multiple configurations (referred to as "targets") within a single project. The multi-task shown in Listing 2-15 has two targets: `mammals` and `birds`. This task can be run against a specific target as shown in Listing 2-16.

Listing 2-16. Running the Grunt Multi-Task Shown in Listing 2-15 Against a Specific Target

```
$ grunt list-animals:mammals
Running "list-animals:mammals" (list-animals) task
Target: mammals
Data: { animals: [ 'Cat', 'Zebra', 'Koala', 'Kangaroo' ] }

Done, without errors.
```

Multi-tasks can also be called without any arguments, in which case they are executed multiple times, once for each available target. Listing 2-17 shows the result of calling this task without specifying a target.

Listing 2-17. Running the Multi-Task Shown in Listing 2-15 Without Specifying a Target

```
$ grunt list-animals
Running "list-animals:mammals" (list-animals) task
Target: mammals
Data: { animals: [ 'Cat', 'Zebra', 'Koala', 'Kangaroo' ] }

Running "list-animals:birds" (list-animals) task
Target: birds
Data: { animals: [ 'Penguin', 'Sparrow', 'Eagle', 'Parrot' ] }
```

In this example, our multi-task ran twice, once for each available target (`mammals` and `birds`). Notice in Listing 2-15 that within our multi-task we referenced two properties: `this.target` and `this.data`. These properties allow our multi-task to fetch information about the target that it is currently running against.

Multi-Task Options

Within a multi-task's configuration object, any values stored under the `options` key (see Listing 2-18) receive special treatment.

Listing 2-18. Grunt Multi-Task with Configuration Options

```
// example-list-animals-options/tasks/list-animals.js

module.exports = function(grunt) {

    grunt.config('list-animals', {
        'options': {
            'format': 'array'
        },
        'mammals': {
            'options': {
                'format': 'json'
            },
            'animals': ['Cat', 'Zebra', 'Koala', 'Kangaroo']
        },
        'birds': {
            'animals': ['Penguin', 'Sparrow', 'Eagle', 'Parrot']
        }
    });

    grunt.registerMultiTask('list-animals', function() {

        var options = this.options();

        switch (options.format) {
            case 'array':
                grunt.log.writeln(this.data.animals);
            break;
            case 'json':
                grunt.log.writeln(JSON.stringify(this.data.animals));
            break;
            default:
                grunt.fail.fatal('Unknown format: ' + options.format);
            break;
        }

    });

};
```

Multi-task options provide developers with a mechanism for defining global options for a task, which can then be overridden at the target level. In this example, a global format in which to list animals ('array') is defined at the task level. The mammals target has chosen to override this value ('json'), while the birds task has not. As a result, mammals will be displayed as JSON, while birds will be shown as an array due to its inheritance of the global option.

The vast majority of Grunt plugins that you will encounter are configurable as multi-tasks. The flexibility afforded by this approach allows you to apply the same task differently under different circumstances. A frequently encountered scenario involves the creation of separate targets for each build environment. For example, when compiling an application, you may want to modify the behavior of a task based on whether you are compiling for a local development environment or in preparation for release to production.

Configuration Templates

Grunt configuration objects support the embedding of template strings, which can then be used to reference other configuration values. The template format favored by Grunt follows that of the Lodash and Underscore utility libraries, which are covered in further detail in a later chapter. For an example of how this feature can be put to use, see Listing 2-19 and Listing 2-20.

Listing 2-19. Sample Gruntfile That Stores the Contents of Its Project's package.json File Under the pkg Key Within Grunt's Configuration Object

```
// example-templates/Gruntfile.js

module.exports = function(grunt) {
    grunt.initConfig({
        'pkg': grunt.file.readJSON('package.json')
    });
    grunt.loadTasks('tasks');
    grunt.registerTask('default', ['test']);
};
```

Listing 2-20. A Subsequently Loaded Task with Its Own Configuration That Is Able to Reference Other Configuration Values Through the Use of Templates

```
// example-templates/tasks/test.js

module.exports = function(grunt) {
    grunt.config('test', {
        'banner': '<%= pkg.name %>-<%= pkg.version %>'
    });
    grunt.registerTask('test', function() {
        grunt.log.writeln(grunt.config('test.banner'));
    });
};
```

Listing 2-19 shows a sample Gruntfile that loads the contents of the project's package.json file using one of several built-in methods for interacting with the file system that are discussed in further detail later in the chapter. The contents of this file are then stored under the pkg key of Grunt's configuration object. In Listing 2-20, we see a task that is able to directly reference this information through the use of configuration templates.

Command-Line Options

Additional options can be passed to Grunt using the following format:

```
$ grunt count --count=5
```

The example shown in Listing 2-21 demonstrates how a Grunt task can access this information via the `grunt.option()` method. The result of calling this task is shown in Listing 2-22.

Listing 2-21. Simple Grunt Task That Counts to the Specified Number

```
// example-options/tasks/count.js

module.exports = function(grunt) {

    grunt.registerTask('count', function() {
        var limit = parseInt(grunt.option('limit'), 10);
        if (isNaN(limit)) grunt.fail.fatal('A limit must be provided (e.g. --limit=10)');
        console.log('Counting to: %s', limit);
        for (var i = 1; i <= limit; i++) console.log(i);
    });

};
```

Listing 2-22. Result of Calling the Task Shown in Listing 2-21

```
$ grunt count --limit=5
Running "count" task
Counting to: 5
1
2
3
4
5

Done, without errors.
```

Providing Feedback

Grunt provides a number of built-in methods for providing feedback to users during the execution of tasks, a few of which you have already seen used throughout this chapter. While we won't list all of them here, several useful examples can be found in Table 2-1.

Table 2-1. *Useful Grunt Methods for Displaying Feedback to the User*

Method	Description
grunt.log.write()	Prints a message to the console
grunt.log.writeln()	Prints a message to the console, followed by a newline character
grunt.log.oklns()	Prints a success message to the console, followed by a newline character
grunt.log.error()	Prints an error message to the console, followed by a newline character
grunt.log.subhead()	Prints a bold message to the console, following by a newline character
grunt.log.debug()	Prints a message to the console only if the - -debug flag was passed

Handling Errors

During the course of task execution, errors can occur. When they do, it's important to know how to appropriately handle them. When faced with an error, developers should make use of Grunt's error API, which is easy to use, as it provides just two methods, shown in Table 2-2.

Table 2-2. *Methods Available via Grunt's error API*

Method	Description
grunt.fail.warn()	Displays a warning and aborts Grunt immediately. Tasks will continue to run if the - -force option is passed.
grunt.fail.fatal()	Displays a warning and aborts Grunt immediately.

Interacting with the File System

As a build tool, it comes as no surprise that the majority of Grunt's plugins interact with the file system in one way or another. Given its importance, Grunt provides helpful abstractions that allow developers to interact with the file system with a minimal amount of boilerplate code.

While we won't list all of them here, Table 2-3 shows several of the most frequently used methods within Grunt's file API.

Table 2-3. *Useful Grunt Methods for Interacting with the File System*

Method	Description
grunt.file.read()	Reads and returns file's contents
grunt.file.readJSON()	Reads a file's contents, parsing the data as JSON, and returns the result
grunt.file.write()	Writes the specified contents to a file, creating intermediate directories, if necessary
grunt.file.copy()	Copies a source file to a destination path, creating intermediate directories, if necessary
grunt.file.delete()	Deletes the specified file path; deletes files and folders recursively
grunt.file.mkdir()	Creates a directory, along with any missing intermediate directories
grunt.file.recurse()	Recurses into a directory, executing a callback for every file that is found

Source-Destination Mappings

Many Grunt tasks that interact with the file system rely heavily on the concept of source-destination mappings, a format that describes a set of files to be processed and a corresponding destination for each. Such mappings can be tedious to construct, but thankfully Grunt provides helpful shortcuts that address this need.

Imagine for a moment that you are working on a project with a `public` folder located at its root. Within this folder are the files to be served over the Web once the project is deployed, as shown in Listing 2-23.

Listing 2-23. Contents of an Imaginary Project's `public` Folder

```
// example-iterate1


.
└── public
    └── images
        ├── cat1.jpg
        ├── cat2.jpg
        └── cat3.png
```

As you can see, our project has an `images` folder containing three files. Knowing this, let's take a look at a few ways in which Grunt can help us iterate through these files.

In Listing 2-24, we find a Grunt multi-task similar to those we've recently been introduced to. The key difference here is the presence of an `src` key within our task's configuration. Grunt gives special attention to multi-task configurations that contain this key, as we'll soon see. When the `src` key is present, Grunt provides a `this.files` property within our task that provides an array containing paths to every matching file that is found via the `node-glob` module. The output from this task is shown in Listing 2-25.

Listing 2-24. Grunt Multi-Task with a Configuration Object Containing an `src` Key

```
// example-iterate1/tasks/list-files.js

module.exports = function(grunt) {

    grunt.config('list-files', {
        'images': {
            'src': ['public/**/*.jpg', 'public/**/*.png']
        }
    });

    grunt.registerMultiTask('list-files', function() {
        this.files.forEach(function(files) {
            grunt.log.writeln('Source:', files.src);
        });
    });

};
```

Listing 2-25. Output from the Grunt Task Shown in Listing 2-24

```
$ grunt list-files
Running "list-files:images" (list-files) task
Source: [ 'public/images/cat1.jpg',
  'public/images/cat2.jpg',
  'public/images/cat3.png' ]

Done, without errors.
```

The combination of the src configuration property and the this.files multi-task property provides developers with a concise syntax for iterating over multiple files. The contrived example that we've just looked at is fairly simple, but Grunt also provides additional options for tackling more complex scenarios. Let's take a look.

As opposed to the src key that was used to configure our task in Listing 2-24, the example in Listing 2-26 demonstrates the use of the files array—a slightly more verbose, but more powerful format for selecting files. This format accepts additional options that allow us to more finely tune our selection. Of particular importance is the expand option, as you'll see in Listing 2-27. Pay close attention to how the output differs from that of Listing 2-26, due to the use of the expand option.

Listing 2-26. Iterating Through Files Using the "Files Array" Format

```
// example-iterate2/tasks/list-files.js

module.exports = function(grunt) {

    grunt.config('list-files', {
        'images': {
            'files': [
                {
                    'cwd': 'public',
                    'src': ['**/*.jpg', '**/*.png'],
                    'dest': 'tmp',
                    'expand': true
                }
            ]
        }
    });

    grunt.registerMultiTask('list-files', function() {
        this.files.forEach(function(files) {
            grunt.log.writeln('Source:', files.src);
            grunt.log.writeln('Destination:', files.dest);
        });
    });

};
```

Listing 2-27. Output from the Grunt Task shown in Listing 2-26

```
$ grunt list-files
Running "list-files:images" (list-files) task
Source: [ 'public/images/cat1.jpg' ]
Destination: tmp/images/cat1.jpg
Source: [ 'public/images/cat2.jpg' ]
Destination: tmp/images/cat2.jpg

Done, without errors.
```

The expand option, when paired with the dest option, instructs Grunt to iterate through our task's this.files.forEach loop once for every entry it finds, within which we can find a corresponding dest property. Using this approach, we can easily create source-destination mappings that can be used to copy (or move) files from one location to another.

Watching for File Changes

One of Grunt's most popular plugins, grunt-contrib-watch, gives Grunt the ability to run predefined tasks whenever files that match a specified pattern are created, modified, or deleted. When combined with other tasks, grunt-contrib-watch enables developers to create powerful workflows that automate actions such as

- Checking JavaScript code for errors (i.e., "linting")
- Compiling Sass/L stylesheets
- Running unit tests

Let's take a look at a few examples that demonstrate such workflows put into action.

Automated JavaScript Linting

Listing 2-28 shows a basic Grunt setup similar to those already shown in this chapter. A default task is registered which serves as an alias to the watch task, allowing us to start watching for changes within our project by simply running $ grunt from the command line. In this example, Grunt will watch for changes within the src folder. As they occur, the jshint task is triggered, which will scan our project's src folder in search of JavaScript errors.

Listing 2-28. Automatically Checking for JavaScript Errors As Changes Occur

```
// example-watch-hint/Gruntfile.js

module.exports = function(grunt) {
    grunt.loadTasks('tasks');
    grunt.registerTask('default', ['watch']);
};

// example-watch-hint/tasks/jshint.js

module.exports = function(grunt) {

    grunt.loadNpmTasks('grunt-contrib-jshint');
```

```
    grunt.config('jshint', {
        'options': {
            'globalstrict': true,
            'node': true,
            'scripturl': true,
            'browser': true,
            'jquery': true
        },
        'all': [
            'src/**/*.js'
        ]
    });

};

// example-watch-hint/tasks/watch.js

module.exports = function(grunt) {

    grunt.loadNpmTasks('grunt-contrib-watch');

    grunt.config('watch', {
        'js': {
            'files': [
                'src/**/*'
            ],
            'tasks': ['jshint'],
            'options': {
                'spawn': true
            }
        }
    });

};
```

Automated Sass Stylesheet Compilation

Listing 2-29 shows an example in which Grunt is instructed to watch our project for changes. This time, however, instead of watching our JavaScript, Grunt is configured to watch our project's Sass stylesheets. As changes occur, the grunt-contrib-compass plugin is called, which compiles our stylesheets into their final form.

Listing 2-29. Automatically Compiling Sass Stylesheets As Changes Occur

```
// example-watch-sass/Gruntfile.js

module.exports = function(grunt) {
    grunt.loadTasks('tasks');
    grunt.registerTask('default', ['watch']);
};
```

```
// example-watch-sass/tasks/compass.js

module.exports = function(grunt) {

    grunt.loadNpmTasks('grunt-contrib-compass');

    grunt.config('compass', {
        'all': {
            'options': {
                'httpPath': '/',
                'cssDir': 'public/css',
                'sassDir': 'scss',
                'imagesDir': 'public/images',
                'relativeAssets': true,
                'outputStyle': 'compressed'
            }
        }
    });

};

// example-watch-compass/tasks/watch.js

module.exports = function(grunt) {

    grunt.loadNpmTasks('grunt-contrib-watch');

    grunt.config('watch', {
        'scss': {
            'files': [
                'scss/**/*'
            ],
            'tasks': ['compass'],
            'options': {
                'spawn': true
            }
        }
    });

};
```

■ **Note** In order for this example to function, you must install Compass, an open source CSS authoring framework. You can find additional information on how to install Compass at http://compass-style.org/install.

Automated Unit Testing

Our final example regarding `grunt-contrib-watch` concerns unit testing. In Listing 2-30, we see a Gruntfile that watches our project's JavaScript for changes. As these changes occur, our project's unit tests are immediately triggered with the help of Grunt's `grunt-mocha-test` plugin.

Listing 2-30. Automatically Running Unit Tests As Changes Occur

```
// example-watch-test/Gruntfile.js

module.exports = function(grunt) {
    grunt.loadTasks('tasks');
    grunt.registerTask('default', ['watch']);
};

// example-watch-test/tasks/mochaTest.js

module.exports = function(grunt) {

    grunt.loadNpmTasks('grunt-mocha-test');

    grunt.config('mochaTest', {
        'test': {
            'options': {
                'reporter': 'spec'
            },
            'src': ['test/**/*.js']
        }
    });

};

// example-watch-test/tasks/watch.js

module.exports = function(grunt) {

    grunt.loadNpmTasks('grunt-contrib-watch');

    grunt.config('watch', {
        'scss': {
            'files': [
                'src/**/*.js'
            ],
            'tasks': ['mochaTest'],
            'options': {
                'spawn': true
            }
        }
    });

};
```

31

Creating Plugins

A large library of community-supported plugins is what makes Grunt truly shine—a library that will allow you to start benefitting from Grunt immediately, without the need to create complex tasks from scratch. If you need to automate a build process within your project, there's a good chance that someone has already done the "grunt" work (zing!) for you.

In this section, you'll discover how you can contribute back to the community with Grunt plugins of your own creation.

Getting Started

One of the first things you'll want to do is create a public GitHub repository in which to store your new plugin. The example that we will be referencing is included with the source code that accompanies this book.

Once your new repository is ready, clone it to your computer. Next, initialize Grunt within it by following the same steps that were outlined earlier in this chapter's "Adding Grunt to Your Project" section. Afterward, the file structure of your new Grunt plugin should resemble that shown in Listing 2-31.

Listing 2-31. File Structure of Your New Grunt Plugin

```
.
├── Gruntfile.js
├── README.md
├── package.json
└── tasks
```

■ **Note** The most important point to note here is that there is no special structure or knowledge required (apart from what has already been covered in this chapter) for the creation of Grunt plugins. The process mirrors that of integrating Grunt into an existing project—the creation of a Gruntfile that loads tasks, along with the tasks themselves. Once published to npm, other Grunt projects will be able to load your plugin in the same way that other plugins have been referenced throughout this chapter.

Creating the Task

By way of an example, let's create a Grunt plugin capable of generating a report that details the type, size, and number of files contained within a project. An example demonstrating the configuration for this plugin is shown in Listing 2-32.

Listing 2-32. Example Demonstrating the Configuration of Our Plugin

```
// example-plugin/Gruntfile.js

module.exports = function(grunt) {

    grunt.config('file-report', {
        'options': {
        },
        'public': {
            'src': ['public/**/*']
        },
```

```
        'images': {
            'src': ['public/**/*.jpg', 'public/**/*.png', 'public/**/*.gif']
        }
    });

    grunt.loadNpmTasks('grunt-file-reporter');
    grunt.registerTask('default', ['file-report']);

};
```

The source code for our plugin is shown in Listing 2-33. Within our plugin, a Grunt multi-task named file-report is registered. When called, the task will iterate through the various target files that were specified in Listing 2-32. As it does so, the plugin will compile a report that details the type, number, and size of the files it finds.

Listing 2-33. Source Code for Our Plugin

```
// example-plugin/node_modules/grunt-file-reporter/Gruntfile.js

var fs = require('fs');
var filesize = require('filesize');
var _ = require('lodash');
_.mixin(require('underscore.string'));

module.exports = function(grunt) {

    var mime = require('mime');
    var Table = require('cli-table');

    grunt.registerMultiTask('file-report', 'Generates a report of file types & sizes used
    within a project', function() {

        var report = {
            'mimeTypes': {},
            'largest': null,
            'smallest': null
        };

        var table = new Table({
            'head': ['Content Type', 'Files Found', 'Total Size',
            'Average Size', 'Largest', 'Smallest']
        });
        var addFile = function(file) {
            if (grunt.file.isDir(file)) return;
            var mimeType = mime.lookup(file);
            if (!report.mimeTypes[mimeType]) {
                report.mimeTypes[mimeType] = {
                    'count': 0,
                    'sizes': [],
                    'largest': null,
                    'smallest': null,
```

33

```
                'oldest': null,
                'newest': null
            };
        }
        var details = report.mimeTypes[mimeType];
        details.count++;
        var stats = fs.statSync(file);
        details.sizes.push(stats.size);
        if (!details.largest || stats.size > details.largest.size) {
            details.largest = { 'file': file, 'size': stats.size };
        }
        if (!report.largest || stats.size > report.largest.size) {
            report.largest = { 'file': file, 'size': stats.size };
        }
        if (!details.smallest || stats.size < details.smallest.size) {
            details.smallest = { 'file': file, 'size': stats.size };
        }
        if (!report.smallest || stats.size < report.smallest.size) {
            report.smallest = { 'file': file, 'size': stats.size };
        }
    };

    var sum = function(arr) {
        return arr.reduce(function(a, b) {
            return a + b;
        });
    };

    var displayReport = function() {
        var totalSum = 0;
        var totalFiles = 0;
        var totalSizes = [];
        _.each(report.mimeTypes, function(data, mType) {
            var fileSum = sum(data.sizes);
            totalSum += fileSum;
            totalFiles += data.sizes.length;
            totalSizes = totalSizes.concat(data.sizes);
            table.push([mType, data.count, filesize(fileSum),
                filesize(fileSum / data.sizes.length),
                _.sprintf('%s (%s)', data.largest.file, filesize(data.largest.size)),
                _.sprintf('%s (%s)', data.smallest.file, filesize(data.smallest.size)),
            ]);
        });
        table.push(['-', totalFiles, filesize(totalSum),
            filesize(totalSum / totalSizes.length),
            _.sprintf('%s (%s)', report.largest.file, filesize(report.largest.size)),
            _.sprintf('%s (%s)', report.smallest.file, filesize(report.smallest.size)),
        ]);
        console.log(table.toString());
    };
```

```
        this.files.forEach(function(files) {
            files.src.forEach(addFile);
        });

        displayReport();

    });

};
```

The output generated by our plugin's `file-report` task is shown in Figure 2-1.

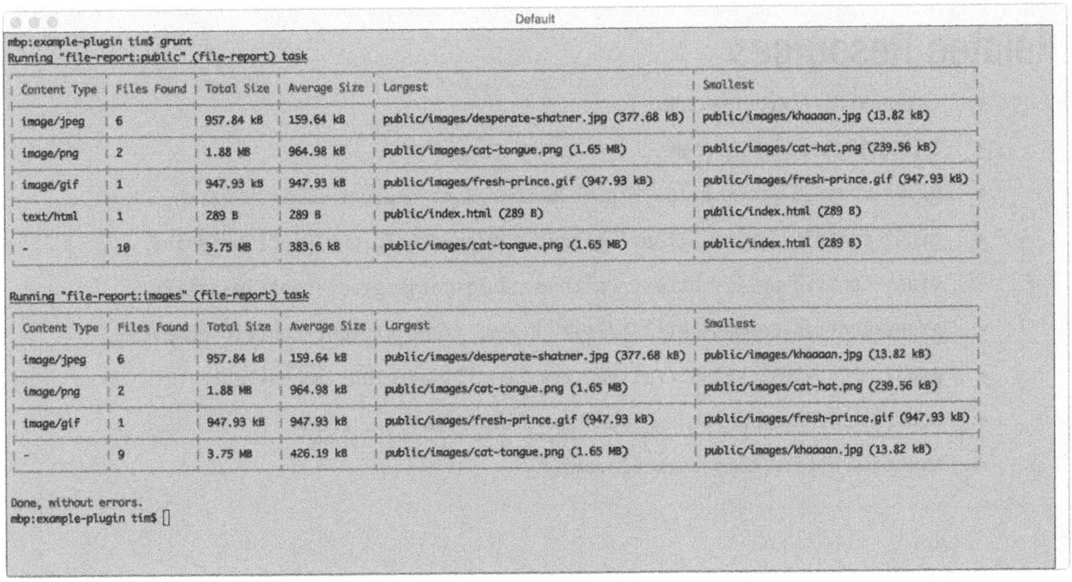

Figure 2-1. The output generated by the `file-report` task

Publishing to npm

Once our plugin is ready and our Git repository is updated with the latest code, the final step toward making it available to others is publishing it via npm:

```
$ npm publish
```

■ **Note** If this is your first time publishing a module to npm, you will be asked to create an account.

Summary

In this chapter, we've looked at how Grunt provides developers with a powerful toolkit for automating many of the repetitive, tedious tasks that often accompany software development. You've discovered

- What makes Grunt tick (tasks, plugins, and configuration objects)

- How to configure tasks and plugins

- How to use many of the helpful built-in utilities that Grunt makes available for providing user feedback and interacting with the file system

- How to create and share your own Grunt plugins

Related Resources

- Grunt: http://gruntjs.com

- JSHint: http://jshint.com

- grunt-contrib-watch: https://github.com/gruntjs/grunt-contrib-watch

- grunt-contrib-jshint: https://github.com/gruntjs/grunt-contrib-jshint

- grunt-contrib-uglify: https://github.com/gruntjs/grunt-contrib-uglify

- grunt-contrib-compass: https://github.com/gruntjs/grunt-contrib-compass

- grunt-mocha-test: https://github.com/pghalliday/grunt-mocha-test

- Syntactically Awesome Stylesheets (Sass): http://sass-lang.com

- Compass: http://compass-style.org

CHAPTER 3

Yeoman

One only needs two tools in life: WD-40 to make things go, and duct tape to make them stop.

—G. Weilacher

The development community has witnessed a role-reversal of sorts take place in recent years. Web applications, once considered by many to be second-class citizens in comparison to their native counterparts, have largely supplanted traditional desktop applications, thanks in large part to the widespread adoption of modern web development technologies and the rise of the mobile Web. But as web applications have grown increasingly sophisticated, so too have the tools on which they rely and the steps required to bootstrap them into existence.

The topic of this chapter, Yeoman, is a popular project "scaffolding" tool that helps to alleviate this problem by automating the tedious tasks associated with bootstrapping new applications off the ground. Yeoman provides a mechanism for creating reusable templates that describe a project's initial file structure, HTML, third-party libraries, and task runner configurations. These templates, which can be shared with the wider development community via npm, allow developers to bootstrap new projects that follow agreed-upon best practices in a matter of minutes.

In this chapter, you will learn how to:

- Install Yeoman

- Take advantage of Yeoman generators that have already been published by the community

- Contribute back to the community with your own Yeoman generators

---

Note   This chapter builds on topics that have already been covered in this book's first two chapters on Bower and Grunt. If you are unfamiliar with either of these tools, you may wish to read the respective chapter for that tool before you continue.

Installing Yeoman

Yeoman's command-line utility, yo, is available via npm. If you have not already installed Yeoman, you should do so before you continue, as shown in Listing 3-1.

Listing 3-1. Installing the yo Command-Line Utility via npm

```
$ npm install -g yo
$ yo --version
1.4.6
```

Creating Your First Project

Yeoman allows developers to quickly create the initial structure of an application through the use of reusable templates, which Yeoman refers to as "generators." To better understand how this process can improve your workflow, let's create a new project with the help of the modernweb generator that was created specifically for this chapter. Afterward, we will look at how this generator was created, providing you with the knowledge you need to create and share your own custom Yeoman generators with the wider development community.

The generator we will be using will create the initial foundations of a project that uses the following tools and libraries:

- Grunt

- Bower

- jQuery

- AngularJS

- Browserify

- Compass

Yeoman generators are installed as global npm modules. That being the case, the command for installing our generator should look familiar:

```
$ npm install -g generator-modernweb
```

■ **Note** This generator's name is prefixed with generator-, which is an important convention that all Yeoman generators must follow. At runtime, Yeoman will determine what (if any) generators have been installed by searching for global modules whose names follow this format.

With our generator now installed, we can move forward with setting up our first project. First, we create a new folder to contain it. Afterward, we instruct Yeoman to create a new project based on the generator that we just installed. Listing 3-2 shows these steps in action, along with several questions the generator is designed to prompt you with.

Listing 3-2. Creating Our First Project with the modernweb Generator

```
$ mkdir my-app
$ cd my-app
$ yo modernweb

? Project Title: My Project
? Package Name: my-project
? Project Description: My awesome project
? Project Author: John Doe
? Express Port: 7000
```

After responding to the generator's questions (you can safely accept the defaults), Yeoman will move forward with creating the project. Afterward, we can easily build and launch it using the project's default Grunt task, which our generator has conveniently set up for us (see Listing 3-3).

Listing 3-3. Our New Project's Default Grunt Task Will Trigger Various Build Steps and Open the Project Within Our Browser

```
$ grunt
Running "concat:app" (concat) task
File public/dist/libs.js created.

Running "compass:app" (compass) task
unchanged scss/style.scss
Compilation took 0.002s

Running "browserify" task

Running "concurrent:app" (concurrent) task
Running "watch" task
Waiting…
Running "open:app" (open) task
Running "server" task
Server is now listening on port: 7000

Done, without errors.
```

As you can see, our new project's default Grunt task executes several additional build steps for us:

- JavaScript libraries are compiled into a single, minified script.

- Sass stylesheets are compiled.

- The source code of the application itself is compiled via Browserify.

- An instance of Express is created to serve our project.

- Various watch scripts are initialized that will automatically recompile our project as changes are made.

The final action of our project's default Grunt task will be to launch our project within a new browser window, as shown in Figure 3-1.

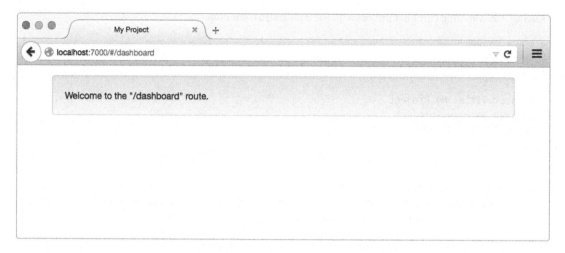

Figure 3-1. *Our new project's home page, opened for us by the default Grunt task*

Now that our new project is ready for further development, let's take a few moments to become familiar with the various templates, scripts, and Grunt tasks that our generator has put in place for us, paying special attention to the contents of these files:

- `bower.json`
- `Gruntfile.js`
- `package.json`
- `public/index.html`

With the help of Yeoman's support for user prompts and templates (which we will discuss in more detail in the next section), the generator has merged our answers to its initial questions with the contents of our project's files, where appropriate. For instance, the values for name, `description`, and `author` within our project's `package.json` file have been set for us (see Listing 3-4).

Listing 3-4. Contents of Our Project's `package.json` File

```
// package.json

{
  "name": "my-project",
  "description": "My awesome project",
  "author": "John Doe",
  "files": [],
  "keywords": [],
  "dependencies": {},
  "browserify": {
    "transform": [
      "brfs",
```

```
        "bulkify",
        "folderify"
    ]
  },
  "browser": {}
}
```

Subcommands

In their simplest form, generators act as configurable project templates that simplify the creation of new projects, but that's not their only purpose. In addition to assisting with the initial creation of new projects, generators can also include other commands that project maintainers will find useful throughout development.

In Listing 3-2, we used the modernweb generator to create a new single-page application built using the AngularJS framework. If you are unfamiliar with Angular, don't worry—the particulars of this framework are unimportant for now. What is important, however, is the contents of the project's public/app/routes folder. Notice that a single folder, dashboard, has been created for us at this location. The contents of this folder is shown in Listing 3-5.

Listing 3-5. Contents of Our Project's public/app/routes/dashboard Folder

```
.
├── index.js
└── template.html
```

```
// public/app/routes/dashboard/index.js

module.exports = {
    'route': '/dashboard',
    'controller': function() {
    },
    'templateUrl': '/app/routes/dashboard/template.html',
    'resolve': {}
};
```

```
// public/app/routes/dashboard/template.html

<div class="well">
    Welcome to the "/dashboard" route.
</div>
```

This project has been set up such that each folder within public/app/routes defines a different "hashbang" route within the application. In this example, the project's dashboard folder defines a route that can be accessed at http://localhost:7000/#/dashboard. Knowing this, suppose that we wanted to add a new users route to our application. To do so, we could manually create the necessary files at the appropriate location. Alternatively, we could use an additional command provided by our generator that simplifies this process (see Listing 3-6).

Listing 3-6. Example of Calling the route Sub-generator to Automate the Process of Creating New Routes Within Our Angular Application

```
$ yo modernweb:route users
   create public/app/routes/users/index.js
   create public/app/routes/users/template.html
Route `users` created.
```

After running this command, refer to the project's /public/app/routes folder and note the existence of a new folder named users. Within this folder, our Yeoman generator has taken care of creating the appropriate files for us. If you happen to still have the server that we created in Listing 3-3 running, you should also be able to see that the watch scripts that were started for us have detected this change and automatically recompiled our application (see Listing 3-7).

Listing 3-7. Grunt Automatically Recompiles Application As Changes Are Made

```
>> File "public/app/routes/users" added.
Running "browserify" task
Done, without errors.
```

Creating Your First Generator

The remainder of this chapter will focus on the creation of a custom Yeoman generator—the same one used in the previous section to bootstrap a new project built around AngularJS (among other tools). Afterward, you will be well prepared to begin creating your own generators that will allow you to quickly get up-and-running with workflows that meet your specific needs.

Yeoman Generators are Node Modules

A Yeoman generator is nothing more than a simple Node module that follows Yeoman's prescribed guidelines. As such, the first step in creating a generator is the creation of a new Node module. Listing 3-8 shows the required commands, along with the resulting package.json file.

Listing 3-8. Creating a New Node Module to Contain the Contents of Our First Yeoman Generator

```
$ mkdir generator-example
$ cd generator-example
$ npm init

// generator-example/package.json
{
  "name": "generator-example",
  "version": "1.0.0",
  "description": "An example Yeoman generator",
  "files": [],
  "keywords": [
    "yeoman-generator"
  ],
  "dependencies": {}
}
```

Yeoman generators have the option of relying on external dependencies, as is the case with any other Node module. At a bare minimum, however, every generator must specify the yeoman-generator module as a local dependency. This module will provide us with the core functionality provided by Yeoman for creating user interactions, interacting with the file system, and other important tasks. This module is installed as a local dependency using the following command:

```
$ npm install yeoman-generator --save
```

Sub-Generators

Yeoman generators consist of one or more commands, each of which can be called separately from the command line. These commands, which Yeoman refers to as "sub-generators," are defined within folders that exist at the root level of the module. For some additional context, refer back to Listing 3-2, in which we created a new project based off of the modernweb generator by running $ yo modernweb from the command line. In that example, we did not specify a command—we simply passed Yeoman the name of a generator. As a result, Yeoman executed that generator's *default* sub-generator, which by convention is always named app. We could have accomplished the same thing by running this command:

```
$ yo modernweb:app
```

To better understand how this works, let's move forward with creating our generator's default app sub-generator. We do so in four steps:

1. Create a folder named app at the root level of our module.

2. Create a folder named templates within our new app folder.

3. Place various files within our templates folder that we want to copy into the target project (e.g., HTML files, Grunt tasks, a Bower manifest, and so forth).

4. Create the script shown in Listing 3-9, which is responsible for driving the functionality for this command.

Listing 3-9. Contents of Our Generator's Default app Command ("Sub-generator")

```
// generator-example/app/index.js

var generators = require('yeoman-generator');

/**
 * We create our generator by exporting a class that extends
 * from Yeoman's `Base` class.
 */
```

```
module.exports = generators.Base.extend({

    'prompting': function() {

    /**
     * Indicates that this function will execute asynchronously. Yeoman
     * will wait until we call the `done()` function before continuing.
     */
        var done = this.async();

    /**
     * Our generator's `prompt` method (inherited from Yeoman's `Base`
     * class) allows us to define a series of questions to prompt the
     * user with.
     */
        this.prompt([
            {
                'type': 'input',
                'name': 'title',
                'message': 'Project Title',
                'default': 'My Project',
                'validate': function(title) {
                    return (title.length > 0);
                }
            },
            {
                'type': 'input',
                'name': 'package_name',
                'message': 'Package Name',
                'default': 'my-project',
                'validate': function(name) {
                    return (name.length > 0 && /^[a-z0-9\-]+$/i.test(name));
                },
                'filter': function(name) {
                    return name.toLowerCase();
                }
            },
            {
                'type': 'input',
                'name': 'description',
                'message': 'Project Description',
                'default': 'My awesome project',
                'validate': function(description) {
                    return (description.length > 0);
                }
            },
            {
                'type': 'input',
                'name': 'author',
                'message': 'Project Author',
                'default': 'John Doe',
```

```
                'validate': function(author) {
                    return (author.length > 0);
                }
            },
            {
                'type': 'input',
                'name': 'port',
                'message': 'Express Port',
                'default': 7000,
                'validate': function(port) {
                    port = parseInt(port, 10);
                    return (!isNaN(port) && port > 0);
                }
            }
        ], function(answers) {
            this._answers = answers;
            done();
        }.bind(this));

},

'writing': function() {

/**
 * Copies files from our sub-generator's `templates` folder to the target
 * project. The contents of each file is processed as a Lodash template
 * before being written to the disk.
 */
    this.fs.copyTpl(
    this.templatePath('**/*'),
    this.destinationPath(),
    this._answers
      );

    this.fs.copyTpl(
        this.templatePath('pkg.json'),
        this.destinationPath('package.json'),
        this._answers
    );

    this.fs.delete(this.destinationPath('pkg.json'));

    this.fs.copyTpl(
     this.templatePath('.bowerrc'),
     this.destinationPath('.bowerrc'),
     this._answers
  );
```

```
/**
 * Writes a Yeoman configuration file to the target project's folder.
 */
    this.config.save();

},

'install': function() {

  /**
   * Installs various npm modules within the project folder and updates
   * `package.json` accordingly.
   */
    this.npmInstall([
        'express', 'lodash', 'underscore.string', 'browserify',
        'grunt', 'grunt-contrib-concat', 'grunt-contrib-watch',
        'grunt-contrib-compass', 'grunt-concurrent', 'bulk-require',
        'brfs', 'bulkify', 'folderify', 'grunt-open'
    ], {
        'saveDev': false
    });

  /**
   * Installs dependencies defined within `bower.json`.
   */
    this.bowerInstall();

},

'end': function() {
    this.log('Your project is ready.');
}

});
```

The contents of our generator's app folder is shown in Figure 3-2.

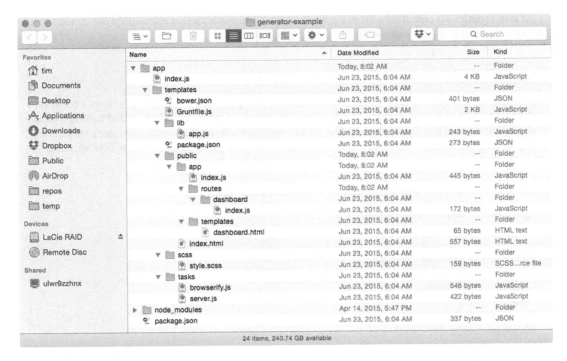

Figure 3-2. *The contents of our generator's app folder. The contents of the* `templates` *folder will be copied into the target project*

In Listing 3-9, our generator's default app command is created by exporting a class that extends from Yeoman's `Base` class. Within this class, four instance methods are defined:

- `prompting()`
- `writing()`
- `install()`
- `end()`

These method names play an important role during execution (they were not arbitrarily chosen). When Yeoman runs a generator, it searches for prototype methods whose names match those listed here:

- `initializing()`: Initialization methods (checking project state, getting configs).
- `prompting()`: Prompting the user for information
- `configuring()`: Saving configuration files.
- `default()`: Prototype methods with names *not* included within this list will be executed during this step.
- `writing()`: Write operations specific to this generator occur here.
- `conflicts()`: Conflicts are handled here (used internally by Yeoman).
- `install()`: Installation procedures occur here (npm, bower).
- `end()`: Last function to be called. Cleanup/closing messages.

Once Yeoman has compiled a list of the various prototype methods that exist within our generator, it will execute them in the priority shown in the preceding list.

Lodash Templates

In Listing 3-9, Yeoman's `fs.copyTpl()` method was used to copy files from our sub-generator's `templates` folder to the target project. This method differs from Yeoman's `fs.copy()` method, in that it also processes each file it finds as a Lodash template. Listing 3-10 shows the contents of our sub-generator's `templates/pkg.json` file, which will be processed in this way before being saved to the folder of the new project as `package.json`.

Listing 3-10. Contents of Our Sub-generator's `templates/pkg.json` File

```
// generator-example/app/templates/pkg.json

{
  "name": "<%= package_name %>",
  "description": "<%= description %>",
  "author": "<%= author %>",
  "files": [],
  "keywords": [],
  "dependencies": {},
  "browserify": {
    "transform": [
      "brfs",
      "bulkify",
      "folderify"
    ]
  },
  "browser": {}
}
```

■ **Note**   The process by which Yeoman generators can modify their behavior and alter the contents of templates based on a user's answers to prompts opens up a lot of exciting possibilities. It allows for the creation of new projects that are dynamically configured according to a user's specific needs. It's this aspect of Yeoman, more than any other, that makes the tool truly useful.

We're now ready to create our first project using our new generator. To do so, open a new terminal window and create a folder to contain it. Next, move into the new folder and run the generator, as shown in Listing 3-11.

Listing 3-11. Running Our New Generator for the First Time

```
$ mkdir new-project
$ cd new-project
$ yo example

Error example
```

You don't seem to have a generator with the name example installed.
You can see available generators with npm search yeoman-generator and then install the
with npm install [name].

Obviously, this isn't the result we were hoping for. To understand what caused this error, recall from earlier in the chapter that when Yeoman is called, it locates generators by searching for modules whose names begin with generator- that have been installed in the global context. As a result, Yeoman is currently unaware of the existence of our new generator. Fortunately, npm provides a handy command that will solve this problem for us. The npm link command creates a symbolic link (symlink) between our new module and Node's global modules folder. The command is executed at the root level of our new module (see Listing 3-12).

Listing 3-12. Creating a Symbolic Link with the npm link Command

```
$ npm link
/Users/tim/.nvm/v0.10.33/lib/node_modules/generator-example -> /opt/generator-example
```

Npm's link command creates a symbolic link between the folder in which it is run and the folder in which globally installed Node modules are stored. By running this command, we place a reference to our new generator in a location that Yeoman can find. With this link in place, let's run our generator again (see Listing 3-13).

Listing 3-13. Successfully Running Our New Generator for the First Time

```
$ yo example

? Project Title: My Project
? Package Name: my-project
? Project Description: My awesome project
? Project Author: John Doe
? Express Port: 7000
```

After responding to the generator's questions, Yeoman will move forward with building our new project, just as it did with the modernweb generator that we used in the first half of this chapter. Once this process is finished, run Grunt's default task—$ grunt—to build and launch the project.

Defining Secondary Commands

In the first half of this chapter, you learned that multiple commands can be included with Yeoman generators—commands whose usefulness can extend well beyond the initial creation of a new project. The modernweb generator demonstrated this by including a route command that automated the process of creating new routes within an Angular application (refer to Listing 3-6 earlier in the chapter). The steps involved in creating this command closely follow those we took when we created our generator's default app command:

1. Create a folder named route at the root level of our module.

2. Create a folder named templates within our new route folder.

3. Place various files within our templates folder that we want to copy into the target project.

4. Create the script shown in Listing 3-14, which is responsible for driving the functionality for the route command.

Listing 3-14. A route Sub-generator That Automates the Creation of New Angular Routes

```
// generator-example/route/index.js

var generators = require('yeoman-generator');

/*
Our generator's default `app` command was created by extending Yeoman's `Base` class.
In this example, we extend the `NamedBase` class, instead. Doing so alerts Yeoman to
the fact that this command expects one or more arguments. For example: $ yo example:route
my-new-route
*/
module.exports = generators.NamedBase.extend({

    'constructor': function(args) {
        this._opts = {
            'route': args[0]
        };
        generators.NamedBase.apply(this, arguments);
    },

    'writing': function() {

        this.fs.copyTpl(
            this.templatePath('index.js'),
            this.destinationPath('public/app/routes/' + this._opts.route + '/index.js'),
            this._opts
        );

        this.fs.copyTpl(
            this.templatePath('template.html'),
            this.destinationPath('public/app/routes/' + this._opts.route +
            '/template.html'),
            this._opts
        );

    },

    'end': function() {
        this.log('Route `' + this._opts.route + '` created.');
    }

});
```

The script shown in Listing 3-14 looks very similar to that shown in Listing 3-9, the primary difference being the use of Yeoman's NamedBase class. By creating a sub-generator that extends from NamedBase, we alert Yeoman to the fact that this command expects to receive one or more arguments.

Listing 3-15 demonstrates the use of our generator's new route command.

Listing 3-15. Creating a New Angular Route Using Our Generator's route Command

```
$ yo example:route users
   create public/app/routes/users/index.js
   create public/app/routes/users/template.html
Route `users` created.
```

Composability

When creating Yeoman generators, it is not uncommon to encounter situations in which having the ability to execute one sub-generator from within another would be useful. For example, consider the generator that we just created. It's easy to imagine a scenario in which we might want our generator to automatically create several default routes when run. To accomplish that goal, it would be helpful if we had the ability to call our generator's route command from *within* its app command. Yeoman's composeWith() method exists for this very reason (see Listing 3-16).

Listing 3-16. Yeoman's composeWith() Method Allows One Sub-generator to Call Another

```
// generator-example/app/index.js (excerpt)

'writing': function() {

    this.fs.copyTpl(
        this.templatePath('**/*'),
        this.destinationPath(),
        this._answers
    );

    this.fs.copy(
        this.templatePath('.bowerrc'),
        this.destinationPath('.bowerrc'),
        this._answers
    );

    /*
    Yeoman's `composeWith` method allows us to execute external generators.
    Here, we trigger the creation of a new route named "dashboard".
    */
    this.composeWith('example:route', {
        'args': ['dashboard']
    });

    this.config.save();

}
```

With the help of Yeoman's composeWith() method, simple sub-generators can be combined (i.e., "composed") with one another to create fairly sophisticated workflows. By taking advantage of this method, developers can create complex, multicommand generators, while avoiding the use of duplicate code across commands.

Summary

Yeoman is a simple but powerful tool that automates the tedious tasks associated with bootstrapping new applications into existence, speeding up the process by which developers can move from concept to prototype. When used, it allows developers to focus their attention where it matters most—on the applications themselves.

At last count, more than 1,500 Yeoman generators have been published to npm, making it easy for developers to experiment with a wide variety of tools, libraries, frameworks, and design patterns (e.g., Bower, Grunt, AngularJS, Knockout, React) with which they may not have experience.

Related Resources

- Yeoman: `http://yeoman.io/`

CHAPTER 4

PM2

Do not wait; the time will never be "just right." Start where you stand, and work with whatever tools you may have at your command, and better tools will be found as you go along.

—George Herbert

The previous chapters within this section have covered a variety of useful web development tools, with our primary focus placed on client-side development. In this chapter, we will round out our coverage of development tools by shifting our focus to the server. We will be exploring PM2, a command-line utility that simplifies many of the tasks associated with running Node applications, monitoring their status, and efficiently scaling them to meet increasing demand. Topics covered include:

- Working with processes
- Monitoring logs
- Monitoring resource usage
- Advanced process management
- Load-balancing across multiple processors
- Zero-downtime deployments

Installation

PM2's command-line utility, pm2, is available via npm. If you have not already installed PM2, you should do so before you continue, as shown in Listing 4-1.

Listing 4-1. Installing the pm2 Command-line Utility via npm

```
$ npm install -g pm2
$ pm2 --version
0.12.15
```

> ■ **Note** Node's package manager (npm) allows users to install packages in one of two contexts: locally or globally. In this example, bower is installed within the global context, which is typically reserved for command-line utilities.

Working with Processes

Listing 4-2 shows the contents of a simple Node application that will form the basis of our first several interactions with PM2. When accessed, it does nothing more than display the message "Hello, world." to users.

Listing 4-2. Simple Express Application

```
// my-app/index.js

var express = require('express');
var morgan = require('morgan');
var app = express();
app.use(morgan('combined'));

app.get('/', function(req, res, next) {
    res.send('Hello, world.\n');
});

app.listen(8000);
```

Figure 4-1 demonstrates the process by which we can launch this application with the help of the pm2 command-line utility. In this example, we instruct PM2 to start our application by executing its index.js script. We also provide PM2 with an (optional) name for our application (my-app), making it easier for us to reference it at a later time. Before doing so, be sure you install the project's dependencies by running $ npm install.

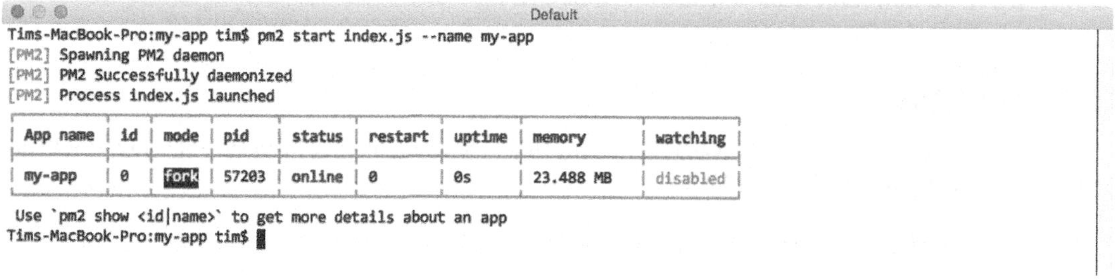

```
● ○ ●                                        Default
Tims-MacBook-Pro:my-app tim$ pm2 start index.js --name my-app
[PM2] Spawning PM2 daemon
[PM2] PM2 Successfully daemonized
[PM2] Process index.js launched

| App name | id | mode | pid   | status | restart | uptime | memory    | watching |
| my-app   | 0  | fork | 57203 | online | 0       | 0s     | 23.488 MB | disabled |

Use `pm2 show <id|name>` to get more details about an app
Tims-MacBook-Pro:my-app tim$ █
```

Figure 4-1. *Launching the application shown in Listing 4-2 with PM2*

After calling PM2's start command, PM2 helpfully displays a table containing information about every Node application it is currently aware of before returning us to the command prompt. The meaning of the columns that we see in this example is summarized in Table 4-1.

Table 4-1. *Summary of Columns Shown in Figure 4-1*

Heading	Description
App name	The name of the process. Defaults to the name of the script that was executed.
id	A unique ID assigned to the process by PM2. Processes can be referenced by name or ID.
mode	The method of execution (fork or cluster). Defaults to fork. Explored in more detail later in the chapter.
pid	A unique number assigned by the operating system to the process.
status	The current status of the process (e.g., online, stopped, etc.).
restart	The number of times the process has been restarted by PM2.
uptime	The length of time the process has been running since last being restarted.
memory	The amount of memory consumed by the process.
watching	Indicates whether PM2 will automatically restart the process when it detects changes within a project's file structure. Particularly useful during development. Defaults to disabled.

As indicated by the output provided by PM2 in Listing 4-3, our application is now online and ready for use. We can verify this by calling our application's sole route using the curl command-line utility, as shown in Figure 4-2.

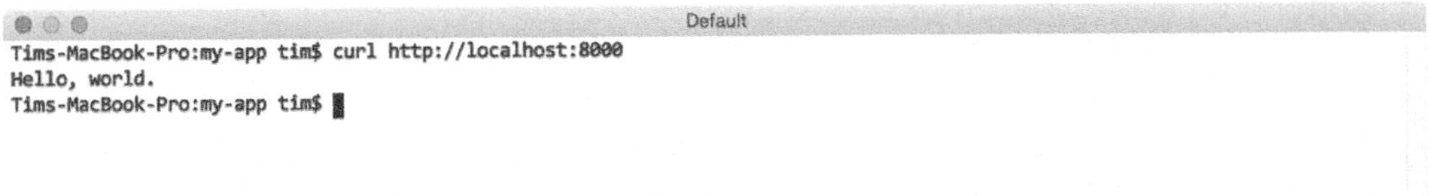

```
Default
Tims-MacBook-Pro:my-app tim$ curl http://localhost:8000
Hello, world.
Tims-MacBook-Pro:my-app tim$ ▇
```

Figure 4-2. *Accessing the sole route defined by our Express application*

■ **Note**   Figure 4-2 assumes the existence of the curl command-line utility within your environment. If you happen to be working in an environment where this utility is not available, you could also verify the status of this application by opening it directly within your web browser.

In addition to the start command, PM2 also provides a number of useful commands for interacting with processes that PM2 is already aware of, the most common of which are shown in Table 4-2.

Table 4-2. *Frequently Used Commands for Interacting with PM2 Processes*

Command	Description
list	Displays an up-to-date version of the table shown in Listing 4-4
stop	Stops the process, without removing it from PM2's list
restart	Restarts the process
delete	Stops the process and removes it from PM2's list
show	Displays details regarding the specified process

Simple commands such as stop, start, and delete require no additional commentary. Figure 4-3, on the other hand, shows the information you can expect to receive when requesting information about a specific PM2 process via the show command.

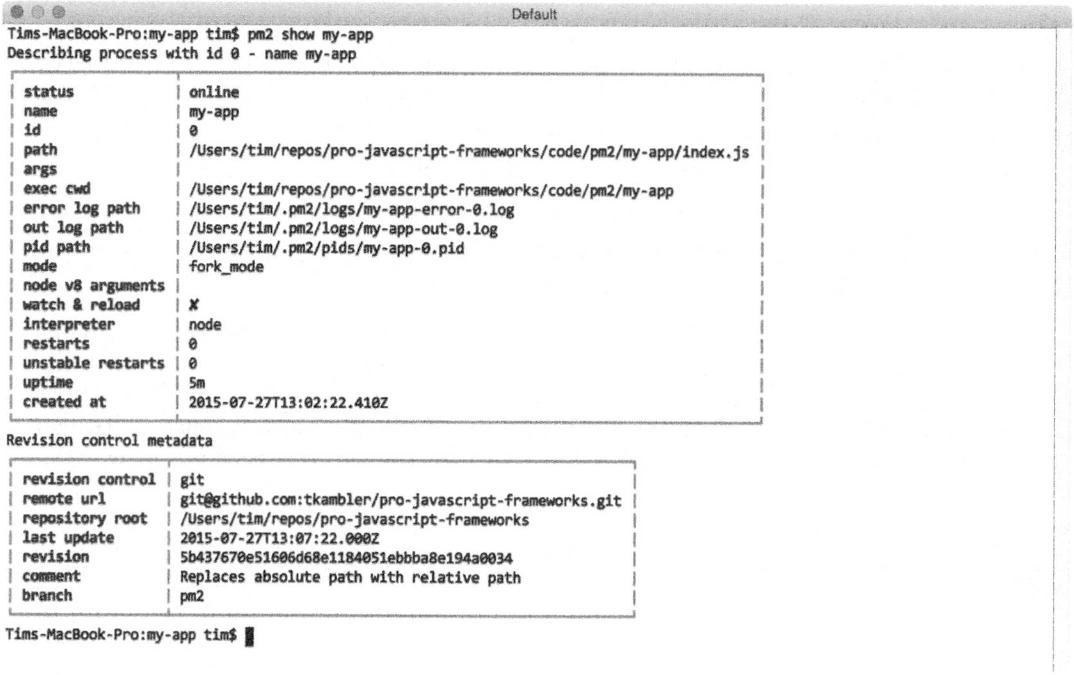

```
● ● ●                                          Default
Tims-MacBook-Pro:my-app tim$ pm2 show my-app
Describing process with id 0 - name my-app

| status            | online                                                            |
| name              | my-app                                                            |
| id                | 0                                                                 |
| path              | /Users/tim/repos/pro-javascript-frameworks/code/pm2/my-app/index.js |
| args              |                                                                   |
| exec cwd          | /Users/tim/repos/pro-javascript-frameworks/code/pm2/my-app        |
| error log path    | /Users/tim/.pm2/logs/my-app-error-0.log                           |
| out log path      | /Users/tim/.pm2/logs/my-app-out-0.log                             |
| pid path          | /Users/tim/.pm2/pids/my-app-0.pid                                 |
| mode              | fork_mode                                                         |
| node v8 arguments |                                                                   |
| watch & reload    | ✗                                                                 |
| interpreter       | node                                                              |
| restarts          | 0                                                                 |
| unstable restarts | 0                                                                 |
| uptime            | 5m                                                                |
| created at        | 2015-07-27T13:02:22.410Z                                          |

Revision control metadata

| revision control | git                                                        |
| remote url       | git@github.com:tkambler/pro-javascript-frameworks.git      |
| repository root  | /Users/tim/repos/pro-javascript-frameworks                 |
| last update      | 2015-07-27T13:07:22.000Z                                   |
| revision         | 5b437670e51606d68e1184051ebbba8e194a0034                   |
| comment          | Replaces absolute path with relative path                  |
| branch           | pm2                                                        |

Tims-MacBook-Pro:my-app tim$ █
```

Figure 4-3. *Viewing details for a specific PM2 process*

Recovering from Errors

At this point, you are now familiar with some of the basic steps involved in interacting with PM2. You've learned how to create new processes with the help of PM2's start command. You've also discovered how you can subsequently manage running processes with the help of commands such as list, stop, restart, delete, and show. We've yet to discuss, however, much of the real value that PM2 brings to the table in regard to managing Node processes. We'll begin that discussion by discovering how PM2 can assist Node applications in automatically recovering from fatal errors.

Listing 4-3 shows a modified version of the application we originally saw in Listing 4-2. In this version, however, an uncaught exception is thrown at a regular interval.

Listing 4-3. Modified Version of Our Original Application That Throws an Uncaught Exception Every Four Seconds

```
// my-bad-app/index.js

var express = require('express');
var morgan = require('morgan');
var app = express();
app.use(morgan('combined'));
```

```
app.get('/', function(req, res, next) {
    res.send('Hello, world.\n');
});

setInterval(function() {
    throw new Error('Uh oh.');
}, 4000);

app.listen(8000);
```

If we were to start this application without the help of PM2 by passing it directly to the node executable, we would quickly find ourselves out of luck the moment our first error was thrown. Node would simply print the error message to the console before dumping us back to the command prompt, as shown in Figure 4-4.

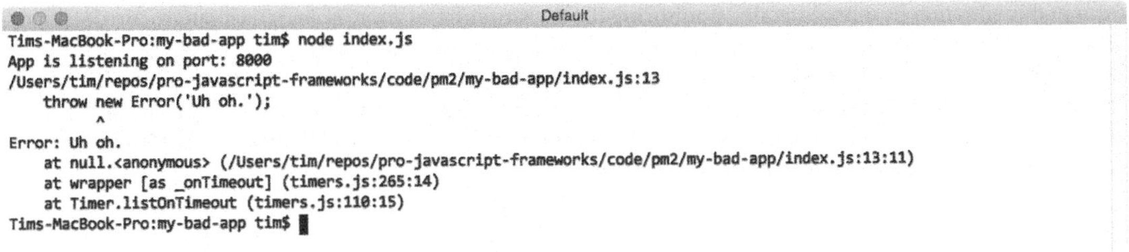

Figure 4-4. Output provided by Node after crashing from the error shown in Listing 4-3

Such behavior won't get us very far in a real usage scenario. Ideally, an application that has been released to a production environment should be thoroughly tested and devoid from such uncaught exceptions. However, in the event of such a crash, an application should at the very least be able to bring itself back online without requiring manual intervention. PM2 can help us accomplish this goal.

In Figure 4-5, we remove our existing process from PM2's list via the delete command and create a new instance of the poorly written application shown in Listing 4-3. Afterward, we wait several seconds before requesting an up-to-date process list from PM2.

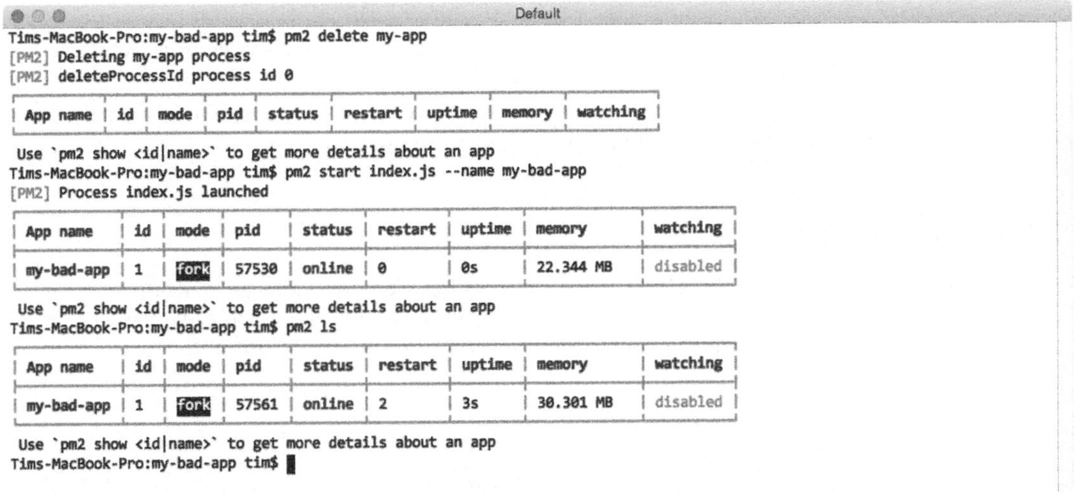

Figure 4-5. PM2 helps Node applications recover from fatal errors

Notice anything interesting here? Based on the values within the status, restart, and uptime columns, we can see that our application has crashed three times already. Each time, PM2 has helpfully stepped in and restarted it for us. The most recent process has been running for a total of two seconds, which means we can expect another crash (and automatic restart) two seconds from now.

PM2's ability to assist applications in recovering from fatal errors in a production environment, while useful, is just one of several useful features the utility provides. PM2 is also equally useful within development environments, as we'll soon see.

Responding to File Changes

Imagine a scenario in which you've recently begun work on a new Node project. Let's assume it's a web API built with Express. Without the help of additional tools, you must manually restart the related Node process in order to see the effects of your ongoing work—a frustrating chore that quickly grows old. PM2 can assist you in this situation by automatically monitoring the file structure of your project. As changes are detected, PM2 can automatically restart your application for you, if you instruct it to do so.

Figure 4-6 demonstrates this process. In this example, we first remove our currently running instance of my-bad-app. Next, we create a new instance of the application that was shown in our original example (see Listing 4-2). This time, however, we pass an additional flag, --watch, which instructs PM2 to monitor our project for changes and to respond accordingly.

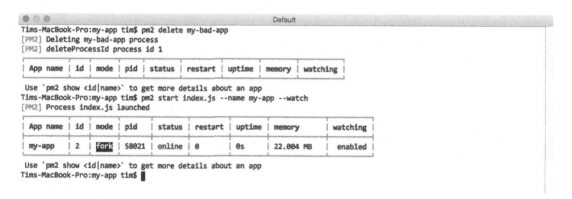

Figure 4-6. *Creating a new PM2 process that will automatically restart itself as changes are detected*

As changes are saved to this project's files, subsequent calls to PM2's list command will indicate how many times PM2 has restarted the application, as seen in a previous example.

Monitoring Logs

Refer back to Listing 4-2 and note this application's use of morgan, a module for logging incoming HTTP requests. In this example, morgan is configured to print such information to the console. We can see the result by running our application directly via the node executable, as shown in Figure 4-7.

```
● ● ●                                    Default
Tims-MacBook-Pro:my-app tim$ node index.js
App is listening on port: 8000
::1 - - [27/Jul/2015:13:17:09 +0000] "GET / HTTP/1.1" 200 14 "-" "Mozilla/5.0 (Macintosh; Intel Mac OS X 10_10_4) AppleWebKit
/537.36 (KHTML, like Gecko) Chrome/44.0.2403.107 Safari/537.36"
::1 - - [27/Jul/2015:13:17:09 +0000] "GET /favicon.ico HTTP/1.1" 404 24 "http://localhost:8000/" "Mozilla/5.0 (Macintosh; Int
el Mac OS X 10_10_4) AppleWebKit/537.36 (KHTML, like Gecko) Chrome/44.0.2403.107 Safari/537.36"
::1 - - [27/Jul/2015:13:17:12 +0000] "GET / HTTP/1.1" 304 - "-" "Mozilla/5.0 (Macintosh; Intel Mac OS X 10_10_4) AppleWebKit/
537.36 (KHTML, like Gecko) Chrome/44.0.2403.107 Safari/537.36"
::1 - - [27/Jul/2015:13:17:14 +0000] "GET / HTTP/1.1" 304 - "-" "Mozilla/5.0 (Macintosh; Intel Mac OS X 10_10_4) AppleWebKit/
537.36 (KHTML, like Gecko) Chrome/44.0.2403.107 Safari/537.36"
::1 - - [27/Jul/2015:13:17:16 +0000] "GET / HTTP/1.1" 304 - "-" "Mozilla/5.0 (Macintosh; Intel Mac OS X 10_10_4) AppleWebKit/
537.36 (KHTML, like Gecko) Chrome/44.0.2403.107 Safari/537.36"
::1 - - [27/Jul/2015:13:17:16 +0000] "GET / HTTP/1.1" 304 - "-" "Mozilla/5.0 (Macintosh; Intel Mac OS X 10_10_4) AppleWebKit/
537.36 (KHTML, like Gecko) Chrome/44.0.2403.107 Safari/537.36"
```

Figure 4-7. *Logging incoming requests to Express with* morgan

We recently explored how to allow PM2 to manage the execution of this application for us via the start command (see Figure 4-1). Doing so provides us with several benefits, but it also causes us to lose immediate insight into the output being generated by our application to the console. Fortunately, PM2 provides us with a simple mechanism for monitoring such output.

In Figure 4-3, we requested information from PM2 regarding a specific process under its control via the show command. Contained within the provided information were paths to two log files that PM2 automatically created for this process—one labeled "out log path" and one labeled "error log path"—to which PM2 will save this process's standard output and error messages, respectively. We could view these files directly, but PM2 provides a much more convenient method for interacting with them, as shown in Figure 4-8.

```
● ● ●                                    Default
Tims-MacBook-Pro:my-app tim$ pm2 logs
[PM2] Starting streaming logs for [all] process
PM2: 2015-07-27 08:19:05: Starting execution sequence in -fork mode- for app name:my-app id:0
PM2: 2015-07-27 08:19:05: App name:my-app id:0 online
my-app-0 (out): App is listening on port: 8000
my-app-0 (out): ::1 - - [27/Jul/2015:13:05:01 +0000] "GET / HTTP/1.1" 200 14 "-" "curl/7.37.1"
my-app-0 (out): App is listening on port: 8000
my-app-0 (out): App is listening on port: 8000
my-app-0 (out): App is listening on port: 8000
my-app-0 (out): ::1 - - [27/Jul/2015:13:19:17 +0000] "GET / HTTP/1.1" 304 - "-" "Mozilla/5.0 (Macintosh; Intel Mac OS X 10_10
_4) AppleWebKit/537.36 (KHTML, like Gecko) Chrome/44.0.2403.107 Safari/537.36"
my-app-0 (out): ::1 - - [27/Jul/2015:13:19:19 +0000] "GET / HTTP/1.1" 304 - "-" "Mozilla/5.0 (Macintosh; Intel Mac OS X 10_10
_4) AppleWebKit/537.36 (KHTML, like Gecko) Chrome/44.0.2403.107 Safari/537.36"
my-app-0 (out): ::1 - - [27/Jul/2015:13:19:21 +0000] "GET / HTTP/1.1" 304 - "-" "Mozilla/5.0 (Macintosh; Intel Mac OS X 10_10
_4) AppleWebKit/537.36 (KHTML, like Gecko) Chrome/44.0.2403.107 Safari/537.36"
```

Figure 4-8. *Monitoring the output from processes under PM2's control*

Here we see how the output from processes under PM2's control can be monitored as needed via the logs command. In this example, we monitor the output from *all* processes under PM2's control. Notice how PM2 helpfully prefixes each entry with information regarding the process from which each line of output originated. This information is particularly useful when using PM2 to manage multiple processes, which we will begin doing in the upcoming section. Alternatively, we can also monitor the output from a specific process by passing the name (or ID) for that process to the logs command (see Figure 4-9).

```
● ● ●                                          Default
Tims-MacBook-Pro:my-app tim$ pm2 logs my-app
[PM2] Starting streaming logs for [my-app] process
PM2: 2015-07-27 08:19:05: Starting execution sequence in -fork mode- for app name:my-app id:0
PM2: 2015-07-27 08:19:05: App name:my-app id:0 online
my-app-0 (out): App is listening on port: 8000
my-app-0 (out): ::1 - - [27/Jul/2015:13:05:01 +0000] "GET / HTTP/1.1" 200 14 "-" "curl/7.37.1"
my-app-0 (out): App is listening on port: 8000
my-app-0 (out): App is listening on port: 8000
my-app-0 (out): App is listening on port: 8000
my-app-0 (out): ::1 - - [27/Jul/2015:13:19:17 +0000] "GET / HTTP/1.1" 304 - "-" "Mozilla/5.0 (Macintosh; Intel Mac OS X 10_10
_4) AppleWebKit/537.36 (KHTML, like Gecko) Chrome/44.0.2403.107 Safari/537.36"
my-app-0 (out): ::1 - - [27/Jul/2015:13:19:19 +0000] "GET / HTTP/1.1" 304 - "-" "Mozilla/5.0 (Macintosh; Intel Mac OS X 10_10
_4) AppleWebKit/537.36 (KHTML, like Gecko) Chrome/44.0.2403.107 Safari/537.36"
my-app-0 (out): ::1 - - [27/Jul/2015:13:19:21 +0000] "GET / HTTP/1.1" 304 - "-" "Mozilla/5.0 (Macintosh; Intel Mac OS X 10_10
_4) AppleWebKit/537.36 (KHTML, like Gecko) Chrome/44.0.2403.107 Safari/537.36"
■
```

Figure 4-9. *Monitoring the output from a specific process under PM2's control*

Should you wish to clear out the content of log files generated by PM2 at any point, you can quickly do so by calling PM2's flush command. The behavior of the utility's logs command can also be tweaked slightly with the use of two optional arguments, which are listed in Table 4-3.

Table 4-3. *Arguments Accepted by PM2's logs Command*

Argument	Description
-raw	Displays the raw content of log files, stripping prefixed process identifiers in the process
-lines <N>	Instructs PM2 to display the last N lines, instead of the default of 20

Monitoring Resource Usage

In the previous section, you learned how PM2 can assist you in monitoring the standard output and errors being generated by processes under its control. In much the same way, PM2 also provides easy-to-use tools for monitoring the health of those processes, as well as for monitoring the overall health of the server on which they are running.

Monitoring Local Resources

Figure 4-10 demonstrates the output that is generated when PM2's monit command is called. Here we see a continuously updated view that allows us to track the amount of CPU processing power as well as the amount of RAM consumed by each process being managed by PM2.

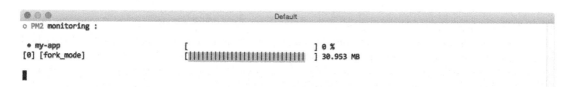

Figure 4-10. *Monitoring CPU and memory usage via PM2's monit command*

Monitoring Remote Resources

The information provided by PM2's `monit` command provides us with a quick and easy method for monitoring the health of its processes. This functionality is particularly helpful during development, when our primary focus is on the resources being consumed within our own environment. It's less helpful, however, as an application moves into a remote, production environment that could easily consist of *multiple* servers, each running its own instance of PM2.

PM2 takes this into account by also providing a built-in JSON API that can be accessed over the Web on port 9615. Disabled by default, the process for enabling it is shown in Figure 4-11.

```
● ● ●                                          Default
Tims-MacBook-Pro:my-app tim$ pm2 web
Launching web interface on port 9615
[PM2] Process /Users/tim/.nvm/versions/node/v0.12.4/lib/node_modules/pm2/lib/HttpInterface.js launched
[PM2] Process launched
┌───────────────────┬────┬──────┬───────┬────────┬─────────┬────────┬───────────┬───────────┐
│ App name          │ id │ mode │ pid   │ status │ restart │ uptime │ memory    │ watching  │
├───────────────────┼────┼──────┼───────┼────────┼─────────┼────────┼───────────┼───────────┤
│ my-app            │ 0  │ fork │ 58211 │ online │ 0       │ 7m     │ 30.953 MB │ disabled  │
│ pm2-http-interface│ 1  │ fork │ 58769 │ online │ 0       │ 0s     │ 21.926 MB │ disabled  │
└───────────────────┴────┴──────┴───────┴────────┴─────────┴────────┴───────────┴───────────┘
Use `pm2 show <id|name>` to get more details about an app
Tims-MacBook-Pro:my-app tim$ ▌
```

Figure 4-11. *Enabling PM2's JSON web API*

In this example, we enable PM2's web-accessible JSON API by calling the utility's web command. PM2 implements this functionality as part of a separate application that runs independently of PM2 itself. As a result, we can see that a new process, `pm2-http-interface`, is now under PM2's control. Should we ever wish to disable PM2's JSON API, we can do so by removing this process as we would any other, by passing its name (or ID) to the `delete` (or `stop`) commands.

Listing 4-4 shows an excerpt of the output that is provided when a GET request is made to the server running PM2 over port 9615. As you can see, PM2 provides us with a number of details regarding each of the processes currently under its control, as well as the system on which it is running.

Listing 4-4. Excerpt of the Information Provided by PM2's JSON API

```json
{
    "system_info": {
        "hostname": "iMac.local",
        "uptime": 2186
    },
    "monit": {
        "loadavg": [1.39794921875],
        "total_mem": 8589934592,
        "free_mem": 2832281600,
        "cpu": [{
            "model": "Intel(R) Core(TM) i5-4590 CPU @ 3.30GHz",
            "speed": 3300,
            "times": {
                "user": 121680,
                "nice": 0,
                "sys": 176220,
```

```
                    "idle": 1888430,
                    "irq": 0
                }
        }],
        "interfaces": {
            "lo0": [{
                "address": "::1",
                "netmask": "ffff:ffff:ffff:ffff:ffff:ffff:ffff:ffff",
                "family": "IPv6",
                "mac": "00:00:00:00:00:00",
                "scopeid": 0,
                "internal": true
            }],
            "en0": [{
                "address": "10.0.1.49",
                "netmask": "255.255.255.0",
                "family": "IPv4",
                "mac": "ac:87:a3:35:9c:72",
                "internal": false
            }]
        }
    },
    "processes": [{
        "pid": 1163,
        "name": "my-app",
        "pm2_env": {
            "name": "my-app",
            "vizion": true,
            "autorestart": true,
            "exec_mode": "fork_mode",
            "exec_interpreter": "node",
            "pm_exec_path": "/opt/my-app/index.js",
            "env": {
                "_": "/usr/local/opt/nvm/versions/node/v0.12.4/bin/pm2",
                "NVM_IOJS_ORG_MIRROR": "https://iojs.org/dist",
                "NVM_BIN": "/usr/local/opt/nvm/versions/node/v0.12.4/bin",
                "LOGNAME": "user",
                "ITERM_SESSION_ID": "w0t0p0",
                "HOME": "/Users/user",
                "COLORFGBG": "7;0",
                "SHLVL": "1",
                "XPC_SERVICE_NAME": "0",
                "XPC_FLAGS": "0x0",
                "ITERM_PROFILE": "Default",
                "LANG": "en_US.UTF-8",
                "PWD": "/opt/my-app",
                "NVM_NODEJS_ORG_MIRROR": "https://nodejs.org/dist",
                "PATH": "/usr/local/opt/nvm/versions/node/v0.12.4/bin",
                "__CF_USER_TEXT_ENCODING": "0x1F5:0x0:0x0",
                "SSH_AUTH_SOCK": "/private/tmp/com.apple.launchd.kEqu8iouDS/Listeners",
                "USER": "user",
```

```
        "NVM_DIR": "/usr/local/opt/nvm",
        "NVM_PATH": "/usr/local/opt/nvm/versions/node/v0.12.4/lib/node",
        "TMPDIR": "/var/folders/y3/2fphz1fd6rg9l4cg2t8t7g840000gn/T/",
        "TERM": "xterm",
        "SHELL": "/bin/bash",
        "TERM_PROGRAM": "iTerm.app",
        "NVM_IOJS_ORG_VERSION_LISTING": "https://iojs.org/dist/index.tab",
        "pm_cwd": "/opt/my-app"
      },
      "versioning": {
        "type": "git",
        "url": "git@github.com:tkambler/pro-javascript-frameworks.git",
        "revision": "18104d13d14673652ee7a522095fc06dcf87f8ba",
        "update_time": "2015-05-25T20:53:50.000Z",
        "comment": "Merge pull request #28 from tkambler/ordered-build",
        "unstaged": true,
        "branch": "pm2",
        "remotes": ["origin"],
        "remote": "origin",
        "branch_exists_on_remote": false,
        "ahead": false,
        "next_rev": null,
        "prev_rev": "b0e486adab79821d3093c6522eb8a24455bfb051",
        "repo_path": "/Users/user/repos/pro-javascript-frameworks"
      }
    },
    "pm_id": 0,
    "monit": {
      "memory": 32141312,
      "cpu": 0
    }
  }]
}
```

Advanced Process Management

Most of this chapter's focus so far has revolved around interactions with PM2 that occur primarily via the command line. On their own, commands such as start, stop, restart, and delete provide us with simple mechanisms for managing processes in a quick, one-off fashion. But what about more complex scenarios? Perhaps an application requires that additional parameters be specified at runtime, or perhaps it expects that one or more environment variables be set.

JSON Application Declarations

To meet these needs, additional configuration is needed, and the best way to accomplish this is with the help of what PM2 refers to as "JSON application configuration" files. An example configuration file that demonstrates most of the various options that are available is shown in Listing 4-5.

Listing 4-5. Sample of the Various Options Available Within a JSON Application Configuration File

```
{
    "name"                 : "my-app",
    "cwd"                  : "/opt/my-app",
    "args"                 : ["--argument1=value", "--flag", "value"],
    "script"               : "index.js",
    "node_args"            : ["--harmony"],
    "log_date_format"      : "YYYY-MM-DD HH:mm Z",
    "error_file"           : "/var/log/my-app/err.log",
    "out_file"             : "/var/log/my-app/out.log",
    "pid_file"             : "pids/my-app.pid",
    "instances"            : 1, // or 0 => 'max'
    "max_restarts"         : 10, // defaults to 15
    "max_memory_restart"   : "1M", // 1 megabytes, e.g.: "2G", "10M", "100K"
    "cron_restart"         : "1 0 * * *",
    "watch"                : false,
    "ignore_watch"         : ["node_modules"],
    "merge_logs"           : true,
    "exec_mode"            : "fork",
    "autorestart"          : false,
    "env": {
        "NODE_ENV": "production"
    }
}
```

JSON application configuration files provide us with a standard format for passing advanced settings to PM2 in a way that is easily repeatable and that can be shared with others. Several of the options that you see here should be familiar, based on previous examples (e.g., name, out_file, error_file, watch, etc.). Others will be touched on later in the chapter. Descriptions for each are provided in Table 4-4.

Table 4-4. Descriptions of the Various Configuration Settings Shown in Listing 4-5

Setting	Description
name	Name of the application.
cwd	Directory from which the application will be launched.
args	Command-line arguments to be passed to the application.
script	Path to the script with which PM2 will launch the application (relative to cwd).
node_args	Command-line arguments to be passed to the node executable.
log_date_format	Format with which log timestamps will be generated.
error_file	Path to which standard error messages will be logged.
out_file	Path to which standout output messages will be logged.
pid_file	Path to which the application's PID (process identifier) will be logged.
instances	The number of instances of the application to launch. Discussed in further detail in the next section.
max_restarts	The maximum number of times PM2 will attempt to restart (consecutively) an failed application before giving up.

(*continued*)

Table 4-4. (*continued*)

Setting	Description
max_memory_restart	PM2 will automatically restart the application if the amount of memory it consumes crosses this threshold.
cron_restart	PM2 will automatically restart the application on a specified schedule.
watch	Whether or not PM2 should automatically restart the application as changes to its file structure are detected. Defaults to false.
ignore_watch	An array of locations for which PM2 should ignore file changes, if watching is enabled.
merge_logs	If multiple instances of a single application are created, PM2 should use a single output and error log file for all of them.
exec_mode	Method of execution. Defaults to fork. Discussed in further detail in the next section.
autorestart	Automatically restart a crashed or exited application. Defaults to true.
vizon	If enabled, PM2 will attempt to read metadata from the application's version control files, if they exist. Defaults to true.
env	Object containing environment variable keys/values to pass to the application.

Included with this chapter is a microservices project that provides a working demonstration of JSON configuration files in action. Contained within this project are two applications: a weather application with an API that returns random temperature information for a specified postal code, and a main application that generates a request to the API every two seconds and prints the result to the console. The main script for each of these applications is shown in Listing 4-6.

Listing 4-6. Source Code for the main and weather Applications

```
// microservices/main/index.js

var request = require('request');

if (!process.env.WEATHER_API_URL) {
    throw new Error('The `WEATHER_API_URL` environment variable must be set.');
}

setInterval(function() {

    request({
        'url': process.env.WEATHER_API_URL + '/api/weather/37204',
        'json': true,
        'method': 'GET'
    }, function(err, res, result) {
        if (err) throw new Error(err);
        console.log('The temperature is: %s', result.temperature.fahrenheit);
    });

}, 2000);
```

```
// microservices/weather/index.js

if (!process.env.PORT) {
    throw new Error('The `PORT` environment variable must be set.');
}

var express = require('express');
var morgan = require('morgan');
var app = express();
app.use(morgan('combined'));

var random = function(min, max) {
    return Math.floor(Math.random() * (max - min + 1) + min);
};

app.get('/api/weather/:postal_code', function(req, res, next) {
    var fahr = random(70, 110);
    res.send({
        'temperature': {
            'fahrenheit': fahr,
            'celsius': (fahr - 32) * (5/9)
        }
    });
});

app.listen(process.env.PORT);
```

A single JSON application configuration file is also included with the `microservices` project, the content of which is shown in Listing 4-7.

Listing 4-7. JSON Application Configuration File for this Chapter's `microservices` Projectmicroservices/pm2/development.json

```
[
    {
        "name"                 : "main",
        "cwd"                  : "../microservices",
        "script"               : "main/index.js",
        "max_memory_restart": "60M",
        "watch"                : true,
        "env": {
            "NODE_ENV": "development",
            "WEATHER_API_URL": "http://localhost:7010"
        }
    },
    {
        "name"                 : "weather-api",
        "cwd"                  : "../microservices",
        "script"               : "weather/index.js",
        "max_memory_restart": "60M",
        "watch"                : true,
        "env": {
```

```
        "NODE_ENV": "development",
        "PORT": 7010
      }
    }
]
```

The application configuration file shown here provides PM2 with instructions on how to launch each of the applications included within this project. In this example, PM2 is instructed to restart each application if changes are detected to either's file structure, or if they begin to consume more than 60MB of memory. The file also provides PM2 with separate environment variables to be passed to each process.

■ **Note**   Before running this example, you will need to adjust the values for the cwd settings within this file so that they reference the absolute path to the microservices folder on your computer. After making the appropriate adjustments, launch both applications with a single call to PM2, as shown in Figure 4-12.

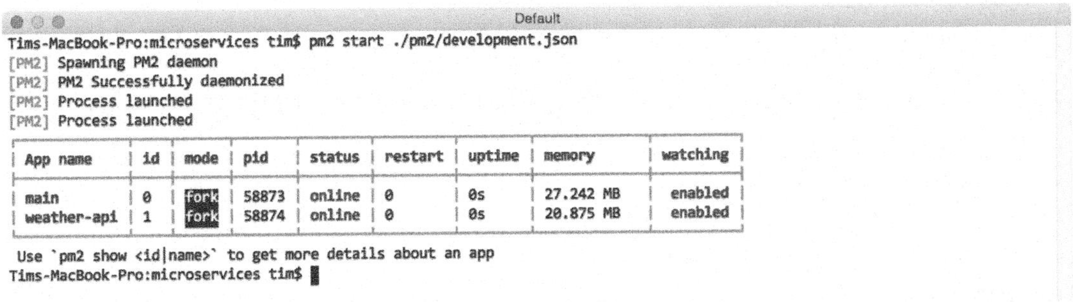

Figure 4-12. Launching the main and weather-api applications with PM2

As expected, PM2 has created two instances for us, one for each of the applications referenced within our configuration file. As in previous examples, we can monitor the output that is generated with the help of PM2's logs command (see Figure 4-13).

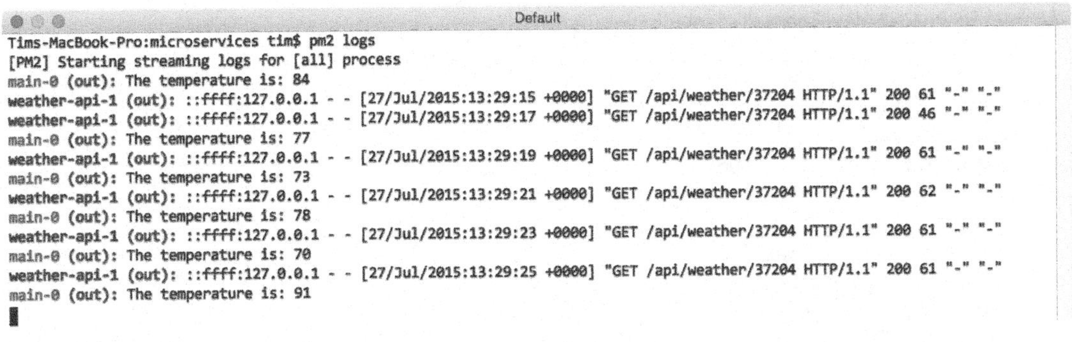

Figure 4-13. Excerpt of the output generated by PM2's logs command

67

Load-Balancing Across Multiple Processors

The single-threaded, nonblocking nature of Node's I/O model makes it possible for developers to create applications capable of handling thousands of concurrent connections with relative ease. While impressive, the efficiency with which Node is capable of processing incoming requests comes with one major expense: an inability to spread computation across multiple CPUs. Thankfully, Node's core cluster module provides a method for addressing this limitation. With it, developers can write applications capable of creating their own child processes—each running on a separate processor, and each capable of sharing the use of ports with other child processes and the parent process that launched it.

Before we close out this chapter, let's take a look at a convenient abstraction of Node's cluster module that is provided by PM2. With this functionality, applications that were not originally written to take advantage of Node's cluster module can be launched in a way that allows them to take full advantage of multiprocessor environments. As a result, developers can quickly scale up their applications to meet increasing demand without immediately being forced to bring additional servers to bear.

Listing 4-8 shows the source code for a simple Express application that we will be scaling across multiple processors with the help of PM2, while Listing 4-9 shows the accompanying JSON application configuration file.

Listing 4-8 Express Application to be Scaled Across Multiple CPUs

```
// multicore/index.js

if (!process.env.port) throw new Error('The port environment variable must be set');

var express = require('express');
var morgan = require('morgan');
var app = express();
app.use(morgan('combined'));

app.route('/')
    .get(function(req, res, next) {
        res.send('Hello, world.');
    });

app.listen(process.env.port);
```

Listing 4-9. JSON Application Configuration File with Which Our Application Will Be Launched

```
// multicore/pm2/development.json

{
    "name": "multicore",
    "cwd": "../multicore",
    "max_memory_restart": "60M",
    "watch": false,
    "script": "index.js",
    "instances": 0, // max
    "exec_mode": "cluster",
    "autorestart": true,
    "merge_logs": true,
    "env": {
        "port": 9000
    }
}
```

The application configuration file shown in Listing 4-9 contains two key items of interest. The first is the instances property. In this example, we specify a value of 0, which instructs PM2 to launch a separate process for every CPU that it finds. The second is the exec_mode property. By specifying a value of cluster, we instruct PM2 to launch its own parent process, which will in turn launch separate child processes for our application with the help of Node's cluster module.

In Figure 4-14, we launch the application by passing the path to our application configuration file to PM2's start command. Afterward, PM2 displays a listing of every known process, as in previous examples. In this instance, we see that PM2 has launched a separate process for each of the eight CPUs available within our environment. We can verify this by monitoring CPU usage for each of these new processes using the monit command, as shown in Figure 4-15.

```
Tims-MacBook-Pro:multicore tim$ pm2 start ./pm2/development.json
[PM2] Spawning PM2 daemon
[PM2] PM2 Successfully daemonized
[PM2] Process launched

| App name  | id | mode    | pid   | status | restart | uptime | memory    | watching |
| multicore | 0  | cluster | 59154 | online | 0       | 0s     | 34.715 MB | disabled |
| multicore | 1  | cluster | 59155 | online | 0       | 0s     | 34.613 MB | disabled |
| multicore | 2  | cluster | 59164 | online | 0       | 0s     | 34.996 MB | disabled |
| multicore | 3  | cluster | 59181 | online | 0       | 0s     | 35.098 MB | disabled |
| multicore | 4  | cluster | 59196 | online | 0       | 0s     | 35.023 MB | disabled |
| multicore | 5  | cluster | 59211 | online | 0       | 0s     | 35.020 MB | disabled |
| multicore | 6  | cluster | 59226 | online | 0       | 0s     | 34.801 MB | disabled |
| multicore | 7  | cluster | 59240 | online | 0       | 0s     | 32.617 MB | disabled |

Use `pm2 show <id|name>` to get more details about an app
Tims-MacBook-Pro:multicore tim$
```

Figure 4-14. *Launching the application on cluster mode with PM2*

```
o PM2 monitoring :

• multicore
[0] [cluster_mode]      [|||    ] 0 %
                                ] 35.781 MB

• multicore
[1] [cluster_mode]      [|||    ] 0 %
                                ] 35.551 MB

• multicore
[2] [cluster_mode]      [|||    ] 0 %
                                ] 36.066 MB

• multicore
[3] [cluster_mode]      [|||    ] 0 %
                                ] 35.941 MB

• multicore
[4] [cluster_mode]      [|||    ] 0 %
                                ] 35.938 MB

• multicore
[5] [cluster_mode]      [|||    ] 0 %
                                ] 35.926 MB

• multicore
[6] [cluster_mode]      [|||    ] 0 %
                                ] 35.680 MB

• multicore
[7] [cluster_mode]      [|||    ] 0 %
                                ] 35.477 MB
```

Figure 4-15. *Monitoring CPU usage with PM2's monit command*

> ▩ **Note** When launching applications in cluster mode, PM2 will print a message to the console warning that this functionality is still a beta feature. According to the lead developer of PM2, however, this functionality is stable enough for production environments, so long as Node v0.12.0 or higher is being used.

Before you continue, you can quickly remove each of the eight processes launched by this example by running `$ pm2 delete multicore`.

Zero-Downtime Deployments

After launching an application in cluster mode, PM2 will begin forwarding incoming requests in a round-robin fashion to each of the eight processes under its control—providing us with an enormous increase in performance. As an added benefit, having our application distributed across multiple processors also allows us to release updates without incurring any downtime, as we will see in a moment.

Imagine a scenario in which an application under PM2's control is running on one or more servers. As updates to this application become available, releasing them to the public will involve two critical steps:

- Copying the updated source code to the appropriate server(s)

- Restarting each of the processes under PM2's control

As these steps take place, a brief period of downtime will be introduced, during which incoming requests to the application will be rejected—unless special precautions are taken. Fortunately, launching applications with PM2 in cluster mode provides us with the tools we need to take those precautions.

To avoid any downtime when relaunching the application we previously saw in Listing 4-8, we will first need to make a minor adjustment to our application's source code and application configuration files. The updated versions are shown in Listing 4-10.

Listing 4-10. Application Designed to Take Advantage of PM2's gracefulReload Command

```
// graceful/index.js

if (!process.env.port) throw new Error('The port environment variable must be set');

var server;
var express = require('express');
var morgan = require('morgan');
var app = express();
app.use(morgan('combined'));

app.route('/')
    .get(function(req, res, next) {
        res.send('Hello, world.');
    });

process.on('message', function(msg) {
    switch (msg) {
        case 'shutdown':
            server.close();
        break;
    }
});
```

```
server = app.listen(process.env.port, function() {
    console.log('App is listening on port: %s', process.env.port);
});

// graceful/pm2/production.json

{
    "name": "graceful",
    "cwd": "../graceful",
    "max_memory_restart": "60M",
    "watch": false,
    "script": "index.js",
    "instances": 0, // max
    "exec_mode": "cluster",
    "autorestart": true,
    "merge_logs": false,
    "env": {
        "port": 9000,
        "PM2_GRACEFUL_TIMEOUT": 10000
    }
}
```

Previous examples have demonstrated the use of PM2's restart command, which immediately stops and starts a specified process. While this behavior is typically not a problem within nonproduction environments, issues begin to surface when we consider the impact it would have on any active requests that our application may be processing at the moment this command is issued. When stability is of the upmost importance, PM2's gracefulReload command serves as a more appropriate alternative.

When called, gracefulReload first sends a shutdown message to each of the processes under its control, providing them with the opportunity to take any necessary precautions to ensure that any active connections are not disturbed. Only after a configurable period of time has passed (specified via the PM2_GRACEFUL_TIMEOUT environment variable) will PM2 then move forward with restarting the process.

In this example, after receiving the shutdown message, our application responds by calling the close() method on the HTTP server that was created for us by Express. This method instructs our server to stop accepting *new* connections, but allows those that have already been established to complete. Only after ten seconds have passed (as specified via PM2_GRACEFUL_TIMEOUT) will PM2 restart the process, at which point any connections managed by this process should already have been completed.

Figure 4-16 demonstrates the process by which this application can be started and subsequently restarted through the use of the gracefulReload command. By doing so, we are able to release updates without interrupting our application's users.

```
● ● ●                                    Default
Tims-MacBook-Pro:graceful tim$ pm2 start ./pm2/production.json
[PM2] Spawning PM2 daemon
[PM2] PM2 Successfully daemonized
[PM2] Process launched
```

App name	id	mode	pid	status	restart	uptime	memory	watching
graceful	0	cluster	60536	online	0	0s	34.563 MB	disabled
graceful	1	cluster	60537	online	0	0s	34.922 MB	disabled
graceful	2	cluster	60544	online	0	0s	35.074 MB	disabled
graceful	3	cluster	60563	online	0	0s	34.953 MB	disabled
graceful	4	cluster	60578	online	0	0s	34.781 MB	disabled
graceful	5	cluster	60593	online	0	0s	35.012 MB	disabled
graceful	6	cluster	60608	online	0	0s	34.801 MB	disabled
graceful	7	cluster	60623	online	0	0s	32.781 MB	disabled

```
 Use `pm2 show <id|name>` to get more details about an app
Tims-MacBook-Pro:graceful tim$ pm2 gracefulReload all
[PM2] Process graceful succesfully reloaded
[PM2] Process graceful succesfully reloaded
[PM2] Process graceful succesfully reloaded
[PM2] Process graceful succesfully reloaded
[PM2] Process graceful succesfully reloaded
[PM2] Process graceful succesfully reloaded
[PM2] Process graceful succesfully reloaded
[PM2] Process graceful succesfully reloaded
```

App name	id	mode	pid	status	restart	uptime	memory	watching
graceful	0	cluster	60674	online	1	67s	34.078 MB	disabled
graceful	1	cluster	60694	online	1	58s	34.633 MB	disabled
graceful	2	cluster	60713	online	1	50s	34.430 MB	disabled
graceful	3	cluster	60865	online	1	42s	34.652 MB	disabled
graceful	4	cluster	60887	online	1	33s	34.520 MB	disabled
graceful	5	cluster	60906	online	1	25s	34.602 MB	disabled
graceful	6	cluster	60925	online	1	16s	34.711 MB	disabled
graceful	7	cluster	61078	online	1	8s	34.668 MB	disabled

```
 Use `pm2 show <id|name>` to get more details about an app
Tims-MacBook-Pro:graceful tim$ █
```

Figure 4-16. *Gracefully reloading each of the processes under PM2's control*

Summary

PM2 provides developers with a powerful utility for managing Node applications that is equally at home in both production and nonproduction environments. Simple aspects, such as the utility's ability to automatically restart processes under its control as source code changes occur, serve as convenient timesavers during development. More advanced features, such as the ability to load balance applications across multiple processors and to *gracefully* restart those applications in a way that does not negatively impact users, also provide critical functionality for using Node in a significant capacity.

Related Resources

- PM2: https://github.com/Unitech/pm2

CHAPTER 5

■ ■ ■

RequireJS

It is more productive to think about what is within my control than to worry and fret about things that are outside of my control. Worrying is not a form of thinking.

—Peter Saint-Andre

While JavaScript now plays a far more significant role in web applications, the HTML5 specification (and therefore modern browsers) does not specify a means to detect dependency relationships among scripts, or how to load script dependencies in a particular order. In the simplest scenario, scripts are typically referenced in page markup with simple `<script>` tags. These tags are evaluated, loaded, and executed in order, which means that common libraries or modules are typically included first, then application scripts follow. (For example, a page might load jQuery and then load an application script that uses jQuery to manipulate the Document Object Model [DOM].) Simple web pages with easily traceable dependency hierarchies fit well into this model, but as the complexity of a web application increases, the number of application scripts will grow and the web of dependencies may become difficult, if not impossible, to manage.

The whole process is made even messier by asynchronous scripts. If a `<script>` tag possesses an async attribute, the script content will be loaded over HTTP in the background and executed as soon as it becomes available. While the script is loading, the remainder of the page, *including any subsequent script tags*, will continue to load. Large dependencies (or dependencies delivered by slow sources) that are loaded asynchronously may not be available when application scripts are evaluated and executed. Even if application `<script>` tags possess async attributes as well, a developer has no means of controlling the order in which all asynchronous scripts are loaded, and therefore no way to ensure that the dependency hierarchy is respected.

■ **Tip** The HTML5 `<script>` tag attribute `defer` is similar to `async` but delays script execution until page parsing has finished. Both of these attributes reduce page rendering delays, thereby improving user experience and page performance. This is especially important for mobile devices.

RequireJS was created to address this dependency orchestration problem by giving developers a standard way to write JavaScript modules ("scripts") that declare their own dependencies before any module execution occurs. By declaring all dependencies up front, RequireJS can ensure that the overall dependency hierarchy is loaded asynchronously while executing modules in the correct order. This pattern, known as Asynchronous Module Definition (AMD), stands in contrast to the CommonJS module-loading pattern adopted by Node.js and the Browserify module-loading library. While there are certainly strong points to be made for using both patterns in a variety of use cases, RequireJS and AMD were developed to address issues specific to web browsers and DOM shortcomings. In reality, the concessions that RequireJS and Browserify make in their implementations are usually mitigated by workflow and community plugins.

For example, RequireJS can create dynamic shims for non-AMD dependencies that it must load (usually remote libraries on content delivery networks or legacy code). This is important because RequireJS assumes that scripts in a web application may come from multiple sources and will not all directly be under a developer's control. By default, RequireJS does not concatenate all application scripts ("packing") into a single file, opting instead to issue HTTP requests for every script it loads. The RequireJS tool r.js, discussed later, produces packed bundles for production environments, but can still load remote, shimmed scripts from other locations. Browserify, on the other hand, takes a "pack-first" approach. It assumes that all internal scripts and dependencies *will* be packed into a single file and that other remote scripts will be loaded separately. This places remote scripts beyond the control of Browserify, but plugins like bromote work within the CommonJS model to load remote scripts during the packing process. For both approaches, the end result is the same: a remote resource is made available to the application at runtime.

Running the Examples

This chapter contains a variety of examples that may be run in a modern web browser. Node.js is necessary to install code dependencies and to run all web server scripts.

To install the example code dependencies, open the code/requirejs directory in a terminal and execute the command npm install. This command will read the package.json file and download the few packages necessary to run each example.

Example code blocks throughout the chapter contain a comment at the top to indicate in which file the source code may be found. The fictitious index.html file in Listing 5-1, for example, would be found in the example-000/public directory. (This directory does not really exist, so don't worry if you can't find it.)

Listing 5-1. An Exciting HTML File

```
<!-- example-000/public/index.html -->
<html>
  <head></head>
  <body><h1>Hello world!</h1></body>
</html>
```

Unless otherwise specified, assume that all example code directories contain an index.js file that launches a very basic web server. Listing 5-2 shows how Node.js would be used in a terminal to run the fictitious web server script example-000/index.js.

Listing 5-2. Launching an Exciting Web Server

```
example-000$ node index.js
>> mach web server started on node 0.12.0
>> Listening on :::8080, use CTRL+C to stop
```

The command output shows that the web server is listening at http://localhost:8080. In a web browser, navigating to http://localhost:8080/index.html would render the HTML snippet in Listing 5-1.

Working with RequireJS

The workflow for using RequireJS in a web application typically includes some common steps. First, RequireJS must be loaded in an HTML file with a <script> tag. RequireJS may be referenced as a stand-alone script on a web server or CDN, or it may also be installed with package managers like Bower and npm, then served from a local web server. Next, RequireJS must be configured so that it knows where scripts and modules live, how to shim scripts that are not AMD compliant, which plugins to load, and so on. Once configuration is complete, RequireJS will load a primary application module that is responsible for loading the major page components, essentially "kicking off" the page's application code. At this point RequireJS evaluates the dependency tree created by modules and begins asynchronously loading dependency scripts in the background. Once all modules are loaded, the application code proceeds to do whatever is within its purview.

Each step in this process is given detailed consideration in the following sections. The examples code used in each section represents the evolution of a simple application that will show inspirational and humorous quotes by (semi-) famous persons.

Installation

The RequireJS script may be downloaded directly from http://requirejs.org. It comes in a few distinct flavors: a vanilla RequireJS script, a vanilla RequireJS script prebundled with jQuery, and a Node.js package that includes both RequireJS and its packing utility, r.js. For most examples in this chapter, the vanilla script is used. The prebundled jQuery script is merely offered as a convenience for developers. If you wish to add RequireJS to a project that is already using jQuery, the vanilla RequireJS script can accommodate the existing jQuery installation with no issues, though older versions of jQuery may need to be shimmed. (Shimmed scripts will be covered later.)

Once acquired, the RequireJS script is referenced in the web application with a `<script>` tag. Because RequireJS is a module loader, it bears the responsibility of loading all other JavaScript files and modules that an application may need. It is therefore very likely that the RequireJS `<script>` tag will be the *only* `<script>` tag that occupies a web page. A simplified example is given in Listing 5-3.

Listing 5-3. Including the RequireJS Script on a Web Page

```
<!-- example-001/public/index.html -->
<body>
  <header>
    <h1>Ponderings</h1>
  </header>
  <script src="/scripts/require.js"></script>
</body>
```

Configuration

After the RequireJS script is loaded on a page, it looks for a configuration which will primarily tell RequireJS where script and modules live. Configuration options can be provided in in one of three ways.

First, a global `require` object may be created *before* the RequireJS script is loaded. This object may contain all of the RequireJS configuration options as well as a "kickoff" callback that will be executed once RequireJS has finished loading all application modules.

The script block in Listing 5-4 shows a newly minted RequireJS configuration object stored in the global `require` variable.

Listing 5-4. Configuring RequireJS with a Global `require` Object

```
<!-- example-001/public/config01.html -->
<body>
  <header>
    <h1>Ponderings</h1>
  </header>
```

```
<section id="quotes"></section>
<script>
/*
 * Will be automatically attached to the
 * global window object as window.require.
 */
var require = {
  // configuration
  baseUrl: '/scripts',
  // kickoff
  deps: ['quotes-view'],
  callback: function (quotesView) {
    quotesView.addQuote('Lorem ipsum dolor sit amet, consectetur adipiscing elit.');
    quotesView.addQuote('Nunc non purus faucibus justo tristique porta.');
  }
};
</script>
<script src="/scripts/require.js"></script>
</body>
```

The most important configuration property on this object, baseUrl, identifies a path relative to the application root where RequireJS should begin to resolve module dependencies. The deps array specifies modules that should be loaded immediately after configuration, and the callback function exists to receive these modules once they are loaded. This example loads a single module, quotes-view. Once the callback is invoked, it may access the properties and methods on this module.

The directory tree in Listing 5-5 shows the position of the quotes-view.js file relative to both config01.html (the page being viewed) and require.js.

Listing 5-5. Application File Locations

```
├── config01.html
├── scripts
│   ├── quotes-view.js
│   └── require.js
└── styles
    └── app.css
```

Notice that the absolute path and file extension for the quotes-view module is omitted in the deps array. By default, RequireJS assumes that any given module is located relative to the *page* being viewed and that it is contained within a single JavaScript file with the appropriate file extension. In this case the latter assumption is true but the first is not, which is why specifying a baseUrl property is necessary. When RequireJS attempts to resolve any module, it will combine any configured baseUrl value and the module name, then append the .js file extension to produce a full path relative to the application root.

When the config01.html page loads, the strings passed to the quotesView.addQuote() method will be displayed on the page.

The second configuration method is similar to the first but uses the RequireJS API to perform configuration *after* the RequireJS script is loaded, as demonstrated in Listing 5-6.

Listing 5-6. Configuration with the RequireJS API

```
<!-- example-001/public/config02.html -->
<body>
  <header>
    <h1>Ponderings</h1>
  </header>
  <section id="quotes"></section>
  <script src="/scripts/require.js"></script>
  <script>
  // configuration
  requirejs.config({
    baseUrl: '/scripts'
  });
  // kickoff
  requirejs(['quotes-view'], function (quotesView) {
    quotesView.addQuote('Lorem ipsum dolor sit amet, consectetur adipiscing elit.');
    quotesView.addQuote('Nunc non purus faucibus justo tristique porta.');
  });
  </script>
</body>
```

In this example a `<script>` block first uses the global `requirejs` object, created by the `require.js` script, to configure RequireJS by invoking its `config()` method. It then invokes `requirejs` to kick off the application. The object passed to the `config()` method resembles the global `require` object from Listing 5-4, but lacks its deps and `callback` properties. The `requirejs` function accepts an array of application dependencies and a callback function instead, a pattern that will become very familiar when module design is covered later.

The net effect is the same: RequireJS uses its configuration to load the `quotes-view` module, and once loaded, the callback function interacts with it to affect the page.

The third configuration method uses the syntax of the second, but moves the configuration and kickoff code into its own script. The RequireJS `<script>` tag in Listing 5-7 uses the `data-main` attribute to tell RequireJS where its configuration and kickoff module live.

Listing 5-7. Configuring RequireJS with an External Script

```
<!-- example-001/public/config03.html -->
<body>
  <header>
    <h1>Ponderings</h1>
  </header>
  <section id="quotes"></section>
  <script src="/scripts/require.js" data-main="/scripts/main.js"></script>
</body>
```

Once RequireJS has loaded, it will look for the `data-main` attribute and, if found, asynchronously load the script specified in the attribute. Listing 5-8 shows the content of `main.js`, which is identical to the `<script>` block in Listing 5-6.

Listing 5-8. The RequireJS Main Module

```
// example-001/public/scripts/main.js
// configuration
requirejs.config({
  baseUrl: '/scripts'
});

// kickoff
requirejs(['quotes-view'], function (quotesView) {
  quotesView.addQuote('Lorem ipsum dolor sit amet, consectetur adipiscing elit.');
  quotesView.addQuote('Nunc non purus faucibus justo tristique porta.');
});
```

■ **Tip**   Because the data-main script is loaded asynchronously, scripts or <script> blocks included immediately *after* RequireJS will likely be run first. If RequireJS manages *all* scripts in an application, or if scripts loaded after RequireJS have no bearing on the application itself (such as advertiser scripts), there will be no conflicts.

Application Modules and Dependencies

RequireJS modules are defined by three things:

1. A module name

2. A list of dependencies (modules)

3. A module closure that will accept the output from each dependency module as function arguments, set up module code, and potentially return something that other modules can use

Listing 5-9 shows each of these points in a fake module definition. Modules are created when the global define() function is invoked. This function takes three arguments, corresponding to the three points above.

Listing 5-9. Module Anatomy

```
define(/*#1*/'m1', /*#2*/['d1', 'd2'], /*#3*/function (d1, d2) {
  /*
   * Variables declared within the module closure
   * are private to the module, and will not be
   * exposed to other modules
   */
  var privateModuleVariable = "can't touch this";

  /*
   * The returned value (if any) will now be available
   * to any other module if they specify m1 as a
   * dependency.
   */
```

```
  return {
    getPrivateModuleVariable: function () {
      return privateModuleVariable;
    }
  };
})
```

A module's name is key. In Listing 5-9 a module name, m1, is explicitly declared. If a module name is omitted (leaving the dependencies and module closure as the only arguments passed to define()), then RequireJS will assume that the name of the module is the file name containing the module script, without its .js extension. This is fairly common in practice, but the module name is shown here for clarity.

■ **Tip** Giving modules specific names can introduce unwanted complexity, as RequireJS depends on script URL paths for loading modules. If a module is explicitly named and the *file name does not match the module name*, then a module alias *that maps the module name to an actual JavaScript file* needs to be defined in the RequireJS configuration. This is covered in the next section.

The dependency list in Listing 5-9 identifies two other modules that RequireJS should load. The values d1 and d2 are the names of these modules, located in script files d1.js and d2.js. These scripts look similar to the module definition in Listing 5-9, but they will load their own dependencies.

Finally, the module closure accepts the output from each dependency module as function arguments. This output is any value returned from each dependency module's closure function. The closure in Listing 5-9 returns its own value, and if another module were to declare m1 as a dependency, it is this returned value that would be passed to that module's closure.

If a module has no dependencies, its dependency array will be empty and it will receive no arguments to its closure.

Once a module is loaded, it exists in memory until the application is terminated. If multiple modules declare the same dependency, that dependency is loaded only once. Whatever value it returns from its closure will be passed to both modules by reference. The state of a given module, then, is shared among all other modules that use it.

A module may return any valid JavaScript value, or none at all if the module exists only to manipulate other modules or simply produce side effects in the application.

Listing 5-10 shows the structure of the example-002/public directory. This looks similar to example-001 but a few additional modules have been added, namely data/quotes.js (a module for fetching quote data) and util/dom.js (a module that wraps the global window object for other modules so that they do not need to access window directly).

Listing 5-10. Public Directory Structure for example-002

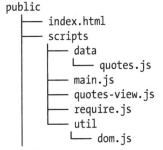

```
public
    ├── index.html
    ├── scripts
        ├── data
        │   └── quotes.js
        ├── main.js
        ├── quotes-view.js
        ├── require.js
        └── util
            └── dom.js
```

Recall that a module's dependencies exist relative to the RequireJS baseUrl value. When a module specifies dependency paths, it does so *relative to the* baseUrl *path*. In Listing 5-11 the main.js file depends on the data/quotes module (public/scripts/data/quotes.js), while the quotes-view.js module depends on util/dom (public/scripts/util/dom.js).

Listing 5-11. Module Dependency Paths

```
// example-002/public/scripts/main.js
requirejs(['data/quotes', 'quotes-view'], function (quoteData, quotesView) {
  // ...
});

// example-002/public/scripts/data/quotes.js
define([/*no dependencies*/], function () {
  // ...
});

// example-002/public/scripts/quotes-view.js
define(['util/dom'], function (dom) {
  // ...
});

// example-002/public/scripts/util/dom.js
define([/*no dependencies*/], function () {
    // ...
});
```

Figure 5-1 shows the logical dependency tree created when these modules are loaded.

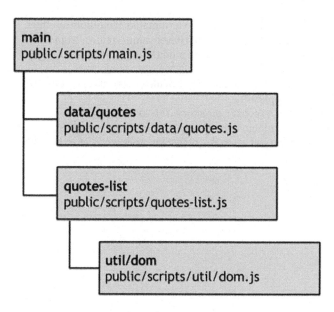

Figure 5-1. *RequireJS dependency tree*

As application dependencies multiply, module pathing can become tedious, but there are two ways to mitigate this.

First, a module may use leading dot notation to specify dependencies relative to itself. For example, a module with the declared dependency ./foo would load foo.js as a sibling file, located on the same URL segment as itself, whereas a module with the dependency ../bar would load bar.js one URL segment "up" from itself. This greatly reduces dependency verbosity.

Second, modules may be named with path aliases, defined in the RequireJS configuration, as described in the next section.

Paths and Aliases

Assigning an alias to a module allows other modules to use the alias as a dependency name instead of the full module pathname. This can be useful for a variety of reasons but is commonly used to simplify vendor module paths, eliminate version numbers from vendor module names, or deal with vendor libraries that declare their own module names explicitly.

The module in Listing 5-12 depends on the vendor library jQuery. If the jquery module script was located at /scripts/jquery.js, no module aliasing would be required to load the dependency; RequireJS would locate the module based on the configured baseUrl configuration value.

Listing 5-12. Specifying a jQuery Module Dependency

```
define(['jquery'], function ($) {
  // ...
});
```

It is unlikely that jquery lives at the module root defined by the baseUrl configuration, however. It is more likely that the jquery script would exist within a vendor directory such as /scripts/vendor/jquery, and that the script name would contain the jQuery version (e.g., jquery-2.1.3.min), as this is how jQuery scripts are distributed. To further complicate matters, jQuery explicitly declares its own module name, jquery. If a module attempted to load jquery using the full path to the jQuery script, /scripts/vendor/jquery/jquery-2.1.3.min, RequireJS would load the script over HTTP and then fail to import the module because its declared name is jquery, not jquery-2.1.3.min.

■ **Tip** Explicitly naming modules is considered bad practice because application modules *must* use a module's declared name, and the script file that contains the module must either share its name or be aliased in the RequireJS configuration. A special concession is made for jQuery because it is a fairly ubiquitous library.

Aliases are specified in the RequireJS configuration hash under the paths property. In Listing 5-13 the alias jquery is assigned to vendor/jquery/jquery-2.1.3.min, a path which is relative to the baseUrl.

Listing 5-13. Configuration Module Path Aliases

```
requirejs.config({
  baseUrl: '/scripts',
  // ... other options ...
  paths: {
    'jquery': 'vendor/jquery/jquery-2.1.3.min'
  }
});
```

In the paths object, aliases are keys and the scripts to which they are mapped are values. Once a module alias is defined, it may be used in any other module's dependency list. Listing 5-14 shows the jquery alias in use.

Listing 5-14. Using a Module Alias in a Dependency List

```
// jquery alias points to vendor/jquery/jquery-2.1.3.min
define(['jquery'], function ($) {
    // ...
});
```

Because module aliases take precedence over actual module locations, RequireJS will resolve the location of the jQuery script before attempting to locate it at /scripts/jquery.js.

■ **Note** Anonymous modules (that do not declare their own module names) may be aliased with any module name, but if named modules are aliased (like jquery) they *must* be aliased with their declared module names.

Loading Plugins with Proxy Modules

Libraries such as jQuery, Underscore, Lodash, Handlebars, and so forth all have plugin systems that let developers extend the functionality of each. Strategic use of module aliases can actually help developers load extensions for these libraries all at once, without having to specify such extensions in every module that makes use of them.

In Listing 5-15 the jquery script location is aliased with the name jquery and a custom module, util/jquery-all, is aliased with the name jquery-all for brevity. All application modules will load jquery by specifying jquery-all as a dependency. The jquery-all module, in turn, loads the normal jquery module and then attaches custom plugins to it.

Listing 5-15. Using Module Aliases to Load jQuery Plugins

```
requirejs.config({
    baseUrl: '/scripts',
    // ... other options ...
    paths: {
        // vendor script
        'jquery': 'vendor/jquery/jquery-2.1.3.min',
        // custom extensions
        'jquery-all': 'util/jquery-all'
    }
});

// example-003/public/scripts/util/jquery-all
define(['jquery'], function ($) {

    $.fn.addQuotes = function () {/*...*/};

    return $;
    // or
    //return $.noConflict(true);
});
```

The `jquery-all` proxy module returns the jQuery object itself, which allows modules that depend on `jquery-all` to access `jquery` with the loaded custom extensions. By default, jQuery registers itself with the global `window` object, even when it is used as an AMD module. If all application modules are accessing jQuery through the `jquery-all` module (or even the plain `jquery` module, as most vendor libraries do), then there is no need for the jQuery global. It may be removed by invoking `$.noConflict(true)`. This will return the `jquery` object and is the alternate return value for the `jquery-all` module in Listing 5-15.

Because jQuery is now part of the example application, the `quotes-view` module, responsible for rendering quote data in the DOM, need no longer rely on the `util/dom` module. It can specify `jquery-all` as a dependency and load `jquery` and the custom `addQuotes()` plugin method all at once. Listing 5-16 shows the changes made to the `quotes-view` module.

Listing 5-16. Loading jQuery and Custom Plugins in the quotes-view Module

```
// example-003/public/scripts/quotes-view.js
define(['jquery-all'], function ($) {
  var $quotes = $('#quotes');

  return {
    render: function (groupedQuotes) {
      for (var attribution in groupedQuotes) {
        if (!groupedQuotes.hasOwnProperty(attribution)) continue;
        $quotes.addQuotes(attribution, groupedQuotes[attribution]);
      }
    }
  };
});
```

The advantage to using a module proxy to load `jquery` is that it eliminates the need to specify both `jquery` and custom plugin modules in other modules that depend on both. Without this technique, for example, application modules would all have multiple dependencies to ensure that the appropriate jQuery plugins are loaded when needed, as shown in Listing 5-17.

Listing 5-17. Loading Plugins Without a Proxy Module

```
// scripts/util/jquery-plugin-1.js
define(['jquery'], function ($) {
    $.fn.customPlugin1 = function () {/*...*/};
});

// scripts/util/jquery-plugin-2.js
define(['jquery'], function ($) {
    $.fn.customPlugin2 = function () {/*...*/};
});

// scripts/*/module-that-uses-jquery.js
define(['jquery', 'util/jquery-plugins-1', 'util/jquery-plugins-2'], function ($) {
  // ...
});
```

In this case, even though `jquery-plugin-1` and `jquery-plugin-2` do not return values, they must still be added as dependencies so that their side effects—adding plugins to the `jquery` module—still occur.

Shims

Libraries that support the AMD module format are straightforward to use with RequireJS. Non-AMD libraries may still be used by configuring RequireJS shims, or by creating a shimmed modules manually.

The data/quotes module in example-003 exposes a groupByAttribution() method that iterates over the collection of quotes. It creates a hash where keys are the names of people and values are arrays of quotes attributed to them. This grouping functionality would likely be useful for other collections as well.

Fortunately, a vendor library, *undrln*, can provide a generalized version of this functionality, but it is not AMD-compatible. A shim would be necessary for other AMD modules to use undrln as a dependency. Undrln is written as a standard JavaScript module within a function closure, shown in Listing 5-18. It assigns itself to the global window object, where it may be accessed by other scripts on a page.

■ **Note** The undrln.js script blatantly mimics a subset of the Lodash API *without* AMD module compatibility, exclusively for this chapter's examples.

Listing 5-18. The Completely Original Undrln Library

```
// example-004/public/scripts/vendor/undrln/undrln.js
/**
 * undrln (c) 2015 l33th@x0r
 * MIT license.
 * v0.0.0.0.1-alpha-DEV-theta-r2
 */
(function () {

  var undrln = window._ = {};

  undrln.groupBy = function (collection, key) {
    // ...
  };

}());
```

Several things must be added to the RequireJS configuration to create a shim. First, a module alias must be created under paths so that RequireJS knows where the shimmed module lives. Second, a shim configuration entry must be added to the shim section. Both are added to the RequireJS configuration in Listing 5-19.

Listing 5-19. Configuration of a Module Shim

```
// example-004/public/scripts/main.js
requirejs.config({
  baseUrl: '/scripts',
  paths: {
    jquery: 'vendor/jquery/jquery-2.1.3.min',
    'jquery-all': 'util/jquery-all',
    // giving undrln a module alias
    undrln: 'vendor/undrln/undrln'
  },
```

```
shim: {
  // defining a shim for undrln
  undrln: {
    exports: '_'
  }
}
});
```

Each key under the shim section identifies the module alias (or name) to be shimmed, and the objects assigned to those keys specify details about how the shim works. Under the hood, RequireJS creates a shim by defining an empty AMD module that returns the *global* object created by a script or library. Undrln creates the global window._ object, and so the name _ is specified in the shim configuration as undrln's *export*. The final, generated RequireJS shim will look something like the module in Listing 5-20. Note that these shims are created dynamically as modules are loaded and do not actually exist as "files" on the web server. (One exception to this rule is the r.js packing utility, discussed later, which writes generated shim output to a bundle file as an optimization measure.)

Listing 5-20. Example RequireJS Shim Module

```
define('undrln', [], function () {
  return window._;
});
```

The quotes module in Listing 5-21 may now use the undrln shim as a dependency.

Listing 5-21. Using the Undrln Shim As a Dependency

```
// example-004/public/scripts/data/quotes.js
define(['undrln'], function (_) {
  //...
  return {
    groupByAttribution: function () {
      return _.groupBy(quoteData, 'attribution');
    },
    //...
  }
});
```

By shimming non-AMD scripts, RequireJS can use its asynchronous module-loading capabilities behind the scenes to load non-AMD scripts when they are dependencies of other AMD modules. Without this capability these scripts would need to be included on every page with a standard <script> tag and loaded synchronously to ensure availability.

Running the web application in example-004 and then browsing to http://localhost:8080/index.html will display a list of quotes. Figure 5-2 shows the rendered page and Chrome's Network panel in which all loaded JavaScript modules are listed. Note that the Initiator column clearly shows that RequireJS is responsible for loading all modules, and that even undrln.js, a non-AMD module, is included in the list.

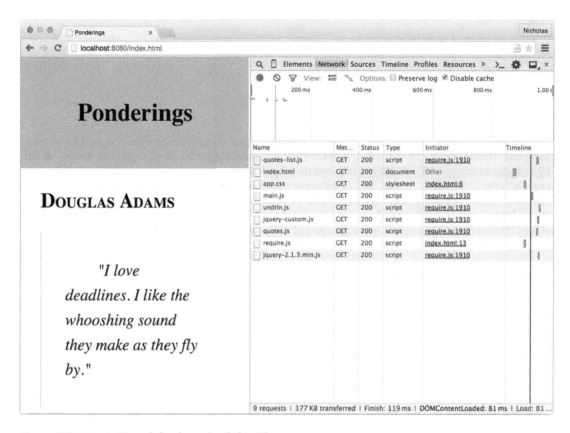

Figure 5-2. *RequireJS modules shown loaded in Chrome*

Shim Dependencies

It is reasonable to expect shimmed scripts to have dependencies, likely objects in the global scope. When AMD modules specify dependencies, RequireJS ensures that the dependencies are loaded first, before the module code is executed. Dependencies for shimmed scripts are specified in a similar manner within the shim configuration. A shimmed script may depend on other shimmed scripts, or even AMD modules if those modules make content available in the global scope (usually a bad idea, but sometimes necessary).

To enhance the example application, a search field has been added to the quote page in example-005. Terms entered into the search field appear highlighted in the text of any quote in which they are found. Up to this point all examples have used a single view, quotes-view, to display the rendered markup. Because the application features are growing, two new modules will be introduced to help manage features: search-view and quotes-state. The search-view module is responsible for monitoring a text field for user input. When this field changes, the view informs the quotes-state module that a search has occurred, passing it the search term. The quotes-state module acts as the single source of state for all views, and when it receives a new search term, it triggers an event to which views may subscribe.

Digging through some legacy source code produced the file public/scripts/util/jquery.highlight.js, a non-AMD jQuery plugin that highlights text in the DOM. When the quotes-view module receives the search event from the quotes-state module, it uses this plugin to highlight text in the DOM based on the search term stored in quotes-state. To use this legacy script, a path and a shim entry are both added to the main.js configuration. The highlight plugin doesn't export any values, but it does need jQuery to be loaded first or the plugin will throw an error when it attempts to access the global jQuery object.

Dependencies have been added to the `highlight` shim with the `deps` property, shown in Listing 5-22. This property contains an array of module names (or aliases) that should be loaded *before* the shim--in this case jQuery.

Listing 5-22. The `highlight` Shim Depends on jQuery

```
// example-005/public/scripts/main.js
requirejs.config({
  baseUrl: '/scripts',
  paths: {
    jquery: 'vendor/jquery/jquery-2.1.3.min',
    'jquery-all': 'util/jquery-all',
    undrln: 'vendor/undrln/undrln',
    ventage: 'vendor/ventage/ventage',
    highlight: 'util/jquery.highlight'
  },
  shim: {
    undrln: {
      exports: '_'
    },
    highlight: {
      deps: ['jquery']
    }
  }
});
```

Once the `highlight` plugin has been shimmed, it may be loaded as a dependency of another module. Since the `jquery-all` module is responsible for loading custom plugins anyway, making the `highlight` module one of its dependencies in Listing 5-23 seems sensible.

Shimmed scripts should only have two kinds of dependencies:

- Other shimmed scripts that execute immediately and potentially create one or more reusable variables or namespaces in the global scope

- AMD modules that also create reusable variables or namespaces in the global scope (such as `window.jQuery`) as a side effect

Because AMD modules *typically* don't meddle with the global scope at all, it is practically useless to use them as dependencies for a shimmed script because there is no way for the shimmed script to access an AMD module's API. If an AMD module adds nothing to the global scope, it is useless to shimed scripts. Also, AMD modules are loaded asynchronously and their closures are executed in a particular order (discussed in the next section), whereas shimmed scripts will be run as soon as they are loaded. (Rembmer: shimmed scripts are *normal* scripts that run once they've been introduced into the DOM. A generated shim module simply delivers the global export created by a non-AMD script to other AMD modules as a dependency.) Even if a shimmed script *could* access an AMD module's API, there is no guarantee that the module would be available when the shimmed script actually runs.

Listing 5-23. Loading the highlight Module As a Dependency of Another Module

```
// example-005/public/scripts/util/jquery-all.js
define(['jquery', 'highlight'], function ($) {

  $.fn.addQuotes = function (attribution, quotes) {
    // ...
  };

  return $;
});
```

With this arrangement there are likely two questions that spring to mind immediately:

1. Since both the highlight and jquery-all modules declare jquery as a dependency, when is jQuery actually loaded?

2. Why isn't a second highlight parameter specified in the jquery-all module closure function?

First, when RequireJS evaluates dependencies among modules, it creates an internal dependency tree based on module hierarchy. By doing this it can determine the optimal time to load any particular module, starting from the leaves and moving toward the trunk. In this case the "trunk" is the jquery-all module, and the furthest leaf is the jquery module on which highlight depends. RequireJS will execute module closures in the following order: jquery, highlight, jquery-all. Because jquery is also a dependency of jquery-all, RequireJS will simply deliver the same jquery instance created for the highlight module.

Second, the highlight module returns no value and is used merely for side effects—for adding a plugin to the jQuery object. No parameter is passed to the jquery-all module because highlight returns none. Dependencies that are used only for side effects should always be placed at the end of a module's dependency list for this reason.

Loader Plugins

There are several RequireJS loader plugins that are so useful, they find a home in most projects. A loader plugin is an external script that is used to conveniently load, and sometimes parse, specific kinds of resources that may then be imported as standard AMD dependencies, even though the resources themselves may not be actual AMD modules.

text.js

The RequireJS text plugin can load a plain text resource over HTTP, serialize it as a string, and deliver it to an AMD module as a dependency. This is commonly used to load HTML templates, or even raw JSON data from HTTP endpoints. To install the plugin, the text.js script must be copied from the project repository and, by convention, placed in the same directory as the main.js configuration file. (Alternative installation methods are listed in the plugin project's README.)

The quotes-view module in the example application uses a jQuery plugin to build up the list of quotes, one DOM element at a time. This is not very efficient and could easily be replaced by a templating solution. The AMD-compatible Handlebars templating library is a popular choice for such tasks. In Listing 5-24 the library has been added to the vendor directory in example-006 and a convenient module alias has been created in the main.js configuration.

Listing 5-24. Handlebars Module Alias

```
// example-006/public/scripts/main.js
requirejs.config({
  baseUrl: '/scripts',
  paths: {
    //...
    Handlebars: 'vendor/handlebars/handlebars-v3.0.3'
  },
  //...
});
```

When the quotes-view module renders itself, it uses quote data in an object hash where the keys are attributions (i.e., the person credited with each quote) and the values are arrays of quotes for each. (A given attribution may be associated with one or more quotes.) Listing 5-25 shows the template that will be bound to this data structure, located in the public/scripts/templates/quotes.hbs file.

Listing 5-25. The quotes-view Handlebars Template

```
<!-- example-006/public/scripts/templates/quotes.hbs -->
{{#each this as |quotes attribution|}}
<section class="multiquote">
  <h2 class="attribution">{{attribution}}</h2>
  {{#each quotes}}
  <blockquote class="quote">
  {{#explode text delim="\n"}}
    <p>{{this}}</p>
  {{/explode}}
  </blockquote>
  {{/each}}
</section>
{{/each}}
```

It is not necessary to be completely familiar with Handlebars syntax to understand that this template iterates over the data object, pulling out each attribution and its associated quotes. It creates an <h2> element for the attribution, then for each quote builds a <blockquote> element to hold the quote text. A special block helper, #explode, breaks the quote text apart at the new line (\n) delimiter, and then wraps each segment of the quote text in a <p> tag.

The #explode helper is significant because it is not native to Handlebars. It is defined and registered as a Handlebars helper in the file public/scripts/util/handlebars-all.js, as shown in Listing 5-26.

Listing 5-26. #explode Handlebars Helper

```
// example-006/public/scripts/util/handlebars-all.js
define(['Handlebars'], function (Handlebars) {
  Handlebars.registerHelper('explode', function (context, options) {
    var delimiter = options.hash.delim || '';
    var parts = context.split(delimiter);
    var processed = '';
    while (parts.length) {
      processed += options.fn(parts.shift().trim());
    }
```

```
    return processed;
  });
  return Handlebars;
});
```

Because this module adds helpers and then returns the Handlebars object, the `quotes-view` module will import it as a dependency instead of the vanilla Handlebars module, in much the same way as the `jquery-all` module is used in lieu of `jquery`. The appropriate module alias has been added to the configuration in Listing 5-27.

Listing 5-27. `handlebars-all` Module Alias

```
// example-006/public/scripts/main.js
requirejs.config({
  baseUrl: '/scripts',
  paths: {
    //...
    Handlebars: 'vendor/handlebars/handlebars-v3.0.3',
    'handlebars-all': 'util/handlebars-all'
  },
  //...
});
```

In Listing 5-28, the `quotes-view` module has been modified to import both `handlebars-all` and the `quotes.hbs` template. The module name for the text template is very specific: it must begin with the prefix `text!` followed by the path to the template file relative to the `baseUrl` path defined in `main.js`.

Listing 5-28. The `quotes.hbs` Template Imported As a Module Dependency

```
// example-006/public/scripts/quotes-view.js
define([
  'jquery-all',
  'quotes-state',
  'handlebars-all',
  'text!templates/quote.hbs'
],
function ($, quotesState, Handlebars, quotesTemplate) {

  var bindTemplate = Handlebars.compile(quotesTemplate);

  var view = {
    // ...
    render: function () {
      view.$el.empty();
      var groupedQuotes = quotesState.quotes;
      view.$el.html(bindTemplate(groupedQuotes));
    },
    // ...
  };

  // ...
});
```

When RequireJS encounters a dependency name with the text! prefix, it automatically attempts to load the text.js plugin script, which will then load and serialize the specified file content as a string. The quotesTemplate function argument in the quotes-view closure will contain the serialized content of the quotes.hbs file, which is then compiled by Handlebars and used to render the module in the DOM.

Page Load

When a web page has fully loaded, it triggers a DOMContentLoaded event (in modern browsers). Scripts that are loaded before the browser has finished building the DOM often listen for this event to know when it is safe to begin manipulating page elements. If scripts are loaded just before the ending </body> tag, they may assume that the bulk of the DOM has already been loaded and that they need not listen for this event. Scripts anywhere else in the <body> element, or more commonly the <head> element, have no such luxury, however.

Even though RequireJS is loaded before the closing </body> tag in the application example, the main.js file (configuration omitted) in Listing 5-29 still passes a function to jQuery that will be executed once the DOMContentLoaded has fired. If the RequireJS <script> tag were moved into the document <head>, nothing would break.

Listing 5-29. Using jQuery to Determine If the DOM Is Fully Loaded

```
// example-006/public/scripts/main.js
// ...

requirejs(['jquery-all', 'quotes-view', 'search-view'],
  function ($, quotesView) {
  $(function () {
    quotesView.ready();
  });
});
```

The domReady plugin is a peculiar kind of "loader" in that it simply stalls the invocation of a module's closure until the DOM is completely ready. Like the text plugin, the domReady.js file must be accessible to RequireJS within the baseUrl path defined in the main.js configuration. By convention it is typically a sibling of main.js.

Listing 5-30 shows a modified version of main.js (configuration omitted) in which the jquery dependency has been removed and the domReady! plugin has been appended to the dependency list. The trailing exclamation mark tells RequireJS that this module acts as a loader plugin rather than a standard module. Unlike the text plugin, domReady actually loads nothing, so no additional information is required after the exclamation mark.

Listing 5-30. Using the domReady Plugin to Determine If the DOM Is Fully Loaded

```
// example-007/public/scripts/main.js
// ...

requirejs(['quotes-view', 'search-view', 'domReady!'],
  function (quotesView) {
    quotesView.ready();
});
```

i18n

RequireJS supports internationalization via the i18n loader plugin. (i18n is a numeronym, which means that the number "18" represents the 18 characters between "i" and "n" in the word "internationalization".) Internationalization is the act of writing a web application such that it can adapt its content to a user's language and locale (also known as National Language Support, or NLS). The i18n plugin is primarily used for translating text in a website's controls and "chrome": button labels, headers, hyperlink text, fieldset legends, and so forth. To demonstrate this plugin's capabilities, two new templates have been added to the example application, one for the page title in the header, and one for the search field with placeholder text. The actual quote data will not be translated because, presumably, it comes from an application server that would be responsible for rendering the appropriate translation. In this application, though, the data is hard-coded in the data/quotes module for simplicity and will always appear in English.

The search.hbs template in Listing 5-31 has also been extracted from the index.html file and now accepts placeholder text for the search field as its only input. The search-view module has been adapted to use this template when it renders content in the DOM.

Listing 5-31. The search.hbs Template Will Display the Placeholder Translation

```
<!-- example-008/public/scripts/templates/search.hbs -->
<form>
  <fieldset>
    <input type="text" name="search" placeholder="{{searchPlaceholder}}" />
  </fieldset>
</form>
```

Listing 5-32 shows the new header.hbs template that will be rendered by the new header-view module. The template accepts a single input, the page title.

Listing 5-32. The header.hbs Template Will Display the Page Title Translation

```
<!-- example-008/public/scripts/templates/header.hbs -->
<h1>{{pageTitle}}</h1>
```

The header-view module in Listing 5-33 demonstrates not only how the template dependency is imported with the text plugin, but also how a language module dependency is imported with the i18n plugin. The familiar loader syntax looks nearly identical: the plugin name followed by an exclamation mark and a module path relative to the configured baseUrl, in this case nls/lang. When a template is loaded, its serialized string content is passed to a module's closure, but the i18n plugin loads a language module that contains translated text data and passes that module's object to the closure. In Listing 5-33 this object will be accessible through the lang parameter.

Listing 5-33. The header-view Module Depends on the i18n Language Object

```
// example-008/public/scripts/header-view.js
define([
  'quotes-state',
  'jquery-all',
  'handlebars-all',
  'text!templates/header.hbs',
  'i18n!nls/lang'
], function (quotesState, $, Handlebars, headerTemplate, lang) {
  // ...
});
```

The language module is a regular AMD module, but instead of passing a list of dependencies and a closure to `define()`, a simple object literal is used. This object literal follows a very specific syntax, shown in Listing 5-34.

Listing 5-34. Default English Language Module

```
// example-008/public/scripts/nls/lang.js
define({
  root: {
    pageTitle: 'Ponderings',
    searchPlaceholder: 'search'
  },
  de: true
});
```

First, a `root` property holds the key/value pairs that will be used to fetch translated data when the plugin resolves the language translations. The keys in this object are simply keys by which the translated text may be accessed programmatically. In the `search` template, for example, `{{searchPlaceholder}}` will be replaced with the string value at the language object's key `searchPlaceholder` when the template is bound to it.

Second, siblings to the `root` property are the various IETF language tags for active and inactive translations that should be resolved based on a browser's language setting. In this example, the German `de` language tag is assigned the value `true`. If a Spanish translation was made available, an `es-es` property with the value `true` could be added. And for a French translation, a `fr-fr` property could be added, and so forth for other languages.

When a new language tag is enabled in the default language module, a directory corresponding to the language code must be made as a sibling to the module file. The `nls/de` directory can be seen in Listing 5-35.

Listing 5-35. Directory Structure for NLS Modules

```
├── nls
│     ├── de
│     │     └── lang.js
│     └── lang.js
```

Once the language-specific directory has been created, a language module file *of the same name as the default language module file* must be created within. This new language module will contain the translated content of the `root` property in the default language module *only*. Listing 5-36 shows the German (de) translation of the `pageTitle` and `searchPlaceholder` properties.

Listing 5-36. German (de) Translation Module

```
// example-008/public/scripts/nls/de/lang.js
define({
  pageTitle: 'Grübeleien',
  searchPlaceholder: 'suche'
});
```

When the default language module is loaded with the i18n plugin, it examines the browser's `window.navigator.language` property to determine what locale and language translation should be used. If the default language module specifies a compatible, enabled locale, the i18n plugin loads the locale-specific module and then merges it with the default language module's `root` object. Missing translations in the locale-specific module will be filled with values from the default language module.

Figure 5-3 shows how the quotes page looks when a Google Chrome browser's language has been set to German.

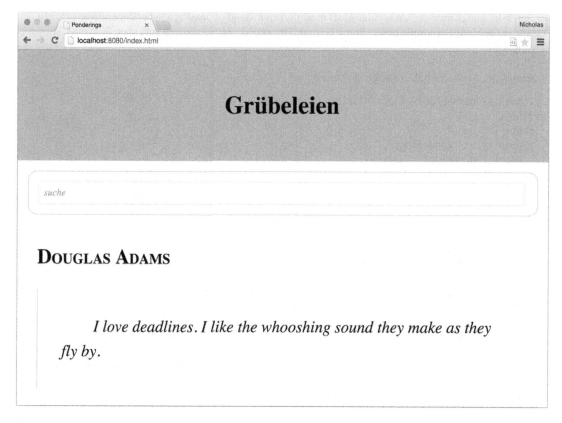

Figure 5-3. *Switching the browser language loads the German translation*

■ **Note** The `window.navigator.language` property is affected by different settings in different browsers. For example, in Google Chrome it only reflects the user's language setting, whereas in Mozilla Firefox it can be affected by an `Accept-Language` header in a page's HTTP response as well.

Cache Busting

Application servers often cache resources like script files, images, stylesheets, and so on to eliminate unnecessary disk access when serving a resource that has not changed since it was last read. Cached resources are often stored in memory and associated with some key, usually the URL of the resource. When multiple requests for a given URL occur within a specified cache period, the resource is fetched from memory using the key (URL). This can have significant performance benefits in a production environment, but invalidating cache in development or testing environments every time a code change is made, or a new resource is introduced, can become tedious.

Certainly caching can be toggled on a per-environment basis, but a simpler solution, at least for JavaScript (or any resource loaded by RequireJS), might be to utilize the RequireJS cache-busting feature. *Cache busting* is the act of mutating the URL for every resource request in such a way that the resource may still be fetched, but will never be found in cache because its "key" is always different. This is commonly done by including a query string parameter that changes whenever a page is reloaded.

A urlArgs property has been added to the configuration script in Listing 5-37. This will append the query string parameter bust={timestamp} to all requests generated by RequireJS. The time stamp is recalculated for each page load to ensure that the parameter value changes, making URLs unique.

Listing 5-37. The urlArgs Configuration Property Can Be Used to Bust Cache

```
// example-009/public/scripts/main.js
requirejs.config({
  baseUrl: '/scripts',
  urlArgs: 'bust=' + (new Date().getTime()),
  paths: {
    // ...
  },
  shim: {
    // ...
  }
});
```

Figure 5-4 shows that the bust parameter is indeed applied to each request initiated by RequireJS, even XHR requests for text resources like header.hbs.

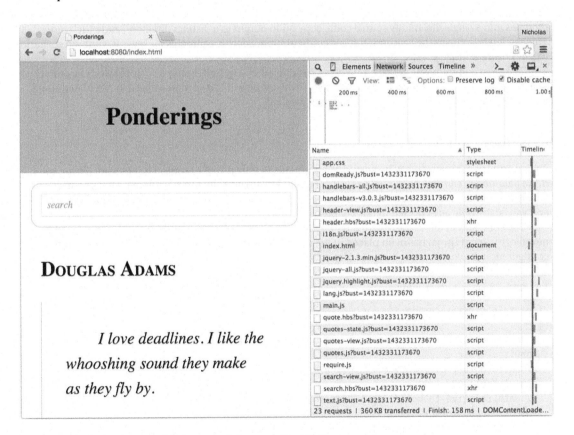

Figure 5-4. The bust parameter is appended to each RequireJS request

While the usefulness of this feature is evident, it can also create a few problems.

First, RequireJS respects HTTP cache headers, so even if urlArgs is used as a cache-busting mechanism, RequireJS may still request (and receive) a cached version of a resource, depending on how cache is implemented. If possible, always serve the appropriate cache headers in each environment.

Second, be aware that some proxy servers drop query string parameters. If a development or staging environment includes proxies to mimic a production environment, a cache-busting query string parameter may be ineffective. Some developers use urlArgs to specify particular resource versions in a production environment (e.g., version=v2), but this is generally discouraged for this very reason. It is an unreliable versioning technique, at best.

Finally, some browsers treat resources with different URLs as distinct, debuggable entities. In Chrome and Firefox, for example, if a debug breakpoint is set in the source code for http://localhost:8080/scripts/quotes-state.js?bust=1432504595280, it will be removed if the page is refreshed, when the new resource URL becomes http://localhost:8080/scripts/quotes-state.js?bust=1432504694566. Resetting breakpoints can become tedious, and though the debugger keyword can be used to circumvent this problem by forcing the browser to pause execution, it still requires a diligent developer to ensure that all debugger breakpoints are removed before code is promoted to production.

RequireJS Optimizer

The RequireJS optimizer, r.js, is a build tool for RequireJS projects. It can be used to concatenate all RequireJS modules into a single file, minify source code, copy build output to a distinct directory, and much more. This section introduces the tool and its basic configuration. Specific examples for several common scenarios will be covered next.

The most common way to use r.js involves installing the RequireJS npm package for Node.js, either as a global package or as a local project package. The examples in this section will use the local RequireJS installation created when all npm modules were installed.

Configuring r.js

A wide array of parameters may be passed as arguments to the r.js tool to control its behavior. Fortunately these parameters can also be passed to r.js in a regular JavaScript configuration file, which makes the terminal command significantly shorter. For non-trivial projects this is the preferred configuration method, and will be the only one covered in this chapter.

The code files in the example-010 directory have been moved into a standard src directory, and a new file, rjs-config.js, has been placed in the directory root. This file, unsurprisingly, contains the r.js configuration. Its contents are shown in Listing 5-38.

Listing 5-38. r.js Configuration

```
// example-010/rjs-config.js
({
  // build input directory for application code
  appDir: './src',
  // build output directory for application code
  dir: './build',
  // path relative to build input directory where scripts live
  baseUrl: 'public/scripts',
  // predefined configuration file used to resolve dependencies
  mainConfigFile: './src/public/scripts/main.js',
```

```
// include all text! references as inline modules
inlineText: true,
// do not copy files that were combined in build output
removeCombined: true,

// specific modules to be built
modules: [
  {
    name: 'main'
  }
],

// uglify the output
optimize: 'uglify'
})
```

Developers who are familiar with build tools will immediately recognize the input/output pattern present in the configuration.

The appDir property specifies the project "input" directory, relative to the configuration file, where uncompiled source code lives.

The dir property specifies the project "output" directory, relative to the configuration file, where compiled and minified output will be written when the r.js tool runs.

The baseUrl property tells r.js where the project scripts are located *relative to the appDir property*. This should not be confused with the baseUrl property in the main.js file, which tells RequireJS where modules are located relative to the web application root.

The mainConfigFile property points to the actual RequireJS (not r.js) configuration. This helps r.js understand how modules are related to each other, and what module aliases and shims exist, if any. It is possible to omit this property and specify all of these paths in the r.js configuration, though that is beyond the scope of this example.

Setting the inlineText property to true ensures that all text files referenced with the text plugin prefix text! will be compiled with RequireJS modules in the final build output. This option is enabled by default but is explicitly set in this project for clarity.

By default, r.js will minify and copy *all* scripts (packed and unpacked) to the output directory. The removeCombined property toggles this behavior. In this case only the packed, compiled script(s) and any other scripts that could not be included in the packed output will be copied to the output directory.

The modules array lists all of the top-level modules to be compiled. Because this is a single-page application, only the actual main module needs to be compiled.

Finally, the optimize property instructs r.js to apply an uglify transform to all scripts, minimizing all JavaScript code.

Running the r.js Command

Building the project is simply a matter of running the r.js command in a terminal, passing it the path to the configuration file via its -o flag as shown in Listing 5-39.

Listing 5-39. Running the r.js Command

```
example-010$ ../node_modules/.bin/r.js -o rjs-config.js
```

Terminal output shows which files are compiled and copied by r.js during the build. Examining the build output files in Listing 5-40 shows what, exactly, r.js optimized and copied.

Listing 5-40. Build Directory Content

```
example-010/build$ tree
.
├── build.txt
├── index.js
└── public
    ├── index.html
    ├── scripts
    │   ├── main.js
    │   ├── nls
    │   │   └── de
    │   │       └── lang.js
    │   ├── require.js
    │   ├── templates
    │   │   ├── header.hbs
    │   │   ├── quote.hbs
    │   │   └── search.hbs
    │   └── vendor
    │       └── ventage
    │           ├── LICENSE
    │           ├── README.md
    │           ├── bower.json
    │           ├── package.json
    │           └── test
    │               ├── index.html
    │               ├── main.js
    │               ├── ventage.clear.js
    │               ├── ventage.create.js
    │               ├── ventage.ctor.js
    │               ├── ventage.off.js
    │               ├── ventage.on.js
    │               ├── ventage.pipe.js
    │               ├── ventage.trigger.js
    │               └── ventage.triggerAsync.js
    └── styles
        └── app.css

9 directories, 24 files
```

Several things immediately stand out in the `public/scripts` directory.

First, the `require.js` and `main.js` scripts are both present. Since these scripts are the only files referenced in `index.html`, their presence here is expected. Other scripts such as the `quotes-view.js` and `quotes-state.js` scripts are noticeably absent, but examining the content of `main.js` reveals why: they have been packed and minified according to the r.js build settings.

Second, the localization file `nls/lang.js` is now missing because it has been included as part of `main.js`. The `nls/de/lang.js` script still remains as part of the build output, though its contents have been minified. Any user browsing the example web page in the default locale will receive an optimized experience, as RequireJS will not have to make an external AJAX call to load the default language translations. Users from Germany will incur the additional HTTP request because the German localization file has not been included in the packed output. This is a limitation of the localization plugin that r.js must respect.

Third, the Handlebars templates, though compiled as part of the build output in `main.js`, have also been copied to the `public/scripts/templates` directory. This happens because RequireJS plugins currently *have no visibility into the build process* and therefore no method of honoring the `removeCombined` option in the r.js configuration file. Fortunately, because these templates have been wrapped in AMD modules and concatenated with `main.js`, RequireJS will *not* attempt to load them with AJAX requests. If deployment size is an issue for this project, a post-build script or task can be created to remove the `templates` directory if needed.

Fourth, the `vendor/ventage` directory has been copied to the `build` directory even though its core module, `ventage.js`, has been concatenated with `main.js`. While RequireJS can automatically remove individual module files (like `ventage.js`) after compilation, it will not clean up other files associated with a module (in this case, unit tests and package definition files like `package.json` and `bower.json`), so they must be removed manually, or as part of a post-build process.

Summary

RequireJS is a very pragmatic JavaScript module loader that works well in a browser environment. Its ability to load and resolve modules asynchronously means that it does not rely solely on bundling or packing scripts for performance benefits. For further optimization, though, the r.js optimization tool may be used to combine RequireJS modules into a single, minified script to minimize the number of HTTP requests necessary to load modules and other resources.

Though RequireJS modules must be defined in AMD format, RequireJS can shim non-AMD scripts so that legacy code may be imported by AMD modules where necessary. Shimmed modules may also have dependencies that can automatically be loaded by RequireJS.

The `text` plugin lets modules import external text file dependencies (such as templates) as strings. These text files are loaded like any other module dependency, and may even be inlined in build output by the r.js optimizer.

Localization is supported by the `i18n` module loader, which can dynamically load text translation modules based on a browser's locale settings. While the primary locale translation module can be optimized and concatenated with r.js, additional locale translation modules will always be loaded with HTTP requests.

Module execution can be deferred by the `pageLoad` plugin, which prevents a module's closure from executing until the DOM has been fully rendered. This can be an effective way to eliminate repeat calls to jQuery's `ready()` function, or fumbling through the cross-browser code necessary to subscribe to the `DOMContentLoaded` event manually.

Finally, the RequireJS configuration can automatically append query string parameters to all RequireJS HTTP requests, providing a cheap but effective cache-busting feature for development environments.

CHAPTER 6

Browserify

Less is more.

—Ludwig Mies van der Rohe

Browserify is a JavaScript module loader that works around the language's current lack of support for importing modules within the browser by serving as a "pre-processor" for your code. In much the same way that CSS extensions such as SASS and LESS have brought enhanced syntax support to stylesheets, Browserify enhances client-side JavaScript applications by recursively scanning their source code for calls to a global `require()` function. When Browserify finds such calls, it immediately loads the referenced modules (using the same `require()` function that is available within Node.js) and combines them into a single, minified file—a "bundle"—that can then be loaded within the browser.

This simple but elegant approach brings the power and convenience of CommonJS (the method by which modules are loaded within Node.js) to the browser, while also doing away with the additional complexity and boilerplate code required by Asynchronous Module Definition (AMD) loaders such as RequireJS (described in Chapter 5).

In this chapter, you will learn how to

- Distinguish between AMD and CommonJS module loaders

- Create modular front-end JavaScript applications that follow the simple patterns for module management popularized by tools such as Node.js

- Visualize a project's dependency tree

- Compile your application as quickly as possible—as changes are made—using Browserify's sister application, Watchify

- Use third-party Browserify plugins ("transforms") to extend the tool beyond its core functionality

---

Note   Portions of this chapter discuss concepts already covered in this book's previous chapters on Bower (Chapter 1) and Grunt (Chapter 2). If you are unfamiliar with these tools, you are encouraged to cover that material before proceeding.

The AMD API vs. CommonJS

The Asynchronous Module Definition API, covered in Chapter 5, serves as a clever workaround to JavaScript's current lack of support for loading external modules inline. Often referred to as a "browser-first" approach, the AMD API accomplishes its goal of bringing modules to the browser by requiring that developers wrap each of their modules within a callback function, which can then be loaded asynchronously (i.e., "lazy loaded") as needed. This process is demonstrated by the modules shown in Listing 6-1.

Listing 6-1. Defining and Requiring an AMD Module

```
// requirejs-example/public/app/weather.js

define([], function() {
    return {
        'getForecast': function() {
            document.getElementById('forecast').innerHTML = 'Partly cloudy.';
        }
    };
});

// requirejs-example/public/app/index.js

define(['weather'], function(weather) {
    weather.getForecast();
});
```

The AMD API is both clever and effective, but many developers also find it to be a bit clumsy and verbose. Ideally, JavaScript applications should be capable of referencing external modules without the added complexity and boilerplate code that the AMD API requires. Fortunately, a popular alternative known as CommonJS exists that addresses this concern.

While most people tend to associate JavaScript with web browsers, the truth is that JavaScript has found widespread use in a number of other environments for quite some time—well before Node.js came on the scene. Examples of such environments include Rhino, a server-side runtime environment created by Mozilla, and ActionScript, a derivative used by Adobe's once-popular Flash platform that has fallen out of favor in recent years. Each of these platforms works around JavaScript's lack of built-in module support by creating its own approach.

Sensing a need for a standard solution to this problem, a group of developers got together and proposed what became known as CommonJS, a standardized approach to defining and using JavaScript modules. Node.js follows a similar approach, as does the next major update to JavaScript (ECMAScript 6, a.k.a. ES6 Harmony). This approach can also be used to write modular JavaScript applications that work in all web browsers in use today, although not without the help of additional tools such as Browserify, the subject of this chapter.

Installing Browserify

Before going any further, you should ensure that you have installed Browserify's command-line utility. Available as an npm package, the installation process is shown in Listing 6-2.

Listing 6-2. Installing the browserify Command-Line Utility via npm

```
$ npm install -g browserify
$ browserify --version
10.2.4
```

■ **Note** Node's package manager (npm) allows users to install packages in one of two contexts: locally or globally. In this example, browserify is installed within the global context, which is typically reserved for command-line utilities.

Creating Your First Bundle

Much of Browserify's appeal lies in its simplicity; JavaScript developers familiar with CommonJS and Node will find themselves immediately at home. By way of an example, consider Listing 6-3, which shows the CommonJS-based equivalent of the simple RequireJS-based application we saw in Listing 6-1.

Listing 6-3. Front-End Application That Requires Modules via CommonJS

```
// simple/public/app/index.js

var weather = require('./weather');
weather.getForecast();

// simple/public/app/weather.js

module.exports = {
    'getForecast': function() {
        document.getElementById('forecast').innerHTML = 'Partly cloudy.';
    }
};
```

Unlike our RequireJS-based example, this application *cannot* be run directly within the browser because the browser lacks a built-in mechanism for loading modules via require(). Before the browser can understand this application, we must first compile it into a bundle with the help of the browserify command-line utility or via Browserify's API.

The command for compiling this application using Browserify's command-line utility is as follows:

```
$ browserify app/index.js -o public/dist/app.js
```

Here we pass the browserify utility the path to our application's main file, public/app/index.js, and specify that the compiled output should be saved to public/dist/app.js, the script referenced within the project's HTML (see Listing 6-4).

Listing 6-4. HTML File Referencing Our Compiled Browserify Bundle

```
// simple/public/index.html

<!DOCTYPE html>
<html>
<head>
    <meta charset="utf-8">
    <meta http-equiv="X-UA-Compatible" content="IE=edge">
    <meta name="viewport" content="width=device-width, initial-scale=1">
    <title>Browserify - Simple Example</title>
</head>
<body>
    <div id="forecast"></div>
    <script src="/dist/app.js"></script>
</body>
</html>
```

In addition to using Browserify's command-line utility, we also have the option of compiling this application programmatically via Browserify's API. Doing so will allow us to easily incorporate this step into a larger build process (developed with tools such as Grunt). Listing 6-5 shows this project's browserify Grunt task.

Listing 6-5. Grunt Task That Compiles the Application via Browserify's API

```
// simple/tasks/browserify.js

module.exports = function(grunt) {

    grunt.registerTask('browserify', function() {
        var done = this.async();
        var path = require('path');
        var fs = require('fs');
        var src = path.join('public', 'app', 'index.js');
        var target = path.join('public', 'dist', 'app.js');
        var browserify = require('browserify')([src]);
        browserify.bundle(function(err, data) {
            if (err) return grunt.fail.fatal(err);
            grunt.file.mkdir(path.join('public', 'dist'));
            fs.writeFileSync(target, data);
            done();
        });
    });

};
```

Visualizing the Dependency Tree

If you happen to be more of a visual learner, the chart shown in Figure 6-1 may go a long way toward conveying what occurs during Browserify's compilation process. Here we see a visualization of the various dependencies encountered by Browserify as it compiled this chapter's advanced project.

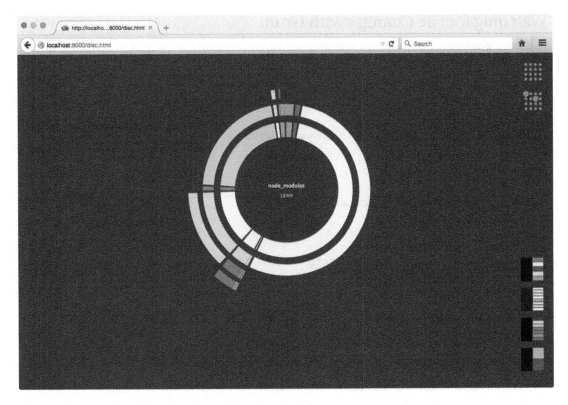

Figure 6-1. *Visualizing the advanced project's dependency tree*

Viewing this chart as a static rendering on a page really does not do it justice. For the full effect, you should compile the project and view the chart within your browser by running npm start from within the project's folder. Doing so will allow you to hover your mouse over the various segments of the chart, each of which represents a dependency encountered by Browserify during its compilation process. While it is not evident in Figure 6-1, an in-depth analysis of the chart indicates that our application's custom code accounts for only a tiny sliver (9.7kB) of the total size of the bundle generated by Browserify. The vast majority of this project's nearly 2MB of code consists of third-party dependencies (e.g., Angular, jQuery, Lodash, etc.), an important fact that will be referenced again later in the chapter.

***

■ **Note**   You may also be interested in investigating the browserify-graph and colony command-line utilities (also available via npm), which you can use to generate additional visualizations of a project's dependency tree.

***

Creating New Bundles As Changes Occur

Projects that take advantage of Browserify cannot be run directly within the browser—they must first be compiled. In order to make the most efficient use of the tool, it is important that projects be set up in such a way as to *automatically* trigger this step as changes occur within their source code. Let's take a look at two methods by which this can be achieved.

Watching for File Changes with Grunt

In Chapter 2 on Grunt, you discovered how plugins such as `grunt-contrib-watch` allow developers to trigger build steps as changes are made within an application's source code. It's easy to see how such tools could be applied to projects using Browserify, triggering the creation of new bundles as changes are detected. An example of this process in action can be seen by running the default Grunt task for this chapter's `simple` project, as shown in Listing 6-6.

Listing 6-6. Triggering the Creation of New Browserify Builds with Grunt

```
$ grunt
Running "browserify" task

Running "concurrent:serve" (concurrent) task
    Running "watch" task
    Waiting...
    Running "server" task
    App is now available at: http://localhost:7000
    >> File "app/index.js" changed.
    Running "browserify" task

    Done, without errors.
    Completed in 0.615s at Fri Jun 26 2015 08:31:25 GMT-0500 (CDT) - Waiting...
```

In this example, running the default Grunt task triggered three steps:

- A Browserify bundle was immediately created.

- A web server was launched to host the project.

- A watch script was executed that triggers the creation of new Browserify bundles as source code changes are detected.

This simple approach typically serves most small projects quite well; however, as small projects gradually evolve into large projects, developers often grow frustrated, understandably, with the ever-increasing build times that accompany it. Having to wait several seconds before you can try out each of your updates can quickly destroy any sense of "flow" that you might hope to achieve. Fortunately, Browserify's sister application, Watchify, can help us in these situations.

Watching for File Changes with Watchify

If Browserify (which compiles applications in their entirety) can be thought of as a meat cleaver, Watchify can be thought of as a paring knife. When invoked, Watchify initially compiles a specified application in its entirety; however, rather than exiting once this process has completed, Watchify continues to run, watching for changes to a project's source code. As changes are detected, Watchify recompiles *only those files that have changed*, resulting in drastically faster build times. Watchify accomplishes this by maintaining its own internal caching mechanism throughout each build.

As with Browserify, Watchify can be invoked via either the command line or a provided API. In Listing 6-7, this chapter's `simple` project is compiled with the help of Watchify's command-line utility. In this example, the `-v` argument is passed to specify that Watchify should run in verbose mode. As a result, Watchify notifies us as changes are detected.

Listing 6-7. Installing Watchify via npm and Running It Against This Chapter's simple Project

```
$ npm install -g watchify
$ watchify public/app/index.js -o public/dist/app.js -v
778 bytes written to public/dist/app.js (0.03 seconds)
786 bytes written to public/dist/app.js (0.01 seconds)
```

As with Browserify, Watchify provides a convenient API that allows us to integrate it into a larger build process (see Listing 6-8). We can do so with just a few small tweaks to the Browserify task previously shown in Listing 6-7.

Listing 6-8. Grunt Task Demonstrating the Use of Watchify's API

```
// simple/tasks/watchify.js

module.exports = function(grunt) {

    grunt.registerTask('watchify', function() {

        var done = this.async();
        var browserify = require('browserify');
        var watchify = require('watchify');
        var fs = require('fs');
        var path = require('path');
        var src = path.join('public', 'app', 'index.js');
        var target = path.join('public', 'dist', 'app.js');
        var targetDir = path.join('public', 'dist');

        var browserify = browserify({
            'cache': {},
            'packageCache': {}
        });
        browserify = watchify(browserify);
        browserify.add(src);

        var compile = function(err, data) {
            if (err) return grunt.log.error(err);
            if (!data) return grunt.log.error('No data');
            grunt.file.mkdir(targetDir);
            fs.writeFileSync(target, data);
        };

        browserify.bundle(compile);

        browserify.on('update', function() {
            browserify.bundle(compile);
        });

        browserify.on('log', function(msg) {
            grunt.log.oklns(msg);
        });

    });

};
```

In this example, we wrap our browserify instance with watchify. Afterward, we recompile the project as needed by subscribing to the update event emitted by our wrapped instance.

Using Multiple Bundles

In the earlier section "Visualizing the Dependency Tree," we looked at an interactive chart that allowed us to visualize the various dependencies encountered by Browserify as it compiled this chapter's advanced project (see Figure 6-1). One of the most important facts that we can take away from this chart is that the project's custom code (found in /app) accounts for only a tiny portion (9.7kB) of the bundle's total size of 1.8MB. In other words, the vast majority of this project's code consists of third-party libraries (e.g., Angular, jQuery, Lodash, etc.) that are unlikely to frequently change. Let's take a look at how we can use this knowledge to our advantage.

This chapter's extracted project is identical to the advanced project in every way, with one exception: instead of compiling a single Browserify bundle, the extracted project's build process creates two separate bundles:

- /dist/vendor.js: Third-party dependencies

- /dist/app.js: Custom application code

By taking this approach, browsers can more efficiently access project updates as they are released. In other words, as changes occur within the project's custom code, browsers only need to re-download /dist/app.js. Contrast this approach with that of the advanced project, in which each update (no matter how small) forces clients to re-download the project's nearly 2MB bundle.

Listing 6-9 shows the HTML file for the extracted project. As you can see, here we reference two separate bundles, /dist/vendor.js and /dist/app.js.

Listing 6-9. HTML for This Chapter's extracted Project

```
// extracted/public/index.html

<!DOCTYPE html>
<html ng-app="app">
<head>
    <meta charset="utf-8">
    <meta http-equiv="X-UA-Compatible" content="IE=edge">
    <meta name="viewport" content="width=device-width, initial-scale=1">
    <title>Browserify - Advanced Example</title>
    <link rel="stylesheet" href="/css/style.css">
</head>
<body class="container">

    <navbar ng-if="user_id"></navbar>

    <div ng-view></div>

    <footer><a href="/disc.html">View this project's dependency tree</a></footer>

    <script src="/dist/vendor.js"></script>
    <script src="/dist/app.js"></script>

</body>
</html>
```

Listing 6-10 shows the extracted project's Gruntfile. Take note of a special configuration value (`browserify.vendor_modules`) that is being set.

Listing 6-10. Gruntfile for This Chapter's extracted Project

```
// extracted/Gruntfile.js

module.exports = function(grunt) {

    grunt.initConfig({
        'browserify': {
            'vendor_modules': [
                'angular',
                'bootstrap-sass',
                'jquery',
                'angular-route',
                'angular-sanitize',
                'restangular',
                'jquery.cookie',
                'lodash',
                'underscore.string',
                'lodash-deep'
            ]
        }
    });

    grunt.loadTasks('tasks');

    grunt.registerTask('default', ['compass', 'browserify', 'browserify-vendor', 'init-db',
'concurrent']);

};
```

Listing 6-11 shows the contents of the extracted project's browserify Grunt task. This task largely mimics the corresponding task in the advanced project, with one major exception. In this task, we iterate through the third-party modules that we defined in the project's Gruntfile, and for each entry, we instruct Browserify to exclude the referenced module from the compiled bundle.

Listing 6-11. The extracted Project's browserify Grunt Task

```
// extracted/tasks/browserify.js

module.exports = function(grunt) {

    grunt.registerTask('browserify', function() {

        var done = this.async();
        var path = require('path');
        var fs = require('fs');
        var target = path.join('public', 'dist', 'app.js');
        var vendorModules = grunt.config.get('browserify.vendor_modules') || [];
```

```
    var browserify = require('browserify')([
        path.join('app', 'index.js')
    ], {
        'paths': ['app'],
        'fullPaths': true,
        'bundleExternal': true
    });

    vendorModules.forEach(function(vm) {
        grunt.log.writelns('Excluding module from application bundle: %s', vm);
        browserify.exclude(vm);
    });

    browserify.bundle(function(err, data) {
        if (err) return grunt.fail.fatal(err);
        grunt.file.mkdir(path.join('public', 'dist'));
        fs.writeFileSync(target, data);
        grunt.task.run('disc');
        done();
    });

    });

};
```

Finally, Listing 6-12 shows the contents of the extracted project's browserify-vendor Grunt task. When run, this task will create a separate Browserify bundle consisting solely of the third-party modules that we defined in Listing 6-10.

Listing 6-12. The extracted Project's browserify-vendor Grunt Task

```
// extracted/tasks/browserify-vendor.js

module.exports = function(grunt) {

    grunt.registerTask('browserify-vendor', function() {

        var done = this.async();
        var path = require('path');
        var fs = require('fs');
        var target = path.join('public', 'dist', 'vendor.js');
        var vendorModules = grunt.config.get('browserify.vendor_modules') || [];

        var browserify = require('browserify')({
            'paths': [
                'app'
            ],
            'fullPaths': true
        });
```

```
    vendorModules.forEach(function(vm) {
        browserify.require(vm);
    });

    browserify.bundle(function(err, data) {
        if (err) return grunt.fail.fatal(err);
        grunt.file.mkdir(path.join('public', 'dist'));
        fs.writeFileSync(target, data);
        done();
    });

    });

};
```

To see this process in action, navigate to the extracted project in your terminal and run $ npm start. Any missing npm modules will be installed, and the project's default Grunt task will be run. As this process occurs, two separate bundles will be created. The bundle containing the project's custom code, /dist/app.js, comes in at only 14kB in size.

The Node Way

As mentioned in this chapter's introduction, Browserify compiles a project by recursively scanning its source code in search of calls to a global require() function. As these calls are found, Browserify loads the modules they reference via the same require() function used by Node. Afterward, Browserify merges them into a single bundle that browsers are capable of understanding.

In this regard, projects that use Browserify are best thought of as client-side Node applications. Many aspects of Browserify that tend to confuse newcomers are more readily understood when this concept—along with everything that it entails—is kept in mind. Let's take a look at two such aspects now: module resolution and dependency management.

Module Resolution and the NODE_PATH Environment Variable

Node applications have the ability to reference modules in a number of ways. For example, here we see a simple Node application that requires a module by providing a relative path to its location:

```
var animals = require('./lib/animals');
```

In a similar manner, this example could also have provided the full, absolute path to this module. Either way, the location at which Node is expected to find this module is rather obvious. Now consider the following example, in which a module is referenced solely by name:

```
var animals = require('animals');
```

In situations such as this, Node will first attempt to locate the referenced module within its core library. This process can be seen in action when loading modules such as fs, Node's file system module. If no match is found, Node will then proceed to search for folders named node_modules, starting with the location of the module that called require() and working its way upward through the file system. As these folders are encountered, Node will check to see if they contain a module (or package) matching that which was requested. This process will continue until a match is found, and if none is found, an exception is thrown.

This simple yet powerful method by which module resolution occurs within Node revolves almost exclusively around the node_modules folder. However, Node provides an often-overlooked method that allows developers to augment this behavior by defining *additional* folders within which Node should be allowed to search for modules, should the previous steps turn up empty-handed. Let's take a look at this chapter's path-env project, which demonstrates how this can be accomplished.

Listing 6-13 shows an excerpt from this project's package.json file. Of particular importance is the start script that has been defined. Based on the settings shown here, when $ npm start is run within this project, the NODE_PATH environment variable will be updated to include a reference to this project's /lib folder before the application is run. As a result, Node will add this folder to those it uses to resolve the location of named modules.

Listing 6-13. This Project's npm start Script Updates the NODE_PATH Environment Variable

```
// path-env/package.json

{
    "name": "path-env",
    "version": "1.0.0",
    "main": "./bin/index.js",
    "scripts": {
            "start": "export NODE_PATH=$NODE_PATH:./lib && node ./bin/index.js"
    }
}
```

■ **Note** On OS X and Linux, environment variables are set from the terminal by running export ENVIRONMENT_VARIABLE=value. The command to be used within the Windows command line is set ENVIRONMENT_VARIABLE=value.

The significance of setting the NODE_PATH environment variable may not be obvious at first glance; however, doing so can have a dramatically positive impact on the cleanliness and maintainability of complex projects. Why? Because when this approach is used, it essentially allows developers to create a namespace through which an application's modules (those that do not exist as independent npm packages) can be referenced by name, rather than by lengthy relative paths. Listing 6-14 shows a simple example of what this looks like in practice.

Listing 6-14. Several of the Modules Contained Within the path-env Project

```
// path-env/bin/index.js

var api = require('app/api');

// path-env/lib/app/api/index.js

var express = require('express');
var path = require('path');
var app = express();
var animals = require('app/models/animal');
app.use('/', express.static(path.join(__dirname, '..', '..', '..', 'public')));
```

```
app.get('/animals', function(req, res, next) {
    res.send(animals);
});
app.listen(7000, function() {
    console.log('App is now available at: http://localhost:7000');
});
module.exports = app;

// path-env/lib/app/models/animal/index.js

module.exports = [
    'Aardvarks', 'Cats', 'Dogs', 'Lemurs', 'Three-Toed Sloths', 'Zebras'
];
```

Take note of this example's lack of relative module references. For example, notice how this project's main script, bin/index.js, is able to load a custom module responsible for initializing Express via require('app/api');. The alternative would be to use a relative path: require('../lib/app/api');. Anyone who has worked within complex Node applications and encountered module references along the line of require('../../../../models/animal'); will quickly come to appreciate the increase in code clarity that this approach affords.

■ **Note**   It is important to bear in mind that the use of the NODE_PATH environment variable only makes sense within the context of a Node (or Browserify) application—*not* a package. When creating a reusable package that is intended to be shared with others, you should rely solely on Node's default module resolution behavior.

Taking Advantage of NODE_PATH Within Browserify

Thus far, we have focused on how the NODE_PATH environment variable can have a positive impact on server-side Node applications. Now that we have laid that groundwork, let's see how this concept can be applied within the context of client-side, browser-based applications compiled with Browserify.

Listing 6-15 shows the browserify Grunt task for this chapter's advanced project, which is responsible for compiling the application via Browserify's API. Of particular importance is the use of the paths option, which allows us to provide Browserify with an array of paths that should be appended to the NODE_PATH environment variable before compilation begins. It is this setting that allows us to easily take advantage of the same benefits demonstrated in this section's previous examples.

Listing 6-15. The browserify Grunt Task for This Chapter's advanced Project

```
// advanced/tasks/browserify.js

module.exports = function(grunt) {

    grunt.registerTask('browserify', function() {
        var done = this.async();
        var path = require('path');
        var fs = require('fs');
        var target = path.join('public', 'dist', 'app.js');
        var browserify = require('browserify')([
```

```
            path.join('app', 'index.js')
        ], {
            'paths': [
                'app'
            ],
            'fullPaths': true
        });
        browserify.bundle(function(err, data) {
            if (err) return grunt.fail.fatal(err);
            grunt.file.mkdir(path.join('public', 'dist'));
            fs.writeFileSync(target, data);
            grunt.task.run('disc');
            done();
        });
    });

};
```

For a simple demonstration of how this approach has positively impacted this project, consider Listing 6-16. Here we see a small module that is responsible for loading lodash and integrating two third-party utilities, underscore.string and lodash-deep. The final, exported value is a single object containing the combined functionality of all three modules.

Listing 6-16. Module Responsible for Loading Lodash and Integrating Various Third-Party Plugins

```
// advanced/app/utils/index.js

var _ = require('lodash');
_.mixin(require('underscore.string'));
_.mixin(require('lodash-deep'));
module.exports = _;
```

As a result of the paths value that was provided to Browserify, our application can now reference this module from any location by simply calling require('app/utils');.

Dependency Management

Up until quite recently, the notion of "dependency management" has (for the most part) been a foreign concept within the context of client-side, browser-based projects. The tide has swiftly turned, however, thanks in large part to the rapidly increasing popularity of Node, along with additional utilities built on top of it—a few of which this book has already covered (e.g., Bower, Grunt, and Yeoman). These utilities have helped to bring desperately needed tooling and guidance to the untamed, "Wild West" that once was (and largely still is) client-side development.

In regard to dependency management, Bower has helped address this need by providing client-side developers with an easy-to-use mechanism for managing the various third-party libraries that applications rely on. For developers who are new to this concept and are not using client-side compilers such as Browserify, Bower has always been and continues to be a viable option for managing a project's dependencies; however, as developers begin to see the advantages afforded by tools such as Browserify, Bower has begun to show signs of age.

At the beginning of this section, we mentioned that projects using Browserify are best thought of as client-side Node applications. In regard to dependency management, this statement is particularly important. Recall that during Browserify's compile process, a project's source code is scanned for calls to a global require() function. When found, these calls are executed within Node, and the returned value is subsequently made available to the client-side application. The important implication here is that when using Browserify, dependency management is significantly simplified when developers rely solely on npm, Node's package manager. While technically, yes, it is possible to instruct Browserify on how to load packages installed by Bower, more often than not, it's simply more trouble than it's worth.

Defining Browser-Specific Modules

Consider a scenario in which you would like to create a new module, which you intend to publish and share via npm. You want this module to work both within Node and within the browser (via Browserify). To facilitate this, Browserify supports the use of a browser configuration setting within a project's package.json file. When defined, this setting allows developers to override the location used to locate a particular module. To better understand how this works, let's take a look at two brief examples.

Listing 6-17 shows the contents of a simple package. Within this package, two modules exist, lib/node.js and lib/browser.js. According to this package's package.json file, the main module for this package is lib/node.js. In other words, when this package is referenced by name within a Node application, this is the module Node will load. Notice, however, that an additional configuration setting has been defined: "browser": "./lib/browser.js". As a result of this setting, Browserify will load this module rather than the one specified by main.

Listing 6-17. Module Exposing Two Distinct Entry Points: One for Node, the Other for Browserify

```
// browser1/package.json

{
  "name": "browser1",
  "version": "1.0.0",
  "main": "./lib/node.js",
  "browser": "./lib/browser.js"
}

// browser1/lib/browser.js

module.exports = {
    'run': function() {
        console.log('I am running within a browser.');
    }
};

// browser1/lib/node.js

module.exports = {
    'run': function() {
        console.log('I am running within Node.');
    }
};
```

As you will see in a moment, Browserify's browser configuration setting need not be limited to simply overriding the location of a package's main module. It can also be used to override the location of *multiple* modules within a package. By way of an example, consider Listing 6-18. In this instance, instead of providing a string for our package.json file's browser setting, we provide an object, allowing us to specify *multiple*, browser-specific overrides.

Listing 6-18. Module Exposing Multiple, Distinct Modules for Node and Browserify

```
// browser2/package.json

{
  "name": "browser2",
  "version": "1.0.0",
  "main": "./lib/node.js",
  "browser": {
    "./lib/node.js": "./lib/browser.js",
    "./lib/extra.js": "./lib/extra-browser.js"
  }
}
```

As in Listing 6-17, a module that implements this pattern will expose distinct entry points into itself: one for Node, and a separate one for applications compiled via Browserify. This example takes this concept a step further, however. As this module is compiled, should it ever attempt to load the module located at lib/extra.js, the module located at lib/extra-browser will be substituted instead. In this way, the browser setting allows us to create modules with behavior that can vary greatly depending on whether those modules are run within Node or within the browser.

Extending Browserify with Transforms

Developers can build upon Browserify's core functionality by creating plugins, called *transforms*, that tap into the compilation process that occurs as new bundles are created. Such transforms are installed via npm and are enabled once their names are included within the browserify.transform array in an application's package.json file. Let's take a look at a few useful examples.

brfs

The brfs transform simplifies the process of loading file contents inline. It extends Browserify's compilation process to search for calls to the fs.readFileSync() method. When found, the contents of the referenced file are immediately loaded and returned.

Listing 6-19 shows an excerpt from the package.json file for this chapter's transforms-brfs project. In this example, the brfs module has been installed and included within the browserify.transform configuration setting.

Listing 6-19. Excerpt from the package.json File for This Chapter's transforms-brfs Project

```
// transforms-brfs/package.json

{
  "name": "transforms-brfs",
  "dependencies": {
    "browserify": "^10.2.4",
    "brfs": "^1.4.0"
  },
  "browserify": {
    "transform": [
        "brfs"
    ]
  }
}
```

Listing 6-20 shows the contents of this project's /app/index.js module. In this example, the brfs transform will load the contents of /app/templates/lorem.html, which is subsequently assigned to the tpl variable.

Listing 6-20. Loading a Template via fs.readFileSync()

```
// transforms-brfs/app/index.js

var fs = require('fs');
var $ = require('jquery');
var tpl = fs.readFileSync(__dirname + '/templates/lorem.html', 'utf8');
$('#container').html(tpl);
```

folderify

Much like the brfs transform, the folderify transform allows you to load the contents of files inline. Rather than operating on a single file at a time, however, folderify allows you to quickly load the contents of *multiple* files. By way of an example, consider Listing 6-21, which shows the contents of this chapter's transforms-folderify application.

Listing 6-21. Loading the Contents of Multiple Files with folderify

```
// transforms-folderify/app/index.js

var $ = require('jquery');
var includeFolder = require('include-folder');
var folder = includeFolder(__dirname + '/templates');

for (var k in folder) {
    $('#container').append('<p>' + k + ': ' + folder[k] + '</p>');
}
```

As in the previous example, the package.json file for this project has been modified to include folderify within its browserify.transform array. When compiled, Browserify will search for references to the include-folder module. When the function it returns is called, Browserify will load the contents of each file it finds within the specified folder and return them in the form of an object.

bulkify

With the bulkify transform, developers can import multiple modules with a single call. To better understand how this works, see Listing 6-22, which shows an excerpt of the contents of the main application file for this chapter's transforms-bulkify project.

Listing 6-22. Main Application File for This Chapter's transforms-bulkify Project

```
// transforms-bulkify/app/index.js

var bulk = require('bulk-require');

var app = angular.module('app', [
    'ngRoute'
]);

var routes = bulk(__dirname, [
    'routes/**/route.js'
]).routes;

app.config(function($routeProvider) {

    var defaultRoute = 'dashboard';

    _.each(routes, function(route, route_name) {
        route = route.route;
        route.config.resolve = route.config.resolve || {};
        $routeProvider.when(route.route, route.config);
    });

    $routeProvider.otherwise({
        'redirectTo': defaultRoute
    });

});
```

This particular example demonstrates the use of Browserify within the context of an Angular application. If you are unfamiliar with Angular (covered in Chapter 8), don't worry—the important aspect of this example is the manner in which the bulk() method allows us to require() multiple modules matching one or more specified patterns (in this case, routes/**/route.js).

Figure 6-2 shows the file structure for this project. As you can see, the app/routes module contains three folders, each representing a route within our Angular application. The bulkify transform has allowed us to quickly require() each of these modules with a single call to bulk(). Afterward, we are able to iterate over the resulting object and pass each route to Angular.

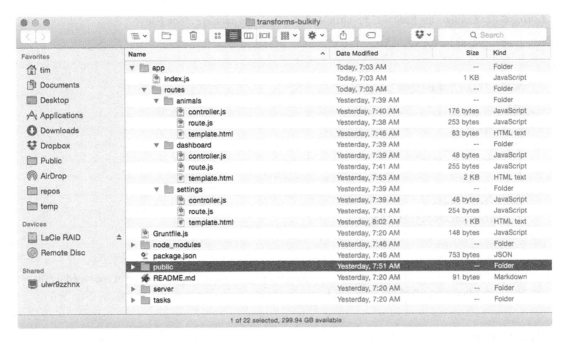

Figure 6-2. File structure for this chapter's transforms-bulkify *project*

Browserify-Shim

Developers using Browserify will occasionally find themselves needing to import modules that do not conform to the CommonJS way of doing things. Consider a third-party Foo library that, once loaded, assigns itself to the global window.Foo variable (see Listing 6-23). Such libraries can be imported with the help of the browserify-shim transform.

Listing 6-23. Third-Party Foo Library That Assigns Itself to the Global Foo Variable

```
// transforms-shim/app/vendor/foo.js

function Foo() {
    console.log('Bar');
}
```

After installing the browserify-shim module locally via npm, enable it by adding its name to the list of enabled transforms within a project's package.json file, as shown previously in Listing 6-19. Next, create a browserify-shim object at the root level of your application's package.json file, which will serve as the configuration object for this transform (see Listing 6-24). In this example, each key within this object represents the path to an improperly exposed module, while the corresponding value specifies the global variable to which the module has assigned itself.

Listing 6-24. Configuring `browserify-shim` Within a Project's `package.json` File

```
// transforms-shim/package.json

{
  "name": "transforms-shim",
  "version": "1.0.0",
  "main": "server.js",
  "browserify": {
    "transform": [
      "browserify-shim"
    ]
  },
  "browserify-shim": {
    "./app/vendor/foo.js": "Foo"
  }
}
```

With the `browserify-shim` transform installed and configured, the module located at app/vendor/foo.js can now be properly imported via `require()`.

Summary

Browserify is a powerful utility that extends the intuitive process by which modules are created and imported within Node to the browser. With its help, browser-based JavaScript applications can be organized as a series of small, easy-to-understand, and tightly focused modules that work together to form a larger and more complicated whole. What's more, there is nothing preventing applications that currently have no module management system in place from putting Browserify to use right away. The process of refactoring a monolithic application down into smaller components is not an overnight process, and is best taken one step at a time. With the help of Browserify, you can do just that—as time and resources allow.

Related Resources

- Browserify: `http://browserify.org`

- Browserify transforms: `https://github.com/substack/node-browserify/wiki/list-of-transforms`

- brfs: `https://github.com/substack/brfs`

- Watchify: `https://github.com/substack/watchify`

CHAPTER 7

Knockout

*Complex systems are characterized by simple elements, acting on local knowledge with
local rules, giving rise to complicated, patterned behavior.*

—David West

Knockout is a JavaScript library concerned with binding HTML markup to JavaScript objects. It is not a full
framework. It has no state router, HTTP AJAX capability, internal message bus, or module loader. Instead,
it focuses on two-way data binding between JavaScript objects and the DOM. When the data in a JavaScript
application changes, HTML elements bound to Knockout views receive automatic updates. Likewise, when
DOM input occurs--through form field manipulation, for example--Knockout captures the input changes
and updates the application state accordingly.

In place of low-level, imperative HTML element manipulation, Knockout uses specialized objects called
observables and a custom binding syntax to express how application data relates to markup. The internal
mechanics are fully customizable so developers can extend Knockout's capabilities with custom binding
syntax and behaviors.

As an independent JavaScript library, Knockout has no dependencies. The presence of other libraries
is often required to fulfill the application functions that Knockout does not perform, however, so it plays
well with many other common libraries like jQuery, Underscore, Q, etc. The Knockout API represents data
binding operations at a much higher level than strict DOM manipulation, and so places Knockout closer to
Backbone or Angular in terms of abstraction, but its slim, view-oriented feature set means it has a far smaller
footprint.

Knockout will fully function in all modern browsers and, as of this writing, extends back to cover
Firefox 3+, Internet Explorer 6+, and Safari 6+. Its backward compatibility is especially impressive in light of
its newest feature, HTML5-compatible components with custom markup tags. The Knockout team has taken
pains to make the Knockout development experience seamless in a variety of browser environments.

This chapter explores Knockout's features and API through an example application that manages
kitchen recipes. All chapter code examples will be prefixed with a comment to indicate in which file
the example code actually resides. For example, in Listing 7-1, the index.js file would be found in the
knockout/example-000 directory distributed with this book's source code.

Listing 7-1. Not a Real Example

```
// example-000/index.js
console.log('this is not a real example');
```

To run examples, first install Node.js (refer to the Node.js documentation for your system) and then run
npm install in the knockout directory to install all example code dependencies. Each example directory
will contain an index.js file that runs a simple Node.js web server. To run each example, it will be necessary

to launch this server and then navigate to a specified URL in a web browser. For example, to run the index.js file in Listing 7-1, navigate to the knockout/example-000 directory at a terminal prompt and run node index.js.

All example pages include the core Knockout script in a <script> tag reference. You can download this script from http://knockoutjs.com or from one of a number of reputable content delivery networks. Knockout can also be installed as a Bower package or npm module and is both AMD and CommonJS compatible. The Knockout documentation contains detailed instructions for all of these installation methods.

Views, Models, and View Models

Knockout distinguishes between two sources of information in an application's user interface: the *data model*, which represents the state of the application, and the *view model*, which represents how that state is displayed or communicated to the user. Both of these models are created in an application as JavaScript objects. Knockout bridges them by giving view models a way to represent a data model in a view (HTML) friendly way, while establishing bidirectional communication between views and data models so that input affects application state, and application state affects how a view represents data.

Since HTML is the technology that represents data in a web browser, Knockout view models can either bind directly to preexisting HTML document elements or create new elements with HTML templates. Knockout can even create complete reusable HTML components (custom HTML tags with their own attributes and behaviors).

The example application included with this chapter, *Omnom Recipes*, displays recipe data ("data model") in a browsable master/detail user interface. Both parts of this interface—the list of recipes and the details presented for each—are logical components situated ideally for Knockout view models. Each will have its own view model, and the application will coordinate the interactions between them. Eventually users will want to add or edit recipes, so additional HTML markup and view models will be introduced for that purpose.

Listing 7-2 shows the example application structure in the example-001 directory as output of the tree command.

Listing 7-2. Example Application Structure

```
example-001$ tree --dirsfirst
.
├── public
│   ├── scripts
│   │   ├── vendor
│   │   │   ├── jquery-2.1.3.min.js
│   │   │   └── knockout-3.3.0.js
│   │   ├── app.js
│   │   ├── recipe-details.js
│   │   └── recipe-list.js
│   ├── styles
│   │   └── app.css
│   ├── index.html
├── index.js
└── recipes.json
```

The index.js file is responsible for launching a web server that will service requests for files in the public directory. When the application's web page makes an AJAX request for recipe data, the web server will serialize the data in recipes.json and return it to the client.

In the `public` directory the `index.html` file will be served up by default when a user visits `http://localhost:8080`. This file contains application markup augmented with Knockout attributes. The `index.html` file also references the `app.css` stylesheet in `public/styles`, the two vendor scripts in `public/scripts/vendor`, and the three application scripts in `public/scripts`.

A Knockout view model can be applied to an entire page, or scoped to specific elements on a page. For nontrivial applications, it is advisable to use multiple view models to maintain modularity. In the *Omnom Recipes* application, the user interface exists as two logical "components": a list of recipes and a detailed view of a selected recipe. Instead of using a monolithic view model for the entire page, the application divides Knockout logic into two JavaScript modules in `public/scripts`: `recipe-list.js` and `recipe-details.js`. The `app.js` module consumes both of these view models and coordinates their activities on the page.

Figure 7-1 shows a screenshot of the rendered application, the recipe list clearly visible on the left and the recipe details on the right.

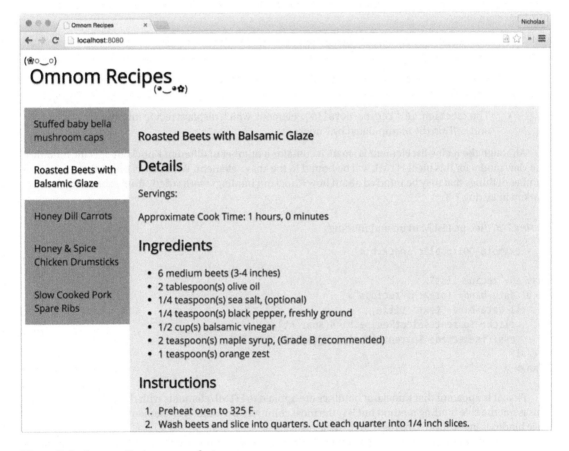

Figure 7-1. *Omnom Recipes screenshot*

■ **Note** To avoid confusion the example application makes use of simple JavaScript closures instead of client-side frameworks or module-oriented build tools to organize modules. These closures often assign a single object to a property on the global `window` object that will be consumed by other scripts. For example, the `recipe-list.js` file creates a global object, `window.RecipeList`, to be used in the `app.js` file. While completely valid, this architectural decision should be viewed in light of the example application's simplistic requirements.

The Recipe List

The `index.html` file, which contains the full page markup and Knockout templates, is divided into three key top-level elements:

- The `<header>` element, which contains static HTML content that will not be manipulated by Knockout

- The `<nav id="recipe-list">` element, which contains an unordered list of recipes and *will* be manipulated by Knockout

- The `<section id="recipe-details">` element, which displays recipe information and *will also* be manipulated by Knockout

Although the recipe list element is small, it contains a number of different Knockout-specific bindings. The view model for this bit of HTML will be bound to the `<nav>` element. With that in mind, there are a number of things that may be inferred about how Knockout bindings work strictly from examining the markup in Listing 7-3.

Listing 7-3. Recipe List Markup and Bindings

```
<!-- example-001/public/index.html -->

<nav id="recipe-list">
  <ul data-bind="foreach: recipes">
    <li data-bind="text: title,
      click: $parent.selectRecipe.bind($parent),
      css: {selected: $parent.isSelected($data)}"></li>
  </ul>
</nav>
```

First, it is apparent that Knockout bindings are applied to HTML elements with the `data-bind` attribute. This is not the sole binding method but it is the most common. Both the `<ul>` element and the `<li>` element have bindings in the form `binding-name: binding-value`.

Second, multiple bindings may be applied to an element as a comma-delimited list, demonstrated by the `<li>` element, which has bindings for `text`, `click`, and `css`.

Third, bindings with more complex values, such as the `css` binding on the `<li>` element, use key/value hashes (`{key: value, ... }`) to define specific binding options.

Finally, binding *values* may refer to JavaScript primitives, view model properties, view model methods, or any valid JavaScript expression.

The recipe list Knockout bindings reveal certain things about the Knockout view model that will be bound to the `<nav>` element. Developers will immediately recognize the `foreach` flow control statement, and correctly infer that `recipes` will be some collection exposed by the view model over which `foreach` will loop.

The <li> element within the unordered list has no HTML content of its own, so it may also be inferred that this element serves as a kind of *template* element that will be bound and rendered for each item in the recipes collection. As with most foreach loops, it is reasonable to expect the object *within* the loop (the loop's "context") to be an element of the collection. The list item's text binding references the title property of the recipe object for the current iteration and will be injected as the text content of the <li> element when rendered.

The click and css bindings both reference the special $parent object, which tells Knockout that the binding values should target the view model bound with foreach and not the current recipe object. (The view model is the "parent" context and the recipe is its "child".)

The click binding invokes the selectRecipe() method on the view model whenever the list item's click event is triggered. It binds the method to the view model specifically, by passing the $parent reference to the method's bind() function. This ensures that the value of this within the selectRecipe() method does not refer to the DOM element on which the handler is attached when it executes (the DOM's default behavior).

In contrast, the isSelected() method on the $parent (view model) object is invoked by the css binding, but Knockout, not the DOM, manages the invocation, ensuring the value of this within the method refers to the view model and not a DOM element.

The css binding instructs Knockout to apply specific CSS classes to a DOM element whenever specific criteria are met. The css binding value is a hash of selector/function pairs that Knockout evaluates whenever the DOM element is rendered. If the isSelected() method returns true, the selected CSS class will be added to the list item element. Another special variable, $data, is passed to isSelected(). The $data variable always refers to the *current* object context in which Knockout is working, in this case an individual recipe object. Some Knockout bindings, like text, operate on the current object context by default; others, like foreach, cause a context switch as a side effect.

In Listing 7-4, the context objects and values of each special variable are shown in HTML comments. Bindings have been abbreviated for clarity.

Listing 7-4. Changing Contexts with Knockout Bindings

```
<!-- example-001/public/index.html -->

<nav id="recipe-list">
  <!-- context: viewmodel -->
  <!-- $parent === undefined -->
  <!-- $data === viewmodel -->
  <ul data-bind="foreach: ...">
    <!-- context: recipe -->
    <!-- $parent === viewmodel -->
    <!-- $data === recipe -->
    <li data-bind="text: ..."></li>
  </ul>
</nav>
```

The recipe list module in Listing 7-5 creates the view model object that Knockout will bind to the recipe list markup when the page is rendered. The module's create() method accepts a list of recipe objects—JSON data loaded from the server—and returns a view model object with data properties and methods. Nearly all Knockout view models will need to access helper functions on the global window.ko object, so it is passed to the module's closure function as an argument.

Listing 7-5. Recipe List View Model

```
// example-001/public/scripts/recipe-list.js
'use strict';
window.RecipeList = (function (ko) {

  return {
    create: function (recipes) {
      var viewmodel = {};

      // properties
      viewmodel.recipes = recipes;
      viewmodel.selectedRecipe = ko.observable(recipes[0]);

      // methods
      viewmodel.selectRecipe = function (recipe) {
        this.selectedRecipe(recipe);
      };

      viewmodel.isSelected = function (recipe) {
        return this.selectedRecipe() === recipe;
      };

      return viewmodel;
    }
  };

}(window.ko));
```

■ **Note** The view model object itself may be created in any manner a developer chooses. In the example code each view model is a simple object literal created by a factory method. It is common to see the JavaScript constructor function pattern used to create view models in the wild, but view models are merely objects and may be constructed as a developer sees fit.

Other than the selectedRecipe property, the recipe list view model is wholly unremarkable. The template's foreach binding is applied to the recipes property (an array of plain JavaScript objects), the click binding on each list item invokes the selectRecipe() method (passing it a specific recipe), and when each list item is rendered, the isSelected() method is called to determine if the recipe being evaluated has been assigned to the selectedRecipe property or not. Actually, that is not entirely correct. The value of selectedRecipe is not actually a recipe object, but a function--a Knockout *observable*.

An observable is a special kind of function that holds a value, and can notify potential subscribers whenever that value changes. Bindings between HTML elements and observables automatically create subscriptions that Knockout manages in the background. Observables are created with special factory functions on the global ko object. The selectedRecipe observable in Listing 7-5 is created when ko. observable(recipes[0]) is called. Its initial value is the first element in the recipes array. When selectedRecipe() is invoked with no argument, it returns the value it contains (in this case, the object in recipes[0]). Any value passed to selectedRecipe() will become its new value. Although the selectedRecipe() property is not bound to any element in the recipe list template, it *is* manipulated when the user interacts with the recipe list via the view model's methods. The changing value of this element will be used as input for the next page component: recipe details.

Recipe Details

When a recipe is clicked in the recipe list, the recipe details are displayed in the right pane (refer to Figure 7-1). The markup in Listing 7-6 shows the HTML elements and Knockout bindings used to render the recipe details view model in the DOM.

Listing 7-6. Recipe Details Markup and Bindings

```html
<!-- example-001/public/index.html -->
<section id="recipe-details">
  <h1 data-bind="text: title"></h1>

  <h2>Details</h2>
  <p>Servings: <span data-bind="text: servings"></span></p>
  <p>Approximate Cook Time: <span data-bind="text: cookingTime"></span></p>

  <h2>Ingredients</h2>

  <ul data-bind="foreach: ingredients">
    <li data-bind="text: $data"></li>
  </ul>

  <h2>Instructions</h2>

  <ol data-bind="foreach: instructions">
    <li data-bind="text: $data"></li>
  </ol>

  <a data-bind="visible: hasCitation,
    attr: {href: citation, title: title}"
    target="_blank">Source</a>

</section>
```

Some bindings, like the `<h1>` text binding, read a value from a view model property and inject its string value into the HTML element.

Because the paragraphs under the "Details" heading have static content (the text "Servings:" and "Approximate Cook Time:"), `<span>` tags are used to anchor the Knockout bindings for the `servings` and `cookingTimes` properties at the end of each paragraph.

The ingredients list iterates over a collection of strings with the `foreach` binding, so the context object within each loop is a string represented by the `$data` variable. Each string becomes the text content of a list item.

The `<a>` tag at the bottom links to the recipe's website of origin as a citation. If the recipe has no citation, the anchor will not be displayed. The element's `visible` binding examines the view model's `hasCitation` observable and if the value is empty, hides the anchor element. Like the `css` binding used in the recipe list, the `attr` binding takes a key/value hash as its binding value. Hash keys (`href` and `title`) are the element attributes to be set on the the anchor, and values are properties on the view model that will be bound to each attribute.

127

The recipe details view model has many more members than the recipe list view model. Listing 7-7 shows that the recipe details view model is created in a similar fashion, by invoking the `RecipeDetails.create()` function with a specific recipe object that will be used to add data to the view model. This module uses several functions on the global ko object, and so, like the recipe list, it is passed as an argument to the module closure.

Listing 7-7. Recipe Details View Model

```
// example-001/public/scripts/recipe-details.js
'use strict';
window.RecipeDetails = (function (ko) {

  return {
    create: function (recipe) {
      var viewmodel = {};
      // add properties and methods...
      return viewmodel;
    }
  };

}(window.ko));
```

For each property on the recipe object, the recipe details view model has a corresponding observable property, shown in Listing 7-8. Observables are really only useful if the value they contain is expected to *change*. If values are expected to be static, plain JavaScript properties and values may be used instead. Observables are used in the recipe details view model because there will only be one instance of the view model bound to the page. When a new recipe is selected in the recipe list, the recipe details view model will be updated with the new recipe's values. Because its properties are observables, the page's markup will change immediately.

Listing 7-8. Recipe Details View Model Properties

```
// example-001/public/scripts/recipe-details.js
// properties
viewmodel.title = ko.observable(recipe.title);
viewmodel.servings = ko.observable(recipe.servings);
viewmodel.hours = ko.observable(recipe.cookingTime.hours);
viewmodel.minutes = ko.observable(recipe.cookingTime.minutes);
viewmodel.ingredients = ko.observableArray(recipe.ingredients);
viewmodel.instructions = ko.observableArray(recipe.instructions);
viewmodel.citation = ko.observable(recipe.citation);

viewmodel.cookingTime = ko.computed(function () {
  return '$1 hours, $2 minutes'
    .replace('$1', this.hours())
    .replace('$2', this.minutes());
}, viewmodel);
```

Listing 7-8 shows two new types of observables: `ko.observableArray()` and `ko.computed()`.

Observable arrays monitor their values (normal JavaScript arrays) for additions, deletions, and index changes, so that if the array mutates, any subscriber to the observable array is notified. While the ingredients and instructions do not change in this example, code will be introduced later to manipulate the collections and show the observable array's automatic binding updates in action.

Computed observables *generate* or *compute* a value based on other values exposed by observables on the view model. The ko.computed() function accepts callback that will be invoked to generate the value of the computed observable, and optionally a context object that acts as the value of this within the callback. When referenced by a template binding, a computed observable's value will be whatever its callback returns. The cookingTime property in Listing 7-8 creates a formatted string interpolated with the values from the hours and minutes observables. If either hours or minutes changes, the cookingTime computed observable will also update its subscribers.

■ **Note**   Because hours and minutes are really *functions* (though they are treated as properties in Knockout binding expressions), each must be invoked in the body of the computed observable in order to retrieve its value.

The recipe details view model methods in Listing 7-9 are fairly straightforward. The hasCitation() method tests the citation property for a nonempty value, while the update() method accepts a recipe and updates observable properties on the view model with new values. This method is not bound to the view, but will be used when a recipe in the recipe lists view model is selected.

Listing 7-9. Recipe Details View Model Methods

```
// example-001/public/scripts/recipe-details.js
// methods
viewmodel.hasCitation = function () {
  return this.citation() !== '';
};

viewmodel.update = function (recipe) {
  this.title(recipe.title);
  this.servings(recipe.servings);
  this.hours(recipe.cookingTime.hours);
  this.minutes(recipe.cookingTime.minutes);
  this.ingredients(recipe.ingredients);
  this.instructions(recipe.instructions);
  this.citation(recipe.citation);
};
```

Binding View Models to the DOM

Both view model factories are attached to the global window object and can be used to create individual view model instances that will be bound to the page. The app.js file, shown in Listing 7-10, is the main script that ties both recipe view models together.

Listing 7-10. Binding View Models to the DOM

```
// example-001/public/scripts/app.js
(function app ($, ko, RecipeList, RecipeDetails) {
  // #1
  var getRecipes = $.get('/recipes');

  // #2
  $(function () {
    // #3
    getRecipes.then(function (recipes) {
      // #4
      var list = RecipeList.create(recipes);
      // #5
      var details = RecipeDetails.create(list.selectedRecipe());
      // #6
      list.selectedRecipe.subscribe(function (recipe) {
        details.update(recipe);
      });
      // #7
      ko.applyBindings(list, document.querySelector('#recipe-list'));
      ko.applyBindings(details, document.querySelector('#recipe-details'));

    }).fail(function () {
      alert('No recipes for you!');
    });
  });

}(window.jQuery, window.ko, window.RecipeList, window.RecipeDetails));
```

The app module is responsible for loading an initial set of recipe data from the server, waiting for the DOM to enter a ready state, and then instantiating view model instances and binding each to the appropriate elements. The following list describes each step comment (e.g., // #1) shown in Listing 7-10.

1. A jQuery promise is created that will resolve at some point in the future, when the data obtained from the GET /recipes request becomes available.

2. The function passed to $() will be triggered when the DOM has been completely initialized to ensure that all Knockout template elements will be present before any binding attempts.

3. When the jQuery promise resolves, it passes the list of recipes to its resolution handler. If the promise fails, an alert is shown to the user indicating that a problem occurred.

4. Once the recipe data has been loaded, the list view model is created. The recipe array is passed as an argument to RecipeList.create(). The return value is the actual recipe list view model object.

5. The recipe details view model is created in a similar fashion. Its factory function accepts a single recipe, and so the selectedRecipe property on the recipe list is queried for a value. (The recipe list view model chooses the very first recipe in its data array for this value, by default.)

6. After the recipe details view model has been created, it subscribes to change notifications on the recipe list's `selectedRecipe` observable. This is the manual equivalent of a DOM subscription created by Knockout when an observable is bound to an HTML element. The function provided to the `subscribe()` method will be invoked whenever `selectedRecipe` changes, receiving the new value as an argument. When the callback fires the recipe details view model uses any newly selected recipe to update itself, thereby changing the values of its own observable properties.

7. Finally, view models are bound to the DOM when the global `ko.applyBindings()` function is invoked. In Listing 7-10 this function receives two arguments: the view model to be bound, and the DOM element to which the view model will be bound. Any binding attribute Knockout encounters on this element or its descendants will be applied to the specified view model. If no DOM element is specified, Knockout assumes that the view model applies to the entire page. For simplistic pages this might be appropriate, but for more complex scenarios, using multiple view models that encapsulate their own data and behavior is the better option.

View Models and Forms

Knockout view model properties may be bound to form controls. Many controls, such as the `<input>` elements, share standard bindings like `value`; but others like `<select>` have element-specific bindings. For example, the `options` binding controls the creation of `<option>` elements within a `<select>` tag. In general, form field bindings behave much like bindings seen in example code up to this point, but complex forms can be tricky beasts and sometimes require more creative binding strategies.

The examples in this section build on the recipe details template and view model. Specifically, an "edit" mode is introduced whereby a user viewing a particular recipe can choose to alter its details through form fields. The same view model is used, but new form field elements have been added to the recipe details template, adding additional complexity to both.

Switching to "Edit" Mode

Three buttons have been added to the top and bottom of the recipe details markup. Figures 7-2 and 7-3 show how the buttons appear when rendered.

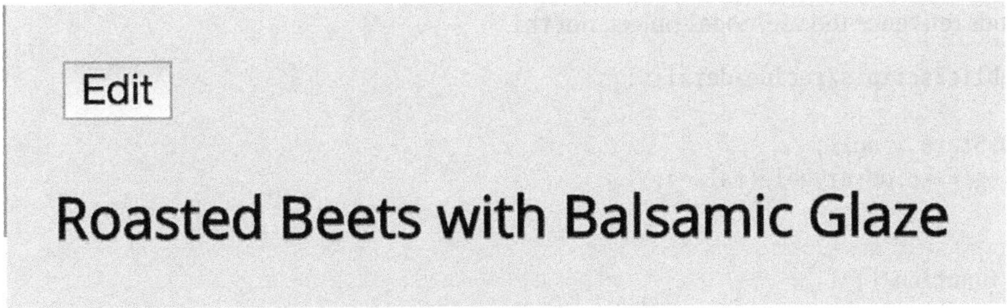

Roasted Beets with Balsamic Glaze

Figure 7-2. *In "view" mode, the Edit button is visible*

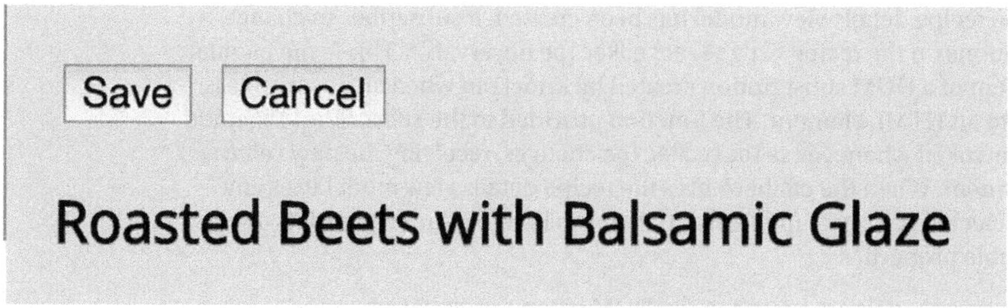

Figure 7-3. *In "edit" mode, the Save and Cancel buttons are visible*

The Edit button switches the page from viewing mode to edit mode (and shows the appropriate form fields for each part of the recipe being viewed). While in edit mode the Edit button itself is hidden, but two other buttons, Save and Cancel, become visible. If the user clicks the Save button any changes made to the recipe will be persisted; in contrast, if the user clicks the Cancel button, the edit session will be aborted and the recipe details will revert to their original states.

The Knockout bindings for each button, shown in Listing 7-11, vary slightly from the bindings discussed so far.

Listing 7-11. Editing Button Markup

```
<!-- example-002/public/index.html -->
<div>
  <!-- in read-only view -->
  <button data-bind="click: edit, visible: !isEditing()">Edit</button>
  <!-- in edit view -->
  <button data-bind="click: save, visible: isEditing">Save</button>
  <button data-bind="click: cancelEdit, visible: isEditing">Cancel</button>
</div>
```

First, each button has a click event handler that calls a method on the view model: edit(), save(), and cancelEdit(). But unlike previous examples, these methods do not use the bind() function to ensure the value of this within the view model. Instead, all occurrences of the keyword this *within the view* model have been replaced with a reference to the object literal viewmodel, shown in Listing 7-12. The new properties and methods for these buttons have also been added to the recipe details view model. For brevity, Listing 7-12 omits the portions of recipe-list.js that have not changed.

Listing 7-12. Methods reference the viewmodel object, not this

```
// example-002/public/scripts/recipe-details.js
// properties
viewmodel.previousState = null;
viewmodel.isEditing = ko.observable(false);

// methods
viewmodel.edit = function () {
  viewmodel.previousState = ko.mapping.toJS(viewmodel);
  viewmodel.isEditing(true);
};
```

```
viewmodel.save = function () {
  // TODO save recipe
  viewmodel.isEditing(false);
};

viewmodel.cancelEdit = function () {
  viewmodel.isEditing(false);
  ko.mapping.fromJS(viewmodel.previousState, {}, viewmodel);
};
```

Because the view model itself is assigned to a variable within the RecipeDetails.create() closure, its methods may reference it by name. By avoiding this altogether, event bindings are simplified and potential bugs are avoided.

Second, each button has a visible binding attached to the view model's isEditing observable, but only the Edit button invokes the method directly as a function. It also possesses the only binding that uses a negation (!) operator, which turns the binding value into an *expression*. Any observable evaluated within an expression must be invoked as a function to retrieve its value. If an observable is itself used as the binding value, as is the case with visible bindings for the Save and Cancel buttons, it will be invoked automatically when Knockout evaluates the binding.

All three methods, edit(), save(), and cancelEdit(), manipulate the value of the isEditing observable, which determines which button or buttons are displayed on the form (and, as shall be demonstrated shortly, which form fields are displayed as well). Editing begins when the edit() method is called and ends when the user either saves the recipe or cancels the editing session.

To ensure that changes to the recipe are discarded when a user cancels the edit session, the view model serializes its state when the editing session begins in anticipation of possible reversion. If the editing session is canceled, the previous state is deserialized and the value of each observable property is effectively reset.

The Knockout mapping plugin is used to serialize and deserialize the view model's state in the edit() and cancelEdit() methods:

```
// serializing the view model
viewmodel.previousState = ko.mapping.toJS(viewmodel);
// deserializing the view model
ko.mapping.fromJS(viewmodel.previousState, {}, viewmodel);
```

■ **Tip**   Knockout's mapping plugin is distributed separately from the core Knockout library. The current version may be downloaded from http://knockoutjs.com/documentation/plugins-mapping.html. To install the plugin, simply add a <script> tag reference to the plugin script *after* the core Knockout <script> tag on an HTML page. It will automatically create the ko.mapping namespace property on the global ko object.

The mapping plugin serializes/deserializes objects that possess observable properties, reading their values during serialization and setting their values during deserialization. When the edit() method calls ko.mapping.toJS(viewmodel), it receives a plain JavaScript object literal whose property names are identical to those of the view model, but contain plain JavaScript data instead of observable functions. To push these values back into the view model's own observables when the edit session is cancelled, the cancelEdit() method invokes ko.mapping.fromJS() with three arguments:

- The plain JavaScript object literal that contains the data to be written to the view model's observable properties

- An object literal that maps properties on the plain JavaScript state object to observable properties on the view model (if this object is empty, it is assumed that the properties for both share the same names)

- The view model that will receive the object literal's data

■ **Note**   The Knockout mapper plugin can serialize/deserialize view models as plain JavaScript object literals with its toJS() and fromJS() functions, or as JSON strings with its toJSON() and fromJSON() functions. These functions can be particularly useful for CRUD (create + read + update + delete) view models that bind JSON data to simple forms.

Although the Save button is present on the form, its method has only been stubbed in the view model. Its functionality will be added in a later example.

Changing the Recipe Title

The recipe title is visible regardless of whether the recipe details view is in edit mode or read-only mode. When the user clicks the Edit button, a label and input field become visible beneath the <h1> tag so the user may update the recipe title if necessary. A visible binding on the containing <div> element controls shows and hides this field by subscribing to the isEditing observable on the view model. The value of the input field is bound to the view model's title observable via the value binding. By default, the value binding will only refresh data in an observable when the field to which the observable is bound looses focus. When the title input in Listing 7-13 looses focus, the <h1> tag's content will be instantly updated with the new title value because both are bound to the title observable. The rendered field is shown in Figure 7-4.

Listing 7-13. Recipe Title Markup

```
<!-- example-002/public/index.html -->
<h1 data-bind="text: title"></h1>
<!-- in edit view -->
<div data-bind="visible: isEditing" class="edit-field">
  <label for="recipe-title">Title:</label>
  <input data-bind="value: title" name="title" id="recipe-title" type="text" />
</div>
```

Roasted Beets with Balsamic Glaze

Title:

Roasted Beets with Balsamic Glaze

Figure 7-4. *Editing the recipe title*

Updating Recipe Servings and Cooking Time

In Listing 7-14 the recipe's read-only serving size `<p>` element is hidden when the form enters edit mode. In its place a `<select>` element is displayed with a number of serving size options from which the user may select. Once again, the `isEditing` observable is used to determine which elements are displayed.

Listing 7-14. Serving Size Markup

```
<!-- example-002/public/index.html -->
<h2>Details</h2>
<!-- in read-only view -->
<p data-bind="visible: !isEditing()">
  Servings: <span data-bind="text: servings"></span>
</p>
<!-- in edit view -->
<div data-bind="visible: isEditing" class="edit-field">
  <label for="recipe-servings">Servings:</label>
  <select data-bind="options: servingSizes,
          optionsText: 'text',
          optionsValue: 'numeral',
          value: servings,
          optionsCaption: 'Choose...'"
          name="recipeServings"
          id="recipe-servings">
  </select>
</div>
```

New, element-specific Knockout bindings are declared for the `<select>` tag in Listing 7-14 to control the manner in which it uses view model data. The `options` binding tells Knockout which property on the view model holds the data set that will be used to create `<option>` elements within the tag. The binding value is the name of the property (in this case `servingSizes`), a plain array of read-only reference data.

For primitive values, like strings or numbers, the `options` binding assumes that each primitive should be both the text and value of its `<option>` element. For complex objects, the `optionsText` and `optionsValue` bindings tell Knockout which properties on each object in the array will be used to generate the text and value of each `<option>` element instead. The serving size objects are defined in Listing 7-15. Notice that the text value is the name of each number, while the numeral value is a corresponding digit. When a serving size is selected by the user the numeral value will be assigned to `viewmodel.servings()`.

Listing 7-15. Recipe Serving Size Data in the View Model

```
// example-002/public/scripts/recipe-details.js
// properties
viewmodel.servings = ko.observable(recipe.servings);
viewmodel.servingSizes = [
  {text: 'one', numeral: 1},
  {text: 'two', numeral: 2},
  {text: 'three', numeral: 3},
  {text: 'four', numeral: 4},
  {text: 'five', numeral: 5},
  {text: 'six', numeral: 6},
  {text: 'seven', numeral: 7},
  {text: 'eight', numeral: 8},
  {text: 'nine', numeral: 9},
  {text: 'ten', numeral: 10}
];
```

The <select> tag's value binding ties the selected value of the drop-down to an observable on the view model. When the <select> tag is rendered, this value will be automatically selected for the user in the DOM; when the user chooses a new value the bound observable will be updated.

Finally, the optionsCaption binding creates a special <option> element in the DOM that appears at the top of the drop-down options list, but will never be set as the selected value on the view model. It is a mere cosmetic enhancement that gives some instruction to the user about how the drop-down is to be used.

Figures 7-5 and 7-6 show a collapsed and expanded serving size drop-down.

Figure 7-5. *Servings drop-down with a pre-selected value*

Figure 7-6. *Choosing a new value from the Servings drop-down*

The cooking time fields, also shown in Figure 7-5, contain no special bindings. Both input fields (hours and minutes) shown in Listing 7-16 are number fields that use simple value bindings to update observables on the view model. They are shown and hidden by the same visibility mechanism discussed earlier.

Listing 7-16. Cooking Time Markup

```
<!-- example-002/public/index.html -->
<!-- in read-only view -->
<p data-bind="visible: !isEditing()">
  Approximate Cook Time: <span data-bind="text: cookingTime"></span>
</p>
<!-- in edit view -->
<div data-bind="visible: isEditing" class="edit-field">
  <label for="recipe-hours">Approximate Cook Time:</label>
  <input data-bind="value: hours"
         name="hours"
         id="recipe-hours"
         type="number" />
  <input data-bind="value: minutes"
         name="minutes"
         id="recipe-minutes"
         type="number" />
</div>
```

Recall that when cooking time is displayed to the user in read-only mode, the cookingTime computed observable in Listing 7-17 is used, not the hours and minutes observables. When the values of these observables change based on the input bindings in Listing 7-16, the computed observable regenerates the formatted string for the view. Also notice that the computed observable no longer has a context argument, because inside the observable the view model variable is referenced by name instead of being resolved with the this keyword.

Listing 7-17. View Model Hours, Minutes, and Computed Cooking Time

```
// example-002/public/scripts/recipe-details.js
// properties
viewmodel.hours = ko.observable(recipe.cookingTime.hours);
viewmodel.minutes = ko.observable(recipe.cookingTime.minutes);
viewmodel.cookingTime = ko.computed(function () {
  return '$1 hours, $2 minutes'
    .replace('$1', viewmodel.hours())
    .replace('$2', viewmodel.minutes());
});
```

Adding and Removing Ingredients

In read-only mode, recipe ingredients are rendered as an unordered list. To maintain form, when the recipe details view enters edit mode, an input is generated for each item in the list, shown in Figure 7-7. A minus button next to each ingredient allows the user to remove any or all ingredients, while an empty input field and a plus button below the input list may be used to add a new ingredient. Text changes made within any ingredient input will update the values in the view model's ingredients array.

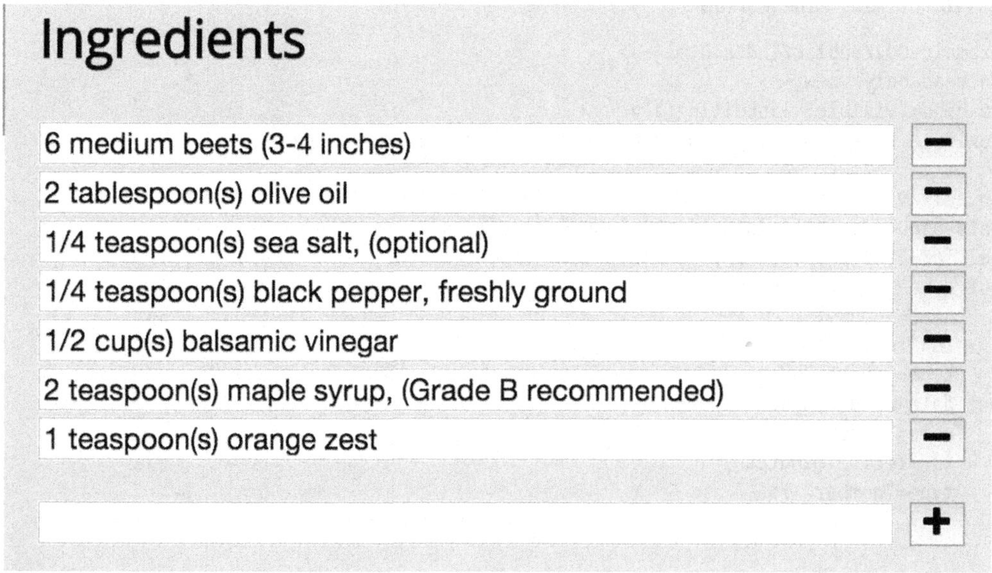

Figure 7-7. *Creating and editing recipe ingredients*

Adding a new ingredient is more straight-forward than editing existing ingredients in place. The markup in Listing 7-18 shows *part* of the changes to the Ingredients section of the form. The read-only unordered list is present, and below it is a `<div>` element that contains all the new form fields. A comment block indicates where the `<input>` elements for *existing* ingredients will go (discussed in a moment), but the new Ingredients fields are shown below it.

Listing 7-18. New Ingredients Markup

```
<!-- example-002/public/index.html -->
<h2>Ingredients</h2>
<!-- in read-only view -->
<ul data-bind="foreach: ingredients, visible: !isEditing()">
  <li data-bind="text: $data"></li>
</ul>
<!-- in edit view -->
<div data-bind="visible: isEditing" class="edit-field">

  <!-- ingredient list inputs here... -->

  <input data-bind="value: newIngredient"
         type="text"
         name="new-ingredient"
         id="recipe-new-ingredient"/>
  <button data-bind="click: commitNewIngredient"
          class="fa fa-plus"></button>
</div>
```

To add a new ingredient a user enters text into the new ingredient `<input>` field and then clicks the plus button next to it. The `<input>` is bound to the `newIngredient` observable on the view model, and the Plus button's `click` event invokes the `commitNewIngredient()` method, both shown in Listing 7-19.

Listing 7-19. Creating a New Ingredient in the View Model

```
// example-002/public/scripts/recipe-details.js
// properties
viewmodel.ingredients = ko.observableArray(recipe.ingredients);
viewmodel.newIngredient = ko.observable('');

// methods
viewmodel.commitNewIngredient = function () {
  var ingredient = viewmodel.newIngredient();
  if (ingredient === '') return;
  viewmodel.ingredients.push(ingredient);
  viewmodel.newIngredient('');
};
```

The `commitNewIngredient()` method evaluates the content of the `newIngredient` observable to determine if it is empty or not. If it is, the user has entered no text into the `<input>`, and so the method returns prematurely. If not, the value of `newIngredient` is pushed into the `ingredients` observable array and the `newIngredient` observable is cleared.

■ **Tip**   Observable arrays share a nearly identical API with normal JavaScript arrays. Most array operations, such as `push()`, `pop()`, `slice()`, `splice()`, and so on, are available on observable arrays and will trigger update notifications to the observable array's subscribers when called.

When the new ingredient is appended to `ingredients`, Knockout updates the DOM to reflect the change. The read-only list, hidden while in edit mode, silently acquires a new list item element, and the editable list of existing `<input>` elements, shown in Listing 7-20, gains a new entry as well.

Listing 7-20. Ingredients Markup

```
<!-- example-002/public/index.html -->
<h2>Ingredients</h2>
<!-- in read-only view -->
<ul data-bind="foreach: ingredients, visible: !isEditing()">
  <li data-bind="text: $data"></li>
</ul>
<!-- in edit view -->
<div data-bind="visible: isEditing" class="edit-field">
  <ul data-bind="foreach: ingredients" class="listless">
    <li>
      <input data-bind="value: $data,
             valueUpdate: 'input',
             attr: {name: 'ingredient-' + $index()},
             event: {input: $parent.changeIngredient.bind($parent, $index())}"
             type="text" />
      <button data-bind="click: $parent.removeIngredient.bind($parent, $index())"
              class="fa fa-minus"></button>
    </li>
  </ul>

  <!-- new ingredient input here... -->
</div>
```

For each ingredient in the `ingredients` observable array, an input is rendered above the new ingredient field. These inputs are nested within an unordered list, and their values are all bound to specific ingredients in the array, denoted by the $data variable within the `foreach` loop. The `attr` binding is used to give a name to each `<input>` element by concatenating the string "ingredient-" with the current index of the loop, exposed by the special $index observable. Like any observable used in a binding *expression*, $index must be invoked to retrieve its value.

It cannot be emphasized enough that the bindings exposed by observable arrays apply only to the arrays themselves and *not* to the elements they contain. When each ingredient is bound to a DOM `<input>` element, it is wrapped in the $data observable, but there is no communication between this observable and the containing observable array. If the value within $data changes because of input, the array will be oblivious and still contain its own copy of the unchanged data. This is a source of consternation, but there are several coping strategies that make it bearable.

First, the observable `ingredients` array could be filled with objects that each expose the ingredient text as an observable property (something like { `ingredient: ko.observable('20 mushrooms')` }). The `value` binding of each `<input>` would then use each object's $data.ingredient property to establish a two-way binding. The observable array still remains ignorant of changes to its members, but because each element is an object that tracks its own data through an observable, this becomes a moot point.

The second approach, taken in Listing 7-20, is to listen for change events on each <input> element through the valueUpdate and event bindings, and then tell the *view model* to replace specific ingredient values in the ingredients observable array as they change. Neither way is "right"—both merely have their own advantages and disadvantages.

The valueUpdate binding first instructs Knockout to change the value of $data each time the DOM input event fires on each <input> element. (Remember: Knockout normally updates $data once an element looses focus, not when it receives input.) Second, a Knockout event binding is added that invokes the changeIngredient() method on the view model every time the DOM input event fires as well. By default Knockout submits the current value of $data to changeIngredient(), but since the new value will replace the old, the view model must know which index in the ingredients array is being targeted. Using bind(), the value of $index is bound to the method as the first argument ensuring that the value of $data will be the second.

The code in Listing 7-21 shows that the changeIngredient() method accesses the actual *underlying* array within the ingredients observable array in order to replace a value at a given index.

Listing 7-21. Changing a Recipe Ingredient in the View Model

```
// example-002/public/scripts/recipe-details.js
// properties
viewmodel.ingredients = ko.observableArray(recipe.ingredients);

// methods
viewmodel.changeIngredient = function (index, newValue) {
  viewmodel.ingredients()[index] = newValue;
};
```

Unfortunately, when an observable array's underlying array structure is changed, the observable array will not automatically notify any subscribers, which means that other DOM elements, such as the read-only unordered list that displays the ingredients, will remain unchanged. To mitigate this, the view model listens to its own isEditing observable, shown in Listing 7-22. When the value passed to the observable is false (meaning that the user has either saved changes to the recipe or canceled the editing session), the view model forcibly notifies any subscribers to the ingredients observable array by calling its valueHasMutated() method. This ensures that the read-only unordered list displayed in "view" mode will accurately reflect any changed values in the ingredients array.

Listing 7-22. Forcing Observable Arrays to Notify Their Subscribers of Underlying Changes

```
// example-002/public/scripts/recipe-details.js
// properties
viewmodel.isEditing = ko.observable(false);
viewmodel.isEditing.subscribe(function (isEditing) {
  if (isEditing) return;
  // force refresh
  //
  viewmodel.ingredients.valueHasMutated();
});
```

Next to each recipe <input> is a minus button used to remove a given ingredient from the ingredients observable array. Its click event is bound to the removeIngredient() method which, like changeIngredient(), must also receive the value of $index so that the view model knows which element to remove. Observable arrays expose a splice() method, shown in Listing 7-23, that may be used to remove an element at a specific index. Using this method instead of manipulating the underlying array directly ensures that subscribers to the ingredients observable array are notified of the change immediately.

141

Listing 7-23. Removing a Recipe Ingredient

```
// example-002/public/scripts/recipe-details.js
// properties
viewmodel.ingredients = ko.observableArray(recipe.ingredients);

// methods
viewmodel.removeIngredient = function (index) {
  viewmodel.ingredients.splice(index, 1);
};
```

Instructions

Recipe instructions are very similar to recipe ingredients but differ in two notable ways. First, instructions are rendered in an *ordered list* because instructions must be followed step-by-step. And second, instructions may be promoted or demoted within the list. Figure 7-8 shows a screenshot of the ordered Instructions fields and the buttons associated with each.

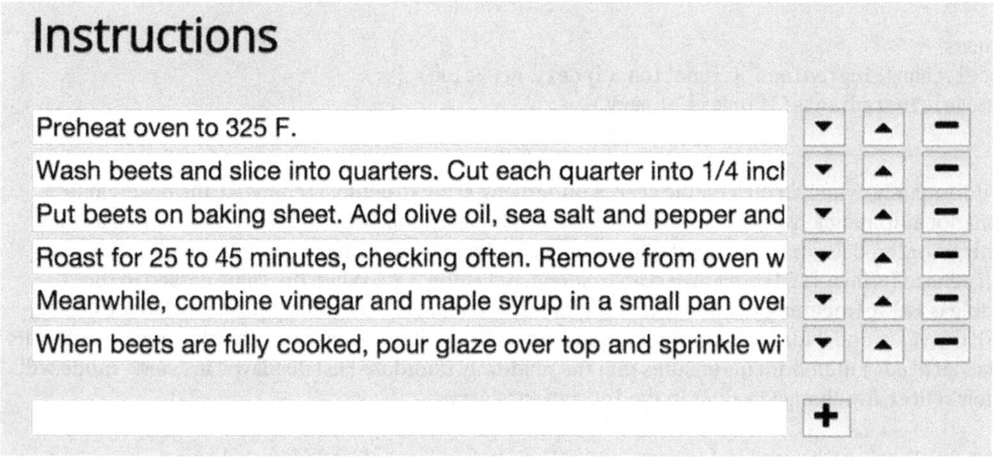

Figure 7-8. *Creating and editing recipe instructions*

The recipe instruction use cases that overlap with ingredient use cases (creating an instruction, removing an instruction, updating an existing instruction) will not be discussed, as the markup, Knockout bindings, and view model structure of both are essentially the same, but operate on the instructions observable array instead. Instruction demotion and promotion within the array are new features, however, represented by the addition of up and down <button> tags in Listing 7-24.

Listing 7-24. Instructions Markup

```
<!-- example-002/public/index.html -->
<h2>Instructions</h2>
<!-- in read-only view -->
<ol data-bind="foreach: instructions, visible: !isEditing()">
  <li data-bind="text: $data"></li>
</ol>
```

```
<!-- in edit view -->
<div data-bind="visible: isEditing" class="edit-field">
  <!-- existing instructions -->
  <ul data-bind="foreach: instructions" class="listless">
    <li>
      <input data-bind="value: $data,
             valueUpdate: 'input',
             attr: {name: 'instruction-' + $index()},
             event: {input: $parent.changeInstruction.bind($parent, $index())}"
             type="text" />
      <button data-bind="click: $parent.demoteInstruction.bind($parent, $index())"
              class="fa fa-caret-down"></button>
      <button data-bind="click: $parent.promoteInstruction.bind($parent, $index())"
              class="fa fa-caret-up"></button>
      <button data-bind="click: $parent.removeInstruction.bind($parent, $index())"
              class="fa fa-minus"></button>
    </li>
  </ul>

  <!-- new instruction input here... -->
</div>
```

Like the minus button, both up and down buttons use Knockout `click` bindings to invoke methods on the view model, passing the associated item index as an argument to each.

Listing 7-25 shows how both methods manipulate the `instructions` observable array. The `promoteInstruction()` method evaluates the index and, if it is zero, exits early (the first instruction cannot be promoted). It then plucks the instruction at the given index from the observable array using its `splice()` method, calculates the new index for the instruction by subtracting one (e.g., going from index 2 to 1 would be a promotion in the list), and then splices the instruction back into the observable array at its new index. The `demoteInstruction()` method does the opposite. It prevents the instruction at the "end" of the list from being demoted further; otherwise it moves instructions down the list by re-splicing the observable array. In both cases any DOM elements bound to the `instructions` property are notified of changes automatically.

Listing 7-25. Promoting and Demoting Recipe Instructions in the View Model

```
// example-002/public/scripts/recipe-details.js
// properties
viewmodel.instructions = ko.observableArray(recipe.instructions);

viewmodel.promoteInstruction = function (index) {
  if (index === 0) return;
  var instruction = viewmodel.instructions.splice(index, 1);
  var newIndex = index - 1;
  viewmodel.instructions.splice(newIndex, 0, instruction);
};

viewmodel.demoteInstruction = function (index) {
  var lastIndex = (viewmodel.instructions.length - 1);
  if (index === lastIndex) return;
  var instruction = viewmodel.instructions.splice(index, 1);
  var newIndex = index + 1;
  viewmodel.instructions.splice(newIndex, 0, instruction);
};
```

143

Citation

The Citation field addition is a fairly vanilla affair considering the complexities involved with instructions and ingredients. A single text <input> uses the value binding to update the view model's citation observable. The rendered field is shown in Figure 7-9.

> **Citation:**
>
> http://www.paleoplan.com/2011/06-09/roasted-beets-with-balsa

Figure 7-9. *Updating a Recipe's Citation*

The visible binding on the citation hyperlink has been changed to a compound expression. Now, the hyperlink in Listing 7-26 will only be displayed if the recipe details view is in read-only mode (!isEditing()) *and* the recipe actually has a citation.

Listing 7-26. Citation Field Markup

```
<!-- example-002/public/index.html -->
<a data-bind="visible: hasCitation() && !isEditing(),
  attr: {href: citation, title: title}"
  target="_blank">Source</a>
<div data-bind="visible: isEditing" class="edit-field">
  <label>Citation:</label>
  <input name="citation" type="text" data-bind="value: citation" />
</div>
```

Custom Components

With inspiration from the popular webcomponents.js polyfill (http://webcomponents.org), Knockout provides a custom component system that produces reusable HTML elements with custom tag names, markup, and behavior.

In the *Omnom Recipes* application, the recipe details view contains two editable lists, Ingredients and Instructions, that share many similar characteristics, both in terms of markup and view model properties and methods. A custom component can, with a little effort, replace both of these lists in the application. The goal is to reduce the complex markup and binding expressions in the DOM to new, custom elements, envisioned in Listing 7-27.

Listing 7-27. Input List Element

```
<!-- example-003/public/index.html -->
<!-- editable ingredients list -->
<input-list params="items: ingredients,
          isOrdered: false"></input-list>

<!-- ... -->

<!-- editable instructions list -->
<input-list params="items: instructions,
          isOrdered: true"></input-list>
```

Knockout components are the intersection of several things:

- A factory function that creates a view model for each instance of the custom component on a page

- An HTML template with its own Knockout bindings that will be injected wherever the component is used

- A custom tag registration that tells Knockout where to find the template and how to instantiate its view model when it encounters component tags on a page

The Input List View Model

The recipe details view model already possesses the properties and methods used to manipulate its ingredients and instructions arrays, but it is necessary to abstract this code and move it into its own module, input-list.js, so that Knockout can use it exclusively for the new input list component.

Listing 7-28 shows an abbreviated version of the input list module. It is structured in the same manner as the other view model factory modules, exposing a create() method on the global InputList object. This factory method accepts a params parameter that will be used to pass the input list component a reference to an observable array (params.items), and a host of optional settings that will determine how the input list will behave when bound to the rendered template: params.isOrdered, params.enableAdd, params.enableUpdate, and params.enableRemove.

The defaultTo() function exists as a simple utility function that returns default values for missing properties on the params object.

Listing 7-28. Input List View Model

```
// example-003/public/scripts/input-list.js
'use strict';
window.InputList = (function (ko) {

  function defaultTo(object, property, defaultValue) {/*...*/}

  return {
    create: function (params) {
      var viewmodel = {};

      // properties
      viewmodel.items = params.items; // the collection
      viewmodel.newItem = ko.observable('');

      viewmodel.isOrdered = defaultTo(params, 'isOrdered', false);
      viewmodel.enableAdd = defaultTo(params, 'enableAdd', true);
      viewmodel.enableUpdate = defaultTo(params, 'enableUpdate', true);
      viewmodel.enableRemove = defaultTo(params, 'enableRemove', true);
```

```
    // methods
    viewmodel.commitNewItem = function () {/*...*/};
    viewmodel.changeItem = function (index, newValue) {/*...*/};
    viewmodel.removeItem = function (index) {/*...*/};
    viewmodel.promoteItem = function (index) {/*...*/};
    viewmodel.demoteItem = function (index) {/*...*/};

    return viewmodel;
  }
};

}(window.ko));
```

The params.items and params.isOrdered properties correspond to the binding attributes in Listing 7-27. When a component is used on a page, the values of its binding attributes are passed, by reference, to the component's view model via the params object. In this scenario, input list components will be given access to the ingredients and instructions observable arrays on the recipe details view model.

Input list methods have been redacted in Listing 7-28 because they are nearly identical to their counterparts in Listing 7-25. Instead of referencing ingredients or instructions, however, these methods reference the abstracted items observable array. The component populates this array with data it receives from params.items. The newItem observable holds the value of the new item input, in exactly the same manner as the newIngredient and newInstruction observables behaved in the recipe-details.js module. It is not shared with the recipe details view model, however, as it only has relevance within the input list.

Since the input list component will now handle the manipulation of the Ingredients and Instructions lists on the page, the properties and methods in the recipe details view model that previously performed these manipulations have been removed.

The Input List Template

A reusable component needs an abstracted, reusable template, so the markup associated with editing instructions and ingredients has also been collected into a single HTML template. Each time an instance of the input list component is created on the page, Knockout will inject the template into the DOM, then bind a new instance of the input list view model to it.

Since the input list component can accommodate both ordered and unordered lists, the template must use Knockout bindings to intelligently decide which kind of list to display. Only ordered lists will have promotion and demotion buttons, while items can be added and removed from both kinds of lists. Since the input list view model exposes boolean properties it receives from its params object, the template can alter its behavior based on the values of those properties. For example, if the view model property isOrdered is true, the template will show an ordered list; otherwise it will show an unordered list. Likewise the fields and buttons associated with adding new items or removing existing items are toggled by the enableAdd and enableRemove properties, respectively.

Template markup is typically added to the DOM in nonparsed elements like <template> or the <script type="text/html"> element. In Listing 7-29, the full component markup and all bindings are shown within a <template> tag. The element's id will be used by Knockout to find the template content within the DOM when the component is registered with the framework.

Listing 7-29. Input List Component Template

```html
<!-- example-003/public/index.html -->
<template id="item-list-template">
  <!-- ko if: isOrdered -->
  <!-- #1 THE ORDERED LIST -->
  <ol data-bind="foreach: items" class="listless">
    <li>
      <input data-bind="value: $data,
                  valueUpdate: 'input',
                  attr: {name: 'item-' + $index()},
                  event: {input: $parent.changeItem.bind($parent, $index())}"
             type="text" />
      <button data-bind="click: $parent.demoteItem.bind($parent, $index())"
              class="fa fa-caret-down"></button>
      <button data-bind="click: $parent.promoteItem.bind($parent, $index())"
              class="fa fa-caret-up"></button>
      <button data-bind="click: $parent.removeItem.bind($parent, $index()),
              visible: $parent.enableRemove"
              class="fa fa-minus"></button>
    </li>
  </ol>
  <!-- /ko -->

  <!-- ko ifnot: isOrdered -->
  <!-- #2 THE UN-ORDERED LIST -->
  <ul data-bind="foreach: items" class="listless">
    <li>
      <input data-bind="value: $data,
                  valueUpdate: 'input',
                  attr: {name: 'item-' + $index()},
                  event: {input: $parent.changeItem.bind($parent, $index())}"
             type="text" />
      <button data-bind="click: $parent.removeItem.bind($parent, $index()),
              visible: $parent.enableRemove"
              class="fa fa-minus"></button>
    </li>
  </ul>
  <!-- /ko -->

  <!-- ko if: enableAdd -->
  <!-- #3 THE NEW ITEM FIELD -->
  <input data-bind="value: newItem"
         type="text"
         name="new-item" />
  <button data-bind="click: commitNewItem"
          class="fa fa-plus"></button>
  <!-- /ko -->
</template>
```

There is a lot of markup to digest in the input list template, but it is really just the combination of both the unordered Ingredients list and the ordered Instructions list, with a shared new item field.

Special binding comments—the ko if and ko ifnot comment blocks—wrap portions of the template to determine if the elements within the comment blocks should be added to the page. These comment blocks evaluate properties on the view model and alter the template processing control flow accordingly. This differs from the visible elements bindings, which merely hide elements that already exist in the DOM.

■ **Tip**   The syntax used within ko comment block bindings is known as *containerless control flow syntax*.

All fields and buttons in the input list template are bound to properties and methods on the input list view model. If a demote button is clicked, for example, the input list view model will manipulate its internal items collection, which is really a reference to the instructions observable array in the recipe details view model, shared via the items binding. The template determines which type of list to display based on the isOrdered property, while the add and remove controls are toggled based on the enableAdd and enableRemove properties. Because these properties are read from the params object in the view model, any of them may be added to the <input-list> component tag as a binding attribute. In this way the component abstracts and encapsulates all operations made against any collection that can be represented as a list of inputs.

Registering the Input List Tag

Once a component view model and template have been defined, the component itself must be registered with Knockout. This tells Knockout how to resolve component instances when it encounters the component's custom tag in the DOM, and also what template and view model to use when rendering the component's contents.

The app.js script has been updated in Listing 7-30 to register the input list component immediately after the DOM becomes ready, but before any Knockout bindings are applied to the page (with ko. applyBindings()). This ensures that Knockout has time to render the component's markup in the DOM so before any view model is bound to it.

Listing 7-30. Registering the Input List Component

```
// example-003/public/scripts/app.js
(function app ($, ko, InputList /*...*/) {
  // ...

  $(function () {
    // register the custom component tag before
    // Knockout bindings are applied to the page
    ko.components.register('input-list', {
      template: {
        element: 'item-list-template'
      },
      viewModel: InputList.create
    });

    // ...
  });

}(window.jQuery, window.ko, window.InputList /*...*/));
```

In Listing 7-30, the `ko.components.register()` function receives two arguments: the name of the new component's custom tag, `input-list`, and an options hash that provides Knockout with the information it needs to construct the component.

Knockout uses the custom tag name to identify the `<input-list>` element in the DOM and replace it with the template content specified in the options hash.

Since markup for the input list element has been defined in a `<template>` element, the Knockout component system only needs to know what element ID it should use to find that element in the DOM. The `template` object in the options hash contains this ID in its `element` property. For smaller components, the entire HTML template could be assigned, as a string, to the `template` property directly.

To construct a view model for the component, a factory function is assigned to the `viewModel` property of the options hash. This property can also reference a regular constructor function, but using factory functions sidesteps potential problems that arise when event bindings reassign the `this` keyword within view models. Regardless of approach, the view model function will receive a `params` object populated with values from the template's binding declarations.

■ **Tip** Knockout can load component templates and view model functions via RequireJS automatically. Consult the Knockout component documentation for more details. The RequireJS module loader is covered in Chapter 5.

Now that the input list component is registered with Knockout, the complicated markup for the editable Ingredients and Instructions lists can be replaced with simple instances of `<input-list>`. Listing 7-31 shows the resulting lighter, cleaner page markup.

Listing 7-31. Editing Instructions and Ingredients with the Input List Component

```
<!-- example-003/public/index.html -->

<h2>Ingredients</h2>
<!-- in read-only view -->
<ul data-bind="foreach: ingredients, visible: !isEditing()">
  <li data-bind="text: $data"></li>
</ul>
<!-- in edit view -->
<div data-bind="visible: isEditing" class="edit-field">
  <input-list params="items: ingredients,
            isOrdered: false"></input-list>
</div>

<h2>Instructions</h2>
<!-- in read-only view -->
<ol data-bind="foreach: instructions, visible: !isEditing()">
  <li data-bind="text: $data"></li>
</ol>
<!-- in edit view -->
<div data-bind="visible: isEditing" class="edit-field">
  <input-list params="items: instructions,
            isOrdered: true"></input-list>
</div>
```

Not only are the complexities of the input list obscured behind the new <input-list> tag, but aspects of the list, such as the ability to add and remove items, are controlled through bound attributes. This promotes both flexibility and maintainability as common behaviors are bundled into a single element.

Subscribables: Cheap Messaging

At this point the recipe details view model manipulates the recipe data but does nothing to persist changes. It also fails to communicate recipe changes to the recipe list, so that even if a user modifies a recipe's title, the recipe list continues to display the recipe's original title. From a use case perspective, the recipe list should only be updated if the recipe details are sent to the server and successfully persisted. A more sophisticated mechanism is needed to facilitate this workflow.

Knockout observables implement the behavior of a Knockout *subscribable*, a more abstract object that does not hold a value but acts as a kind of eventing mechanism to which other objects may subscribe. Observables take advantage of the subscribable interface by publishing their own changes through subscribables, to which DOM bindings (and perhaps even other view models) listen.

Subscribables may be directly, attached to view models as properties, or passed around by reference to any object interested in their events. In Listing 7-32 a subscribable is constructed in the app.js file and passed as an argument to both the recipe list and recipe details modules. Note that, unlike an observable, subscribables must be instantiated with the new keyword.

Listing 7-32. Knockout Subscribable Acting As a Primitive Message Bus

```
// example-004/public/scripts/app.js
var bus = new ko.subscribable();
var list = RecipeList.create(recipes, bus);
var details = RecipeDetails.create(list.selectedRecipe(), bus);
```

To effectively publish an updated recipe to the subscribable, the recipe details view model has been modified in several ways.

First, the subscribable is passed to the recipe details factory function as an argument named bus (shorthand for "poor developer's message bus"). The recipe details module will use this subscribable to raise events when recipe details change.

Second, the view model now tracks the recipe's ID since this value will be used to update recipe data on the server. The recipe list will also use the ID to replace stale recipe data after changes have been saved.

Finally, the save() method has been updated to trigger the recipe.saved event on the bus subscribable, passing the modified recipe data as an argument that will be delivered to any subscribers. The modified save() method is shown in Listing 7-33.

Listing 7-33. Recipe Details View Model Saving a Modified Recipe

```
// example-004/public/scripts/recipe-details.js
viewmodel.save = function () {
  var savedRecipe = {
    id: viewmodel.id,
    title: viewmodel.title(),
    ingredients: viewmodel.ingredients(),
    instructions: viewmodel.instructions(),
    cookingTime: {
      hours: viewmodel.hours(),
      minutes: viewmodel.minutes()
    },
```

```
    servings: viewmodel.servings(),
    citation: viewmodel.citation()
  };
  bus.notifySubscribers(savedRecipe, 'recipe.saved');
  viewmodel.isEditing(false);
};
```

The `notifySubscribers()` method on a subscribable accepts two arguments—the data object subscribers will receive and the name of the event being raised. The `app.js` module subscribes to the `recipe.saved` event on the subscribable bus, shown in Listing 7-34, and initiates an AJAX request to send the modified recipe data to the server. Because the recipe details view model and the `app.js` module share a reference to the bus object, any events triggered by the recipe details view model can be handled in the `app.js` module.

Listing 7-34. Saved Recipe Is Persisted to the Server

```
// example-004/public/scripts/app.js
var bus = new ko.subscribable();

bus.subscribe(function (updatedRecipe) {
  $.ajax({
    method: 'PUT',
    url: '/recipes/' + updatedRecipe.id,
    data: updatedRecipe
  }).then(function () {
    bus.notifySubscribers(updatedRecipe, 'recipe.persisted');
  })
}, null, 'recipe.saved');
```

The subscribable's `subscribe()` method accepts three arguments:

- The callback function to be executed when the specified event is triggered on the subscribable

- The context object that will be bound to the `this` keyword within the callback function (or `null`, if the `this` keyword is never used within the callback)

- The name of the event to which the callback is subscribed (e.g., `recipe.saved`)

If the AJAX update succeeds, the app.js module triggers a `recipe.persisted` event on the subscribable to notify listeners. A reference to the bus subscribable has also been passed to the recipe list view model, which actively listens for the `recipe.persisted` event. When the event fires, the recipe list receives the saved data in Listing 7-35 and updates its internal recipes collection and selected recipe based on the persisted recipie's ID.

Listing 7-35. Updating the Recipe List with a Persisted Recipe

```
// example-004/public/scripts/recipe-list.js
window.RecipeList = (function (ko) {

  return {
    create: function (recipes, bus) {
      var viewmodel = {};
```

```
    // properties
    viewmodel.recipes = ko.observableArray(recipes);
    viewmodel.selectedRecipe = ko.observable(recipes[0]);

    // ...
    bus.subscribe(function (updatedRecipe) {

      var recipes = viewmodel.recipes();
      var i = 0,
        count = recipes.length;
      while (i < count) {
        if (recipes[i].id !== updatedRecipe.id) {
          i += 1;
          continue;
        }
        recipes[i] = updatedRecipe;
        viewmodel.recipes(recipes);
        viewmodel.selectRecipe(recipes[i]);
        break;
      }

    }, null, 'recipe.persisted');
    // ...
  }
};

}(window.ko));
```

Though subscribables aren't the only way to raise events in an application, they can be effective for straightforward uses cases, creating a decoupled communication chain between modules.

Summary

Many front-end frameworks offer suites of compelling features and plugins, but Knockout really focuses on the interaction between the HTML view and data model in an application. Knockout's observables alleviate the pain of manually pulling data from, and pushing data to, HTML DOM elements. Developers can add data-bind attributes to any element on a page, gluing the markup to one or more view models through two-way bindings.

While form data can be directly bound to view model properties, DOM event bindings can also invoke methods on Knockout view models as well. Any changes these methods make to view model observable properties are immediately reflected in the DOM. Bindings like visible and css determine how an element is displayed to the user, while bindings like text and value determine an element's content.

Observables are special objects that hold view model data values. When their values change, observables notify any interested subscribers, including bound DOM elements. Primitive observables hold single values, while observable arrays hold collections. Mutations that happen on observable arrays can be tracked and mirrored by HTML elements that are bound to the collection. The foreach binding is especially useful when iterating over an observable array's elements, though special considerations must be taken if individual members of an observable array are changed or replaced.

Knockout templates and view models can be abstracted into reusable components with unique HTML tags. These components can be added to a page and bound to other view model properties, just as any standard HTML elements would be bound. Encapsulating state and behavior in a component reduces the total markup on a page, and also guarantees that similar portions of an application (for example, a list of inputs bound to a collection) behave the same wherever used.

Finally, subscribable objects—the basic building blocks behind observables—can be used as primitive message busses, notifying subscribers of published events and potentially delivering payloads of data where needed.

Related Resources

- Knockout website: `http://knockoutjs.com/`

- KnockMeOut.net: `http://www.knockmeout.net/`

CHAPTER 8

AngularJS

The secret to building large apps is never build large apps. Break your applications into small pieces. Then, assemble those testable, bite-sized pieces into your big application.

—Justin Meyer, creator of JavaScriptMVC

AngularJS has managed to attract a tremendous amount of attention within the developer community, and with good reason: the framework's unique approach to solving many of the challenges typically associated with single-page application development differs significantly from those of popular alternatives. These differences have won Angular a legion of devoted fans, as well as an increasingly vocal group of critics.

As you progress through this chapter, you will be introduced to several of the unique features that distinguish Angular from alternative single-page application frameworks. We will also provide some guidance as to what types of projects might best be able to benefit from Angular, as well as for what types of projects other alternatives may be better suited. Before we close out the chapter, we will also spend a brief bit of time discussing Angular's history, its current state, and what the future holds for the framework.

A Declarative Approach to Building Web Applications

Angular's most distinguishing characteristic is the manner in which it allows developers to create web applications in a so-called "declarative" fashion, as opposed to the "imperative" approach that most developers are accustomed to. The difference between these two approaches is subtle, but it must be understood to truly appreciate the unique benefits that Angular brings to the table. Let's take a look at two examples that demonstrate each approach.

The Imperative Approach

> *imperative: having the form that expresses a command rather than a statement or a question*
>
> —Merriam-Webster.com

When most people think of "programming," the imperative approach is typically what they have in mind. Using this approach, a developer instructs a computer on how to do something. As a result, a desired behavior is (hopefully) achieved. By way of an example, consider Listing 8-1, which shows a simple web application that uses an imperative approach to display an unordered list of animals.

Listing 8-1. Simple, Imperative Web Application

```
// example-imperative/public/index.html

<!DOCTYPE html>
<html lang="en">
<head>
    <meta charset="utf-8">
    <title>Imperative App</title>
</head>
<body>

    <ul id="myList">
    </ul>

    <script src="/bower_components/jquery/dist/jquery.js"></script>

    <script>
    var App = function App() {
        this.init = function() {
            var animals = ['cats', 'dogs', 'aardvarks', 'hamsters', 'squirrels'];
            var $list = $('#myList');
            animals.forEach(function(animal) {
                $list.append('<li>' + animal + '</li>');
            });
        };
    };

    var app = new App();
    app.init();
    </script>

</body>
</html>
```

In this example, our application's desired behavior—the creation of a list of animals—is achieved as a result of our having *explicitly* instructed the computer on how to go about creating it:

1. We start our application by creating a new instance of the App class and calling its init() method.

2. We specify our list's entries in the form of an array (animals).

3. We create a reference to the desired container of our list ($list).

4. Finally, we iterate through each of our array's entries and append them, one by one, to the container.

When an application is created with an imperative approach, that application's source code serves as the primary source of control behind what that application does and when it does it. Put simply, imperative applications *tell* computers how to behave.

The Declarative Approach

declarative: *having the form of a statement rather than a question or a command*

—Merriam-Webster.com

The declarative approach to programming takes the traditional, imperative approach with which most are familiar and flips it on its head. When developers use this approach, they focus their efforts on describing a desired result, leaving the steps necessary to achieve that result up to the computer itself.

By way of an example, Listing 8-2 shows a simple web application very similar to that shown in Listing 8-1. Here, an unordered list of animals is displayed using a more declarative approach with the help of Angular.

Listing 8-2. Declarative Web Application Developed with Angular

```
// example-declarative/public/index.html

<!DOCTYPE html>
<html lang="en" ng-app="app">
<head>
    <meta charset="utf-8">
    <title>Declarative App</title>
</head>
<body>

    <div ng-controller="BodyController">
        <ul>
            <li ng-repeat="animal in animals">{{animal}}</li>
        </ul>
    </div>

    <script src="/bower_components/angularjs/angular.js"></script>
    <script>
    var app = angular.module('app', []);
    app.controller('BodyController', function($scope) {
        $scope.animals = ['cats', 'dogs', 'aardvarks', 'hamsters', 'squirrels'];
    });
    </script>

</body>
</html>
```

The HTML shown in Listing 8-2 contains several items of importance, but for the moment, direct your attention to the various nonstandard attributes that are used throughout the page (e.g., ng-app, ng-controller, and ng-repeat). These attributes demonstrate the use of directives, one of Angular's most prominent and popular features.

Put simply, Angular directives allow developers to enhance HTML's syntax with their own custom extensions. These extensions can occur in the form of classes, custom attributes, comments, and even entirely new DOM elements, as we'll soon see. When Angular encounters these directives, it automatically executes whatever functionality has been associated with them. This could include the execution of a function, the loading of a template, and much more. Angular also includes several of its own built-in directives (such as those used in Listing 8-2), many of which we will be covering throughout this chapter.

When a web application is created with a declarative approach, the responsibility for determining the flow of control within that application shifts from its source code to its interface. Rather than explicitly stating what needs to occur once our application has loaded (as shown in Listing 8-1), we allow our application's interface to describe for itself what needs to occur. Angular directives help make this possible.

For newcomers, the differences between the imperative and declarative approaches to application development may seem subtle, but as we continue, I think you will find that there is much to be excited about.

Modules: A Foundation for Building Loosely Coupled Applications

Complex applications cease to be complex when we approach them not as a single entity, but instead as a collection of small components that work together to achieve a desired goal. Angular modules, which serve as the fundamental building blocks of all Angular projects, provide us with a convenient pattern for structuring our applications in this way.

Take another look at Listing 8-2 and take note of this example's call to Angular's module() method, which serves as both a setter and a getter. Here we create a module representing our application as a whole. To define a new module using the setter syntax, we supply the name of our new module, along with an array of names referencing other modules that this module depends on. In this example, our module has no dependencies, but we still pass an empty array in order to use the setter syntax. Listing 8-3, on the other hand, demonstrates the creation of a new app module with two dependencies.

Listing 8-3. Creating a New Angular Module with Dependencies

```
/**
 * Creates a new module that depends on two other modules - `module1` and `module2`
 */
var app = angular.module('app', ['module1', 'module2']);
```

Once a module has been defined, we can get a reference to it later by using the module() method's getter syntax, as shown in Listing 8-4.

Listing 8-4. Angular's module() Method Serves As a Getter when No Dependencies Array Is Passed

```
/**
 * Returns a reference to a pre-existing module named `app`
 */
var app = angular.module('app');
```

Throughout this chapter, we will take a look at a number of tools that Angular provides for building applications. As we do so, bear in mind that these tools are always used within the context of a module. Every Angular application is itself a module that relies on other modules. Knowing this, we can visualize the general structure of an Angular application as resembling that shown in Figure 8-1.

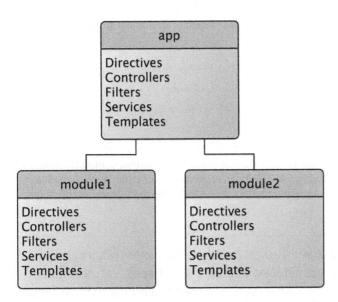

Figure 8-1. *Every Angular application is a module, and Angular modules may specify other modules as dependencies*

Specifying a Bootstrap Module

Significant architectural projects in the physical world often begin with the laying of a cornerstone, the first block around which all other blocks are set in reference to. Similarly, every Angular project has what can be considered a cornerstone of its own—a module representing the application itself. The process by which this module (along with its dependencies) is initialized is referred to as Angular's "bootstrap" process, and can be kicked off in one of two possible ways.

Automatic Bootstrapping

Refer back to Listing 8-2 and take note of the ng-app directive that is attached to the page's html tag. When this page has finished loading, Angular will automatically check for the presence of this directive. If it is found, the module that it references will serve as the application's foundational module—the module representing the application itself. This module will automatically be initialized, at which point the application will be ready.

Manual Bootstrapping

For most applications, Angular's automatic bootstrapping process should suffice. However, in certain situations it can be useful to exert a greater degree of control over when this process occurs. In such cases, it is possible to manually initiate Angular's bootstrap process, as shown in Listing 8-5.

Listing 8-5. Deferring Angular's Bootstrap Process Until the Completion of an Initial jQuery-based AJAX Request

```
$.ajax({
    'url': '/api/data',
    'type': 'GET'
}).done(function() {
    angular.bootstrap(document, ['app']);
});
```

In this example, we defer Angular's bootstrap process until an initial AJAX request completes. Only then do we call Angular's `bootstrap()` method, passing a DOM object to serve as a container for our application (its "root element"), along with an array that specifies a module named app (the module representing our application) as a dependency.

■ **Note**   Most of the time, an Angular application will exist as the only such application within a page; however, *multiple* Angular applications can coexist within the same page. When they do, only one may take advantage of Angular's automatic bootstrap process, while others must manually bootstrap themselves at the appropriate time.

Directives: An Abstraction Layer for the DOM

Through the use of prototypical inheritance, JavaScript provides developers with a mechanism for creating named functions (the JavaScript equivalent of a class) with custom, built-in behavior. Other developers can then instantiate and use such classes, without being required to understand the inner workings of how they function. The example shown in Listing 8-6 demonstrates this process.

Listing 8-6. Prototypal Inheritance in Action

```
// example-prototype/index.js

function Dog() {
}

Dog.prototype.bark = function() {
    console.log('Dog is barking.');
};

Dog.prototype.wag = function() {
    console.log('Tail is wagging.');
};

Dog.prototype.run = function() {
    console.log('Dog is running.');
};

var dog = new Dog();
dog.bark();
dog.wag();
dog.run();
```

This process by which complex behavior is abstracted behind simple interfaces is a fundamental object-oriented programming concept. In much the same way, Angular directives can be thought of as an abstraction layer for the DOM, one that provides developers with a mechanism for creating complex web components that can be used through the use of nothing more than simple HTML markup. Listing 8-7 provides an example that should help to clarify this concept.

Listing 8-7. Example Demonstrating the Creation of a Simple Angular Directive

```
// example-directive1/public/index.html

<!DOCTYPE html>
<html lang="en" ng-app="app">
<head>
    <meta charset="utf-8">
    <title>Example Directive</title>
    <link rel="stylesheet" href="/css/style.css">
    <link rel="stylesheet" href="/bower_components/bootstrap/dist/css/bootstrap.css">
</head>
<body class="container">

    <news-list></news-list>

    <script src="/bower_components/angularjs/angular.js"></script>
    <script>
    var app = angular.module('app', []);
    app.directive('newsList', function() {
        return {
            'restrict': 'E',
            'replace': true,
            'templateUrl': '/templates/news-list.html'
        };
    });
    </script>

</body>
</html>
```

After creating a module for our application, we define a new directive by calling our module's directive() method, passing a name and a factory function responsible for returning an object that describes our new directive to Angular. Several different options may be specified by the object that our factory function returns, but in this simple example, only three are used:

> restrict: Specifies whether this directive should be paired with matching attributes (A), classes (C), or DOM elements (E) that Angular finds (or any combination of the three). In this example, a value of E specifies that Angular should only pair our directive with DOM elements whose tag names match. We could have easily specified all three by passing AEC.

replace: A value of true indicates that our component should completely replace the DOM element that it has been paired with. A value of false would allow us to create a directive that simply augments an existing DOM element in some way, instead of completely replacing it with something else.

templateUrl: The markup that Angular finds at this URL will represent our directive once it has been inserted into the DOM. It is also possible to pass in the contents of a template directly through the use of the template option.

■ **Note**   In regard to the name of our new directive, note the use of camelCase formatting when we created it within Angular and the use of dash-delimited formatting when we referenced it within HTML. This difference is due to the case-insensitive nature of HTML markup. As Angular parses our HTML, it will automatically resolve these differences in naming conventions for us.

Now when we load our application in the browser, Angular will automatically pair our newly defined directive with any matching DOM elements that it finds. As a result, all instances of the <news-list> tag will be replaced with the element shown in Figure 8-2.

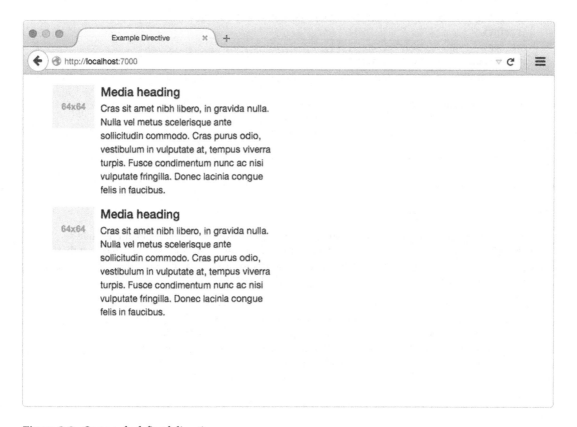

Figure 8-2. *Our newly defined directive*

The basic example that we've just covered did little more than replace a custom DOM element with a different template (we'll build on this example by adding our own custom logic in the next section). However, you should already be starting to notice the power and convenience that Angular directives afford developers. The ability to inject complex components into an application through the use of simple tags such as the one seen in Listing 8-7 provides developers with a convenient mechanism for abstracting complex functionality behind simple facades that are much easier to manage.

Taking Control

In the previous section, we stepped through the creation of a simple Angular directive that, in the end, did little more than replace a custom DOM element with a separate template of our choosing. This is a useful application of directives in and of itself, but in order to appreciate the full power of directives, we'll need to take this example a step further by applying our own custom logic that will allow instances of our directive to behave in interesting ways. We can do so with the help of scopes and controllers.

Scopes and Prototypal Inheritance

Angular scopes can be a bit tricky to grasp at first because they are directly related to one of the more confusing aspects of JavaScript in general: prototypal inheritance. Newcomers to Angular often find scopes to be one of its more confusing concepts, but a solid understanding of them is essential to working with the framework. Before we continue, let's take a few minutes to explore their purpose and how they work.

Within most "classical" object-oriented languages, inheritance is accomplished through the use of classes. JavaScript, on the other hand, implements an entirely different inheritance structure known as prototypal inheritance, in which all inheritance is accomplished through the use of objects and functions. Listing 8-8 show an example of this process in action.

Listing 8-8. Example of Prototypal Inheritance, in Which Car Extends Vehicle

```
// example-prototype2/index.js

/**
 * @class Vehicle
 */
var Vehicle = function Vehicle() {
    console.log(this.constructor.name, 'says: I am a vehicle.');
};

Vehicle.prototype.start = function() {
    console.log('%s has started.', this.constructor.name);
};

Vehicle.prototype.stop = function() {
    console.log('%s has stopped.', this.constructor.name);
};
```

163

```
/**
 * @class Car
 */
var Car = function Car() {
    console.log(this.constructor.name, 'says: I am a car.');
    Vehicle.apply(this, arguments);
};

Car.prototype = Object.create(Vehicle.prototype);
Car.prototype.constructor = Car;

Car.prototype.honk = function() {
    console.log('%s has honked.', this.constructor.name);
};

var vehicle = new Vehicle();
vehicle.start();
vehicle.stop();

var car = new Car();
car.start();
car.honk();
car.stop();

/* Result:
Vehicle says: I am a vehicle.
Vehicle has started.
Vehicle has stopped.
Car says: I am a car.
Car says: I am a vehicle.
Car has started.
Car has honked.
Car has stopped.
*/
```

In this example, a Vehicle function is defined. We assign start() and stop() instance methods to it by augmenting its prototype. Afterward, we define a Car function, only this time, we replace its prototype with one that inherits from that of Vehicle. Finally, we assign a honk instance method to Car. When running this example, take note of the fact that new instances of Vehicle can start and stop, while new instances of Car can start, stop, *and* honk. This is prototypal inheritance at work.

This is an important concept to grasp—during Angular's bootstrap phase, a similar process occurs in which a parent object (referred to as $rootScope) is created and attached to the application's root element. Afterward, Angular will continue parsing the DOM in search of directives (Angular refers to this process as "compilation"). As these directives are encountered, Angular will create new objects which inherit from their nearest ancestor and assign them to the DOM element each directive is attached to. Angular is, in effect, creating a special sandbox—in Angular terms, a "scope"—for each component within our application. The result can be visualized as something like that which is shown in Figure 8-3.

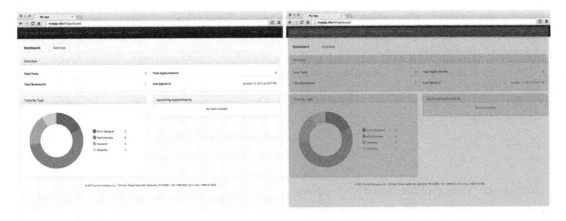

Figure 8-3. *A web application with various components created with the help of directives. On the right, portions of the DOM are highlighted where new scopes have been created*

Manipulating Scope with Controllers

An Angular controller is nothing more than a function whose sole purpose is to manipulate a scope object, and it is here that we can begin to add some intelligence to our application's components. Listing 8-9 shows an extended version of the example we looked at in Listing 8-7. The only difference is the addition of a controller property to the object responsible for describing our directive. The contents of the template this directive uses are shown in Listing 8-10.

Listing 8-9. Extended Version of Listing 8-7 Example That Adds Custom Behavior to Our New Directive

```
// example-directive2/public/index.html

<!DOCTYPE html>
<html lang="en" ng-app="app">
<head>
    <meta charset="utf-8">
    <title>Example Directive</title>
    <link rel="stylesheet" href="/css/style.css">
    <link rel="stylesheet" href="/bower_components/bootstrap/dist/css/bootstrap.css">
</head>
<body class="container">

    <news-list></news-list>

    <script src="/bower_components/angularjs/angular.js"></script>
    <script>
    var app = angular.module('app', []);
    app.directive('newsList', function() {
        return {
            'restrict': 'E',
            'replace': true,
            'controller': function($scope, $http) {
```

```
                $http.get('/api/news').then(function(result) {
                    $scope.items = result.data;
                });
            },
            'templateUrl': '/templates/news-list.html'
        };
    });
    </script>

</body>
</html>
```

Listing 8-10. Contents of Our Directive's Template

```
// example-directive2/public/templates/news-list.html

<div class="row">
    <div class="col-xs-8">
        <div ng-repeat="item in items">
            <div class="media">
                <div class="media-left">
                    <a href="#">
                        <img class="media-object" ng-src="{{item.img}}">
                    </a>
                </div>
                <div class="media-body">
                    <h4 class="media-heading" ng-bind="item.title"></h4>
                </div>
            </div>
        </div>
    </div>
</div>
```

In Listing 8-9, look specifically at the portion where we assign a function to our directive's `controller` property. Take note of the fact that our controller function receives two arguments: `$scope` and `$http`. For the moment, don't concern yourself with how these arguments came to be passed to our controller—we'll discuss that in the upcoming section on services. For now, the important thing to realize is that within our controller, the `$scope` variable refers to the object that Angular automatically created for us when it first encountered our directive in the DOM. At this point, our controller has the opportunity to alter that object and, as a result, to see those changes reflected in the DOM due to Angular's support for two-way data binding.

Two-Way Data Binding

Data binding describes Angular's ability to link a template with a JavaScript object (i.e., a scope), allowing the template to reference properties within the scope that are then rendered to the browser. Figure 8-4 illustrates this process.

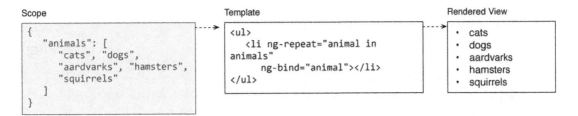

Figure 8-4. *Process by which data binding allows Angular applications to render data that is referenced within a scope object*

Angular's support for data binding doesn't stop with this one-way process by which data referenced within a scope is displayed within a view. The framework also provides directives that enable the inverse effect, allowing a directive's scope to update as changes occur within its view (e.g., when a form field's value changes). When Angular's implementation of data binding is described as "two-way," this is what is being referred to.

■ **Note**   The topic of two-way data binding will be discussed in greater detail later in the chapter in the "Creating Complex Forms" section.

In Listing 8-9, our controller uses Angular's $http service to fetch an array from our API that contains headlines from National Public Radio and *The Onion*. It then assigns that array to the items property of our directive's $scope object. To see how this information gets reflected within the DOM, direct your attention to the ng-repeat directive shown in Listing 8-10. This core Angular directive allows us to iterate over our array from within our template, creating new <div class="media">...</div> elements for each item it contains. Finally, Angular's built-in ng-src and ng-bind directives allow us to dynamically assign image URLs and textual content to the appropriate elements within our template.

The final result after having loaded this application in the browser can be seen in Figure 8-5.

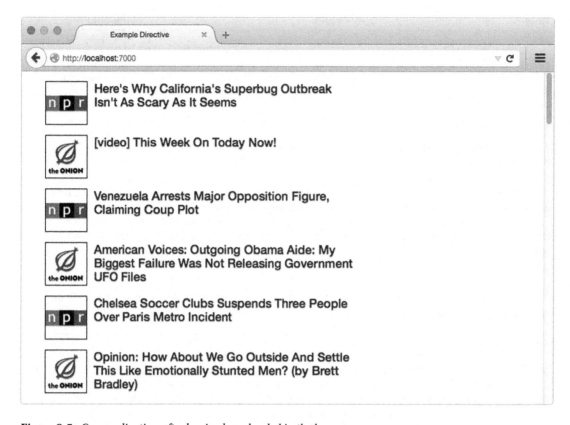

Figure 8-5. Our application after having been loaded in the browser

Loose Coupling Through Services and Dependency Injection

In the previous section, you were introduced to the basic process by which Angular applications are organized as a series of nested scopes, which can be manipulated by controllers and referenced by templates via two-way data binding. Using only these concepts, it is possible to build fairly simple applications (as demonstrated by some of the examples included in this chapter), but without planning, attempts to build anything more complex will quickly run into growing pains. In this section, we'll discover how services can support developers in building loosely coupled Angular applications that are designed to accommodate growth.

Dependency Injection

Before we dive into services, it's important that we take a minute to talk about dependency injection, a concept that is fairly new to the world of client-side frameworks and one that is relied on heavily by Angular.

First, take a look at Listing 8-11, which shows a very basic Node.js application with a single dependency, the `fs` module. In this example, our module has the responsibility of retrieving the `fs` module via the `require()` method.

Listing 8-11. Node.js Application That Depends on the fs Module

```
var fs = require('fs');
fs.readFile('~/data.txt', 'utf8', function(err, contents) {
    if (err) throw new Error(err);
    console.log(contents);
});
```

The pattern that we see here, in which a module "requires" a dependency, intuitively makes sense. A module needs another component, so it goes out and gets it. The concept of dependency injection, however, flips this concept on its head. Listing 8-12 shows a simple example of dependency injection in action within Angular.

Listing 8-12. Dependency Injection in Action Within Angular

```
var app = angular.module('app', []);
app.controller('myController', function($http) {
    $http.get('/api/news').then(function(result) {
        console.log(result);
    });
});
```

Frameworks such as Angular that implement dependency injection prescribe a common pattern by which modules can register themselves with a central point of control. In other words, as an application is initialized, modules are given the opportunity to say, "This is my name, and this is where you can find me." Afterward and throughout the execution of that program, modules that are loaded can reference their dependencies simply by specifying them as arguments to their constructor function (or class). The order in which they are specified makes no difference.

Refer back to Listing 8-12. In this example, we create a new app module to represent our application. Next, we create a controller named myController within our application's module, passing a constructor function that will be called whenever a new instance is needed. Take note of the $http argument that is passed into our controller's constructor; this is an example of dependency injection at work. The $http dependency that our controller refers to is a module included within Angular's core codebase. During our application's bootstrap phase, Angular registered this module in the form of a service—the same type of service that you're about to learn how to create for yourself.

■ **Note** By convention, core services, APIs, and properties provided by Angular are prefixed with $. To prevent possible collisions, it is best if you avoid following this convention within your own code.

Thin Controllers and Fat Services

ake another look at Listing 8-9, which demonstrates the process by which controllers can be used to add intelligence to an application's directives. In this example, our controller creates an AJAX request that returns an array of news headlines from our API. While that works, this example doesn't address the very real and foreseeable need to share this information throughout our application.

While we could have other interested components duplicate this AJAX request themselves, that wouldn't be ideal for a number of reasons. We would be in a much better position if we could instead abstract the logic for gathering these headlines into a centralized API that could be reused throughout our application. Doing so would provide us with a number of benefits, including the ability to change the URL at which this information is fetched in a single location, unbeknownst to consumers of the API.

As we'll see in a moment, Angular services provide us with the tools we need to accomplish this goal. Services provide us with a mechanism for creating well-defined interfaces that can be shared and reused throughout an application. When the bulk of an Angular application's logic is structured in this way, we can begin to see controllers for what they really are: little more than a thin layer of glue responsible for binding scopes with services in ways that make the most sense for a particular view.

Within Angular, three broad categories of service types (one of which is confusingly named "service") exist: factories, services, and providers. Let's take a look at each of them.

Factories

The example shown in Listing 8-13 builds on Listing 8-9 by moving the logic required for fetching our headlines into a factory.

Listing 8-13. Angular headlines Factory That Provides an API for Fetching News Headlines

```
// example-directive3/public/index.html

<!DOCTYPE html>
<html lang="en" ng-app="app">
<head>
    <meta charset="utf-8">
    <title>Example Directive</title>
    <link rel="stylesheet" href="/css/style.css">
    <link rel="stylesheet" href="/bower_components/bootstrap/dist/css/bootstrap.css">
</head>
<body class="container">

    <news-list></news-list>

    <script src="/bower_components/angularjs/angular.js"></script>
    <script>
    var app = angular.module('app', []);
    app.directive('newsList', function() {
        return {
            'restrict': 'E',
            'replace': true,
            'controller': function($scope, headlines) {
                headlines.fetch().then(function(items) {
                    $scope.items = items;
                });
            },
            'templateUrl': '/templates/news-list.html'
        };
    });
    app.factory('headlines', function($http) {
        return {
```

```
        'fetch': function() {
            return $http.get('/api/news').then(function(result) {
                return result.data;
            });
        }
    };
});
</script>

</body>
</html>
```

In Listing 8-13, the headlines factory returns an object with a fetch() method that, when called, will query our API for headlines and return them in the form of a promise.

In most Angular applications, factories are by far the most commonly used type of service. The first time a factory is referenced as a dependency, Angular will invoke the factory's function and return the result to the requestor. Subsequent references to the service will receive the same result that was originally returned the first time the service was referenced. In other words, factories can be thought of as singletons, in that they are never invoked more than once.

Services

The example shown in Listing 8-14 builds on Listing 8-9 by moving the logic required for fetching our headlines into a service.

Listing 8-14. Angular headlines Service That Provides an API for Fetching News Headlines

```
// example-directive4/public/index.html

<!DOCTYPE html>
<html lang="en" ng-app="app">
<head>
    <meta charset="utf-8">
    <title>Example Directive</title>
    <link rel="stylesheet" href="/css/style.css">
    <link rel="stylesheet" href="/bower_components/bootstrap/dist/css/bootstrap.css">
</head>
<body class="container">

    <news-list></news-list>

    <script src="/bower_components/angularjs/angular.js"></script>
    <script>
    var app = angular.module('app', []);
    app.directive('newsList', function() {
        return {
            'restrict': 'E',
            'replace': true,
            'controller': function($scope, headlines) {
                headlines.fetch().then(function(items) {
                    $scope.items = items;
```

171

```
                });
            },
            'templateUrl': '/templates/news-list.html'
        };
    });
    app.service('headlines', function($http) {
        this.fetch = function() {
            return $http.get('/api/news').then(function(result) {
                return result.data;
            });
        };
    });
    </script>

</body>
</html>
```

Within Angular, services function almost identically to factories, with one key difference. While factory functions are simply invoked, service functions are called as constructors via the new keyword, allowing them to be defined in the form of a class that is instantiated. Which you choose to use largely depends on style preferences, as the same end result can be achieved with both.

In this example, instead of returning an object as we did within our factory, we assign a fetch() method to this, the object ultimately returned by our service's constructor function.

Providers

The example shown in Listing 8-15 builds on Listing 8-9 by moving the logic required for fetching our headlines into a provider.

Listing 8-15. Angular headlines Provider That Provides an API for Fetching News Headlines

```
// example-directive5/public/index.html

<!DOCTYPE html>
<html lang="en" ng-app="app">
<head>
    <meta charset="utf-8">
    <title>Example Directive</title>
    <link rel="stylesheet" href="/css/style.css">
    <link rel="stylesheet" href="/bower_components/bootstrap/dist/css/bootstrap.css">
</head>
<body class="container">

    <news-list></news-list>

    <script src="/bower_components/angularjs/angular.js"></script>
    <script>
    var app = angular.module('app', []);
    app.directive('newsList', function() {
        return {
            'restrict': 'E',
```

```
            'replace': true,
            'controller': function($scope, headlines) {
                headlines.fetch().then(function(items) {
                    $scope.items = items;
                });
            },
            'templateUrl': '/templates/news-list.html'
        };
    });
    app.config(function(headlinesProvider) {
        headlinesProvider.limit = 10;
    });
    app.provider('headlines', function() {
        this.$get = function($http) {
            var self = this;
            return {
                'fetch': function() {
                    return $http.get('/api/news', {
                        'params': {
                            'limit': self.limit || 20
                        }
                    }).then(function(result) {
                        return result.data;
                    });
                }
            };
        };
    });
    </script>

</body>
</html>
```

Unlike factories and services, which are fully responsible for determining their own settings, Angular providers allow developers to configure them during their parent module's configuration phase. In this way, providers can be thought of as configurable factories. In this example, we define a headlines provider that functions identically to the factory we created in Listing 8-13, only this time, the fetch() method passes a configurable limit parameter to our API that allows it to specify a limit for the number of results it will receive.

In Listing 8-15, we define a factory function at this.$get within our provider. When the headlines provider is referenced as a dependency, Angular will invoke this function and return its result to the requestor, much like it did with our factory in Listing 8-13. In contrast, notice how our provider's fetch() method is able to reference a limit property that was defined within the module's config block.

Creating Routes

So-called "single-page applications" built with frameworks such as Angular provide their users with fluid experiences that are more akin to that of traditional desktop applications. They do so by preloading all (or most) of the various resources they require (e.g., scripts, stylesheets, etc.) within a single, up-front page load. Subsequent requests for different URLs are then intercepted and processed via background AJAX requests, rather than requiring a full refresh of the page. In this section, you'll learn how to manage such requests with the help of Angular's ngRoute module.

Listing 8-16 builds on the example that was previously shown in Listing 8-13. This time, however, we have added two routes to our application that allow users to navigate to sections labeled "Dashboard" and "News Headlines." Only after the user navigates to the /#/headlines route will our newsList directive be injected into the page. The following steps are taken to achieve this goal:

1. Define a configuration block that will be executed during our application's bootstrap phase. Within this function, we reference the $routeProvider service provided by Angular's angular-route package, which must be installed in addition to Angular's core library.

2. Define an array, routes, within which objects are placed that define the various routes to be made available by our application. In this example, each object's route property defines the location at which the route will be loaded, while the config property allows us to specify a controller function and template to be loaded at the appropriate time.

3. Iterate through each entry of the routes array and pass the appropriate properties to the when() method made available by the $routeProvider service. This approach provides us with a simple method by which multiple routes can be defined. Alternatively, we could have made two separate, explicit calls to the $routeProvider.when() method without using an array.

4. Utilize the $routeProvider.otherwise() method to define a default route to be loaded in the event that no route (or an invalid route) is referenced by the user.

Listing 8-16. Angular Application That Defines Two Routes, dashboard and headlines

```
// example-router1/public/index.html

<!DOCTYPE html>
<html lang="en" ng-app="app">
<head>
    <meta charset="utf-8">
    <title>Routing Example</title>
    <link rel="stylesheet" href="/css/style.css">
    <link rel="stylesheet" href="/bower_components/bootstrap/dist/css/bootstrap.css">
</head>
<body class="container">

    <ng-view></ng-view>

    <script src="/bower_components/angularjs/angular.js"></script>
    <script src="/bower_components/angular-route/angular-route.js"></script>
    <script src="/modules/news-list.js"></script>
    <script>
    var app = angular.module('app', ['ngRoute', 'newsList']);
    app.config(function($routeProvider) {
        var routes = [
            {
                'route': '/dashboard',
                'config': {
```

```
                'templateUrl': '/templates/dashboard.html'
            }
        },
        {
            'route': '/headlines',
            'config': {
                'controller': function($log) {
                    $log.debug('Welcome to the headlines route.');
                },
                'templateUrl': '/templates/headlines.html'
            }
        }
    ];
    routes.forEach(function(route) {
        $routeProvider.when(route.route, route.config);
    });
    $routeProvider.otherwise({
        'redirectTo': '/dashboard' // Our default route
    });
});
</script>

</body>
</html>
```

Route Parameters

In practice, most of the routes that exist within a typical Angular application are designed to serve up dynamic content that varies based on the value of one or more parameters that each route expects. The example shown in Listing 8-17 demonstrates how this can be accomplished.

Listing 8-17. Angular Application with Routes That Vary Their Content Based on the Value of an Expected Parameter

```
// example-router2/public/index.html

<!DOCTYPE html>
<html lang="en" ng-app="app">
<head>
    <meta charset="utf-8">
    <title>Routing Example</title>
    <link rel="stylesheet" href="/css/style.css">
    <link rel="stylesheet" href="/bower_components/bootstrap/dist/css/bootstrap.css">
</head>
<body class="container">

    <ng-view></ng-view>
```

```
<script src="/bower_components/angularjs/angular.js"></script>
<script src="/bower_components/angular-route/angular-route.js"></script>
<script>
var app = angular.module('app', ['ngRoute']);
app.config(function($routeProvider) {
    var routes = [{
        'route': '/dashboard',
        'config': {
            'templateUrl': '/templates/dashboard.html',
            'controller': function($scope, $http) {
                return $http.get('/api/animals').then(function(result) {
                    $scope.animals = result.data;
                });
            },
        }
    },
    {
        'route': '/animals/:animalID',
        'config': {
            'templateUrl': '/templates/animal.html',
            'controller': function($scope, $route, $http) {
                $http.get('/api/animals/' + $route.current.params.animalID).
then(function(result) {
                    $scope.animal = result.data;
                });
            }
        }
    }];
    routes.forEach(function(route) {
        $routeProvider.when(route.route, route.config);
    });
    $routeProvider.otherwise({
        'redirectTo': '/dashboard' // Our default route
    });
});
</script>

</body>
</html>
```

Route Resolutions

If done correctly, single-page applications can provide their users with an experience that is substantially improved over that of their standard counterparts. That said, these improvements don't come without a cost. Coordinating the various API calls that occur throughout a single-page application's life cycle can be quite challenging. Before we move on, let's touch on a particularly useful feature provided by Angular's ngRoute module that can help us tame some of this complexity: resolutions.

Resolutions allow us to define one or more steps that must take place before a transition to a specific route can occur. If any of the resolutions defined for a route happen to return promises, the transition to the desired route will complete only after each of them has been resolved. The example shown in Listing 8-18 shows route resolutions in action.

Listing 8-18. Route Resolutions in Action

```
// example-router3/public/index.html

<!DOCTYPE html>
<html lang="en" ng-app="app">
<head>
    <meta charset="utf-8">
    <title>Routing Example</title>
    <link rel="stylesheet" href="/css/style.css">
    <link rel="stylesheet" href="/bower_components/bootstrap/dist/css/bootstrap.css">
</head>
<body class="container">

    <ng-view></ng-view>

    <script src="/bower_components/angularjs/angular.js"></script>
    <script src="/bower_components/angular-route/angular-route.js"></script>
    <script>
    var app = angular.module('app', ['ngRoute']);
    app.config(function($routeProvider) {
        $routeProvider.when('/dashboard', {
            'templateUrl': '/templates/dashboard.html',
            'controller': function($scope, animals, colors) {
                $scope.animals = animals;
                $scope.colors = colors;
            },
            'resolve': {
                'animals': function($http) {
                    return $http.get('/api/animals').then(function(result) {
                        return result.data;
                    });
                },
                'colors': function($http) {
                    return $http.get('/api/colors').then(function(result) {
                        return result.data;
                    });
                }
            }
        });
        $routeProvider.otherwise({
            'redirectTo': '/dashboard' // Our default route
        });
    });
    </script>

</body>
</html>
```

In this example, a single route is defined that displays a list of animals and colors after making two corresponding calls to an API to fetch this information. Rather than request this information directly from within our route's controller, we create requests within the route's `resolve` object. As a result, when our route's controller function is called, we can know with certainty that the requests have already been completed.

Creating Complex Forms

HTML forms can be frustratingly difficult to manage. A major concern is *validation*, the process by which users are made aware of problems (e.g., a required field that has not been filled out) and guided to their resolution. In addition, complex forms frequently require additional logic that allows them to vary their content based on the user's answers to previous questions. Throughout the next several pages, we'll take a look at a few examples that demonstrate how Angular can help simplify some of these challenges.

Validation

Well-designed HTML forms give careful consideration to user experience. They don't assume that users fully understand what is being asked of them. They also go out of their way to notify users when problems exist, along with the steps that are required to resolve them. Fortunately, Angular's declarative syntax allows developers to easily create forms that abide by these rules.

Listing 8-19 shows the HTML for our first example, while Listing 8-20 shows the accompanying controller.

Listing 8-19. HTML Form That Implements Validation and Displays Dynamic Feedback to the User

```
// example-form1/public/index.html

<!DOCTYPE html>
<html lang="en" ng-app="app">
<head>
    <meta charset="utf-8">
    <title>Example Form</title>
    <link rel="stylesheet" href="/css/style.css">
</head>
<body ng-controller="formController">

    <form name="myForm" ng-class="formClass" ng-submit="submit()" novalidate>

        <div class="row">

            <div ng-class="{
                'has-error': !myForm.first_name.$pristine && !myForm.first_name.$valid,
                'has-success': !myForm.first_name.$pristine && myForm.first_name.$valid
            }">
                <label>First Name</label>
                <input
                    type="text"
                    name="first_name"
                    ng-model="model.first_name"
                    class="form-control"
```

```
                ng-minlength="3"
                ng-maxlength="15"
                ng-required="true">
        <p ng-show="
            !myForm.first_name.$pristine &&
            myForm.first_name.$error.required">
            First name is required.
        </p>
        <p ng-show="
            !myForm.first_name.$pristine &&
            myForm.first_name.$error.minlength">
            First name must be at least 3 characters long.
        </p>
        <p ng-show="
            !myForm.first_name.$pristine &&
            myForm.first_name.$error.maxlength">
            First name can have no more than 15 characters.
        </p>
</div>

<div ng-class="{
    'has-error': !myForm.last_name.$pristine && !myForm.last_name.$valid,
    'has-success': !myForm.last_name.$pristine && myForm.last_name.$valid
}">
    <label>Last Name</label>
    <input
        type="text"
        name="last_name"
        ng-model="model.last_name"
        class="form-control"
        ng-minlength="3"
        ng-maxlength="15"
        ng-required="true">
        <p ng-show="
            !myForm.last_name.$pristine &&
            myForm.last_name.$error.required">
            Last name is required.
        </p>
        <p ng-show="
            !myForm.last_name.$pristine &&
            myForm.last_name.$error.minlength">
            Last name must be at least 3 characters long.
        </p>
        <p ng-show="
            !myForm.last_name.$pristine &&
            myForm.last_name.$error.maxlength">
            Last name can have no more than 15 characters.
        </p>
</div>
```

```
        </div>

        <div class="row">
            <div>
                <button type="submit" ng-disabled="myForm.$invalid">Submit</button>
                <button type="button" ng-click="reset()">Reset</button>
            </div>
        </div>

    </form>

    <hr>

    <div class="output" ng-bind="output"></div>

    <script src="/bower_components/angularjs/angular.js"></script>
    <script src="/app/index.js"></script>

</body>
</html>
```

Listing 8-20. Controller That Has Been Attached to the Document's <body> Element

```
// example-form1/public/app/index.js

var app = angular.module('app', []);
app.controller('formController', function($scope, $http, $log) {

    $scope.formClass = null;
    $scope.model = {};

    $http.get('/api/model').then(function(result) {
        $scope.model = result.data;
    });

    $scope.submit = function() {
        if (!$scope.myForm.$valid) return;
        $http.post('/api/model', {
            'model': $scope.model
        }).then(function() {
            alert('Form submitted.');
        }).catch(function(err) {
            alert(err);
        });
    };

    $scope.reset = function() {
        $scope.model = {};
        $http.post('/api/model', {
            'model': $scope.model
        });
    };
```

```
/**
 * Angular's built-in `$watch()` method (available within every controller)
 * enables us to watch for and respond to changes that occur within variables
 * defined at the `$scope` level. Here we save the contents of our a form as
 * a JSON string to `$scope.output`, which is referenced by our template.
 */
$scope.$watch('model', function() {
    $scope.output = angular.toJson($scope.model, 4);
}, true);

});
```

As Angular compiles our application, it will apply a built-in form directive to the <form> element contained within our template. This directive will create a new instance of a special controller, FormController, that Angular reserves for managing form instances. Finally, based on the value of our form's name attribute (in this case, myForm), Angular will assign a reference to the newly created instance of FormController to the form's parent scope, allowing our controller to interact with our newly created form at $scope.myForm.

Instances of FormController provide a number of useful properties and methods, which you can see referenced throughout Listing 8-19 and Listing 8-20. For instance, note how we are able to dynamically enable or disable our form's submit button with the help of the ng-disabled directive. In this example, we've set this directive to reference our form's $invalid property, which will always return TRUE or FALSE to indicate whether any of the inputs contained within our form are in an invalid state.

Listing 8-19 also applies additional built-in Angular directives (ng-minlength, ng-maxlength, and ng-required) to implement some simple validation rules within our form. Directly below each of these inputs, our template references various properties on the myForm object to determine what, if any, errors currently exist. Based on this information, it can then hide or show the appropriate feedback to the user.

Note the use of the ng-model directive in Listing 8-19 on each of our form's input fields. This directive (which is specifically designed to be used with form controls) allows us to implement two-way data binding, a concept that was briefly mentioned earlier in the chapter. As the values entered within each of these fields is changed, so too will our scope be updated, at the properties referenced by ng-model. Thanks to two-way data binding, the inverse effect also holds. If our controller were to modify a value referenced by ng-model, the matching form input would also update accordingly. It's important to note that the ng-model directive is the preferred method by which we can determine a form's input values. Within Angular, an input's name attribute is used solely for purposes of validation.

Figure 8-6, Figure 8-7, and Figure 8-8 show the end result that users will see in their browsers.

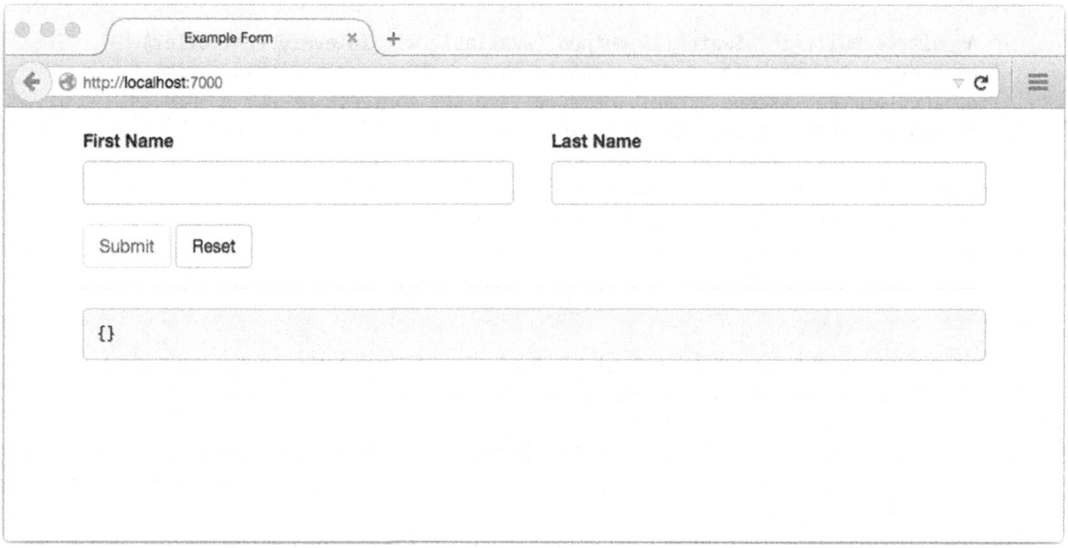

Figure 8-6. *Our form in its initial state. The example that is included with this chapter includes a preview of our scope's* model *object that will automatically update as data is entered into the form*

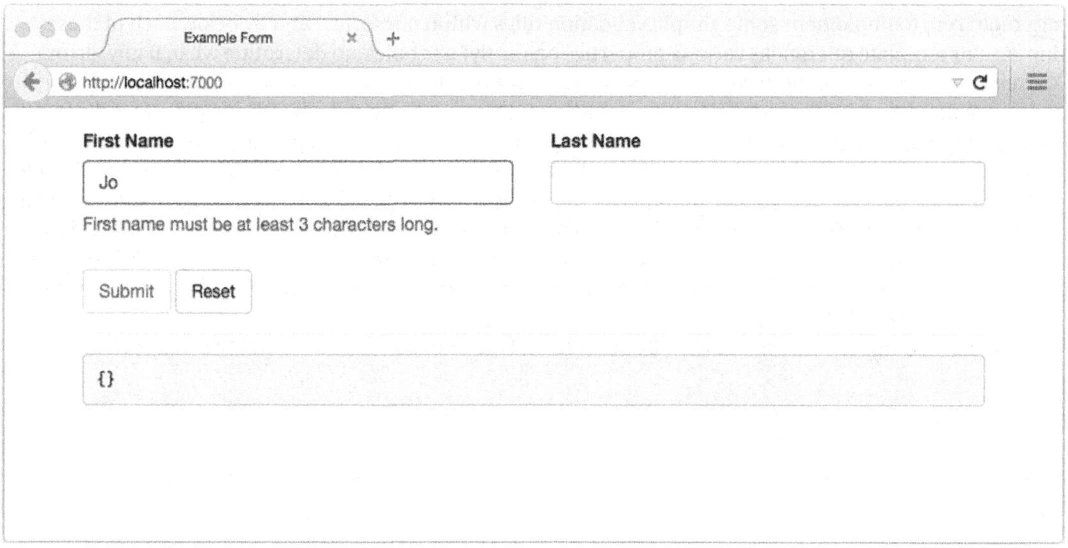

Figure 8-7. *As the user enters their information, the form dynamically displays the appropriate feedback, based on the information that has been submitted. Here we notify the user that the "First Name" field should be at least three characters long*

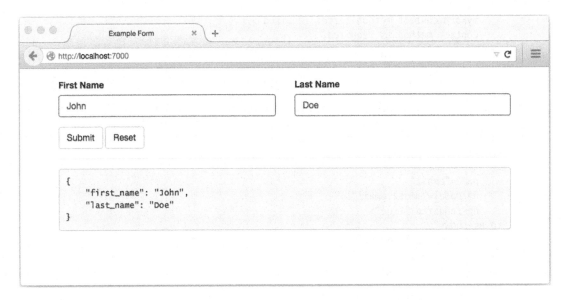

Figure 8-8. Our form in its final state, after the user has entered all of their information

Conditional Logic

Forms often require additional logic to determine under what circumstances certain questions or other information should be presented. A commonly encountered scenario would involve a form that asks a user for their e-mail address only after they have selected "Email" as their preferred method of contact. Our next example, shown in Listing 8-21, will build on the previous one by demonstrating how such logic can be implemented through the use of the ng-if directive. Figure 8-9 and Figure 8-10 show the end result, as rendered within the browser.

Listing 8-21. Excerpt from Our Example's Template Showing the HTML Added to Our Previous Example

```
// example-form2/public/index.html

<div class="row">

    <div ng-class="{
        'has-error': !myForm.contact_method.$pristine && !myForm.contact_method.$valid,
        'has-success': !myForm.contact_method.$pristine && myForm.contact_method.$valid
    }">
        <label>Contact Method</label>
        <select
            name="contact_method"
            ng-model="model.contact_method"
            ng-required="true">
            <option value="">Select One</option>
            <option value="email">Email</option>
            <option value="phone">Phone</option>
        </select>
        <p ng-show="
            !myForm.contact_method.$pristine &&
```

```
                    myForm.contact_method.$error.required">
                Contact method is required.
            </p>
        </div>

        <div ng-if="model.contact_method == 'email'" ng-class="{
            'has-error': !myForm.email.$pristine && !myForm.email.$valid,
            'has-success': !myForm.email.$pristine && myForm.email.$valid}">
            <label>Email Address</label>
            <input
                type="email"
                name="email"
                ng-model="model.email"
                ng-required="true">
            <p ng-show="
                !myForm.email.$pristine &&
                myForm.email.$error.required">
                Email address is required.
            </p>
        </div>

        <div ng-if="model.contact_method == 'phone'" ng-class="{
            'has-error': !myForm.phone.$pristine && !myForm.phone.$valid,
            'has-success': !myForm.phone.$pristine && myForm.phone.$valid}">
            <label>Phone Number</label>
            <input
                type="tel"
                name="phone"
                ng-model="model.phone"
                ng-required="true">
            <p ng-show="
                !myForm.phone.$pristine &&
                myForm.phone.$error.required">
                Phone number is required.
            </p>
        </div>

    </div>
```

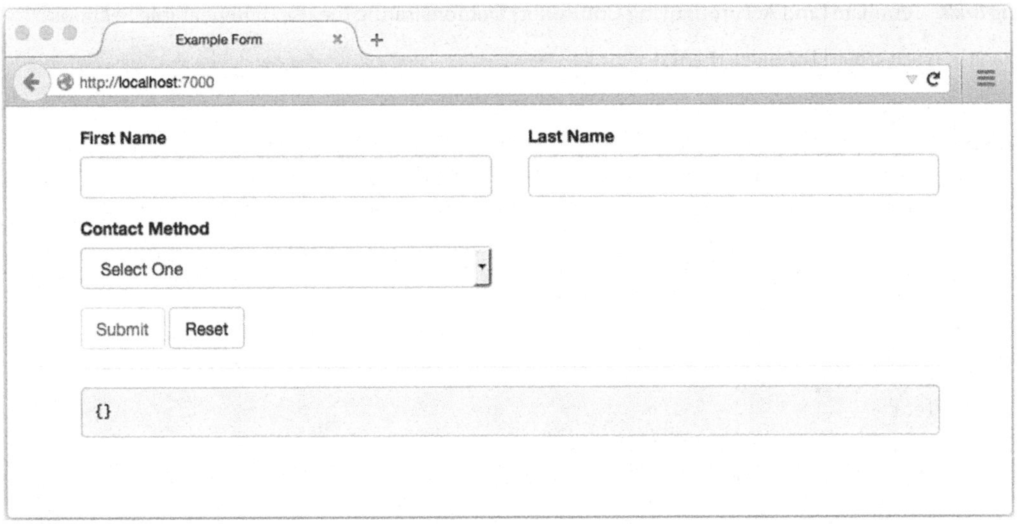

Figure 8-9. *The initial state of our form, before a value has been selected for "Contact Method"*

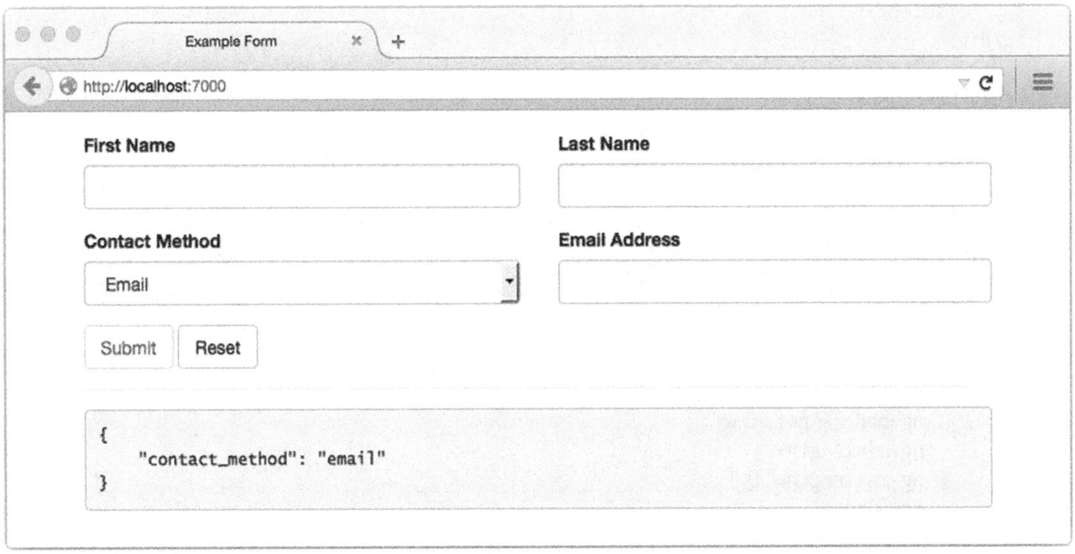

Figure 8-10. *Our form displaying the appropriate input field once a value has been chosen for "Contact Method"*

Repeatable Sections

For our final example, let's see how Angular can assist us in creating a form that employs repeatable sections, based on input from the user. In Listing 8-22, we create a form that asks the user to create "Type" and "Name" entries for each of their pets. Once added, each entry also provides a link that allows the user to remove it.

Listing 8-22. Template (and Accompanying Controller) Demonstrating the use of Repeatable Sections

```
// example-form3/public/index.html

<div class="row">
    <div>
        <h2>Pets</h2> <small><a ng-click="addPet()">Add Pet</a></small>
    </div>
</div>

<div class="row" ng-repeat="pet in model.pets">

    <div>
        <label>Pet Type</label>
        <select
            ng-attr-name="pet_type{{$index}}"
            ng-model="pet.type"
            required>
            <option value="">Select One</option>
            <option value="cat">Cat</option>
            <option value="dog">Dog</option>
            <option value="Goldfish">Goldfish</option>
        </select>
    </div>

    <div ng-class="{
        'has-error': !myForm.last_name.$pristine && !myForm.last_name.$valid,
        'has-success': !myForm.last_name.$pristine && myForm.last_name.$valid
    }">
        <label>
        Pet's Name <small class="pull-right">
        <a ng-click="removePet(pet)">Remove Pet</a></small>
        </label>
        <input
            type="text"
            ng-attr-name="pet_name{{$index}}"
            ng-model="pet.name"
            ng-minlength="3"
            ng-maxlength="15"
            required>
        <p ng-show="
            !myForm.last_name.$pristine &&
            myForm.last_name.$error.required">
            Last name is required.
        </p>
```

```
    <p ng-show="
        !myForm.last_name.$pristine &&
        myForm.last_name.$error.minlength">
        Last name must be at least 3 characters long.
    </p>
    <p ng-show="
        !myForm.last_name.$pristine &&
        myForm.last_name.$error.maxlength">
        Last name can have no more than 15 characters.
    </p>
</div>

</div>
// example-form5/public/app/index.js

$scope.addPet = function() {
    $scope.model.pets.push({});
};

$scope.removePet = function(pet) {
    $scope.model.pets.splice($scope.model.pets.indexOf(pet), 1);
};
```

In Listing 8-22, we use Angular's ng-repeat directive to iterate over entries in our scope's model.pets array. Note how we are able to reference {{$index}} within the scope created by ng-repeat to determine our current position within the array. Using this information, we assign a unique name to each entry for validation purposes.

Our template provides the user with a global "Add Pet" link at the top of the section that, when clicked, calls the addPet() method that has been defined within our controller. Doing so appends an empty object to our scope's model.pets array. As our ng-repeat directive iterates over each entry, we also provide the user with a link for removal. Clicking this link passes the current entry from our model.pets array to our scope's removePet() method, which removes it from the array.

Figure 8-11 shows the final result, as rendered within the browser.

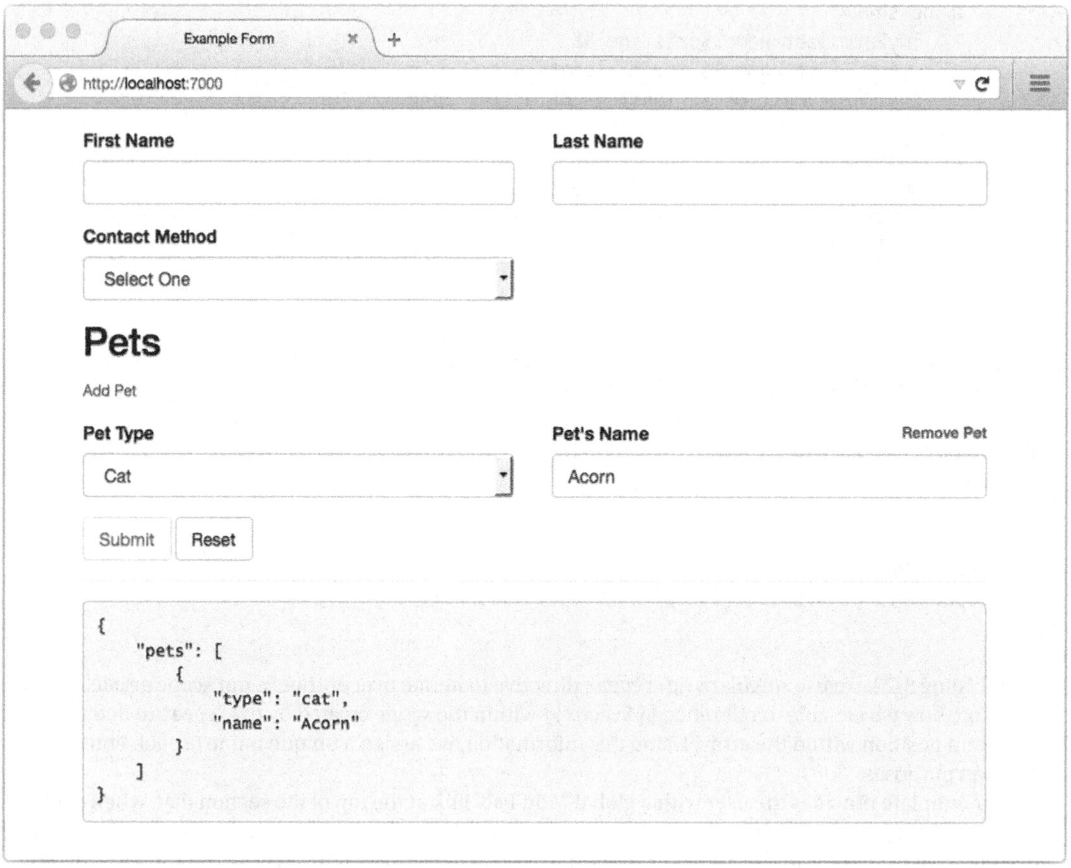

Figure 8-11. *Our final example, as presented to the user*

Summary

At the start of this chapter, we took a moment to compare the traditional, "imperative" approach to development with the "declarative" approach favored by Angular. While each approach has its pros and cons, it's hard to deny that Angular's approach is particularly well suited to solving problems associated with form development. This is not a coincidence.

Over time, Angular has slowly evolved into a framework capable of supporting large applications, but that was not its original intent. Angular's original focus was in fact on form development, as one of the co-creators behind Angular, Miško Hevery, readily admits. This is an important fact to be aware of, because it speaks to the types of projects that Angular is particularly well suited for (as well as those for which more appropriate alternatives may exist).

Angular has attracted a tremendous amount of commentary, mostly positive, since its initial release. The framework's implementation of directives and dependency injection has had a drastic impact on the landscape of client-side development and has raised great questions as to what developers should be expecting from similar frameworks.

That said, the number of developers with valid criticisms of the framework has been steadily increasing for some time. The bulk of this criticism revolves around performance concerns related to Angular's use of so-called "dirty checking" as part of its implementation of two-way data binding. This criticism is fair, because Angular's implementation of two-way data binding *is* inefficient. This author's experience, however, is that Angular's performance is more than adequate for the vast majority of use cases for which it was designed. At the time of this book's publication, a major rewrite (version 2.0) was also underway, which should address many, if not all, of these concerns.

If you are currently wondering whether Angular is a good fit for your project, there is no simple "yes" or "no" answer; it depends entirely upon your specific needs. Generally speaking, however, I am a big fan. Web-based applications are growing more complex and feature-rich by the day. Developers can only create and maintain such applications when they have tools that allow them to abstract complexity behind simple interfaces. Through the use of tools such as directives, Angular extends this well-understood concept to the DOM in very exciting ways.

Related Resources

- AngularJS: `https://angularjs.org/`

CHAPTER 9

Kraken

An organization's ability to learn, and translate that learning into action rapidly, is the ultimate competitive advantage.

—Jack Welch

As development platforms go, Node is still the new kid on the block. But as many well-known and respected organizations will attest, the benefits afforded by JavaScript as a server-side language have already had a tremendous impact on the manner in which they develop and deploy software. Among the many accolades for Node, Michael Yormark, Project Manager at Dow Jones, has proclaimed "The simple truth is Node has reinvented the way we create websites. Developers build critical functionality in days, not weeks." (https://www.joyent.com/blog/the-node-firm-and-joyent-offer-node-js-training)

Kiran Prasad, Director of Mobile Engineering at LinkedIn, has stated "On the server side, our entire mobile software stack is completely built in Node. One reason was scale. The second is Node showed us huge performance gains." (https://nodejs.org/download/docs/v0.6.7/)

Node is certainly generating some rather large waves in the development community, especially when you consider its relatively young age. All that said, however, let's be clear: the platform is far from perfect. JavaScript is beautifully expressive and flexible, but it's also flexible in a way that is easily abused. While Node-based projects enjoy rapid development cycles and impressive performance gains, they frequently suffer at the hands of an overall lack of convention both within the language itself and throughout the development community as a whole. While this problem may not be obvious within small, centralized development teams, it can quickly rear its head as teams grow in size and distribution—just ask Jeff Harrell, Director of Engineering at PayPal (www.paypal-engineering.com/2013/11/):

> We especially liked the ubiquity of Express, but found it didn't scale well in multiple development teams. Express is non-prescriptive and allows you to set up a server in whatever way you see fit. This is great for flexibility, but bad for consistency in large teams... Over time we saw patterns emerge as more teams picked up node.js and turned those into Kraken.js; it's not a framework in itself, but a convention layer on top of express that allows it to scale to larger development organizations. We wanted our engineers to focus on building their applications and not just focus on setting up their environments.

This chapter will introduce you to Kraken, a secure and scalable layer for Express-based applications brought to you by the developers at PayPal. Topics covered within this chapter include

- Environment-aware configuration
- Configuration-based middleware registration
- Structured route registration
- The Dust template engine
- Internationalization and localization
- Enhanced security techniques

■ **Note**   Kraken builds on the already firm foundation of Express, the minimalist web framework for Node whose API has become the de facto standard for frameworks in this category. As a result, this chapter assumes the reader already has a basic, working familiarity with Express. Portions of this chapter also discuss concepts covered in this book's chapters on Grunt, Yeoman, and Knex/Bookshelf. If you are unfamiliar with these subjects, you may wish to read those chapters before you continue.

Environment-Aware Configuration

As applications are developed, tested, staged, and deployed, they naturally progress through a series of corresponding environments, each requiring its own unique set of configuration rules. For example, consider Figure 9-1, which illustrates the process by which an application moves through a continuous integration and delivery deployment pipeline.

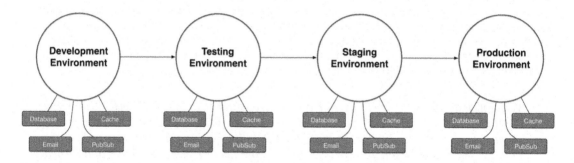

Figure 9-1. *Application that requires unique settings based on its environment*

As the application in Figure 9-1 progresses through each environment, the settings that tell it how to connect to the various external services on which it relies must change accordingly. Kraken's confit library provides developers with a standard convention for accomplishing this goal by offering a simple, environment-aware configuration layer for Node applications.

Confit operates by loading a default JSON configuration file (typically named config.json). Confit then attempts to load an additional configuration file based on the value of the NODE_ENV environment variable. If an environment-specific configuration file is found, any settings it specifies are recursively merged with those defined within the default configuration.

This chapter's `confit-simple` project provides a simple application that relies on `confit` for determining its configuration. Listing 9-1 demonstrates the process by which `confit` is initialized, while Listing 9-2 shows the contents of the project's `/config` folder, from which `confit` is instructed to search for configuration files.

Listing 9-1. Initializing confit

```
// confit-simple/index.js

var confit = require('confit');
var prettyjson = require('prettyjson');
var path = require('path');
var basedir = path.join(__dirname, 'config');

confit(basedir).create(function(err, config) {
    if (err) {
        console.log(err);
        process.exit();
    }
    console.log(prettyjson.render({
        'email': config.get('email'),
        'cache': config.get('cache'),
        'database': config.get('database')
    }));
});
```

Listing 9-2. Contents of the `/config` Folder

```
// Default configuration
// confit-simple/config/config.json

{
    // SMTP server settings
    "email": {
        "hostname": "email.mydomain.com",
        "username": "user",
        "password": "pass",
        "from": "My Application <noreply@myapp.com>"
    },
    "cache": {
        "redis": {
            "hostname": "cache.mydomain.com",
            "password": "redis"
        }
    }
}
```

```
// Development configuration
// confit-simple/config/development.json

{
    "database": {
        "postgresql": {
            "hostname": "localhost",
            "username": "postgres",
            "password": "postgres",
            "database": "myapp"
        }
    },
    "cache": {
        "redis": {
            "hostname": "localhost",
            "password": "redis"
        }
    }
}
```

```
// Production configuration
// confit-simple/config/production.json

{
    "database": {
        "postgresql": {
            "hostname": "db.myapp.com",
            "username": "postgres",
            "password": "super-secret-password",
            "database": "myapp"
        }
    },
    "cache": {
        "redis": {
            "hostname": "redis.myapp.com",
            "password": "redis"
        }
    }
}
```

Before continuing, notice that our project's default configuration file provides connection settings for an e-mail server under the email property, while neither of the project's environment-specific configuration files provides such information. In contrast, the default configuration provides connection settings for a Redis cache server under the nested cache:redis property, while both of the environment-specific configurations provide overriding information for this property.

Notice also that the default configuration file includes a comment above the email property. Comments, which are *not* part of the JSON specification, would normally result in an error being thrown if we attempted to use Node's require() method to parse the contents of this file. Confit, however, will strip out such comments before attempting to parse the file, allowing us to embed comments within our configuration as needed.

Listing 9-3 shows the output that is logged to the console when the project is run with the NODE_ENV environment variable set to development.

Listing 9-3. Running the confit-simple Project in development Mode

```
$ export NODE_ENV=development && node index

email:
  hostname: email.mydomain.com
  username: user
  password: pass
  from:     My Application <noreply@myapp.com>
cache:
  redis:
    hostname: localhost
    password: redis
database:
  postgresql:
    hostname: localhost
    username: postgres
    password: postgres
    database: myapp
```

■ **Note**　In Listing 9-3, $ export NODE_ENV=development is run from the terminal to set the value of the NODE_ENV environment variable. This command applies only to Unix and Unix-like systems (including OS X). Windows users will instead need to run $ set NODE_ENV=development. It's also important to remember that if the NODE_ENV environment variable is not set, confit will assume the application is running in the development environment.

As you can see in Listing 9-3, confit compiled our project's configuration object by merging the contents of the config/development.json environment configuration file with the default config/config.json file, giving priority to any settings specified in development.json. As a result, our configuration object inherited the email settings that only exist in config.json, along with the cache and database settings defined within the configuration file for the development environment. In Listing 9-1, these settings are accessed through the use of the configuration object's get() method.

■ **Note**　In addition to accessing top-level configuration settings (e.g., database, as shown in Listing 9-1), our configuration object's get() method can also be used to access deeply nested configuration settings using: as a delimiter. For example, we could have referenced the project's postgresql settings directly with config.get('database:postgresql').

In Listing 9-4, we run the confit-simple project again, only this time we set the NODE_ENV environment variable with a value of production. As expected, the output shows that our configuration object inherited the email property from config.json, while also inheriting the cache and database properties from production.json.

Listing 9-4. Running the `confit-simple` Project in production Mode

```
$ export NODE_ENV=production && node index

email:
  hostname: email.mydomain.com
  username: user
  password: pass
  from:     My Application <noreply@myapp.com>
cache:
  redis:
    hostname: redis.myapp.com
    password: redis
database:
  postgresql:
    hostname: db.myapp.com
    username: postgres
    password: super-secret-password
    database: myapp
```

Shortstop Handlers

Confit is designed for processing JSON configuration files, as previous examples have shown. As a configuration format, JSON is easy to work with, but it can occasionally leave a bit to be desired in terms of flexibility. Confit helpfully makes up for this shortcoming with support for plugins that it refers to as "shortstop handlers." By way of an example, consider Listing 9-5, in which the two shortstop handlers included within `confit`'s core library, import and config, are used.

Listing 9-5. Demonstrating the Use of the `import` and `config` Shortstop Handlers

```
// confit-shortstop/config/config.json

{
    // The `import` handler allows us to set a property's value to the contents
    // of the specified JSON configuration file.
    "app": "import:./app",
    // The `config` handler allows us to set a property's value to that of the
    // referenced property. Note the use of the `.` character as a delimiter,
    // in this instance.
    "something_else": "config:app.base_url"
}

// confit-shortstop/config/app.json

{
    // The title of the application
    "title": "My Demo Application",
    // The base URL at which the web client can be reached
    "base_url": "https://myapp.com",
    // The base URL at which the API can be reached
    "base_api_url": "https://api.myapp.com"
}
```

Listing 9-6 shows the output that is printed to the console when this chapter's confit-shortstop project is run. In this example, the import shortstop handler has allowed us to populate the app property with the contents of a separate JSON file, making it possible for us to break down particularly large configuration files into smaller and more easily manageable components. The config handler has allowed us to set a configuration value by referencing a preexisting value in another section.

Listing 9-6. Output of This Chapter's confit-shortstop Project

```
$ node index.js

app:
  title:           My Demo Application
  base_url:        https://myapp.com
  base_api_url:    https://api.myapp.com
something_else:    https://myapp.com
```

While confit itself only includes support for the two shortstop handlers that we've just covered (import and config), several additional handlers that are quite useful can be found in the shortstop-handlers module. Let's take a look at four examples.

The main script (index.js) from this chapter's confit-shortstop-extras project is shown in Listing 9-7. This script largely mirrors the one we've already seen in Listing 9-1, with a few minor differences. In this example, additional handlers are imported from the shortstop-handlers module. Also, instead of instantiating confit by passing the path to our project's config folder (basedir), we pass an object of options. Within this object, we continue to specify a value for basedir, but we also pass a protocols object, providing confit with references to the additional shortstop handlers we'd like to use.

Listing 9-7. index.js Script from the confit-shortstop-extras Project

```
// confit-shortstop-extras/index.js

var confit = require('confit');
var handlers = require('shortstop-handlers');
var path = require('path');
var basedir = path.join(__dirname, 'config');
var prettyjson = require('prettyjson');

confit({
    'basedir': basedir,
    'protocols': {
        // The `file` handler allows us to set a property's value to the contents
        // of an external (non-JSON) file. By default, the contents of the file
        // will be loaded as a Buffer.
        'file': handlers.file(basedir /* Folder from which paths should be resolved */, {
            'encoding': 'utf8' // Convert Buffers to UTF-8 strings
        }),
        // The `require` handler allows us to set a property's value to that
        // exported from a module.
        'require': handlers.require(basedir),
        // The `glob` handler allows us to set a property's value to an array
        // containing files whose names match a specified pattern
        'glob': handlers.glob(basedir),
```

```
        // The path handler allows us to resolve relative file paths
        'path': handlers.path(basedir)
    }
}).create(function(err, config) {
    if (err) {
        console.log(err);
        process.exit();
    }
    console.log(prettyjson.render({
        'app': config.get('app'),
        'something_else': config.get('something_else'),
        'ssl': config.get('ssl'),
        'email': config.get('email'),
        'images': config.get('images')
    }));
});
```

In this example, four additional shortstop handlers (imported from the shortstop-handlers module) are used:

- file: Sets a property using the contents of a specified file

- require: Sets a property using the exported value of a Node module (particularly useful for dynamic values that can only be determined at runtime)

- glob: Sets a property to an array containing files whose names match a specified pattern

- path: Sets a property to the absolute path of a referenced file

Listing 9-8 shows the default configuration file for this project. Finally, Listing 9-9 shows the output that is printed to the console when this project is run.

Listing 9-8. Default Configuration File for the confit-shortstop-extras Project

```
// confit-shortstop-extras/config/config.json

{
    "app": "import:./app",
    "something_else": "config:app.base_url",
    "ssl": {
        "certificate": "file:./certificates/server.crt",
     "certificate_path": "path:./certificates/server.crt"
    },
    "email": "require:./email",
    "images": "glob:../public/images/**/*.jpg"
}
```

Listing 9-9. Output from the `confit-shortstop-extras` Project

```
$ export NODE_ENV=development && node index

app:
  title:        My Demo Application
  base_url:     https://myapp.com
  base_api_url: https://api.myapp.com
something_else: https://myapp.com
ssl:
  certificate_path: /opt/confit-shortstop-extras/config/certificates/server.crt
  certificate:
    """

    -----BEGIN CERTIFICATE-----
    MIIDnjCCAoYCCQDy8G1RKCEz4jANBgkqhkiG9woBAQUFADCBkDELMAkGA1UEBhMC
    VVMxEjAQBgNVBAgTCVRlbm5lc3NlZTESMBAGA1UEBxMJTmFzaHZpbGxlMSEwHwYD
    VQQKExhJbnRlcm5ldCBXaWRnaXRzIFB0eSBMdGQxFDASBgNVBAMUCyoubXlhcHAu
    Y29tMSAwHgYJKoZIhvcNAQkBFhFzdXBwb3J0QG15YXBwLmNvbTAeFw0xNTAOMTkw
    MDA4MzRaFw0xNjAOMTgwMDA4MzRaMIGQMQswCQYDVQQGEwJVUzESMBAGA1UECBMJ
    VGVubmVzc2VlMRIwEAYDVQQHEwlOYXNodmlsbGUxITAfBgNVBAoTGEludGVybmVo
    IFdpZGdpdHMgUHR5IEx0ZDEUMBIGA1UEAxQLKi5teWFwcC5jb20xIDAeBgkqhkiG
    9woBCQEWEXN1cHBvcnRAbXlhcHAuY29tMIIBIjANBgkqhkiG9woBAQEFAAOCAQ8A
    MIIBCgKCAQEAyBFxMVlMjP7VCU5w7OokfJX/oEytrQIl1ZOAXnErryQQWwZpHOlu
    ZhTuZ8sBJmMBH3jju+rx4C2dFlXxWDRp8nYt+qfd1aiBKjYxMda2QMwXviTOTd9b
    kPFBCaPQpMrzexwTwK/edoaxzqs/IxMs+n1PfvpuwOuPk6UbwFwWc8UQSWrmbGJw
    UEfs1X9kOSvt85IdrdQ1hQP2fBhHvt/xVVPfi1ZW1yBrWscVHBOJO4RyZSGclayg
    7LP+VHMvkvNmOau/cmCWThHtRt3aXhxAztgkI9IT2G4B9R+7ni8eXw5TLl65bhr1
    Gt7fMK2HnXclPtd3+vy9EnM+XqYXahXFGwIDAQABMAOGCSqGSIb3DQEBBQUAA4IB
    AQDH+QmuWkOBx1kqUoL1Qxtqgf7s81eKoW5X3Tr4ePFXQbwmCZKHEudC98XckI2j
    qGA/SViBr+nbofq6ptnBhAoYVOIQd4YT3qvO+m3otGQ7NQkO2HwD3OUG9khHe2mG
    k8Z7pFOpwu3lbTGKadiJsJSsS1fJGs9hy2vSzRulgOZozT3HJ+2SJpiwy7QAROaF
    jqMC+HcP38zZkTWj1sO45HRCU1HdPjroU3oJtupiU+HAmNpf+vdQnxS6aM5nzc7G
    tZq74ketSxEYXTU8gjfMlR4gBewfPmu2KGuHNV51GAjWgm9wLfPFvMMYjcIEPB3k
    Mla9+pYx1YvXiyJmOnUwsaop
    -----END CERTIFICATE-----

    """
email:
  hostname: smtp.myapp.com
  username: user
  password: pass
  from:      My Application <noreply@myapp.com>
images:
  - /opt/confit-shortstop-extras/public/images/cat1.jpg
  - /opt/confit-shortstop-extras/public/images/cat2.jpg
  - /opt/confit-shortstop-extras/public/images/cat3.jpg
```

Configuration-Based Middleware Registration

Express processes incoming HTTP requests by pushing them through a series of configurable "middleware" functions, as shown in Figure 9-2.

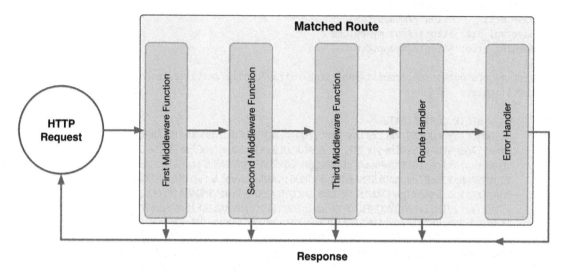

Figure 9-2. *Series of Express middleware calls*

At each step of this process, the active middleware function has the ability to

- Modify the incoming request object

- Modify the outgoing response object

- Execute additional code

- Close the request-response cycle

- Call the next middleware function in the series

By way of an example, consider Listing 9-10, which shows a simple Express application that relies on three middleware modules: morgan, cookie-parser, and ratelimit-middleware. As this application processes incoming HTTP requests, the following steps occur:

1. The morgan module logs the request to the console.

2. The cookie-parser module parses data from the request's Cookie header and assigns it to the request object's cookies property.

3. The ratelimit-middleware module rate-limits clients that attempt to access the application too frequently.

4. Finally, the appropriate route handler is called.

Listing 9-10. Express Application That Relies on Three Middleware Modules

```
// middleware1/index.js

var express = require('express');
// Logs incoming requests
var morgan = require('morgan');
// Populates `req.cookies` with data parsed from the `Cookie` header
var cookieParser = require('cookie-parser');
// Configurable API rate-limiter
var rateLimit = require('ratelimit-middleware');

var app = express();
app.use(morgan('combined'));
app.use(cookieParser());
app.use(rateLimit({
    'burst': 10,
    'rate': 0.5,
    'ip': true
}));

app.get('/animals', function(req, res, next) {
    res.send(['squirrels', 'aardvarks', 'zebras', 'emus']);
});

app.listen(7000);
```

This approach provides developers with a considerable degree of flexibility, allowing them to execute their own logic at any point during the request-response cycle. It also allows Express to maintain a relatively small footprint by delegating responsibility for performing nonessential tasks to third-party middleware modules. But as flexible as this approach is, it can also prove troublesome to manage as applications and the teams that develop them grow in size and complexity.

Kraken's meddleware module simplifies middleware management by providing a configuration-based middleware registration process for Express applications. In doing so, it provides developers with a standardized approach for specifying which middleware modules an Express application should rely on, in what order they should be loaded, and the options that should be passed to each. Listing 9-11 shows an updated version of the previous example, in which the meddleware module manages the registration of all middleware functions.

Listing 9-11. Configuration-based Middleware Registration with the meddleware Module

```
// middleware2/index.js

var express = require('express');
var confit = require('confit');
var meddleware = require('meddleware');
var app = express();
var path = require('path');
```

```
confit(path.join(__dirname, 'config')).create(function(err, config) {
    app.use(meddleware(config.get('middleware')));
    app.get('/animals', function(req, res, next) {
        res.send(['squirrels', 'aardvarks', 'zebras', 'emus']);
    });
    app.listen(7000);
});


// middleware2/config/config.json

{
    "middleware": {
        "morgan": {
            // Toggles the middleware module on / off
            "enabled": true,
            // Specifies the order in which middleware should be registered
            "priority": 10,
            "module": {
                // The name of an installed module (or path to a module file)
                "name": "morgan",
                // Arguments to be passed to the module's factory function
                "arguments": ["combined"]
            }
        },
        "cookieParser": {
            "enabled": true,
            "priority": 20,
            "module": {
                "name": "cookie-parser"
            }
        },
        "rateLimit": {
            "enabled": true,
            "priority": 30,
            "module": {
                "name": "ratelimit-middleware",
                "arguments": [{
                    "burst": 10,
                    "rate": 0.5,
                    "ip": true
                }]
            }
        }
    }
}
```

With the help of Kraken's meddleware module, all aspects of third-party middleware management within this application have been moved from code to standardized configuration files. The result is an application that is not only more organized, but also easier to understand and modify.

Event Notifications

As middleware functions are registered with Express via the `meddleware` module, corresponding events are emitted by the application, providing developers with an easy method for determining what middleware functions are being loaded and in what order (see Listing 9-12).

Listing 9-12. Events Are Emitted As Middleware s Registered via the `meddleware` Module

```
var express = require('express');
var confit = require('confit');
var meddleware = require('meddleware');
var app = express();
var path = require('path');

confit(path.join(__dirname, 'config')).create(function(err, config) {

    // Listening to all middleware registrations
    app.on('middleware:before', function(data) {
        console.log('Registering middleware: %s', data.config.name);
    });

    // Listening for a specific middleware registration event
    app.on('middleware:before:cookieParser', function(data) {
        console.log('Registering middleware: %s', data.config.name);
    });

    app.on('middleware:after', function(data) {
        console.log('Registered middleware: %s', data.config.name);
    });

    app.on('middleware:after:cookieParser', function(data) {
        console.log('Registered middleware: %s', data.config.name);
    });

    app.use(meddleware(config.get('middleware')));

    app.get('/animals', function(req, res, next) {
        res.send(['squirrels', 'aardvarks', 'zebras', 'emus']);
    });

    app.listen(7000);

});
```

Structured Route Registration

In the previous section, you learned how Kraken's `meddleware` module can simplify middleware function registration by moving the logic required for loading and configuring those functions into standardized JSON configuration files. In much the same way, Kraken's `enrouten` module applies the same concept to bring structure where there often is none to be found—Express routes.

Simple Express applications with a small number of routes can often make due with a single module in which every available route is defined. However, as applications gradually grow in depth and complexity, such an organizational structure (or lack thereof) can quickly become unwieldy. Enrouten solves this problem by providing three approaches with which Express routes can be defined in a consistent, structured fashion.

Index Configuration

Using enrouten's index configuration option, the path to a single module can be specified. This module will then be loaded and passed an Express Router instance that has been mounted to the root path. This option provides developers with the simplest method for defining routes, as it does not enforce any specific type of organizational structure. While this option provides a good starting point for new applications, care must be taken not to abuse it. This option is often used in combination with enrouten's directory and routes configuration options, which we will cover shortly.

Listing 9-13 shows a simple Express application whose routes are configured with the help of confit, meddleware, and enrouten, along with the accompanying confit configuration file. Listing 9-14 shows the contents of the module that is passed to enrouten's index option. Subsequent examples within this section will build on this example.

Listing 9-13. Express Application Configured with confit, meddleware, and enrouten

```
// enrouten-index/index.js

var express = require('express');
var confit = require('confit');
var handlers = require('shortstop-handlers');
var meddleware = require('meddleware');
var path = require('path');
var configDir = path.join(__dirname, 'config');
var app = express();

confit({
    'basedir': configDir,
    'protocols': {
        'path': handlers.path(configDir),
        'require': handlers.require(configDir)
    }
}).create(function(err, config) {
    app.use(meddleware(config.get('middleware')));
    app.listen(7000);
    console.log('App is available at: http://localhost:7000');
});

// enrouten-index/config/config.json

{
    "middleware": {
        "morgan": {
            "enabled": true,
            "priority": 10,
            "module": {
```

```
                "name": "morgan",
                "arguments": ["combined"]
            }
        },
        "enrouten": {
            "enabled": true,
            "priority": 30,
            "module": {
                "name": "express-enrouten",
                "arguments": [
                    {
                        "index": "path:../routes/index"
                    }
                ]
            }
        }
    }
}
```

Listing 9-14. Contents of the Module Passed to Enrouten's index Option

```
// enrouten-index/routes/index.js

module.exports = function(router) {

    router.route('/')
    .get(function(req, res, next) {
        res.send('Hello, world.');
    });

    router.route('/api/v1/colors')
    .get(function(req, res, next) {
        res.send([
        'blue', 'green', 'red', 'orange', 'white'
        ]);
    });

};
```

Directory Configuration

Listing 9-15 demonstrates the use of enrouten's directory configuration option. When set, enrouten will recursively scan the contents of the specified folder, searching for modules that export a function accepting a single argument. For each module it finds, enrouten will pass an Express Router instance that has been mounted to a path predetermined by that module's location within the directory structure—a "convention over configuration" approach.

Listing 9-15. Setting Enrouten's directory Configuration Option

```
// enrouten-directory/config/config.json

{
    "middleware": {
        "enrouten": {
            "enabled": true,
            "priority": 10,
            "module": {
                "name": "express-enrouten",
                "arguments": [{ "directory": "path:../routes" }]
            }
        }
    }
}
```

Figure 9-3 shows the structure of this project's /routes folder, while Listing 9-16 shows the contents of the /routes/api/v1/accounts/index.js module. Based on this module's location within the /routes folder, the URLs for each route that it defines will be prefixed with /api/v1/accounts.

```
Tims-MacBook-Pro:routes tim$ tree .
.
└── api
    └── v1
        ├── accounts
        │   └── index.js
        └── users
            └── index.js

4 directories, 2 files
Tims-MacBook-Pro:routes tim$
```

Figure 9-3. Structure of This Project's /routes Folder

Listing 9-16. The /api/v1/accounts Controller

```
// enrouten-directory/routes/api/v1/accounts/index.js

var _ = require('lodash');
var path = require('path');

module.exports = function(router) {

    var accounts = require(path.join(APPROOT, 'models', 'accounts'));

    /**
     * @route /api/v1/accounts
     */
    router.route('/')
        .get(function(req, res, next) {
            res.send(accounts);
        });
```

```
/**
 * @route /api/v1/accounts/:account_id
 */
router.route('/:account_id')
    .get(function(req, res, next) {
    var account = _.findWhere(accounts, {
        'id': parseInt(req.params.account_id, 10)
    });
    if (!account) return next(new Error('Account not found'));
        res.send(account);
    });

};
```

Routes Configuration

Enrouten's directory configuration option provides an approach that favors "convention over configuration" by automatically determining the structure of an application's API based on the layout of a specified folder. This approach provides a quick and easy method for structuring Express routes in an organized and consistent way. However, complex applications may eventually come to find this approach to be rather confining.

Applications with APIs that feature a number of complex, deeply nested routes will likely find greater benefit from enrouten's routes configuration option, which allows developers to create completely separate modules for *each* of the application's routes. API endpoints, methods, handlers, and route-specific middleware are then specified within configuration files—an organized approach that allows for the greatest degree of flexibility, at the expense of being slightly more verbose.

Listing 9-17 shows an excerpt from the configuration file for this chapter's enrouten-routes project. Here we pass an array of objects to enrouten's routes configuration option, the entries of which describe the various routes to be made available by Express. Note that in addition to specifying a route, HTTP method, and handler, each entry also has the option of specifying an array of route-specific middleware functions. As a result, this application is able to apply a middleware function responsible for authorizing incoming requests on a route-by-route basis. As shown in Listing 9-17, the auth middleware function is *not* applied to the route at which users initially sign in, allowing them to sign in before making subsequent requests.

Listing 9-17. Specifying Individual Routes via Enrouten's routes Configuration Option

```
// enrouten-routes/config/config.json (excerpt)

"arguments": [{
    "index": "path:../routes",
    "routes": [
        {
            "path": "/api/v1/session",
            "method": "POST",
            "handler": "require:../routes/api/v1/session/create"
        },
    {
        "path": "/api/v1/session",
        "method": "DELETE",
        "handler": "require:../routes/api/v1/session/delete",
        "middleware": [
```

```
            "require:../middleware/auth"
        ]
    },
        {
          "path": "/api/v1/users",
          "method": "GET",
          "handler": "require:../routes/api/v1/users/list",
          "middleware": [
              "require:../middleware/auth"
          ]
        },
        // ...
    ]
}]
```

Listing 9-18 shows the contents of the module responsible for handling incoming GET requests to this application's /api/v1/users route. The module exports a single function, which accepts the standard req, res, next Express route handler signature.

Listing 9-18. The /routes/api/v1/users/list Route Handler

```
var models = require('../../../../lib/models');

module.exports = function(req, res, next) {

    models.User.fetchAll()
        .then(function(users) {
            res.send(users);
        })
        .catch(next);

};
```

Dust Templates

Many popular JavaScript template engines (e.g., Mustache and Handlebars) tout themselves as being "logic-less"—an attribute that describes their ability to help developers maintain a clear separation of concerns between an application's business logic and its presentation layer. When properly maintained, this separation makes it possible for significant changes to occur within the interface that users are presented with, while requiring minimal (if any) accompanying changes behind the scenes (and vice versa).

So-called "logic-less" template engines accomplish this goal by enforcing a strict set of rules that prevents developers from creating what is often referred to as "spaghetti code," a tangled mess that combines code with presentation in a way that is hard to grasp and even harder to unravel. Anyone who has ever had to deal with a PHP script resembling that shown in Listing 9-19 will immediately grasp the importance of maintaining a layer of separation between these two concerns.

Listing 9-19. Spaghetti Code, an Unmaintainable Mess

```php
<?php

print "<!DOCTYPE html><head><title>";
$result = mysql_query("SELECT * FROM settings") or die(mysql_error());
print $result[0]["title"] . "</title></head><body><table>";
print "<thead><tr><th>First Name</th><th>Last Name</th></tr></thead><tbody>";
$users = mysql_query("SELECT * FROM users") or die(mysql_error());
while ($row = mysql_fetch_assoc($users)) {
    print "<tr><td>" . $row["first_name"] . "</td><td>" . $row["last_name"] . "</td></tr>";
}
print "</tbody></table></body></html>";

?>
```

Logic-less template engines attempt to prevent developers from creating spaghetti code by banning the use of logic within an application's views. Such templates are typically capable of referencing values within a provided payload of information, iterating through arrays, and toggling specific portions of their content on and off based on simple boolean logic.

Unfortunately, this rather heavy-handed approach often brings about the very problems it hoped to prevent, albeit in an unexpected way. Although logic-less template engines such as Handlebars prevent the use of logic within templates themselves, they do not negate the need for that logic to exist in the first place. The logic required for preparing data for template use must exist *somewhere*, and more often than not, the use of logic-less template engines results in presentation-related logic spilling over into the business layer.

Dust, which is the JavaScript template engine favored by Kraken, seeks to solve this problem by taking an approach that is better thought of as "less-logic" rather than strictly "logic-less." By allowing developers to embed slightly more advanced logic within their templates in the form of "helpers," Dust allows presentation logic to remain where it belongs, in the *presentation* layer, rather than the *business* layer.

Context and References

When using Dust templates, two primary components come into play: the template itself and an (optional) object literal containing any data to be referenced from within the template. In Listing 9-20, this process is demonstrated by an Express application that has specified Dust as its rendering engine. Note the use of the adaro module in this example. The adaro module serves as a convenient wrapper for Dust, abstracting away some additional setup that would otherwise be necessary to integrate Dust with Express. It also includes some convenient helper functions by default that we will be covering later in the chapter.

Listing 9-20. Express Application Using Dust As Its Rendering Engine

```javascript
// dust-simple/index.js

var express = require('express');
var adaro = require('adaro');
var app = express();

/**
 * By default, Dust will cache the contents of an application's templates as they are
 * loaded. In a production environment, this is usually the preferred behavior.
 * This behavior will be disabled in this chapter's examples, allowing you to modify
```

```
* templates and see the result without having to restart Express.
*/
app.engine('dust', adaro.dust({
    'cache': false
}));

app.set('view engine', 'dust');
app.use('/', express.static('./public'));

var data = {
    'report_name': 'North American Countries',
    'languages': ['English', 'Spanish'],
    'misc': {
        'total_population': 565000000
    },
    'countries': [
        {
            'name': 'United States',
            'population': 319999999,
            'english': true,
            'capital': { 'name': 'Washington D.C.', 'population': 660000 }
        },
        {
            'name': 'Mexico',
            'population': 118000000,
            'english': false,
            'capital': { 'name': 'Mexico City', 'population': 9000000 }
        },
        {
            'name': 'Canada',
            'population': 35000000,
            'english': true,
            'capital': { 'name': 'Ottawa', 'population': 880000 }
        }
    ]
};

app.get('/', function(req, res, next) {
    res.render('main', data);
});

app.listen(8000);
```

In Listing 9-20, an object literal containing an array of North American countries (referred to by Dust as a "context") is passed to a Dust template, the content of which is shown in Listing 9-21. Within this template, data is referenced by wrapping the desired key within a single pair of curly brackets. Nested properties can also be referenced through the use of dot notation ({misc.total_population}).

Listing 9-21. Accompanying main Dust Template

```
// dust-simple/views/main.dust

<!DOCTYPE html>
<html lang="en">
<head>
    <meta charset="utf-8">
    <meta http-equiv="X-UA-Compatible" content="IE=edge">
    <meta name="viewport" content="width=device-width, initial-scale=1">
    <title>App</title>
    <link href="/css/style.css" rel="stylesheet">
</head>
<body>
    {! Dust comments are created using this format. Data is referenced by wrapping the
    desired key within a single pair of curly brackets, as shown below. !}
    <h1>{report_name}</h1>
    <table>
        <thead>
            <tr>
                <th>Name</th>
                <th>Population</th>
                <th>Speaks English</th>
                <th>Capital</th>
                <th>Population of Capital</th>
            </tr>
        </thead>
        <tbody>
            {! Templates can loop through iterable objects !}
            {#countries}
            <tr>
                <td>{name}</td>
                <td>{population}</td>
                <td>{?english}Yes{:else}No{/english}</td>
                {#capital}
                    <td>{name}</td>
                    <td>{population}</td>
                {/capital}
            </tr>
            {/countries}
        </tbody>
    </table>
    <h2>Languages</h2>
    <ul>
        {#languages}
        <li>{.}</li>
        {/languages}
    </ul>
    <h2>Total Population: {misc.total_population}</h2>
</body>
</html>
```

Sections

As Dust goes about its rendering process, it fetches referenced data by applying one or more "contexts" to the template in question. The simplest templates have a single context that references the outermost level of the JSON object that was passed. For example, consider the template shown in Listing 9-21, in which two references are used, {report_name} and {misc.total_population}. Dust processes these references by searching for matching properties (starting at the outermost level) within the object shown in Listing 9-20.

Dust sections provide a convenient method by which additional contexts can be created, allowing a template to access nested properties without requiring references that start at the outermost level. For example, consider Listing 9-22, in which a new context, {#misc}...{/misc}, is created, allowing nested properties to be accessed using a shorter syntax.

Listing 9-22. Creating a New Dust Section

```
// Template
<h1>{report_name}</h1>
{#misc}
<p>Total Population: {total_population}</p>
{/misc}


// Rendered Output
<h1>Information About North America</h1>
<p>Total Population: 565000000</p>
```

Iteration

In the previous example, a new Dust section (and corresponding context) was created. As a result, the contents of the new section received direct access to the properties of the object literal that was referenced. In much the same way, Dust sections can also be used to iterate through the entries of an array. Listing 9-23 demonstrates this process by creating a new section that references the countries array. Unlike the section from the previous example, which was applied only once, the {#countries} ... {/countries} section will be applied multiple times, once for each entry within the array that it references.

Listing 9-23. Iterating Through an Array with Sections

```
// Template
{#countries}
{! The current position within the iteration can be referenced at `$idx` !}
{! The size of the object through which we are looping can be referenced at `$len` !}
<tr>
    <td>{name}</td>
    <td>{population}</td>
    <td>{capital.name}</td>
    <td>{capital.population}</td>
</tr>
{/countries}

// Rendered Output
<tr>
    <td>United States</td>
    <td>319999999</td>
```

```
        <td>Washington D.C.</td>
        <td>660000</td>
    </tr>
    <tr>
        <td>Mexico</td>
        <td>118000000</td>
        <td>Mexico City</td>
        <td>9000000</td>
    </tr>
    <tr>
        <td>Canada</td>
        <td>35000000</td>
        <td>Ottawa</td>
        <td>880000</td>
    </tr>
```

Listing 9-24 demonstrates the process by which a template can loop through an array whose entries are primitive data types (i.e., not objects). For each iteration, the value itself can be directly referenced via the {.} syntax.

Listing 9-24. Iterating Through an Array Containing Primitive Data Types

```
// Template
<ul>
    {#languages}<li>{.}</li>{/languages}
</ul>

// Rendered Output
<ul>
    <li>English</li>
    <li>Spanish</li>
</ul>
```

Conditionality

Dust provides built-in support for *conditionally* rendering content, based on whether a simple truth test is passed. The template shown in Listing 9-25 demonstrates this concept by rendering the text "Yes" or "No" based on whether each country's english property references a "truthy" value.

Listing 9-25. Applying Conditionality Within a Dust Template

```
// Template
{#countries}
<tr>
    <td>{name}</td>
    <td>{?english}Yes{:else}No{/english}</td>
    {!
        The opposite logic can be applied as shown below:
        <td>{^english}No{:else}Yes{/english}</td>
    !}
</tr>
```

```
{/countries}

// Rendered Output
<tr>
    <td>United States</td>
    <td>Yes</td>
</tr>
<tr>
    <td>Mexico</td>
    <td>No</td>
</tr>
<tr>
    <td>Canada</td>
    <td>Yes</td>
</tr>
```

■ **Note**   When applying conditionality within a template, it is important to understand the rules that Dust
will apply as it determines the "truthiness" of a property. Empty strings, boolean false, empty arrays, null, and
undefined are all considered to be false. The number 0, empty objects, and string-based representations for
"0", "null", "undefined", and "false" are all considered to be true.

Partials

One of Dust's most powerful features, partials, allows developers to include templates *within* other templates.
As a result, complex documents can be broken down into smaller components (i.e., "partials") that are easier
to manage and reuse. A simple example that demonstrates this process is shown in Listing 9-26.

Listing 9-26. Dust Template That References an External Template (i.e., "Partial")

```
// Main Template
<h1>{report_name}</h1>
<p>Total Population: {misc.total_population}</p>
{>"countries"/}
{!
    In this example, an external template - `countries` - is included by a parent
    template which references it by name (using a string literal that is specified
    within the template itself). Alternatively, the name of the external template
    could have been derived from a value held within the template's context, using
    Dust's support for "dynamic" partials. To do so, we would have wrapped the
    `countries` string in a pair of curly brackets, as shown here:
    {>"{countries}"/}
!}

// "countries" template
{#countries}
<tr>
    <td>{name}</td>
```

```
    <td>{population}</td>
    <td>{capital.name}</td>
    <td>{capital.population}</td>
</tr>
{/countries}

// Rendered Output
<h1>Information About North America</h1>
<p>Total Population: 565000000</p>
<tr>
    <td>United States</td>
    <td>Yes</td>
</tr>
<tr>
    <td>Mexico</td>
    <td>No</td>
</tr>
<tr>
    <td>Canada</td>
    <td>Yes</td>
</tr>
```

Blocks

Consider a commonly encountered scenario in which a complex web application consisting of multiple pages is created. Each of these pages displays a unique set of content, while at the same time sharing common elements, such as headers and footers, with the other pages. With the help of Dust blocks, developers can define these shared elements in a single location. Afterward, templates that wish to inherit from them can, while also retaining the ability to overwrite their content when necessary.

Let's take a look at an example that should help to clarify this point. Listing 9-27 shows the content of a Dust template that defines the overall layout of a site. In this instance, a default page title is specified, {+title}App{/title}, along with an empty placeholder for body content.

Listing 9-27. Dust Block from Which Other Templates Can Inherit

```
// dust-blocks/views/shared/base.dust

<!DOCTYPE html>
<html lang="en">
<head>
    <meta charset="utf-8">
    <meta http-equiv="X-UA-Compatible" content="IE=edge">
    <meta name="viewport" content="width=device-width, initial-scale=1">
    <title>{+title}App{/title}</title>
    <link href="/css/style.css" rel="stylesheet">
</head>
<body>
    {+bodyContent/}
</body>
</html>
```

Listing 9-28 shows the content of a Dust template that inherits from the example presented in Listing 9-27. It does so by first embedding the parent template within itself as a partial ({>"shared/base"/}). Next, it injects content into the {+bodyContent/} placeholder that was defined, {<bodyContent}...{/bodyContent}. In this instance, our template chooses *not* to overwrite the default page title that was specified in our parent template.

Listing 9-28. Dust Template Inheriting from a Block

```
// dust-blocks/views/main.dust
```

```
{>"shared/base"/}
```

```
{<bodyContent}
    <p>Hello, world!</p>
{/bodyContent}
```

Filters

Dust includes several built-in filters that allow a template to modify a value before it is rendered. By way of an example, consider the fact that Dust will automatically HTML escape any values referenced within a template. In other words, if a context were to contain a content key with a value matching that shown here:

```
<script>doBadThings();</script>
```

Dust would automatically render this value as

```
&lt;script&gt;doBadThings()&lt;/script&gt;
```

While the behavior that we see here is typically desired, it is not uncommon to run into situations in which this behavior needs to be disabled. This can be accomplished through the use of a filter:

```
{content|s}
```

In this example, the |s filter disables auto-escaping for the referenced value. Table 9-1 contains a list of the built-in filters provided by Dust.

Table 9-1. List of Built-in Filters Provided by Dust

Filter	Description
s	Disables HTML escaping
h	Forces HTML escaping
j	Forces JavaScript escaping
u	Encodes with encodeURI()
uc	Encodes with encodeURIComponent()
js	Stringifies a JSON literal
jp	Parses a JSON string

Creating Custom Filters

In addition to providing several core filters, Dust also makes it easy for developers to extend this behavior by creating their own custom filters, such as that shown in Listing 9-29. In this example, a custom formatTS filter is created. When applied, this filter will convert a referenced timestamp to a human-readable format (e.g., Jul. 4, 1776).

Listing 9-29. Defining a Custom Dust Filter

```
// dust-filters/index.js

var express = require('express');
var adaro = require('adaro');
var app = express();
var moment = require('moment');

app.engine('dust', adaro.dust({
    'cache': false,
    'helpers': [
        function(dust) {
            dust.filters.formatTS = function(ts) {
                return moment(ts, 'X').format('MMM. D, YYYY');
            };
        }
    ]
}));

app.set('view engine', 'dust');
app.use('/', express.static('./public'));

app.get('/', function(req, res, next) {
    res.render('main', {
        'events': [
            { 'label': 'Moon Landing', 'ts': -14558400 },
            { 'label': 'Fall of Berlin Wall', 'ts': 626616000 },
            { 'label': 'First Episode of Who\'s the Boss', 'ts': 464529600 }
        ]
    });
});

// dust-filters/views/main.dist (excerpt)

<tbody>
    {#events}
    <tr>
        <td>{label}</td>
        <td>{ts|formatTS}</td>
    </tr>
    {/events}
</tbody>
```

Context Helpers

In addition to storing data, Dust contexts are also capable of storing functions (referred to as "context helpers"), the output of which can later be referenced by the templates to which they are passed. In this way, a Dust context can be thought of as more than a simple payload of raw information, but rather as a *view model*, a mediator between an application's business logic and its views, capable of formatting information in the most appropriate manner along the way.

This feature is demonstrated by the example shown in Listing 9-30, in which an application presents the user with a table of servers. Each entry displays a name, along with a message indicating whether each server is online. A header displays the overall health of the system, which is generated by the systemStatus() context helper. Note that the template is able to reference our context helper just as it would any other type of value (e.g., object literals, arrays, numbers, strings).

Listing 9-30. Dust Context Helper

```
// dust-context-helpers1/index.js (excerpt)

app.all('/', function(req, res, next) {
    res.render('main', {
        'servers': [
            { 'name': 'Web Server', 'online': true },
            { 'name': 'Database Server', 'online': true },
            { 'name': 'Email Server', 'online': false }
        ],
        'systemStatus': function(chunk, context, bodies, params) {
            var offlineServers = _.filter(this.servers, { 'online': false });
            return offlineServers.length ? 'Bad' : 'Good';
        }
    });
});
```

```
// dust-context-helpers1/views/main.dust (excerpt)

<h1>System Status: {systemStatus}</h1>
<table>
    <thead><tr><th>Server</th><th>Online</th></tr></thead>
    <tbody>
        {#servers}
            <tr>
                <td>{name}</td>
                <td>{?online}Yes{:else}No{/online}</td>
            </tr>
        {/servers}
    </tbody>
</table>
```

As shown in this example, every Dust context helper receives four arguments: chunk, context, bodies, and params. Let's take a look at a few examples that demonstrate their usage.

chunk

A context helper's chunk argument provides it with access to the current portion of the template being rendered—referred to by Dust as a "chunk." By way of an example, consider Listing 9-31, in which a context helper is paired with default content that is defined within the template. In this example, the systemStatus() context helper can choose to override the chunk's default content, "Unknown," with its own value by calling the chunk.write() method. The helper can indicate that it has chosen to do so by returning chunk as its value.

Listing 9-31. Dust Context Helper Paired with Default Content

```
// dust-context-helpers2/index.js (excerpt)

app.all('/', function(req, res, next) {
    res.render('main', {
        'servers': [
            { 'name': 'Web Server', 'online': true },
            { 'name': 'Database Server', 'online': true },
            { 'name': 'Email Server', 'online': false }
        ],
        'systemStatus': function(chunk, context, bodies, params) {
            if (!this.servers.length) return;
            if (_.filter(this.servers, { 'online': false }).length) {
                return chunk.write('Bad');
            } else {
                return chunk.write('Good');
            }
        }
    });
});
```

```
// dust-context-helpers2/views/main.dust (excerpt)

<h1>System Status: {#systemStatus}Unknown{/systemStatus}</h1>
```

context

The context argument provides context helpers with convenient access to the *active* section of the context, as determined by the template. The template shown in Listing 9-32 demonstrates this by referencing the isOnline() context helper once for every server it has been passed. Each time, the isOnline() helper fetches the value of the active section's online property via context.get().

Listing 9-32. The context Argument Provides Context Helpers with Access to the Active Section

```
// dust-context-helpers3/index.js (excerpt)

app.all('/', function(req, res, next) {
    res.render('main', {
        'servers': [
            { 'name': 'Web Server', 'online': true },
            { 'name': 'Database Server', 'online': true },
            { 'name': 'Email Server', 'online': false }
```

```
        ],
        'systemStatus': function(chunk, context, bodies, params) {
            return _.filter(this.servers, { 'online': false }).length ? 'Bad': 'Good';
        },
        'isOnline': function(chunk, context, bodies, params) {
            return context.get('online') ? 'Yes' : 'No';
        }
    });
});


// dust-context-helpers3/views/main.dust (excerpt)

<h1>System Status: {systemStatus}</h1>
<table>
    <thead><tr><th>Server</th><th>Online</th></tr></thead>
    <tbody>
        {#servers}
            <tr>
                <td>{name}</td>
                <td>{isOnline}</td>
            </tr>
        {/servers}
    </tbody>
</table>
```

bodies

Imagine a scenario in which large portions of a template's content are determined by one or more context helpers. Instead of forcing developers to concatenate strings in an unwieldy fashion, Dust allows such content to remain where it belongs—in the template—available as options from which a context helper can choose to render.

Listing 9-33 demonstrates this by passing four different bodies of content to the description() context helper. The helper's bodies argument provides it with references to this content, which it can then choose to render by passing the appropriate value to chunk.render().

Listing 9-33. Selectively Rendering Portions of a Template via the bodies Argument

```
// dust-context-helpers4/index.js (excerpt)

app.all('/', function(req, res, next) {
    res.render('main', {
        'servers': [
            { 'name': 'Web Server', 'online': true },
            { 'name': 'Database Server', 'online': true },
            { 'name': 'Email Server', 'online': false },
            { 'name': 'IRC Server', 'online': true }
        ],
        'systemStatus': function(chunk, context, bodies, params) {
            return _.filter(this.servers, { 'online': false }).length ? 'Bad': 'Good';
        },
        'isOnline': function(chunk, context, bodies, params) {
```

```
            return context.get('online') ? 'Yes' : 'No';
        },
        'description': function(chunk, context, bodies, params) {
            switch (context.get('name')) {
                case 'Web Server':
                    return chunk.render(bodies.web, context);
                break;
                case 'Database Server':
                    return chunk.render(bodies.database, context);
                break;
                case 'Email Server':
                    return chunk.render(bodies.email, context);
                break;
            }
        }
    });
});

// dust-context-helpers4/index.js (excerpt)

<h1>System Status: {systemStatus}</h1>
<table>
    <thead><tr><th>Server</th><th>Online</th><th>Description</th></tr></thead>
    <tbody>
        {#servers}
            <tr>
                <td>{name}</td>
                <td>{isOnline}</td>
                <td>
                    {#description}
                        {:web}
                            A web server serves content over HTTP.
                        {:database}
                            A database server fetches remotely stored information.
                        {:email}
                            An email server sends and receives messages.
                        {:else}
                            -
                    {/description}
                </td>
            </tr>
        {/servers}
    </tbody>
</table>
```

params

In addition to referencing properties of the context in which it is called (via `context.get()`), a context helper can also access parameters that have been passed to it by a template. The example shown in Listing 9-34 demonstrates this by passing each server's `uptime` property to the `formatUptime()` context helper. In this example, the helper converts the provided value, `params.value`, into a more easily readable form before writing it out to the chunk.

Listing 9-34. Context Helpers Can Receive Parameters via the `params` Argument

```
// dust-context-helpers5/index.js (excerpt)

app.all('/', function(req, res, next) {
    res.render('main', {
        'servers': [
            { 'name': 'Web Server', 'online': true, 'uptime': 722383 },
            { 'name': 'Database Server', 'online': true, 'uptime': 9571 },
            { 'name': 'Email Server', 'online': false, 'uptime': null }
        ],
        'systemStatus': function(chunk, context, bodies, params) {
            return _.filter(this.servers, { 'online': false }).length ? 'Bad': 'Good';
        },
        'formatUptime': function(chunk, context, bodies, params) {
            if (!params.value) return chunk.write('-');
            chunk.write(moment.duration(params.value, 'seconds').humanize());
        }
    });
});
```

```
// dust-context-helpers5/views/main.dust (excerpt)

{#servers}
    <tr>
        <td>{name}</td>
        <td>{?online}Yes{:else}No{/online}</td>
        <td>{#formatUptime value=uptime /}</td>
    </tr>
{/servers}
```

In Listing 9-35, we see a slightly more complex demonstration of context helper parameters at work. In this example, the `parseLocation()` helper receives a string in which context properties are referenced: `value="{name} lives in {location}"`. In order for these references to be correctly interpreted, the parameter must first be evaluated with the help of Dust's `helpers.tap()` method.

Listing 9-35. Parameters That Reference Context Properties Must Be Evaluated

```
// dust-context-helpers6/index.js

var express = require('express');
var adaro = require('adaro');
var app = express();
var morgan = require('morgan');
app.use(morgan('combined'));
var engine = adaro.dust();
var dust = engine.dust;

app.engine('dust', engine);

app.set('view engine', 'dust');
app.use('/', express.static('./public'));

app.all('/', function(req, res, next) {
    res.render('main', {
        'people': [
            { 'name': 'Joe', 'location': 'Chicago' },
            { 'name': 'Mary', 'location': 'Denver' },
            { 'name': 'Steve', 'location': 'Oahu' },
            { 'name': 'Laura', 'location': 'Nashville' }
        ],
        'parseLocation': function(chunk, context, bodies, params) {
            var content = dust.helpers.tap(params.value, chunk, context);
            return chunk.write(content.toUpperCase());
        }
    });
});

app.listen(8000);

// dust-context-helpers6/views/main.dust

{#people}
    <li>{#parseLocation value="{name} lives in {location}" /}</li>
{/people}
```

Asynchronous Context Helpers

Helper functions provide Dust with much of its power and flexibility. They allow a context object to serve as a view model—an intelligent bridge between an application's business logic and its user interface, capable of fetching information and formatting it appropriately for a specific use case before passing it along to one or more views for rendering. But as useful as this is, we've really only begun to scratch the surface in terms of how these helper functions can be applied to powerful effect.

In addition to returning data directly, Dust helper functions are also capable of returning data *asynchronously*, a process that is demonstrated by the example shown in Listing 9-36. Here we create two context helpers, cars() and trucks(). The former returns an array, while the latter returns a promise that *resolves* to an array. From the template's perspective, both of these functions are consumed identically.

Listing 9-36. Helper Functions Can Return Promises

```
// dust-promise1/index.js (excerpt)

app.get('/', function(req, res, next) {
    res.render('main', {
        'cars': function(chunk, context, bodies, params) {
            return ['Nissan Maxima', 'Toyota Corolla', 'Volkswagen Jetta'];
        },
        'trucks': function(chunk, context, bodies, params) {
            return new Promise(function(resolve, reject) {
                resolve(['Chevrolet Colorado', 'GMC Canyon', 'Toyota Tacoma']);
            });
        }
    });
});
```

```
// dust-promise1/views/main.dust (excerpt)

<h1>Cars</h1>
<ul>{#cars}<li>{.}</li>{/cars}</ul>
<h2>Trucks</h1>
<ul>{#trucks}<li>{.}</li>{/trucks}</ul>
```

Dust also provides a convenient method for conditionally displaying content, in the event that a promise is rejected. This process is demonstrated by Listing 9-37.

Listing 9-37. Handling Rejected Promises

```
// dust-promise2/index.js (excerpt)

app.get('/', function(req, res, next) {
    res.render('main', {
        'cars': function(chunk, context, bodies, params) {
            return ['Nissan Maxima', 'Toyota Corolla', 'Volkswagen Jetta'];
        },
        'trucks': function(chunk, context, bodies, params) {
            return new Promise(function(resolve, reject) {
                reject('Unable to fetch trucks.');
            });
        }
    });
});
```

```
// dust-promise2/views/main.dust (excerpt)

<h1>Cars</h1>
<ul>{#cars}<li>{.}</li>{/cars}</ul>
<h2>Trucks</h1>
<ul>{#trucks}
    <li>{.}</li>
    {:error}
    An error occurred. We were unable to get a list of trucks.
{/trucks}</ul>
```

Having the ability to feed information to a template in the form of promises is useful for a number of reasons, but things begin to get much more interesting when this functionality is paired with Dust's streaming interface. To better understand this, consider Listing 9-38, which largely mirrors our previous example. In this instance, however, we take advantage of Dust's streaming interface to push portions of our template down to the client *as they are rendered*, rather than waiting for the entire process to complete.

Listing 9-38. Streaming a Template to the Client As Data Becomes Available

```
// dust-promise2/index.js

var Promise = require('bluebird');
var express = require('express');
var adaro = require('adaro');
var app = express();
var engine = adaro.dust();
var dust = engine.dust;
app.engine('dust', engine);
app.set('view engine', 'dust');
app.use('/', express.static('./public'));

app.get('/', function(req, res, next) {
    dust.stream('views/main', {
        'cars': ['Nissan Maxima', 'Toyota Corolla', 'Volkswagen Jetta'],
        'trucks': function(chunk, context, bodies, params) {
            return new Promise(function(resolve, reject) {
                setTimeout(function() {
                    resolve(['Chevrolet Colorado', 'GMC Canyon', 'Toyota Tacoma']);
                }, 4000);
            });
        }
    }).pipe(res);
});

app.listen(8000);
```

Depending on the complexity of the template in question, the impact this approach can have on user experience can often be dramatic. Rather than forcing users to wait for an entire page to load before they can proceed, this approach allows us to push content down to the client as it becomes available. As a result, the delay that users perceive when accessing an application can often be reduced significantly.

Dust Helpers

In the previous section, we explored how context objects can be extended to include logic that is relevant to a specific view through the use of context helpers. In a similar manner, Dust allows helper functions to be defined at a global level, making them available to all templates without being explicitly defined within their contexts. Dust comes packaged with a number of such helpers. By taking advantage of them, developers can more easily solve many of the challenges that are often encountered when working with stricter, logic-less template solutions.

Listing 9-39 shows an excerpt of the JSON data that will be referenced by the rest of this section's examples.

Listing 9-39. Excerpt of the JSON Data Passed to a Dust Template

```
// dust-logic1/people.json (excerpt)

[{
    "name": "Joe", "location": "Chicago", "age": 27,
    "education": "high_school", "employed": false, "job_title": null
}, {
    "name": "Mary", "location": "Denver", "age": 35,
    "education": "college", "employed": true, "job_title": "Chef"
}]
```

Logic Helpers

Listing 9-40 demonstrates the usage of a Dust logic helper, @eq, with which we can perform a strict comparison between two specified values, key and value. In this example, the first value, job_title, references a property within the current context. The second value, "Chef", is defined as a literal value from within the template.

Listing 9-40. Using a Dust Logic Helper to Conditionally Display Content

```
// dust-logic1/views/main.dust (excerpt)

{#people}
    {@eq key=job_title value="Chef"}
        <p>{name} is a chef. This person definitely knows how to cook.</p>
        {:else}
        <p>{name} is not a chef. This person may or may not know how to cook.</p>
    {/eq}
{/people}
```

Knowing this, imagine a scenario in which we want to perform a strict equality check between two numbers, one of which is referenced as a context property, while the other is specified as a literal from within the template. In order to do so, we must *cast* our literal value to the appropriate type, as shown in Listing 9-41.

Listing 9-41. Casting a Literal Value to the Desired Type

```
{#people}
    {@eq key=age value="27" type="number"}
        <p>{name} is 27 years old.</p>
    {/eq}
{/people}
```

Dust provides a number of logic helpers with which simple comparisons can be made. Their names and descriptions are listed in Table 9-2.

Table 9-2. *Logic Helpers Provided by Dust*

Logic Helper	Description
@eq	Strictly equal to
@ne	Not strictly equal to
@gt	Greater than
@lt	Less than
@gte	Greater than or equal to
@lte	Less than or equal to

Switch Statements

The frequently used @select helper provides a method by which we can mimic switch (...) statements, making it possible for a template to specify *multiple* variations of content based on a specified value (see Listing 9-42).

Listing 9-42. Mimicking a switch Statement with the @select Helper

```
{@gte key=age value=retirement_age}
    <p>{name} has reached retirement age.</p>
    {:else}
        <p>
        {@select key=job_title}
            {@eq value="Chef"}Probably went to culinary school, too.{/eq}
            {@eq value="Professor"}Smarty pants.{/eq}
            {@eq value="Accountant"}Good with numbers.{/eq}
            {@eq value="Astronaut"}Not afraid of heights.{/eq}
            {@eq value="Pilot"}Travels frequently.{/eq}
            {@eq value="Stunt Double"}Fearless.{/eq}
            {! @none serves as a `default` case !}
            {@none}Not sure what I think.{/none}
        {/select}
        </p>
{/gte}
```

Iteration Helpers

Dust provides three useful helpers for tackling problems that are frequently encountered when dealing with iteration. For example, Listing 9-43 demonstrates the use of the @sep helper, with which we can define content that will be rendered for every iteration *except* the last.

Listing 9-43. Ignoring Content During a Loop's Last Iteration with @sep

```
// dust-logic1/views/main.dust (excerpt)
{#people}{name}{@sep}, {/sep}{/people}

// output
Joe, Mary, Wilson, Steve, Laura, Tim, Katie, Craig, Ryan
```

Dust provides a total of three helpers for tackling iteration challenges. These are listed in Table 9-3.

Table 9-3. *Iteration Helpers*

Iteration Helper	Description
@sep	Renders content for every iteration, except the last
@first	Renders content only for the first iteration
@last	Renders content only for the last iteration

Mathematical Expressions

Using Dust's @math helper, templates can adjust their content based on the result of a mathematical expression. Such adjustments can take place in one of two ways. The first is demonstrated in Listing 9-44, in which the result of a mathematical expression is referenced directly within a template. The second is demonstrated in Listing 9-45, in which content is conditionally rendered based on the result of a call to the @math helper.

Listing 9-44. Directly Referencing the Result of a Mathematical Expression

```
// dust-logic1/views/main.dust (excerpt)

{#people}
    {@lt key=age value=retirement_age}
        <p>{name} will have reached retirement age in
        {@math key=retirement_age method="subtract" operand=age /} year(s).</p>
    {/lt}
{/people}
```

Listing 9-45. Conditionally Rendering Content Based on the Result of a Call to the @math Helper

```
// dust-logic1/views/main.dust (excerpt)

{#people}
    {@lt key=age value=retirement_age}
        {@math key=retirement_age method="subtract" operand=age}
            {@lte value=10}{name} will reach retirement age fairly soon.{/lte}
            {@lte value=20}{name} has quite a ways to go before they can retire.{/lte}
            {@default}{name} shouldn't even think about retiring.{/default}
        {/math}
    {/lt}
{/people}
```

The various "methods" supported by Dust's @math helper include: add, subtract, multiply, divide, mod, abs, floor, and ceil.

Context Dump

Useful during development, Dust's @contextDump helper allows you to quickly render the current context object (in JSON format), providing insight into the values Dust sees within the section in which it is called. An example of its usage is shown here:

```
{#people}<pre>{@contextDump /}</pre>{/people}
```

Custom Helpers

Earlier in the chapter, you learned how to create context helpers with which context objects can be extended to include custom functionality. In the same way, custom Dust helpers can also be created at the global level. Listing 9-46 provides a demonstration of how this can be applied.

Listing 9-46. Creating and Using a Custom Dust Helper

```
// dust-logic1/index.js (excerpt)

dust.helpers.inRange = function(chunk, context, bodies, params) {
    if (params.key >= params.lower && params.key <= params.upper) {
        return chunk.render(bodies.block, context);
    } else {
        return chunk;
    }
}
```

```
// dust-logic1/views/main.dust (excerpt)

{#people}
    {@gte key=age value=20}
        {@lte key=age value=29}<p>This person is in their 20's.</p>{/lte}
    {/gte}
    {@inRange key=age lower=20 upper=29}<p>This person is in their 20's.</p>{/inRange}
{/people}
```

In this example's template, a loop is created in which we iterate through each person defined within the context. For each person, a message is displayed if they happen to fall within the twenty-something age bracket. First, this message is displayed using a combination of preexisting logic helpers, @gte and @lt. Next, the message is displayed again, using a custom @inRange helper that has been defined at the global level.

Now that you are familiar with many of the fundamental components that Kraken relies on, let's move forward with creating our first real Kraken application.

Let's Get Kraken

In this book's first section on development tools, we covered four useful utilities that help manage many of the tasks associated with web development - among them: Bower, Grunt, and Yeoman. Kraken relies on each of these tools, along with a Yeoman generator that will assist us in building out the initial structure of our project. If you have not already done so, you should install these modules globally via npm, as shown here:

```
$ npm install -g yo generator-kraken bower grunt-cli
```

Creating a new Kraken project with Yeoman is an interactive process. In this example, we pass the generator a name for our new project (app), at which point it begins to prompt us with questions. Figure 9-4 shows the steps that were taken to create this chapter's app project.

Figure 9-4. Creating a Kraken application using the Yeoman generator

Once you have answered these questions, the generator will create the project's initial file structure and begin installing the necessary dependencies. Afterward, you should find a new app folder containing the contents of the project, which should resemble that shown in Figure 9-5.

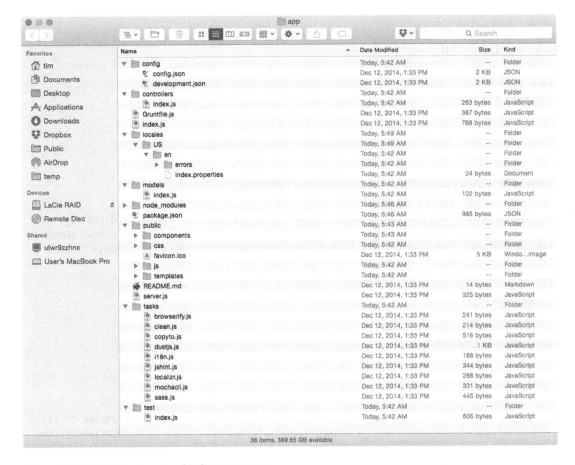

Figure 9-5. *Initial file structure for the app project*

Kraken's Yeoman generator has automated the process of creating a new Express application that is organized using modules that were previously covered in this chapter. We can immediately launch the project in its current state as shown in Listing 9-47. Afterward, the project can be accessed at a local address (see Figure 9-6).

Listing 9-47. Launching the Project for the First Time

```
$ npm start

> app@0.1.0 start /Users/tim/temp/app
> node server.js

Server listening on http://localhost:8000
Application ready to serve requests.
Environment: development
```

Hello, index!

Figure 9-6. *Viewing the Project in the Browser for the First Time*

As you can see, our project has been preconfigured (with the help of confit and meddleware) to use a number of helpful middleware modules (e.g., cookieParser, session, etc.). For some additional insight into how all of this comes together, Listing 9-48 shows the contents of the project's index.js script.

Listing 9-48. Contents of Our New Project's index.js Script

```
// app/index.js

var express = require('express');
var kraken = require('kraken-js');

var options, app;

/*
 * Create and configure application. Also exports application instance for use by tests.
 * See https://github.com/krakenjs/kraken-js#options for additional configuration options.
 */
options = {
    onconfig: function (config, next) {
        /*
         * Add any additional config setup or overrides here. `config` is an initialized
         * `confit` (https://github.com/krakenjs/confit/) configuration object.
         */
        next(null, config);
    }
};

app = module.exports = express();

app.use(kraken(options));
app.on('start', function () {
    console.log('Application ready to serve requests.');
    console.log('Environment: %s', app.kraken.get('env:env'));
});
```

The kraken-js module, which we see here, is nothing more than a standard Express middleware library. However, instead of simply augmenting Express with some small bit of additional functionality, Kraken takes responsibility for configuring a complete Express application. It will do so with the help of many other modules, including those that have already been covered in this chapter: confit, meddleware, enrouten, and adaro.

As shown in Listing 9-48, Kraken is passed a configuration object containing an onconfig() callback function, which will be called after Kraken has taken care of initializing confit for us. Here we can provide any last-minute overrides that we may not want to define directly within the project's JSON configuration files. In this example, no such overrides are made.

Controllers, Models, and Tests

In this chapter's "Structured Route Organization" section, we discovered how enrouten can help bring order to the often haphazard manner in which Express routes are defined. By default, a new Kraken project is set up to use enrouten's directory configuration option, allowing it to recursively scan the contents of a specified folder, searching for modules that export a function accepting a single argument (i.e., router). For each module it finds (referred to as a "controller"), enrouten will pass an Express Router instance that has been mounted to a path predetermined by that module's location within the directory structure. We can see this process in action by looking at the default controller that Kraken has created for our project, shown in Listing 9-49.

Listing 9-49. Our Project's Default Controller

```
// app/controllers/index.js

var IndexModel = require('../models/index');

module.exports = function (router) {

    var model = new IndexModel();

    /**
     * The default route served for us when we access the app at: http://localhost:8000
     */
    router.get('/', function (req, res) {
        res.render('index', model);
    });

};
```

In addition to creating a default controller for our project, Kraken has also taken care of creating a corresponding model, IndexModel, which you can see referenced in Listing 9-49. We will discuss Kraken's relationship with models shortly, but first, let's walk through the process of creating a new controller of our own.

Chapter 3, which covered Yeoman, demonstrated that generators have the ability to provide subcommands capable of providing developers with functionality whose usefulness extends well beyond the initial creation of a project. Kraken's Yeoman generator takes advantage of this by providing a controller subcommand, with which new controllers can quickly be created. By way of an example, let's create a new controller that will be responsible for managing a collection of RSS feeds:

```
$ yo kraken:controller feeds
```

After specifying our desired path, feeds, to the generator's controller subcommand, five new files are automatically created for us:

- controllers/feeds.js: Controller

- models/feeds.js: Model

- test/feeds.js: Test suite

- public/templates/feeds.dust: Dust template

- locales/US/en/feeds.properties: Internationalization settings

For the moment, let's place our focus on the first three files listed here, starting with the model. We'll take a look at the accompanying Dust template and internalization settings file in the next section.

The Model

Listing 9-50 shows the initial state of our project's new feeds model. If you were expecting something sophisticated, you will likely be disappointed. As you can see, this file serves as little more than a generic stub that we are expected to replace with our own persistence layer.

Listing 9-50. Initial Contents of the feeds Model

```
// models/feeds.js

module.exports = function FeedsModel() {
    return {
        name: 'feeds'
    };
};
```

Unlike many other "full-stack" frameworks that attempt to provide developers with tools that address every conceivable need (including data persistence), Kraken takes a minimalistic approach that does not attempt to reinvent the wheel. This approach recognizes that developers already have access to a wide variety of well-supported libraries for managing data persistence, two of which are covered by this book: Knex/Bookshelf and Mongoose.

By way of an example, let's update this module so that it exports a Bookshelf model capable of fetching and storing information within a feeds table stored in a SQLite database. Listing 9-51 shows the updated contents of the feeds model.

Listing 9-51. Updated feeds Model That Uses Knex/Bookshelf

```
// models/feeds.js

var bookshelf = require('../lib/bookshelf');
var Promise = require('bluebird');
var feedRead = require('feed-read');

var Feed = bookshelf.Model.extend({
    'tableName': 'feeds',
    'getArticles': function() {
```

```
        var self = this;
        return Promise.fromNode(function(callback) {
            feedRead(self.get('url'), callback);
        });
    }
});

module.exports = Feed;
```

■ **Note** The updated model shown in Listing 9-51 assumes that you already familiar with the Knex and Bookshelf libraries, along with the steps necessary to configure them. If that is not the case, you may want to read Chapter 12. Regardless, this chapter's app project provides a fully functioning demonstration of the code shown here.

The Controller

Listing 9-52 shows the initial contents of our project's new feeds controller. As with the original controller that accompanied our project, this controller references a corresponding model that Kraken has conveniently created for us, which we have already seen.

Listing 9-52. Initial Contents of the feeds Controller

```
// controllers/feeds.js

var FeedsModel = require('../models/feeds');

/**
 * @url http://localhost:8000/feeds
 */
module.exports = function (router) {
    var model = new FeedsModel();
    router.get('/', function (req, res) {
    });
};
```

In its default state, the feeds controller accomplishes very little. Let's update this controller to include a few additional routes that will allow clients to interact with our application's Feed model. The updated version of the feeds controller is shown in Listing 9-53.

Listing 9-53. Updated feeds Controller

```
var Feed = require('../models/feeds');

module.exports = function(router) {

    router.param('feed_id', function(req, res, next, id) {
        Feed.where({
            'id': id
        }).fetch({
```

```
            'require': true
        }).then(function(feed) {
            req.feed = feed;
            next();
        }).catch(next);
    });

    /**
     * @url http://localhost:8000/feeds
     */
    router.route('/')
        .get(function(req, res, next) {
            return Feed.where({})
                .fetchAll()
                .then(function(feeds) {
                    if (req.accepts('html')) {
                        return res.render('feeds', {
                            'feeds': feeds.toJSON()
                        });
                    } else if (req.accepts('json')) {
                        return res.send(feeds);
                    } else {
                        throw new Error('Unknown `Accept` value: ' + req.headers.accept);
                    }

                })
                .catch(next);
        });

    /**
     * @url http://localhost:8000/feeds/:feed_id
     */
    router.route('/:feed_id')
        .get(function(req, res, next) {
            res.send(req.feed);
        });

    /**
     * @url http://localhost:8000/feeds/:feed_id/articles
     */
    router.route('/:feed_id/articles')
        .get(function(req, res, next) {
            req.feed.getArticles()
                .then(function(articles) {
                    res.send(articles);
                })
                .catch(next);
        });

};
```

With these updates in place, clients now have the ability to

- List feeds
- Fetch information regarding a specific feed
- Fetch articles from a specific feed

In the next section, we will take a look at the test suite that Kraken has created for this portion of our application. With this test suite, we can verify that the routes we have defined work as expected.

The Test Suite

Listing 9-54 shows the initial contents of the test suite that Kraken has created for our new controller. Here we see a single test, which is defined with the help of SuperTest, which is an extension of SuperAgent, a simple library for making HTTP requests.

Listing 9-54. Test Suite for the feeds Controller

```
// test/feeds.js

var kraken = require('kraken-js');
var express = require('express');
var request = require('supertest');

describe('/feeds', function() {

    var app, mock;

    beforeEach(function(done) {
        app = express();
        app.on('start', done);
        app.use(kraken({
            'basedir': process.cwd()
        }));
        mock = app.listen(1337);
    });

    afterEach(function (done) {
        mock.close(done);
    });

    it('should say "hello"', function(done) {
        request(mock)
            .get('/feeds')
            .expect(200)
            .expect('Content-Type', /html/)
            .expect(/"name": "index"/)
            .end(function (err, res) {
                done(err);
            });
    });

});
```

In this example, a GET request is made to our application's /feeds endpoint, and the following assertions are made:

- The server should respond with an HTTP status code of 200.

- The server should respond with a Content-Type header containing the string html.

- The body of the response should contain the string "name": "index".

Given the recent updates that we have made to our new controller, these assertions no longer apply. Let's replace them with a few tests that are relevant. Listing 9-55 shows the updated contents of the test suite.

Listing 9-55. Updated Contents of the feeds Test Suite

```
// test/feeds/index.js

var assert = require('assert');
var kraken = require('kraken-js');
var express = require('express');
var request = require('supertest');

describe('/feeds', function() {

    var app, mock;

    beforeEach(function(done) {
        app = express();
        app.on('start', done);
        app.use(kraken({'basedir': process.cwd()}));
        mock = app.listen(1337);
    });

    afterEach(function(done) {
        mock.close(done);
    });

    it('should return a collection of feeds', function(done) {
        request(mock)
            .get('/feeds')
            .expect('Content-Type', /json/)
            .expect(200)
            .end(function(err, res) {
                if (err) return done(err);
                assert(res.body instanceof Array, 'Expected an array');
                done();
            });
    });
});
```

```
it('should return a single feed', function(done) {
    request(mock)
        .get('/feeds/1')
        .expect('Content-Type', /json/)
        .expect(200)
        .end(function(err, res) {
            if (err) return done(err);
            assert.equal(typeof res.body.id, 'number',
                'Expected a numeric `id` property');
            done();
        });
});

it('should return articles for a specific feed', function(done) {
    request(mock)
        .get('/feeds/1/articles')
        .expect('Content-Type', /json/)
        .expect(200)
        .end(function(err, res) {
            if (err) return done(err);
            assert(res.body instanceof Array, 'Expected an array');
            done();
        });
});

});

});
```

Our updated test suite now contains three tests designed to verify that each of our new controller's routes are functioning correctly. Consider the first test, for instance, which will make a GET request to our application's /feeds endpoint and make the following assertions:

- The server should respond with an HTTP status code of 200.

- The server should respond with a Content-Type header containing the string json.

- The server should return one or more results in the form of an array.

■ **Note**   Recall that our application's Feed model was created with the help of the Knex and Bookshelf libraries. The data that you see referenced in this project originates from a Knex "seed" file (seeds/developments/00-feeds.js) with which we can populate our database with sample data. At any point, this project's SQLite database can be reset to its initial state by running $ grunt reset-db from the command line. If these concepts are unfamiliar to you, you may want to read Chapter 12.

Figure 9-7 shows the output that is printed to the console when our project's test Grunt task is called.

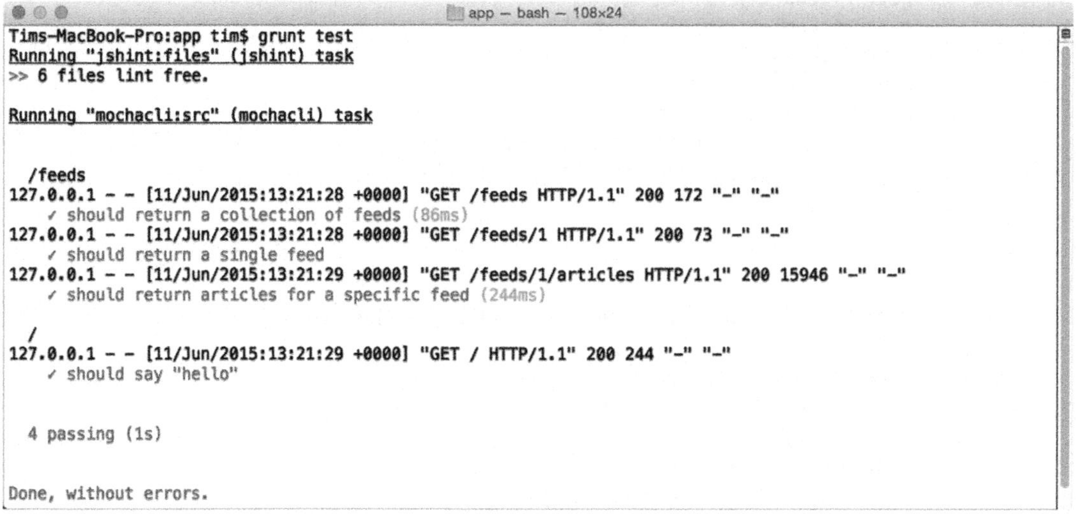

```
● ○ ○                          📄 app — bash — 108×24
Tims-MacBook-Pro:app tim$ grunt test
Running "jshint:files" (jshint) task
>> 6 files lint free.

Running "mochacli:src" (mochacli) task


  /feeds
127.0.0.1 - - [11/Jun/2015:13:21:28 +0000] "GET /feeds HTTP/1.1" 200 172 "-" "-"
    ✓ should return a collection of feeds (86ms)
127.0.0.1 - - [11/Jun/2015:13:21:28 +0000] "GET /feeds/1 HTTP/1.1" 200 73 "-" "-"
    ✓ should return a single feed
127.0.0.1 - - [11/Jun/2015:13:21:29 +0000] "GET /feeds/1/articles HTTP/1.1" 200 15946 "-" "-"
    ✓ should return articles for a specific feed (244ms)


  /
127.0.0.1 - - [11/Jun/2015:13:21:29 +0000] "GET / HTTP/1.1" 200 244 "-" "-"
    ✓ should say "hello"


  4 passing (1s)


Done, without errors.
```

Figure 9-7. *Running the test suite*

Internationalization and Localization

Kraken provides built-in support for creating applications that are capable of adapting themselves to meet the unique needs of multiple languages and regions, an important requirement for most products that hope to see widespread use across multiple, diverse markets. In this section we'll take a look at the two steps by which this is accomplished, internationalization and localization, and how they can be applied within the context of a Kraken application whose templates are generated on the server.

Internationalization (frequently shortened to i18n) refers to the act of developing applications that are *capable* of supporting multiple regions and dialects. In practice, this is accomplished by avoiding the direct use of locale-specific words, phrases, and symbols (e.g., currency symbols) within an application's templates. Placeholders are instead used, which are later populated at the moment a template is requested, based on the location or settings of the user who is making the request. By way of an example, consider the Dust template that is shown in Listing 9-56, which is responsible for rendering the home page of this chapter's app project.

Listing 9-56. Dust Template for the Home Page of app Project

```
// app/public/templates/index.dust

{>"layouts/master" /}

{<body}

    <div class="panel panel-default">
        <div class="panel-heading">
            <h3 class="panel-title">{@pre type="content" key="greeting" /}</h3>
        </div>
        <div class="panel-body">
```

```
<form method="post" action="/sessions">
    <div class="form-group">
        <label>{@pre type="content" key="email_address" /}</label>
        <input type="email" name="email" class="form-control">
    </div>
    <div class="form-group">
        <label>{@pre type="content" key="password" /}</label>
        <input type="password" name="password" class="form-control">
    </div>
    <button type="submit" class="btn btn-primary">
        {@pre type="content" key="submit" /}
    </button>
</form>

    </div>
</div>

{/body}
```

The basic semantics at work here should be familiar, based on material that was previously covered in this chapter's section on Dust. As you can see, instead of directly embedding content, this template relies on a special Dust helper provided by Kraken, @pre, with which we can reference content that is stored in separate, locale-specific content files. The corresponding content files for this particular template are shown in Listing 9-57.

Listing 9-57. Corresponding Content Files for the Dust Template Shown in Listing 9-56

```
// app/locales/US/en/index.properties
# Comments are supported
greeting=Welcome to Feed Reader
submit=Submit
email_address=Email Address
password=Password

// app/locales/ES/es/index.properties
greeting=Bienvenida al Feed Reader
submit=Presentar
email_address=Correo Electrónico
password=Contraseña
```

■ **Note**   Take note of the location of this example's template, `public/templates/index.dust`, and the location of its corresponding content property files, `locales/US/en/index.properties` and `locales/ES/es/index.properties`. Kraken is configured to pair Dust templates with content property files such as these on a one-to-one basis, by matching them based on their paths and filenames.

In contrast to internationalization (i18n), which is primarily concerned with the creation of applications that are *capable* of supporting the injection of localized content, localization (l10n) refers to the process by which locale- and dialect-specific content files, such as those shown in this example, are created. The controller shown in Listing 9-58 demonstrates how Kraken helps developers brings these concepts together to provide users with content that is tailored to meet their specific needs.

Listing 9-58. Serving a Locale-Specific Version of the Home Page

```
// app/controllers/index.js

module.exports = function (router) {

    /**
     * The default route served for us when we access the app
     * at http://localhost:8000
     */
    router.get('/', function (req, res) {
        res.locals.context = { 'locality': { 'language': 'es', 'country': 'ES' } };
        res.render('index');
    });

};
```

This example is an updated version of the controller that we originally saw in Listing 9-49, which is responsible for rendering our application's home page. Here we specify the country and language to be used for locating content files by assigning them to the locals.context property of the incoming Express response object. If no such value is specified, Kraken's default behavior is to use US English. The English and Spanish versions of the rendered template are shown in Figure 9-8 and Figure 9-9, respectively.

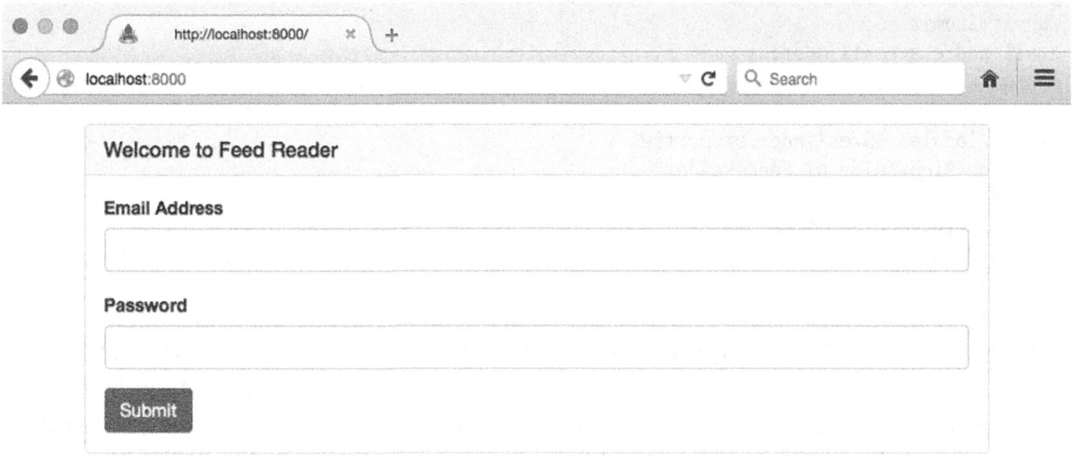

Figure 9-8. *English version of the application's home page*

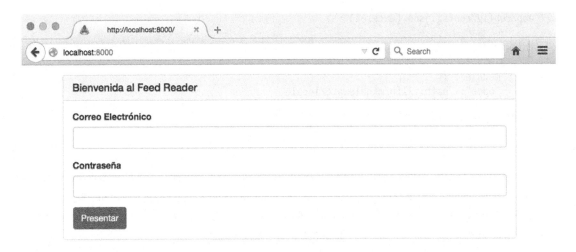

Figure 9-9. *Spanish version of the application's home page*

Detecting Locality

The example shown in Listing 9-58 demonstrates the process by which specific regional settings can be manually assigned to an incoming request. What it does *not* demonstrate, however, is the process by which a user's desired localization settings can be *automatically* detected.

Listing 9-59 demonstrates a simple method for determining locality based on the value of the accept-language HTTP request header. In this example, we have removed the logic for determining a user's locality from our route and placed it in a more appropriate location - a middleware function that will be called for *every* incoming request.

Listing 9-59. Detecting Locality Based on the Value of the accept-language HTTP Request Header

```
// app/lib/middleware/locale.js

var acceptLanguage = require('accept-language');

/**
 * Express middleware function that automatically determines locality based on the value
 * of the `accept-language` header.
 */
module.exports = function() {

    return function(req, res, next) {
        var locale = acceptLanguage.parse(req.headers['accept-language']);
        res.locals.context = {
            'locality': { 'language': locale[0].language, 'country': locale[0].region }
        };
        next();
    };

};
```

```
// app/config/config.json (excerpt)

"middleware":{
    "locale": {
        "module": {
          "name": "path:./lib/middleware/locale"
        },
        "enabled": true
    }
}
```

■ **Note**   While helpful, the accept-language HTTP request header does not always reflect the desired localization settings of the user making the request. Always be sure to provide users with a method for manually specifying such settings on their own (e.g., as part of a "Settings" page).

Security

Given Kraken's origins at PayPal, a worldwide online payments processor, it should come as no surprise that the framework focuses heavily on security. Kraken does so with the help of Lusca, a library that extends Express with a number of enhanced security techniques, as suggested by the Open Web Application Security Project (OWASP). These extensions are provided in the form of multiple, independently configurable middleware modules. In this section, we will briefly examine two ways in which Kraken can help secure Express against commonly encountered attacks.

■ **Note**   This material should by no means be considered exhaustive. It is merely intended to serve as a starting point for implementing security within the context of a Kraken/Express application. Readers with a hand in implementing security on the Web are highly encouraged to delve further into this topic by reading a few of the many great books that are devoted entirely to this subject.

Defending Against Cross-Site Request Forgery Attacks

To understand the basic premise behind cross-site request forgery (CSRF) attacks, it is important to understand the method by which most web applications authenticate their users: cookie-based authentication. This process is illustrated in Figure 9-10.

Figure 9-10. *Cookie-based authentication*

In a typical scenario, a user will submit their credentials to a web application, which will then compare them with those it has on file. Assuming the credentials are valid, the server will then create a new session—essentially, a record representing the user's successful sign-in attempt. A unique identifier belonging to this session is then transmitted to the user in the form of a cookie, which is automatically stored by the user's browser. Subsequent requests to the application made by the browser will automatically attach the information stored in this cookie, allowing the application to look up the matching session record. As a result, the application has the ability to verify the user's identity without requiring the user to resubmit their username and password along with every request.

A CSRF attack takes advantage of the trusted relationship (i.e., session) that exists between an application and a user's browser, by tricking that user into submitting an unintended request to the application. Let's take a look at an example that should help explain how this works. Figure 9-11 illustrates the process by which a user signs into a trusted application—in this case, the csrf-server project that is included with this chapter's source code.

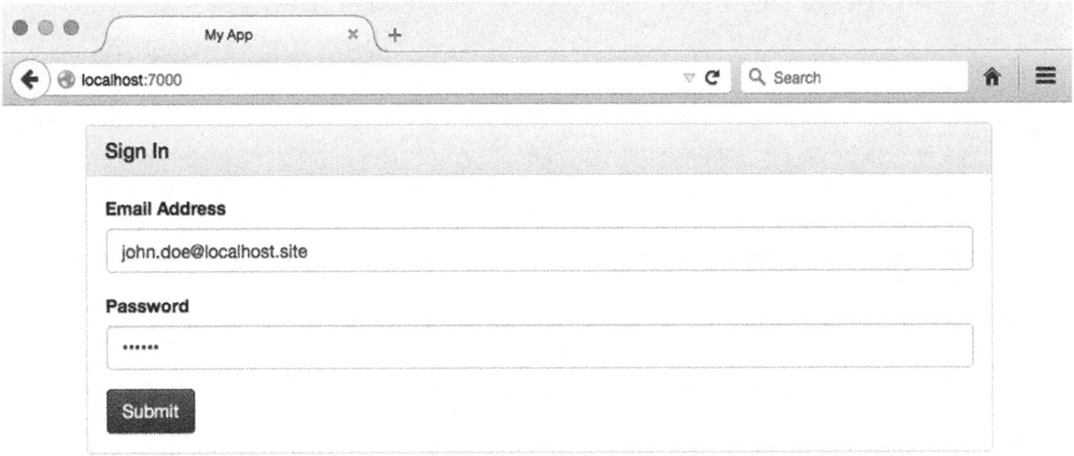

Figure 9-11. *Signing into a trusted application*

Figure 9-12 shows the welcome screen that the user is presented with after successfully signing into the application. Here we see some basic information about the user, including their name and when their account was created.

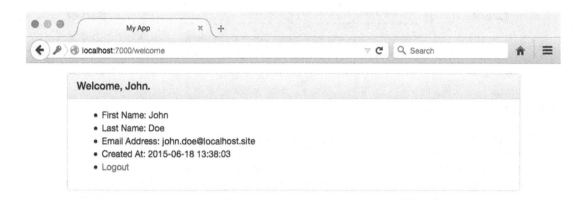

Figure 9-12. *Successful sign-in attempt*

At this point, imagine a scenario in which the user leaves the application (without signing out) and visits another site, which, unbeknownst to the user, has malicious intent (see Figure 9-13). A copy of this malicious site can be found in this chapter's `csrf-attack` project. In this example, the malicious site lures the user into clicking a button with the tempting promise of free candy and butterflies.

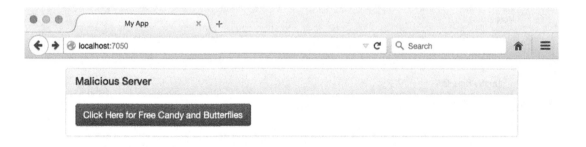

Figure 9-13. *Malicious web site attempting to convince the user to click a button*

Listing 9-60 shows an excerpt from the HTML for this malicious site, which should help explain what is going to happen when the user clicks this button. As you can see, clicking the button will trigger the creation of a POST request to the original application's `/transfer-funds` route.

Listing 9-60. Malicious Web Form

```
// csrf-attack/views/index.dust (excerpt)

<form method="post" action="http://localhost:7000/transfer-funds">
    <button type="submit" class="btn btn-primary">
        Click Here for Free Candy and Butterflies
    </button>
</form>
```

After clicking the button, instead of receiving the free candy and butterflies that they were promised, the user is greeted with a message indicating that all of the funds have been transferred out of their account, as shown in Figure 9-14.

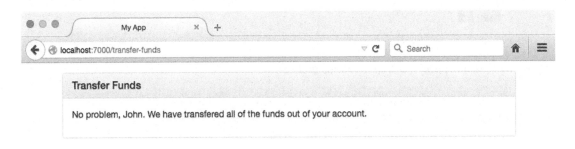

Figure 9-14. *Successful CSRF attack*

Several different steps can be taken to defend against attacks of this nature. The method by which Kraken defends against them is referred to as the "synchronizer token pattern." In this approach, a random string is generated for each incoming request, which the client can subsequently access as part of a template's context or via a response header. Importantly, this string is *not* stored as a cookie. The next POST, PUT, PATCH, or DELETE request made by the client must include this string, which the server will then compare with the one it previously generated. The request will only be allowed to proceed if a match is made.

Let's take a look at how this works in practice. Figure 9-15 shows the sign-in page for this chapter's app project. Refer back to Listing 9-56 to see the underlying HTML for this page.

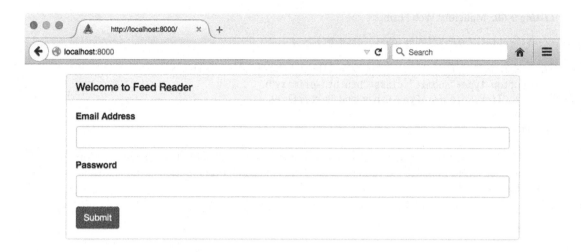

Figure 9-15. *Sign-in page for this chapter's* app *project*

In its current state, any attempt to sign-in using this form will result in the error shown in Figure 9-16. Here we see an error message from Kraken warning us of a missing "CSRF token."

Figure 9-16. *Kraken's "CSRF token missing" Error*

This error can be resolved with the addition of a single, hidden input to our application's login form. Listing 9-61 shows an excerpt from our application's updated Dust template, along with an excerpt from the rendered output.

Listing 9-61. Inserting a Hidden _csrf Field into the Sign-In Form

```
// app/public/templates/index.dust (excerpt)

<form method="post" action="/sessions">
    <input type="hidden" name="_csrf" value="{_csrf}">
    <!-- ... ->
</form>

// Rendered output

<form method="post" action="/sessions">
    <input type="hidden" name="_csrf" value="OERRGi9AGNPEYnNWj8skkfL9fOJIWJp3uKK8g=">
    <!-- ... ->
</form>
```

Here we create a hidden input with the name _csrf, the value for which Lusca has automatically passed to our template's context under a property with the same name. The value that we see rendered in this example, OERRGi9AGNPEYnNWj8skkfL9fOJIWJp3uKK8g=, is a random hash that Lusca has generated for us (i.e., the "synchronizer token"). When we submit this form, Lusca will verify that this value matches the one it previously gave us. If they match, the request is allowed to proceed. Otherwise, an error is thrown. This approach allows applications to defend against CSRF attacks by requiring additional, identifying information that is *not* stored as part of a cookie, making it much more difficult for attackers to trick users into performing unintended actions.

Configuring Content Security Policy Headers

Lusca provides developers with a convenient mechanism for configuring an application's Content Security Policy (CSP). These rules provide instructions to supporting browsers regarding the locations from which various resources (e.g., scripts, stylesheets, images, etc.) can be loaded. When defined, these rules are conveyed to browsers in the form of the Content-Security-Policy response header.

By way of an example, see Listing 9-62, in which Lusca's csp middleware module is provided with a configuration object specifying that *only* images may be loaded from any domain. All other resources must originate from the application's domain.

Listing 9-62. Configuring an Application's Content Security Policy

```
app.use(lusca({
    'csp': {
    'default-src': '\'self\'',
    'img-src': '*'
    }
});
```

■ **Note**   For a full list of the various options that can be configured via the Content-Security-Policy header, visit the Open Web Application Security Project (OWASP) at https://owasp.org.

Summary

The Node community is heavily influenced by the so-called "Unix philosophy," which promotes (among other things) the creation of small, tightly focused modules that are designed to do one thing well. This approach has allowed Node to thrive as a development platform by fostering a large ecosystem of open source modules. PayPal has taken this philosophy to heart by structuring Kraken not as a single, monolithic framework, but rather as a collection of modules that extends and provides structure to Express-based applications. By taking this approach, PayPal has managed to contribute several modules to the Node ecosystem from which developers can benefit, regardless of whether they choose to use Kraken as a whole.

Related Resources

- Kraken: `http://krakenjs.com/`
- Confit: `https://github.com/krakenjs/confit`
- Meddleware: `https://github.com/krakenjs/meddleware`
- Enrouten: `https://github.com/krakenjs/express-enrouten`
- Dust.js: `http://www.dustjs.com`
- SuperAgent: `https://github.com/visionmedia/superagent`
- SuperTest: `https://github.com/visionmedia/supertest`
- Mocha: `http://mochajs.org`
- Open Web Application Security Project (OWASP): `https://owasp.org`
- Lusca: `https://github.com/krakenjs/lusca`

CHAPTER 10

Mach

It is better to have a system omit certain anomalous features and improvements, but to reflect one set of design ideas, than to have one that contains many good but independent and uncoordinated ideas.

—Frederick P. Brooks

There is no shortage of Node.js web servers. Express/Connect, Kraken, and Sails are all popular choices. Mach is a relatively young project in this space, though its predecessor, Strata.js, enjoyed a strong following for several years. Mach was created by Michael Jackson, a former Twitter developer, with a few explicit principles in mind:

- HTTP requests are seamlessly passed to JavaScript functions.

- A promise-oriented interface allows HTTP responses to be asynchronously deferred. HTTP errors may also be propagated through promise chains. (See Chapter 14 for a detailed description of how promises work.)

- Requests and responses can both take advantage of Node.js streams, so that large amounts of data may be sent and received in chunks.

- Composable middleware easily expands Mach's core capabilities.

The choice of which web server to use—indeed, the choice of any library, framework, or programming language in general—should be driven by a project's particular use cases. And while Mach has much to offer for *any* web-based application, it can also be an HTTP client and proxy, route requests to virtual hosts (like Apache and nginx), and rewrite URLs (like Apache's mode_rewrite module). Mach functions as a Node.js module, but some of its features can be used *in the browser* as well, making its use case surface area even wider.

Chapter Examples

This chapter contains a number of runnable examples included with the chapter's sample code. Where applicable, code listings refer to their corresponding file(s) with a comment at the top of the listing, as shown in Listing 10-1.

Listing 10-1. Not a Real Example

```
// example-000/no-such-file.js
console.log('this is not a real example');
```

Most examples in this chapter launch a Node.js web server. Unless otherwise specified, assume that the server may be launched by running the JavaScript file referred to in each listing. For example, the command in Listing 10-2 will run the index.js file, launching the Mach web server in the example-001 directory.

Listing 10-2. Launching an Example Web Server

```
example-001$ node index.js
>> mach web server started on node 0.10.33
>> Listening on 0.0.0.0:8080, use CTRL+C to stop
```

Installation

Mach is a Node.js module that may be installed with the Node.js package manager, npm. The examples in this chapter also use the Q promise library and a handful of other npm modules. All are listed as dependencies in the example code's package.json file, so simply running npm install in the example code directory will download and install each module:

```
code/mach$ npm install
```

Mach, the Web Server

The Mach web server is superficially similar to many other web servers, taking inspiration from proven patterns and designs, and only reinventing the wheel when it has something significant to offer. Creating routes to handle HTTP requests in a Mach web server is a fairly straightforward process, and should be familiar to developers who have used other REST-oriented web servers like Express (JavaScript), Sinatra (Ruby), Nancy (.NET), and so forth.

After importing Mach as an application dependency, Mach application stacks are created by calling mach.stack(). This is the first step to servicing HTTP requests. Listing 10-3 assigns the stack to the app variable.

Listing 10-3. Creating the Application Stack

```
// example-001/index.js
'use strict';
var mach = require('mach');
// ... load other modules ...

// create a stack
var app = mach.stack();

// ...
```

Each Mach application is called a "stack" because each HTTP connection will travel through layers of middleware—small bits of composable functionality—which may manipulate the request before it is delivered to a route, and the response before it is delivered to a calling client. Middleware may also create other side-effects that are important to the web server environment.

Mach itself comes with common web server middleware, which will be covered in the next section. The web server in Listing 10-4 uses a piece of middleware, mach.logger, to print HTTP diagnostic information to the terminal when the web server is receiving requests.

Listing 10-4. Adding Middleware to the Application Stack

```
// example-001/index.js
'use strict';
var mach = require('mach');
// ... load other modules ...

// create a stack
var app = mach.stack();

// add some middleware
app.use(mach.logger);

// ...
```

A *route* is simply a function paired with a particular HTTP method and URL pattern that will handle HTTP requests when they are received by the server. Routes are typically added to an application stack last, after middleware, so that middleware have a chance to parse request information before, and manipulate response information after, a route has an opportunity to interact with each.

The application stack exposes function methods mapped to standard HTTP request methods, as shown in Listing 10-5. Routes are attached to the stack by invoking the appropriate method, followed by a URL pattern and a route callback. When a route is matched to an incoming request, it will receive a connection (typically abbreviated as conn) with which it may respond to the request.

Listing 10-5. Adding HTTP Routes to the Application Stack

```
// example-001/index.js

// add some routes

app.get('/book', function (conn) {/*...*/});

app.get('/book/:id', function (conn) {/*...*/});

app.delete('/book/:id', function (conn) {/*...*/});

app.post('/book', function (conn) {/*...*/});

app.put('/book/:id', function (conn) {/*...*/});

app.get('/author', function (conn) {/*...*/});

app.get('/library', function (conn) {/*...*/});

app.get('/', function (conn) {/*...*/});

// ...
```

When all middleware and routes have been attached to an application stack, the web server is ready to listen for requests. Passing the application stack to Mach.serve() creates an HTTP listener to service requests at the default HTTP scheme, host, and port: http://localhost:5000. Additional options may be added to change this default behavior. In Listing 10-6 a new port number (8080) is passed as a second argument to Mach.serve() to force the HTTP listener to service that port.

Listing 10-6. Serving Up the Application Stack on Port 8080

```
// example-001/index.js

// serve the stack on a port
mach.serve(app, 8080);
// or mach.serve(app, {port: 8080});
```

If more options are necessary, they may be passed to `Mach.serve()` as an options hash instead. The keys and values are described in Table 10-1. The examples in this chapter will make use of the port number shorthand for convenience.

Table 10-1. *Mach Server Options*

Option Property	Description
host	Listen for connections to this hostname, only. No restriction by default.
port	Listen for connections on this port. Defaults to 5000.
socket	Listen for connections via Unix socket. Host and port are ignored.
quiet	true to suppress startup and shutdown messages. Defaults to `false`.
timeout	Duration to wait after receiving SIGINT or SIGTERM signals before forcibly closing connections and terminating.
key	Private key for SSL connections (HTTPS).
cert	Public X509 certificate for SSL connections (HTTPS).

HTTP Routes

Mach routes can handle requests from the most common HTTP methods, and even some uncommon ones:

- GET
- POST
- PUT
- DELETE
- HEAD
- OPTIONS
- TRACE

The HTTP GET route in Listing 10-7 looks up all books in a fake database and delivers the records to the client as an array of JSON objects.

Listing 10-7. Anatomy of a Route

```
// example-001/index.js
app.get('/book', function (conn) {
  /*
   * 1. Routes return promises. Q can adapt the callback-
   * driven database module so that its result (or error)
   * is passed through a promise chain. The makeNodeResolver()
```

```
 * method will provide a callback to feed the deferred.
 */
var deferred = Q.defer();
db.books.all(deferred.makeNodeResolver());
/*
 * 2. Adding handlers to the promise chain by calling
 * promise.then()
 */
return deferred.promise.then(function (books) {
  /*
   * 3. The Connection.json() method returns a promise.
   * The HTTP status code will be sent as an HTTP header
   * in the response, and the array of books will be
   * serialized as JSON.
   */
  return conn.json(200, books);
}, function (err) {
  /*
   * 4. An HTTP 500 will be delivered to the client on
   * error. The error's message will be used in the
   * serialized JSON response.
   */
  return conn.json(500, {error: err.message});
});
});
```

Several things happen in this route that will be common to nearly every route created.

First, a deferred is created that will eventually generate a promise to be returned from the route. (Refer to Chapter 14 for a detailed explanation of how promises work, specifically how values and errors can be passed along a promise chain.) Here the Q promise library creates a deferred, then creates a special callback with makeNodeResolver(). This callback is passed directly to the database.books.all() method, and will feed any value or error generated to the promise chain.

Second, two handlers are attached to the deferred's promise: a handler to receive the book data that needs to be returned to client, and a handler to receive any error from the database should the record fetch fail.

Third, each handler turns its respective data into an HTTP response by calling conn.json() with an HTTP status and a payload. This method is syntactic sugar that encapsulates the conn.send() method (which will be covered in detail later), setting the appropriate Content-Type header, serializing the JSON object, and returning a promise to be passed along the promise chain. When this promise is resolved, the actual HTTP response will be sent.

In a terminal session the curl HTTP utility can make an HTTP GET request to the /book route. The response body contains serialized book data in JSON form:

```
example-001$ curl -X GET http://localhost:8080/book
[{"id":1,"title":"God Emperor of Dune","author":"Frank Herbert"... }]
```

In the terminal session running the Mach server, the mach.logger middleware writes the request details for GET /book to standard output:

```
example-001$ node index.js
>> mach web server started on node 0.12.0
>> Listening on :::8080, use CTRL+C to stop
    ::1 - - [17/Mar/2015 19:58:07] "GET /book HTTP/1.1" 200 - 0.002
```

URL Parameters

URL parameters are segments of a URL path that represent application data, such as unique identifiers. It is common to see REST URLs written in patterns similar to /<entity-type>/<entity-id>/<entity-particular>. The code in Listing 10-8 defines a route for fetching a specific book by its identifier. The actual parameter, :id, is identified by a colon prefix. A route may have any number of parameters, but each must have a unique name and must be an entire URL segment.

Parameters will be available to the route as properties on the conn.params object. Each property name will be the URL parameter name *without* the colon prefix. All property values are also parsed by Mach as strings. Because IDs are numeric in the database, this parameter is converted using the Number function before it is consumed by the database query.

Listing 10-8. REST Route with a Single URL Parameter

```
// example-001/index.js
app.get('/book/:id', function (conn) {
  var id = Number(conn.params.id);
  var deferred = Q.defer();
  db.book.findByID(id, deferred.makeNodeResolver());
  return deferred.promise.then(function (book) {
    if (!book) {
      return conn.json(404);
    }
    return conn.json(200, book);
  }, function (err) {
    return conn.json(500, {error: err.message});
  });
});
```

Unlike the general /book route in Listing 10-8, this route searches for a specific entity that may or may not exist in the database. If the database operation succeeds but the fetched book object is null, no record for that ID exists, and the route resolves with an empty HTTP 404 response.

Query Strings and Request Bodies

While Mach parses URL parameters automatically and makes them available on the conn.params object, the getParams() method must be invoked to parse the query string and the request body. Because request bodies are streamed, parsing is not performed automatically, by default. It remains up to the developer to decide if, and when, the parsing should occur. (If this sounds tedious, don't worry: the params middleware, covered later, can automate this process.)

In Listing 10-9 the /author route accepts a query parameter, genre, and then delivers a JSON array of authors who write books in that genre. The connection's getParams() method returns a promise, passing a parsed params object to the resolution callback. Each property on the params object will be a named parameter from the URL, query string, or request body.

Listing 10-9. Extracting Values from a Query String

```
// example-001/index.js
app.get('/author', function (conn) {
  return conn.getParams().then(function (params) {
    var deferred = Q.defer();
    db.author.findByGenre(params.genre, deferred.makeNodeResolver());
```

```
      return deferred.promise.then(function (authors) {
        return conn.json(200, authors);
      }, function (err) {
        return conn.json(500, {error: err.message});
      });
    });
  });
```

The curl command in Listing 10-10 sends the *Horror* genre parameter to the server, and the response contains a single author record with a matching entry in the genres array.

Listing 10-10. Using cURL to Send a Request with a Query String

```
example-001$ curl -X GET http://localhost:8080/author?genre=Horror
[{"id":6,"name":"Dan Simmons","website":"http://www.dansimmons.com/",
"genres":["Science Fiction","Fantasy","Literature","Horror"]}]
```

The getParams() method has two other useful features. It accepts a single object argument where keys represent whitelisted parameters to be parsed, and the values represent the parsing function for each parameter. When the request body is parsed in Listing 10-11, any body parameter not specified in the whitelist will be ignored. The primitive JavaScript functions String, Number, and Date all parse strings and return deserialized objects. When the params object is passed to the promise's resolution callback, each property will be correctly typed. Custom functions may be used to deserialize request body parameters with proprietary data formats as well.

Once the parameters have been parsed, a new book record is created in the database, then serialized and returned to the client in the response body.

Listing 10-11. Extracting Values from a Request Body

```
// example-001/index.js
app.post('/book', function (conn) {
  return conn.getParams({
    title: String,
    author: String,
    seriesTitle: String,
    seriesPosition: Number,
    publisher: String,
    publicationDate: Date
  }).then(function (params) {
    var book = Book.fromParams(params);
    var deferred = Q.defer();
    db.book.save(book, deferred.makeNodeResolver());
    return deferred.promise.then(function (result) {
      return conn.json(result.isNew ? 201 : 200, book);
    }, function (err) {
      return conn.json(500, {error: err.message});
    });
  });
});
```

Mach can deserialize request bodies in URL-encoded, multipart, and JSON formats. For other formats, custom middleware can be added to deserialize the request body before it arrives at a route handler, or the raw request body stream may be accessed at `conn.request.content`.

Listing 10-12 shows two curl commands that POST new book data in URL-encoded and JSON formats, and the output generated from each HTTP response.

Listing 10-12. Sending a POST Request Body with cURL

```
example-001$ curl -X POST http://localhost:8080/book \
    -H "Content-Type: application/x-www-form-urlencoded" \
    -d "title=Leviathan%20Wakes&author=James%20S.A.%20Corey&publisher=Orbit&publication
    Date=2011-06-15T05%3A00%3A00.000Z"
{"id":10,"title":"Leviathan Wakes","author":"James S.A. Corey","publisher":"Orbit"...}

example-001$ curl -X POST http://localhost:8080/book \
    -H "Content-Type: application/json" \
    -d @new-book.json
{"id":11,"title":"Ready Player One","author":"Ernest Cline","publisher":"Random House
NY"...}
```

When parameters from different sources (i.e., URL parameter, query string parameter, body parameter) have the same name, the following resolution scheme applies:

1. URL parameters always take precedence over query string and request body parameters.

2. Query string parameters take precedence over request body parameters.

3. Nonconflicting request body parameters are included.

Sending Responses

So far the routes have only delivered JSON responses, but Mach can stream any valid HTTP response content to a client.

The lowest-level response method on the `Connection` object is `Connection.send()`. This method accepts an HTTP status code and a stream, buffer, or string to deliver in the response body. Many of the other response methods (such as `json()` or `html()`) on the `Connection` object are merely facades that manipulate the response by adding appropriate headers before calling `send()`.

Table 10-2 shows each Mach response method, the type of content generally passed to each, and the default values each method uses (if any) for various HTTP response headers. With the exception of `back()`, an HTTP status code may be specified as the first parameter to each of these methods, followed by the response body content. While the status code is an optional parameter, the examples in this chapter always explicitly set it.

Table 10-2. *Mach Response Methods*

Method	Payload	Response Header Defaults
`Connection.send()`	Stream, buffer, or string	(none)
`Connection.redirect()`	Location	`302 Redirect Location:`
`Connection.back()`	Location	`302 Redirect Location:`
`Connection.text()`	Text string	`Content-Type: text/plain`
`Connection.html()`	HTML string	`Content-Type: text/html`
`Connection.json()`	JSON object or string	`Content-Type: application/json`
`Connection.file()`	File content (stream, buffer, string, or path)	`Content-Type` is set if an appropriate MIME type can be determined by the file extension.
		`Content-Length` is set if a specified size is passed to `file()` in an options hash, or if the payload is a file path that can Node.js can resolve and stat to determine file size.

The `redirect()` and `back()` methods do not deliver a response body, but instead manipulate the `Location` header in the response to direct the client to another page. The `file()` method accepts either file content (in the form of a stream, buffer, or string) *or* a file path that is then read into a stream, and delivers the content of the file to the client.

Perhaps the most common response a web server will deliver to web browsers is an HTML response. HTML pages are rarely stored as complete files anymore, however; developers break up HTML into reusable components, mix markup with templating languages, and bind templates to dynamic data to create valid HTML.

In Listing 10-13, the swig templating library compiles two swig templates into functions, `library()` (to display a user's book library) and `err500()` (to display any server errors). When the route handles an incoming request, it loads book data from the database and binds that data to the `library.swig` template using the `library()` function. This produces a valid HTML string, which is then passed as the response body to `conn.html()`. If an error occurs during this process, the `err500()` function does the same with the error template and the error message.

Listing 10-13. Sending an HTML Response

```
// example-001/index.js
var swig = require('swig');
// ...

var library = swig.compileFile('./library.swig');
var err500 = swig.compileFile('./err500.swig');

app.get('/library', function (conn) {
  var deferred = Q.defer();
  db.book.all(deferred.makeNodeResolver());
  return deferred.promise.then(function (books) {
    return conn.html(200, library({books: books}));
  }, function (err) {
    return conn.html(500, err500({err: err.message}));
  });
});
```

The advantage of using conn.html() over conn.send() in Listing 10-13 is purely one of convenience, as html() will set the appropriate Content-Type: text/html header automatically. The conn.text() method would do likewise with the text/plain content type.

For content types that Mach does not wrap, headers can be set manually before conn.send() is called. For example, the route in Listing 10-14 delivers library data as XML instead of HTML by explicitly setting a Content-Type: application/xml header on the connection's response before the promise is returned from the route. The book data is then serialized as an XML string before being sent to the client.

Listing 10-14. Setting the Content-Type Header Manually

```
// example-001/index.js
var xmlify = require('./xmlify');
// ...

app.get('/library.xml', function (conn) {
  var deferred = Q.defer();
  db.book.all(deferred.makeNodeResolver());
  conn.response.setHeader('Content-Type', 'application/xml');
  return deferred.promise.then(function (books) {
    return conn.send(200, xmlify('books', data));
  }, function (err) {
    return conn.send(500, xmlify('err', err.message));
  });
});
```

Not all response methods send content. The conn.redirect() method will send a Location header to the HTTP client with a URL that it should follow, presumably because the content requested is no longer available at the given route. The conn.back() method, in contrast, merely directs the client back to its referer. An optional URL parameter acts as a fallback, in the event that the request's Referer header is blank (e.g., the user typed the address directly into the browser's URL bar).

Listing 10-15 shows a simple redirect from the root of the web application to the /library route.

Listing 10-15. Sending a Redirect Response

```
// example-001/index.js
// ...

app.get('/', function (conn) {
  return conn.redirect('/library');
});
```

Making Connections

By now it should be obvious that the Connection object is the locus of all communication with a client. It holds technical details about each HTTP request and response, and gives middleware and routes the means to interact with and manipulate HTTP responses.

A Connection object has several properties of import to both middleware and routes:

- location
- request
- response

Location

The `Connection.location` property contains information about the URL target of the connection's *request*. Table 10-3 shows the properties and data it contains.

Table 10-3. *Connection Location Data*

Location Property	Description	Example
href	The full URL.	http://user:pass@webapp.com:8080/admin/dashboard.html#news?showWelcome=1
protocol	The URL scheme with trailing colon.	http:, https:
auth	URL authentication credentials (if provided).	user:pass
host	Full URL host, including any nonstandard port number (e.g., not 80 or 443).	webapp.com:8080
hostname	URL hostname.	webapp.com
port	URL host port.	8080
pathname	URL path without query string.	/admin/dashboard.html#news
search	URL query string with the question mark prefix.	?showWelcome=1
queryString	URL query string without the question mark prefix.	showWelcome=1
query	URL query string parsed as an object hash.	{showWelcome: 1}

If the location object's API looks familiar, it's because Mach takes some inspiration here from the window.location object in modern web browsers.

A few `Connection` properties act as helpful facades for combining `Location` and header data, shown in Table 10-4.

Table 10-4. *Location Property Facades on the* `Connection` *Object*

Connection Property	Description	Example
path	Location.pathname + Location.search.	/admin/dashboard.html#news?showWelcome=1
auth	Value of the Authorization header, or Location.auth.	user:pass
isSSL	true if Location.protocol is "https:", otherwise false.	true

Request and Response Messages

Connections expose request and response properties, which are both instances of Message, an internal Mach type that encapsulates HTTP message plumbing.

Message Headers

The example in Listing 10-14 illustrates how to set a single header on the response message by using conn. response.setHeader(). The response message also exposes an addHeader() method that performs the same function as Message.setHeader(), but with a caveat. If a header is *set*, it will overwrite any previous header key/value pair with the same name. If a header is *added*, Mach assumes that it should be appended to any preexisting header with the same name, effectively creating a multivalue header.

To fetch a specific header, call Message.getHeader() with the desired header name. The value will be returned if the header is present in the message.

Headers may be manipulated en masse through the Message.headers property, which gets and sets the internal header hash, the keys of which are header names (such as Content-Type) with associated header values.

Message Cookies

HTTP requests and responses carry cookie values to and from HTTP servers. These cookies are key/value pairs that are stored in Cookie and Set-Cookie headers, respectively. Mach messages parse these cookie values and expose them as an object hash via the Message.cookies property, while the Message. getCookie() and Message.setCookie() methods behave like their header-oriented counterparts.

Message Content

Request and response bodies exist as streams in each object's Message.content property. These streams may be piped through other transformation streams, or replaced on each Message object entirely. If a string is used instead of a stream when setting the content property value, it will be converted to a stream automatically.

Several Message methods provide alternative access to its content stream. The Message. bufferContent() method will read the stream into a memory buffer and return a promise for the result. When the promise resolves, the buffer will be available for consumption by calling code. An optional length parameter may be passed to restrict the amount of data read into the buffer. If the actual buffer length is exceeded, the promise will fail. This method is useful when consuming code needs to deal with a request or response body as a whole. If a Message has been buffered, its isBuffered property will return true.

The Message.stringifyContent() method returns a promise for the string value of the content. Optional length and encoding arguments may be supplied to limit the amount of data converted and to encode it appropriately. Like Message.bufferContent(), if a maximum length is supplied and the string exceeds that length, the promise will fail.

The Connection.getParams() method calls the Message.parseContent() method under the hood, but this method may also be called directly, perhaps in middleware if necessary. It applies the appropriate parser to the message content based on media type (e.g., URL-encoded) and returns a promise for the parsed result string. It also accepts a maximum length parameter.

Common Middleware

Mach comes bundled with a number of common middleware modules that encapsulate fairly standard web server functionality, though a web server *can* operate without using a single piece of middleware. They are all optional and may be added as needed.

Each example in this chapter has used the mach.logger middleware to write HTTP request/response output to the terminal while a Mach web server is running. Listing 10-16 shows this piece of middleware being attached to the application stack by passing it to the app.use() method.

Listing 10-16. mach.logger Middleware

```
// example-002/index.js

// add some middleware
app.use(mach.logger);

// add some routes...
```

Under the hood, middleware are simply functions with a specific signature. This concept will be examined in depth later, but in general, the app.use() method will accept the middleware function first followed by optional configuration parameters.

The order in which middleware is added to a Mach application is important, as each middleware may modify the request and response. Some middleware, like Mach.file, may prevent the connection from ever reaching other middleware or a route handler at all.

When the web server receives a request, it passes it through middleware in an *upstream* fashion. Each middleware handles the request in succession, passing it along until the chain is terminated by a piece of middleware, handled by a route, or generates an error if it cannot be properly handled. Once the request *is* handled, however, the connection passes back through the middleware chain going *downstream*, giving each middleware a chance to evaluate the response. The diagram in Figure 10-1 illustrates, crudely, how middleware is evaluated relative to request and response flow.

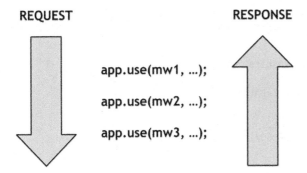

REQUEST   **RESPONSE**

```
app.use(mw1, ...);

app.use(mw2, ...);

app.use(mw3, ...);
```

Figure 10-1. *Order in which Mach middleware evaluates requests and responses*

The impact that middleware order can have on an application will become more apparent as more middleware are added to examples.

What Manner of Content Is This?

The Mach.contentType and Mach.charset middleware are two very simple functions that automatically adjust the Content-Type response header if it is missing altogether, or does not specify a charset value. These can be useful if routes serve homogeneous content (such as XML data) with Message.send(). Instead of manipulating the Content-Type header in each route, a global override can be specified in middleware. Both middleware are added to the application stack in Listing 10-17.

Listing 10-17. Setting Default Header Values with Mach.contentType and Mach.charset

```
// example-002/index.js
// ...

app.use(mach.charset);
app.use(mach.contentType, 'application/xml');

// ...
```

By default, Mach.charset uses the utf-8 encoding, which is sufficient for most purposes. An alternative encoding may be specified with a second string parameter passed to app.use(). Mach.contentType will use text/html by default, but in this case the alternative application/xml value is specified instead.

As stated, the order in which middleware is added to the application stack is important. In this case, Mach.charset is added *before* Mach.contentType, which may seem counterintuitive considering that a charset value is *part of* the Content-Type header value (implying that the header value needs to be set first). Recall, though, that responses pass through middleware in a "downstream" direction. And since the content type and character set of a response cannot be determined until *after* a route has added content to the response, these middleware will perform their work in reverse order.

The curl command in Listing 10-18 shows a simple route that streams an XML file from disk *without specifying a* Content-Type *header in the route*. The verbose curl request output shows that the Content-Type header has been set with the default content type and character set specified by Mach middleware.

Listing 10-18. Automatically Setting XML Content Headers

```
// example-002/index.js
// ...
app.use(mach.charset);
app.use(mach.contentType, 'application/xml');

var insultsFilePath = path.join(__dirname, 'insults.xml');
app.get('/insults', function (conn) {
  conn.send(200, fs.createReadStream(insultsFilePath));
});

example-002$ curl -v -X GET http://localhost:8080/insults
* Hostname was NOT found in DNS cache
*    Trying ::1...
* Connected to localhost (::1) port 8080 (#0)
> GET /insults HTTP/1.1
> User-Agent: curl/7.37.1
> Host: localhost:8080
> Accept: */*
>
< HTTP/1.1 200 OK
< Content-Type: application/xml;charset=utf-8
< Date: Sat, 28 Mar 2015 18:05:13 GMT
< Connection: keep-alive
< Transfer-Encoding: chunked
```

```
<
<?xml version="1.0" encoding="UTF-8"?>
<insults source="The Curse of Monkey Island">
  <insult value="Throughout the Caribbean my great deeds are celebrated!">
    <reply>Too bad they're all fabricated.</reply>
  </insult>
  <insult value="Coming face to face with me must leave you petrified.">
    <reply>Is that your face? I thought it was your backside!</reply>
  </insult>
  <insult value="I can't tell which of my traits has you the most intimidated.">
    <reply>Your odor alone makes me aggravated, agitated, and infuriated!</reply>
  </insult>
</insults>
```

My Kingdom for a File

The Mach.file middleware serves static files (e.g., .html, .css, .js) from a physical directory on disk. When a request enters the application stack pipeline, Mach.file attempts to match the request URL pathname to a path on disk, and if the match is successful, Mach.file streams the static file content to the connection response. If no static file matches the request path, the connection is passed to the next middleware (or route).

Using Mach.file middleware is simply a matter of attaching the middleware function to the application stack and specifying the directory from which static file content will be served. In Listing 10-19 an options hash is passed to app.use() as a second argument. This object contains the few options used to configure Mach.file, including the required root directory option. In this example the example-003/public directory is specified.

Listing 10-19. Mach.file Middleware

```
// example-003/index.js
var path = require('path');
// ...

var publicDir = path.join(__dirname, 'public');
app.use(mach.file, {
  root: publicDir
  // ...other options...
});

// routes
```

■ **Tip** Because root is the only *required* option for Mach.file, the directory path string may be used as the second argument to app.use() in lieu of the options hash.

The directory tree in Listing 10-20 shows the static content that will be served from the example-003/public directory. Mach treats this directory as part of the web server root, so static files and directories will all have URLs relative to / (e.g., http://localhost:8080/styles/index.css).

Listing 10-20. Content of the Public Directory

```
├── images
│   ├── bat-cat.jpg
│   ├── computing.gif
│   ├── llama.gif
│   ├── no-idea.jpg
│   └── swine.gif
├── index.html
├── scripts
│   └── index.js
└── styles
    └── index.css
```

Since static file content is read-only, Mach.file will only service requests with the HTTP methods GET and HEAD. It will also reject requests that attempt to access a file path outside of the specified static file directory, sending a 403 Forbidden response back to the client.

After launching the web server, a browser may be pointed at http://localhost:8080/index.html. Mach will serve the static index.html page and its assets, all magnificently depicted in Figure 10-2.

Figure 10-2. *Serving a static HTML page with Mach.file*

You may have noticed that the index.html file is explicitly included in the URL. It is common practice to map an index.html (or some equivalent "default" .html file) to the web server root, or some other nested directory path. If the file name is removed from the URL, however, the Mach.file middleware will generate a 404 Not Found response. To change this behavior and serve an index file automatically, an index property may be added to the options hash. If this property is "truthy," Mach.file will automatically search for an index.html file at any terminating segment in a URL path, including the application root. If more granular control is required, this property may also contain an array of file names for which to search, prioritized by array order. Listing 10-21 shows this property and its possible values.

Listing 10-21. The Mach.file index Option Searches for Index Files at Directory Paths

```
// example-003/index.js
// ...

app.use(mach.file, {
  root: publicDir,
  index: true
  //or, index: ['index.html', 'index.htm', ...]
});
```

After the index option has been added and the web server restarted, visiting http://localhost:8080 will automatically serve the index.html file to the browser.

The Mach.file middleware can also generate directory listings for directories with no index file. The autoIndex option in Listing 10-22 activates this feature.

Listing 10-22. The Mach.file autoIndex Option Creates a Directory Listing for Directories Without Index Files

```
// example-003/index.js
// ...

app.use(mach.file, {
  root: publicDir,
  autoIndex: true
});
```

Browsing to http://localhost:8080/images displays a directory listing of all images, their sizes, MIME types, and last modified timestamps, shown in Figure 10-3.

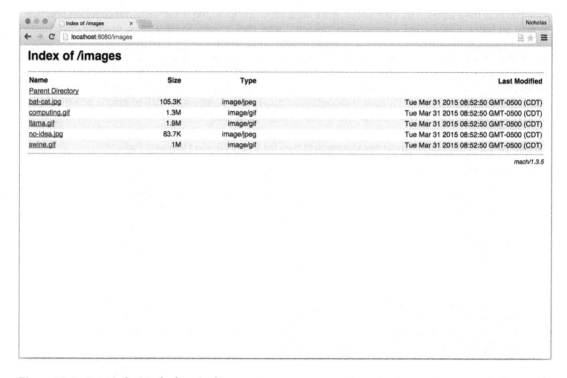

Figure 10-3. *Auto-indexing the* images *directory*

Each image file name is a hyperlink to the image itself, while the Parent Directory hyperlink directs the browser to the parent URL segment, in this case, the website root. If both the index and autoIndex options are used together, any index page identified with the index option takes precedence and will be displayed instead of a directory listing.

Zip It

Modern browsers automatically request compressed resources from a web server by issuing an Accept-Encoding: gzip header with each request. Compression can dramatically reduce response size, improving the speed and bandwidth required to fulfill each HTTP request. In exchange, a minor compression cost is paid by the server and a decompression cost is paid by the browser.

Mach's gzip middleware automatically compresses any response with the following Content-Type headers:

- text/*

- application/javascript

- application/json

Response bodies are compressed with the Node.js zlib module, and the following headers are set on compressed response:

- Content-Encoding: gzip

- Content-Length: [compressed content length]

- Vary: Accept-Encoding

■ **Tip** The Vary header tells any intermediary HTTP cache that variations of this response should be cached according to a particular header, in this case, Accept-Encoding. If Browser-A requests an uncompressed response and Browser-B requests a compressed response *for the same URL*, HTTP caches will store *both* responses instead of storing only the first.

The code in Listing 10-23 introduces the Mach.gzip middleware *before* setting up a static file server. When a response travels upstream, Mach.gzip will evaluate the request headers to see if Accept-Encoding: gzip is present, then evaluate the response headers to determine if the Content-Type is a candidate for compression. If both conditions are true, the response body will be compressed, as the curl request in Listing 10-23 demonstrates.

Listing 10-23. Mach.gzip Compresses Response Bodies

```
// example-004/index.js
// ...

app.use(mach.gzip);

var publicDir = path.join(__dirname, 'public');
app.use(mach.file, {
  root: publicDir,
  index: true
});
```

```
example-004$ curl -X GET -H "Accept-Encoding: gzip" -v http://localhost:8080/index.html
* Hostname was NOT found in DNS cache
*    Trying ::1...
* Connected to localhost (::1) port 8080 (#0)
> GET /index.html HTTP/1.1
> User-Agent: curl/7.37.1
> Host: localhost:8080
> Accept: */*
> Accept-Encoding: gzip
>
< HTTP/1.1 200 OK
< Content-Type: text/html
< Last-Modified: Tue, 31 Mar 2015 13:52:50 GMT
< Content-Encoding: gzip
< Vary: Accept-Encoding
< Date: Tue, 31 Mar 2015 14:14:09 GMT
< Connection: keep-alive
< Transfer-Encoding: chunked
<
```

H��� ��tvu�{������y���•
���vM�Fy^�
         =[�:$R��Z�•��6�
Y��Ť4XsF �p1����g�?�#���J\���mY��bЛ�@<��g��.x��L��
⊕�t�t•�:�5���|�oIHd'1(�
�1�l
q�lyD��SR1�$�8��9�q"�U����������Өn/�V8q�?T�Gq•
�L�•s^�����d0#��|�L9E�5��dG�ɫ���I�`

For fine-grained control over the compression algorithm (compression level, memory consumption, compression strategy, etc.), a zlib options object may be passed to the application stack when the Mach. gzip middleware is attached. The technical details of each option are beyond the scope of this chapter. Refer to the Node.js zlib documentation for more details.

Look at That Body

Earlier, in Listing 10-11, the Connection.getParams() method was used to parse and extract data from query strings and POST request bodies. Performing this step within individual routes can quickly become tedious, however. The Mach.params middleware relieves the developer of this responsibility, parsing query strings and request body data automatically, affixing data to Connection.params (where URL parameter data lives) before the connection is passed to a route.

In Listing 10-24, when data is POSTed to the route, the POST body parameters are appended to the conn.params object. This object is then added as a database record. Output from the curl command shows that the Mach.params middleware performed as expected.

Listing 10-24. Parsing a Request Body Automatically with Mach.params

```
// example-005/index.js
// ...

// Mach.params
app.use(mach.params);

app.post('/hero', function (conn) {
  var deferred = Q.defer();
  db.hero.save(conn.params, deferred.makeNodeResolver());
  return deferred.promise.then(function (result) {
    return conn.json(201, result);
  }, function (err) {
    return conn.json(500, {err: err.message});
  });
});

example-005$ curl -X POST http://localhost:8080/hero \
  -H "Content-Type: application/x-www-form-urlencoded" \
  -d "name=Minsc&race=Human&class=Ranger&subclass=Berserker&alignment=Neutral%20
Good&companion=Boo"
{"id":6,"isNew":true}
```

■ **Tip**   Remember, URL parameters will always take precedence over query string and request body parameters. If a naming conflict exists between any parameter source, Mach favors URL parameters first, then query string parameters, and finally request body parameters.

To verify that the POSTed data was in fact added to the database, a request may be sent to the route in Listing 10-25 with two query string parameters, skip and take. These parameters allow clients to page through what might conceivably be a large collection of heroes by defining an offset (skip) from which to start, and the quantity (take) of heroes to load from that offset. Because Mach.params handles both request bodies and query strings, there is no need to parse them manually.

The two following `curl` requests can be used to query records 1–3 and 4–6 respectively. The POSTed hero, Minsc, is the last hero in the last page of data.

Listing 10-25. Parsing a Query String Automatically with `Mach.params params`

```
// example-005/index.js
// ...

// Mach.params
app.use(mach.params);

// ...

app.get('/hero'/*?skip=#&take=#*/, function (conn) {
  var skip = Number(conn.params.skip || 0),
    take = Number(conn.params.take || 0);
  var deferred = Q.defer();
  db.hero.page(skip, take, deferred.makeNodeResolver());
  return deferred.promise.then(function (heroes) {
    return conn.json(200, heroes);
  }, function (err) {
    return conn.json(500, {err: err.message});
  })
});
```

```
example-005$ curl -X GET http://localhost:8080/hero?skip=0\&take=3
[{"id":1,"name":"Dynaheir"...},{"id":2,"name":"Imoen"...},{"id":3,"name":"Khalid"...}]

example-005$ curl -X GET http://localhost:8080/hero?skip=3\&take=3
[{"id":4,"name":"Xan"...},{"id":5,"name":"Edwin"...},{"id":6,"name":"Minsc"...}]
```

Who Goes There?

Identifying and tracking users in web applications is a topic unto itself. Mach provides basic authentication support for simple security use cases, and persistent session support that can accomodate many more.

The `Mach.basicAuth` middleware is added to the application stack like all other middleware, and requires a simple validation function as its only parameter. This function takes two arguments, username and password, both parsed from the authentication credentials sent along with the request. The validation function may return one of three values:

- The username of a validated user

- A "falsy" value if validation fails

- A promise that will be resolved with the username of a validated user, or rejected with a falsy value

The web server in Listing 10-26 will serve an `index.html` file to any authenticated user. The `Mach.basicAuth` middleware will intercept each request and query the database for any provided credentials. The `db.user.byCredential()` method returns a promise that will be resolved with the authenticated user or rejected with an error. If resolved, the username is returned and propagated through the promise chain, finally being set as the value of `Connection.remoteUser`. If an error occurs, a Boolean `false` is returned, sending a `401 Unauthorized` response to the client with the appropriate `WWW-Authenticate` header value.

Listing 10-26. Securing Routes with Basic Authentication

```
// example-006/index.js
// ...

// Mach.basicAuth
app.use(mach.basicAuth, function (username, password) {
  return db.user.byCredential(username, password).then(function (user) {
    return user.username;
  }, function (/*err*/) {
    return false;
  });
});

var indexPath = path.join(__dirname, 'index.html');

app.get('/', function (conn) {
  return conn.html(200, fs.createReadStream(indexPath));
});
```

When the server is running and a user attempts to visit http://localhost:8080, he will be prompted for credentials in response to the Basic Authentication challenge. Figure 10-4 shows the modal window that Chrome displays.

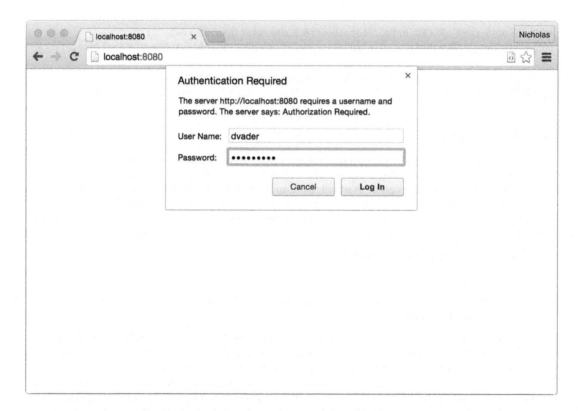

Figure 10-4. *A browser prompts the user for credentials when Basic Authentication fails*

The Velocity of an Unladen Session

Once a user has been authenticated, it is typical to track user-specific data in a server session. Adding the Mach.session middleware to the application stack enables session cookie support automatically. The only configuration property required on the Mach.session options object is a secret session key that will be used to encrypt session data. Listing 10-27 shows session middleware added to the stack before any routes are defined.

Listing 10-27. Adding Session Middleware to the Application Stack

```
// example-007/index.js
// ...

var sessionSecret = 'c94ac0cf8f3b89bf9987d1901863f562592b477b450c26751a5d6964cbdce9eb085
c013d5bd48c7b4ea64a6300c2df97825b9c8b677c352a46d12b8cc5879554';

// Mach.session
app.use(mach.session, {
  secret: sessionSecret
});

var quizView = swig.compileFile('./quiz.swig');

app.get('/', function (conn) {
  return conn.html(200, quizView(conn.session));
});

// ...
```

The route in Listing 10-27 sends an HTML quiz to the browser, shown in Listing 10-28. This quiz is a swig template that interpolates the name, quest, and colour properties of the session object as values for each input. The first time this route is accessed, the session object will be empty, and so these inputs will have no values.

Listing 10-28. A Perplexing Quiz (What Will Be Your Answers?)

```
<h1>Questions, three.</h1>
<form method="post" action="/questions/three">
  <fieldset>
    <h2>What... is your name?</h2>
    <div>
      <input name="name" type="text" value="{{name}}" />
    </div>
    <h2>What... is your quest?</h2>
    <div>
      <input name="quest" type="text" value="{{quest}}" />
    </div>
    <h2>What... is your favourite colour?</h2>
    <div>
      <input name="colour" type="text" value="{{colour}}" />
    </div>
```

```
  <div>
    <button>Cross the Bridge of Death</button>
  </div>
  </fieldset>
</form>
```

When the form is POSTed to the /questions/three route, shown in Listing 10-29, the form values are extracted from the request and the session object, and are used to populate the session object. The user is then redirected to a success page where he or she is given the option to take the quiz again.

Listing 10-29. Setting Session Properties in a Route

```
// example-007/index.js
// ...

var successView = swig.compileFile('./success.swig');
var errView = swig.compileFile('./err.swig');

app.post('/questions/three', function (conn) {
  return conn.getParams().then(function (params) {
    conn.session.name = params.name;
    conn.session.quest = params.quest;
    conn.session.colour = params.colour;
    return conn.html(201, successView());
  }, function (err) {
    return conn.html(500, errView(err));
  });
});
```

When the user returns to the quiz page, the fields are automatically populated with the answers last given to each question. Recall that in Listing 10-28 the session is being bound to the quiz template, and since values were previously stored on the session object, they are now available to the template as well. Figure 10-5 shows the prepopulated form values as well as the session cookie used to connect the browser to the server-side session.

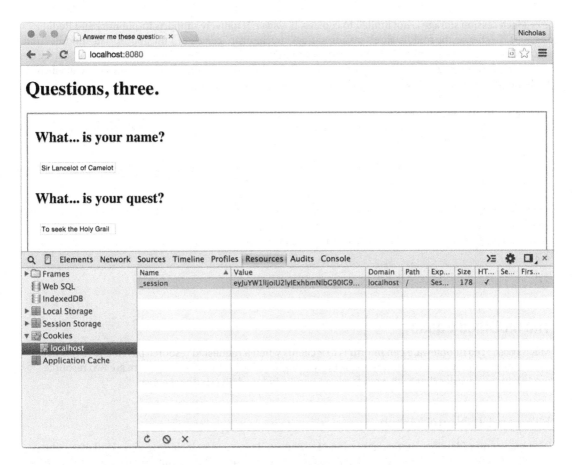

Figure 10-5. *Mach session cookie*

Since Mach.session uses cookie storage by default, there are a number of additional cookie-specific option properties that may be set when the middleware is added to the stack, as described in Table 10-5.

Table 10-5. *Mach.session cookie options*

Property	Description
name	Name of the cookie. Defaults to _session.
path	Cookie path. Defaults to /.
domain	Cookie domain. Defaults to null.
secure	true to send the cookie over HTTPS only. Defaults to false.
expireAfter	Seconds after which the cookie expires. Defaults to 0 (never expires).
httpOnly	true to restrict this cookie to HTTP/S APIs. Defaults to true.

Mach session storage is not limited to cookies, however. It natively supports in-memory and Redis sessions. To change the middleware's session storage mechanism, `require()` the appropriate module from `mach/middleware/session/*`. Add a new instance of that module to the session configuration by setting the `store` property on the options object. Listing 10-30 shows how the default cookie session store can easily be replaced with a Redis session store.

Listing 10-30. Using Redis As a Session Store

```
// example-008/index.js
// ...

var RedisStore = require('mach/lib/middleware/session/RedisStore');

// Mach.session
app.use(mach.session, {
 store: new RedisStore({url: 'redis://127.0.0.1:6379'})
});

// ...
```

The MODified Squad

Mach's `modified` middleware can inform HTTP clients when a requested resource has not been modified since the last request for that resource, simply by using standard HTTP headers. There are two resource modification scenarios that `Mach.modified` can handle before delivering a response.

ETag and If-None-Match

Web servers may identify a particular version of a requested resource by including some kind of version identifier (commonly a message digest) in a response's `ETag` header. This identifier can be sent back to the server in the `If-None-Match` request header on subsequent requests for the same resource. If the resource has not changed—that is, if its version identifier has not changed—the web server may respond with a `304 Not Modified` response, omitting the actual resource from the response body. When this happens, the client knows that the resource has not changed, and that it must continue to use the data it received from its previous request. The code in Listing 10-31 shows how a digest of each book object is being added as the `ETag` response header in each book route.

Listing 10-31. Adding the `ETag` Header to Each Book Response

```
// example-009/index.js
var jsonHash = require('./json-hash');
// ...

app.use(mach.modified);

app.get('/book/:id', function (conn) {
  var id = Number(conn.params.id);
  var deferred = Q.defer();
  db.book.findByID(id, deferred.makeNodeResolver());
  return deferred.promise.then(function (book) {
```

```
    if (!book) {
      return conn.json(404);
    }
    conn.response.setHeader('ETag', jsonHash(book));
    return conn.json(200, book);
  }, function (err) {
    return conn.json(500, {error: err.message});
  });
});

app.put('/book/:id', function (conn) {
    var book = Book.fromParams(conn.params);
    var deferred = Q.defer();
    db.book.save(book, deferred.makeNodeResolver());
    return deferred.promise.then(function (result) {
      conn.response.setHeader('ETag', jsonHash(book));
      return conn.json(result.isNew ? 201 : 200, book);
    }, function (err) {
      return conn.json(500, {error: err.message});
    });
});
```

The first curl request in Listing 10-32 fetches a single book, *Dune* by Frank Herbert. The ETag header in the response shows the message digest cf0fdc372106caa588f794467a17e893, and the response body contains the serialized JSON book data. (The ETag message digest may vary based on your operating system. For each curl command, use the ETag you receive in the HTTP response headers for further comparison.)

The second curl request uses the same URL but also includes an If-None-Match header with the ETag value sent in the previous response. Because the book entity has not changed on the server (and thus its message digest remains the same), Mach sends a 304 Not Modified response with no response body.

Listing 10-32. Using ETag and If-None-Match Headers to Test for Content Modification

```
example-009$ curl -v -X GET http://localhost:8080/book/1
...
< HTTP/1.1 200 OK
< ETag: cf0fdc372106caa588f794467a17e893
< Content-Type: application/json
< Date: Mon, 06 Apr 2015 01:39:11 GMT
< Connection: keep-alive
< Transfer-Encoding: chunked
<
{"id":1,"title":"God Emperor of Dune","author":"Frank Herbert"...}

example-009$ curl -v -H "If-None-Match: cf0fdc372106caa588f794467a17e893" -X GET http://
localhost:8080/book/1
...
< HTTP/1.1 304 Not Modified
< ETag: cf0fdc372106caa588f794467a17e893
< Content-Type: application/json
< Content-Length: 0
< Date: Mon, 06 Apr 2015 01:39:31 GMT
< Connection: keep-alive
<
```

In Listing 10-33, the first curl request performs an HTTP PUT that assigns Frank Herbert's full name to the book *Dune*. The second curl request is identical to the second request in Listing 10-32, but this time the server responds with an HTTP 200 OK because the message digest is different, reflecting the updated book resource. Subsequent fetches would use the newer message digest in the response's ETag header.

Listing 10-33. Updated ETag Header Passes the If-None-Match Check

```
example-009$ curl -X PUT http://localhost:8080/book/1 \
    -H "Content-Type: application/x-www-form-urlencoded" \
    -d "title=God%20Emperor%20of%20Dune&author=Franklin%20Patrick%20
    Herbert&publisher=Victor%20Gollancz&publicationDate=2003-03-13T06:00:00.000Z&series
    Title=Dune%20Chronicles&seriesPosition=4"
{"id":1,"title":"God Emperor of Dune","author":"Franklin Patrick Herbert"...}

example-009$ curl -v -H "If-None-Match: cf0fdc372106caa588f794467a17e893" -X GET http://
localhost:8080/book/1
...
< HTTP/1.1 200 OK
< ETag: 2595cd82c364b04473358bb2d0153774
< Content-Type: application/json
< Date: Mon, 06 Apr 2015 01:54:33 GMT
< Connection: keep-alive
< Transfer-Encoding: chunked
<
{"id":1,"title":"God Emperor of Dune","author":"Franklin Patrick Herbert"...}
```

Last-Modified and If-Modified-Since

The Last-Modified response header is analogous to the ETag header mentioned in the previous section, but instead of a version identifier it contains a timestamp indicating the last time the resource changed. When an HTTP client makes a request, it may supply the timestamp in an If-Modified-Since header, which is then compared to the resource's timestamp on the server. The web server will deliver only newer versions of the resource; otherwise, it will issue a 304 Not Modified response, indicating that the client should depend on the previous resource as the unmodified resource will not be included in the response body.

The code in Listing 10-34 uses the lastModified timestamp on each author record to set the Last-Modified header value in each response. This timestamp is changed automatically by the database when an author record is updated.

Listing 10-34. Adding the Last-Modified Header to Each Author Response

```
// example-009/index.js

app.get('/author/:id', function (conn) {
  var id = Number(conn.params.id);
  var deferred = Q.defer();
  db.author.findByID(id, deferred.makeNodeResolver());
  return deferred.promise.then(function (author) {
    if (!author) {
      return conn.json(404);
    }
```

```
    conn.response.setHeader('Last-Modified', author.lastModified);
    return conn.json(200, author);
  }, function (err) {
    return conn.json(500, {error: err.message});
  });
});

app.put('/author/:id', function (conn) {
  var author = Author.fromParams(conn.params);
  var deferred = Q.defer();
  db.author.save(author, deferred.makeNodeResolver());
  return deferred.promise.then(function (result) {
    conn.response.setHeader('Last-Modified', author.lastModified);
    return conn.json(result.isNew ? 201 : 200, author);
  }, function (err) {
    return conn.json(500, {error: err.message});
  });
});
```

In Listing 10-35, the first `curl` request fetches the author Hugh Howey, and the response informs the client that the last time Hugh's record was modified was on `2015-04-06T00:26:30.744Z`. In the second request, this ISO date string is used as the value of the `If-Modified-Since` header, in response to which Mach sends a `304 Not Modified` Response.

Listing 10-35. Using `Last-Modified` and `If-Modified-Since` Headers to Test for Content Modification

```
example-009$ curl -v -X GET http://localhost:8080/author/1
...
< HTTP/1.1 200 OK
< Last-Modified: 2015-04-06T00:26:30.744Z
< Content-Type: application/json
< Date: Mon, 06 Apr 2015 01:41:31 GMT
< Connection: keep-alive
< Transfer-Encoding: chunked
<
{"id":1,"name":"Hugh Howey","website":"http://www.hughhowey.com"...}

example-009$ curl -v -H "If-Modified-Since: 2015-04-06T00:26:30.744Z" -X GET
http://localhost:8080/author/1
...
< HTTP/1.1 304 Not Modified
< Last-Modified: 2015-04-06T00:26:30.744Z
< Content-Type: application/json
< Content-Length: 0
< Date: Mon, 06 Apr 2015 01:42:27 GMT
< Connection: keep-alive
<
```

Predictably, once the record has been updated (and thus, its `lastModified` date changed), Mach's response will now contain the updated JSON data in the response body, as well as a new `Last-Modified` response header. Listing 10-36 shows this exchange with two `curl` requests.

Listing 10-36. Updated Last-Modified Header Passes the If-Modified-Since Check

```
example-009$ curl -X PUT http://localhost:8080/author/1 \
    -H "Content-Type: application/x-www-form-urlencoded" \
-d "name=Hugh%20C.%20Howey&website=http%3A%2F%2Fwww.hughhowey.com&genres=Science%20
Fiction%2CFantasy%2CShort%20Stories"
{"id":1,"name":"Hugh C. Howey","website":"http://www.hughhowey.com"...}


example-009$ curl -v -H "If-Modified-Since: 2015-04-06T00:26:30.744Z" -X GET http://
localhost:8080/author/1
...
< HTTP/1.1 200 OK
< Last-Modified: 2015-04-06T02:09:01.783Z
< Content-Type: application/json
< Date: Mon, 06 Apr 2015 02:09:09 GMT
< Connection: keep-alive
< Transfer-Encoding: chunked
<
{"id":1,"name":"Hugh C. Howey","website":"http://www.hughhowey.com"...}
```

These Are Not the Routes You're Looking for...

Mach can rewrite request URLs with the Mach.rewrite middleware. While not as complex as tools like Apache's mod_rewrite module, Mach.rewrite is both simple and flexible enough to handle common rewrite use cases.

Two required parameters must be supplied when Mach.rewrite is added to the application stack:

- A regular expression object (or string that will be cast to a regular expression object) that matches incoming request URLs

- A route path to which the request will be silently forwarded

Consider a use case in which an author migrates his blog from a PHP-based system to a Node.js system running Mach. Search engines have already indexed his valuable contributions to the world, and so his URLs are solidified in perpetuity. By setting up a rewrite rule with Mach.rewrite, he can ensure that his old URLs are still made available to the outside world while mapping them to his new routing scheme.

The Mach.rewrite middleware in Listing 10-37 uses a complicated regular expression object to establish capture groups for parameters that will act as URL parameter inputs for the new blog post route: year, month, day, and slug. After the regular expression, a string representing the rewritten URL route is defined with placeholders for each of the extracted capture groups, in positional order. Under the hood Mach.rewrite uses the String.prototype.replace() method to interpolate the extracted values.

Listing 10-37. Rewriting a URL with Parameters

```
// example-010/index.js

var blogView = swig.compileFile(path.join(__dirname, 'blog.swig'));
var errView = swig.compileFile(path.join(__dirname, 'err.swig'));

app.use(
  mach.rewrite,
  // converts: /index.php/blog/2015-04-02/bacon-ipsum-dolor-amet
  new RegExp('\/index\.php\/blog\/([\\d]{4})-([\\d]{2})-([\\d]{2})\/([^\/]+)'),
```

```
  // into: /blog/2015/04/02/bacon-ipsum-dolor-amet
  '/blog/$1/$2/$3/$4'
);

// :year=$1, :month=$2, :day=$3, :slug=$4
app.get('/blog/:year/:month/:day/:slug', function (conn) {
  var year = Number(conn.params.year || 0),
    month = Number(conn.params.month || 0),
    day = Number(conn.params.day || 0),
    slug = conn.params.slug || '';
  var deferred = Q.defer();
  db.posts.find(year, month, day, slug, deferred.makeNodeResolver());
  return deferred.promise.then(function (post) {
    if (post) {
      return conn.html(200, blogView({posts: [post]}));
    }
    return conn.html(404, errView({message: 'I haven\t written that yet.'}))
  }, function (err) {
    return conn.html(500, errView(err));
  });
});
```

To an HTTP client, such as the web browser shown in Figure 10-6 (or a search engine bot), rewritten URLs are still completely valid, though internally they are morphed into something different. This differs from HTTP redirects or forwards where the *client* is responsible for interpreting response headers and then loading another page. In this case the client is none the wiser.

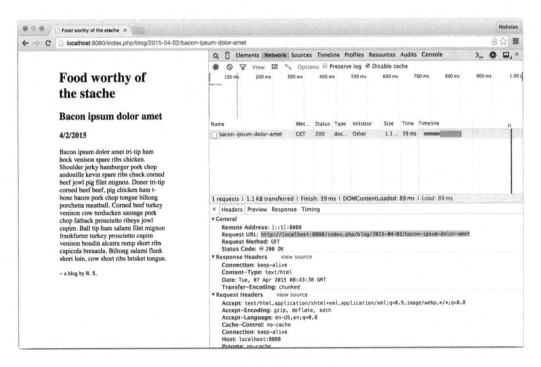

Figure 10-6. *Rewritten URLs appear unmodified to the HTTP client*

The rewrite rule in Listing 10-38 performs the same exact work, but uses a simple string instead of a regular expression for the request URL match because it captures no parameters. Be aware that Mach. rewrite will auto-escape any *string* before converting it to a regular expression. If you escape these strings yourself, they will become doubly escaped and your match rule will fail.

Listing 10-38. Rewriting a URL with No Parameters

```
// example-010/index.js

app.use(
  mach.rewrite,
  '/index.php/blog',
  '/blog'
);

app.get('/blog', function (conn) {
  var deferred = Q.defer();
  db.posts.all(deferred.makeNodeResolver());
  return deferred.promise.then(function (posts) {
    return conn.html(200, blogView({posts: posts}));
  }, function (err) {
    return conn.html(500, errView(err));
  });
});
```

The Hosts with the Most

Mach.mapper is unique in that it performs its own manner of routing on top of Mach's normal routing mechanism. Up to this point it has been assumed that route paths exist for a single host (localhost) and are all relative to that host's name. The Mach.mapper middleware changes this paradigm by introducing a middleware filter that can route requests by both hostname *and* URL pathname, in much the same spirit as Apache's virtual hosts, though with a much lighter footprint.

To demonstrate how Mach's mapping feature works, execute the echo commands in Listing 10-39 to add two aliases to the /etc/hosts file on your computer. Because /etc/hosts is protected on Unix-like systems, the sudo command is used to elevate permissions. If this command fails, you may also add the aliases manually to /etc/hosts with a text editor like vim or nano. The cat command will output the content of /etc/hosts to the terminal so you can verify that the entries have been added.

Listing 10-39. Adding Aliases to /etc/hosts

```
example-011$ sudo echo "127.0.0.1 house-atreides.org" >> /etc/hosts
example-011$ sudo echo "127.0.0.1 house-harkonnen.org" >> /etc/hosts
example-011$ cat /etc/hosts
...
127.0.0.1 house-atreides.org
127.0.0.1 house-harkonnen.org
```

■ **Tip** If your computer runs the Microsoft Windows operating system, you will need to modify the file C:\Windows\System32\drivers\etc\hosts. This file is typically protected by Windows, so you will need to use a text editor running with administrator privileges to modify it.

Once the /etc/hosts file has been modified, use the ping command as shown in Listing 10-40 to verify that each alias resolves to 127.0.0.1 (localhost).

Listing 10-40. Using ping to Test Aliases in /etc/hosts

```
example-011$ ping -t 3 house-atreides.org
PING house-atreides.org (127.0.0.1): 56 data bytes
64 bytes from 127.0.0.1: icmp_seq=0 ttl=64 time=0.044 ms
64 bytes from 127.0.0.1: icmp_seq=1 ttl=64 time=0.118 ms
64 bytes from 127.0.0.1: icmp_seq=2 ttl=64 time=0.074 ms

--- house-atreides.org ping statistics ---
3 packets transmitted, 3 packets received, 0.0% packet loss
round-trip min/avg/max/stddev = 0.044/0.079/0.118/0.030 ms
```

The web server in Listing 10-41 demonstrates how Mach.mapper works. It begins like any normal Mach web server: an application stack is created, a few bits of middleware are added, and then things diverge a bit. Two additional independent application stacks—atreidesApp and harkonnenApp—are also created, and each of these stacks is assigned a route. In fact, *all* of the application stacks are given the *same* route, GET / about.

Listing 10-41. Mach.mapper Middleware Maps Apps to Hostnames

```
// example-011/index.js
// ...

var app = mach.stack();

app.use(mach.logger);
app.use(mach.params);
app.use(mach.file, path.join(__dirname, 'public'));

var atreidesApp = mach.stack();

atreidesApp.get('/about', function (conn) {
  var pagePath = path.join(__dirname, 'atreides.html');
  return conn.html(200, fs.createReadStream(pagePath));
});

var harkonnenApp = mach.stack();

harkonnenApp.get('/about', function (conn) {
  var pagePath = path.join(__dirname, 'harkonnen.html');
  return conn.html(200, fs.createReadStream(pagePath));
});

app.use(mach.mapper, {
  'http://house-atreides.org/': atreidesApp,
  'http://house-harkonnen.org/': harkonnenApp
});
```

```
app.get('/about', function (conn) {
  var pagePath = path.join(__dirname, 'about.html');
  return conn.html(200, fs.createReadStream(pagePath));
});
```

It is clear from examining the body of each route function that these apps all render different HTML pages when invoked. These routes can all coexist because the Mach.mapper middleware maps the atreidesApp application stack to the hose-atreides.org hostname and the harkonnenApp to the house-harkonnen.org hostname in its options hash. When requests are received by the web server, they are passed through the Mach.mapper middleware where the Connection.hostname property is evaluated. If it matches any key on the mapping options object, the connection is passed to the application stack associated with that key for further processing. This has several interesting consequences:

- Application stacks that vary by hostname may have the same routes, such as GET / about.

- Since middleware are attached directly to application stacks, each stack may have different middleware.

- Any middleware added to the hosting application stack *before* Mach.mapper will be applied to *all* application stacks that Mach.mapper manages.

- Any routes added to the hosting application stack *before* Mach.mapper will be evaluated *before* Mach.mapper has a chance to do hostname-based routing. Because the hostname is *not* evaluated without Mach.mapper, routes on the hosting application stack with the same URL *pathname* value would resolve, regardless of hostname.

- Any routes added to the hosting application stack *after* Mach.mapper will act as "fall-through" routes. If no mapped application stack can handle a request for the connection's hostname, these routes will then be evaluated.

■ **Tip** When adding a host to Mach.mapper, the protocol matters but the port number does not, so the port number may be safely omitted. Mach only listens on *one* port. Hostname keys should always end with a trailing slash.

Run the web server, then launch a web browser and navigate to the URL http://localhost:8080/ about. This will open the page shown in Figure 10-7, which comes from the /about route defined on the hosting application stack. This route handled the request because the hostname, localhost, did not match any hostname in the Mach.mapper configuration.

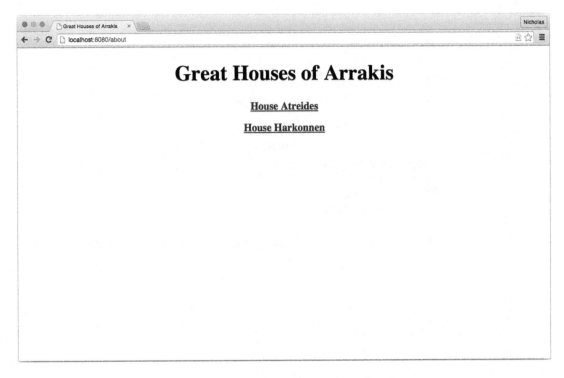

Figure 10-7. *The /about route from* `localhost`

The page source in Listing 10-42 reveals that the two hyperlink anchors, one for House Atreides and one for House Harkonnen, both link to different hosts. Clicking on either link will render the page from the mapped routes defined by `Mach.mapper`. Note that, though the port number is immaterial when declaring mapped application stacks, they must be included in the page hyperlinks or the browser will attempt to use port 80 automatically.

Listing 10-42. Anchors on the Default /about Page Link to Different Hosts

```
<h1>Great Houses of Arrakis</h1>
<h2>
  <a href="http://house-atreides.org:8080/about">House Atreides</a>
</h2>
<h2>
  <a href="http://house-harkonnen.org:8080/about">House Harkonnen</a>
</h2>
```

Figure 10-8 shows the House Atreides "about" page, fully rendered. Figure 10-9 shows the House Harkonnen "about" page.

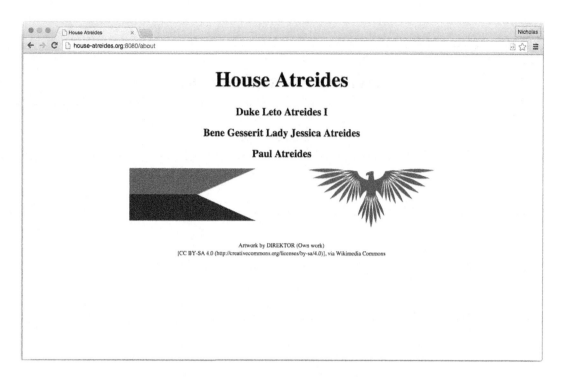

Figure 10-8. *The /about route from house-atreides.org*

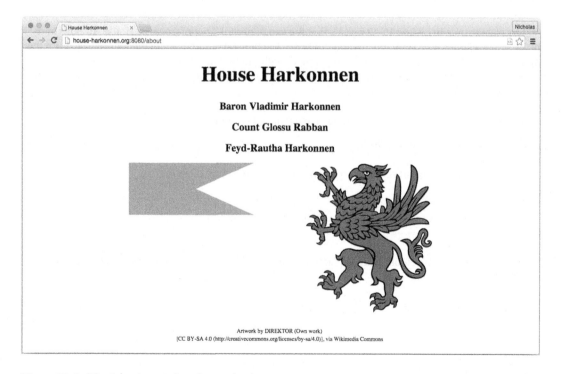

Figure 10-9. *The /about route from house-harkonnen.org*

Looking at the source code for both "about" pages reveals something interesting. Images referenced on both pages, such as the src attribute in Listing 10-43, do not specify a hostname prefix.

Listing 10-43. Images Do Not Have Hostname Prefixes

```
<img class="flag" src="/images/Atreides_guidon_pennant.svg" />
```

This is possible because the Mach.file middleware, which exposes the example-011/public directory as a static resource directory, was added to the hosting application stack before Mach.mapper, thus affecting *all* application stacks upstream. All static resources—images, fonts, scripts, and so on—can be stored in the same location, available to all application stacks regardless of hostname. Each application stack can, of course, use an alternative Mach.file middleware to expose different static asset directories if needed.

Custom Middleware

Creating custom Mach middleware is relatively straightforward. There are generally three "layers" involved when creating custom middleware:

1. A top-level function that is responsible for capturing an "app" and any options that are passed to the middleware via app.use(). This layer returns...

2. a function that will receive an incoming request connection. This function may do one of two things. It may manipulate the connection directly and send a response without passing the connection through the remainder of the application stack (an authentication failure, for example), or...

3. it may send the request downstream and then handle the response when the application stack's promise chain has resolved.

The middleware in Listing 10-44 shows all three stages at work.

Listing 10-44. Custom Middleware Module That Adds an API Version Header to the Response

```
// example-012/api-version.js
'use strict';

// layer 1
function apiVersion(app, options) {
  // layer 2
  return function (conn) {
    // layer 3
    return conn.call(app).then(function () {
      conn.response.headers['X-API-Version'] = options.version;
    });
  };
}

module.exports = apiVersion;
```

The top-level function, apiVersion(),is exposed via module.exports. It will be passed to app.use() when the middleware is attached to an application stack. It captures the application instance and the options object (layer 1), holding both in a closure for further processing. When a request is received, the returned function (layer 2) receives the connection object and makes a decision. This particular middleware is only concerned with adding an "API version" header to the response, so at this point it invokes the Connection.call() method, passing the app itself as the sole argument.

At this point some disambiguation is necessary. In Mach, the "application stack" created by invoking Mach.stack() is a function that accepts a connection and returns the value of Connection.call(). *This process is identical to what a Mach middleware function does.* In fact, this is nearly identical to what a route does: both Connection.call() and all routes return promise objects that exist as a single promise chain!

The practical implication of this similitude is that the "app" a Mach middleware function receives may be either another piece of downstream middleware or a route, depending on the order of middleware/routes added to the application stack. By passing the app object to conn.call(), then, the custom middleware propagates the connection to everything downstream, whatever that may be. When the promise returned by conn.call() resolves (layer 3), all downstream middleware and/or a route have already dealt with the connection object and the custom middleware may decide what, if anything, it must do with the response.

In Listing 10-44, the API version number is assigned to the custom X-API-Version header on the response object once the response is moving upstream again. Had this middleware been designed to modify the request *before* passing it downstream, it would have done so before invoking conn.call().

Custom middleware are attached to the application stack in the same manner as Mach's native middleware, as shown in Listing 10-45. In this example the apiVersion middleware will receive an options object with the version number 1.2, which will be added to each response as a custom header value. Note that Mach.gzip is added to the stack *after* apiVersion, which means that the "app" argument that the apiVersion middleware receives will be the middleware function for Mach.gzip, since it exists just downstream in the stack.

Listing 10-45. Adding Custom Middleware to the Application Stack

```
// example-012/index.js
var apiVersion = require('./api-version');

// create a stack
var app = mach.stack();

// custom middleware
app.use(apiVersion, {version: '1.2'});

// out-of-the-box middleware
app.use(mach.gzip);

app.get('/numbers', function (conn) {
  return conn.json(200, [4, 8, 15, 16, 23, 42]);
});
```

When the web server is queried in Listing 10-46, the X-API-Version header may be seen in the detailed response.

Listing 10-46. API Version Middleware Response Header

```
example-012$ curl -v -X GET http://localhost:8080/numbers
* Hostname was NOT found in DNS cache
*    Trying ::1...
* Connected to localhost (::1) port 8080 (#0)
> GET /numbers HTTP/1.1
> User-Agent: curl/7.37.1
```

```
> Host: localhost:8080
> Accept: */*
>
< HTTP/1.1 200 OK
< Content-Type: application/json
< X-API-Version: 1.2
< Date: Fri, 10 Apr 2015 01:41:42 GMT
< Connection: keep-alive
< Transfer-Encoding: chunked
<
[4,8,15,16,23,42]
```

Mach, the HTTP Client

Mach is much more than an HTTP server. Its internal architecture allows it to play multiple roles in multiple environments. In fact, an examination of the Mach source code reveals that the portions of Mach that are server-specific are implemented as *extensions*. This means that Mach's core objects, such as Connection, Location, and Message, can span multiple use cases.

The code in Listing 10-47 resembles the web server examples presented so far. A Mach application stack is created to service HTTP requests, file middleware is added to serve static content from example-013/ public, and a single route, GET /mach/tags, is registered with the stack. The code within this route, however, takes advantage of Mach's HTTP client features to send a GET request for all of Mach's repository tags to the Github API.

Listing 10-47. Mach As Both Server and Client

```
// example-013/index.js
var app = mach.stack();
app.use(mach.logger);
app.use(mach.file, {
  root: path.join(__dirname, 'public'),
  index: true
});

app.get('/releases', function (conn) {
  function addUserAgent(conn) {
    conn.request.setHeader('User-Agent', 'nicholascloud/mach');
  }
  return mach.get('https://api.github.com/repos/mjackson/mach/tags', addUserAgent);
}).then(function (conn) {
  var tags = [];
  JSON.parse(conn.responseText).forEach(function (tagData) {
    tags.push(tagData.name);
  });
  return tags.sort(semver.rcompare);
}).then(function (tags) {
  return conn.json(200, tags);
}, function (err) {
  return conn.json(500, {err: err.message});
});
});
```

289

Mach's HTTP client methods look much like Mach's routing methods, but they exist on the Mach module itself, not on an application stack. Mach can issue requests for any standard HTTP method.

In Listing 10-47 the `Mach.get()` method receives the request URL as its first parameter and an optional function to modify the connection's request *before* it has been sent as its second. This request connects to the Github API and fetches tag information for the `mjackson/mach` repository. Because the Github API requires a `User-Agent` header in all incoming requests, the `addUserAgent()` function modifies the outgoing request by adding my own source code fork as the agent (per Github's guidelines).

Like other parts of the Mach API, the `Mach.get()` method returns a promise. If the promise resolves, its value will be the connection object with a response message property. If rejected, an error will be passed to the failure callback.

The Github JSON data exists as a string at the `Connection.responseText` property (or as the stream at `Connection.response.content`). Once this data is deserialized, the tag names are extracted, sorted in descending order, and then passed along the promise chain.

When the web server is queried with `curl` in Listing 10-48, all of Mach's release tags are delivered as a JSON array.

Listing 10-48. Fetching Mach Releases with cURL

```
example-013$ curl http://localhost:8080/releases
["v1.3.4","v1.3.3","v1.3.2","v1.3.1","v1.3.0"...]
```

This JSON data is consumed by the HTML page in Listing 10-49. Notice that it *also* uses `Mach.get()` to connect to the local web server. Because Mach's environment-dependent features are implemented as extensions, Mach can be useful in both server and browser code.

■ **Note** Because Mach is a Node.js module, it can be used by any CommonJS module loader, such as Browserify or WebPack. All other uses, such as the plain script inclusion shown in Listing 10-49, should use the global Mach build from the Mach Github repository.

Browse to `http://localhost:8080` to see a list of links to all Mach releases.

Listing 10-49. `Mach.get()` in the Browser

```html
<!-- example-013/public/index.html -->
<h1>Mach Releases</h1>
<h2>Git you one!</h2>
<ul id="tags"></ul>
<script src="/vendor/mach.min.js"></script>
<script>
(function (mach, document) {
  var href = 'https://github.com/mjackson/mach/releases/tag/:tag';
  var ul = document.querySelector('#tags');

  mach.get('/releases').then(function (conn) {
    var tags = JSON.parse(conn.responseText);
    tags.forEach(function (tag) {
      var li = document.createElement('li');
```

```
    var a = document.createElement('a');
    a.innerHTML = tag;
    a.setAttribute('href', href.replace(':tag', tag));
    a.setAttribute('target', '_blank');
    li.appendChild(a);
    ul.appendChild(li);
  });
 });
}(window.mach, window.document))
</script>
```

Mach, the HTTP Proxy

While technically middleware, Mach's HTTP proxy functionality can be used by itself to create a full HTTP proxy server, or integrated with an existing application stack to proxy certain routes. This can be a useful tool for migrating web applications piecemeal while still proxying calls to a legacy web application, or for avoiding same-origin concerns in the browser by proxying calls to an external or third-party service through the web application itself.

The code in Listing 10-50 creates a simple Mach application that serves both a root application route and static files from the public directory. *After* the route declaration, a proxy application is created by calling Mach.proxy() with the HTTP scheme, hostname, and port of another server. For this example, when the web application is run it will listen for some requests on port 8080 while proxying other requests to another web server running on port 8090. This proxy application stack becomes the middleware options argument for Mach.proxy when both are passed to app.use().

Listing 10-50. Proxying Requests to Another Web Server

```
// example-014/web.js
var app = mach.stack();
app.use(mach.logger);
app.use(mach.file, path.join(__dirname, 'public'));

app.get('/', function (conn) {
  var pagePath = path.join(__dirname, 'index.html');
  return conn.html(200, fs.createReadStream(pagePath));
});

var apiProxy = mach.createProxy('http://localhost:8090');

app.use(mach.proxy, apiProxy);

mach.serve(app, 8080);
```

Typically middleware are added to an application stack before routes so that they have a chance to examine the request and interrupt the middleware promise chain if some condition isn't met, or modify the request and pass it along for further processing. Unfortunately, Mach.proxy is fairly dumb, which means that it does not discriminate among requests; any request that passes through Mach.proxy *will* be sent to the proxy server. If an application uses a mix of local and proxied routes, there are two ways to deal with this "limitation":

- Add the proxy middleware *after* application routes have been added. This ensures that if an application route can handle a request, it *will* handle it, stopping the propagation of the connection before it reaches Mach.proxy. This is the approach taken in Listing 10-50.

- Wrap the proxy middleware in a lightweight custom middleware function that discriminates among and only forwards certain requests to the proxy. Because it filters requests, the custom middleware can be added to the stack before any routes. This alternative approach is illustrated in Listing 10-51.

Listing 10-51. Wrapping a Proxy Application in Custom Middleware

```
// example-014/web2.js
var apiProxy = mach.createProxy('http://localhost:8090');

app.use(function (app) {
  return function (conn) {
    if (conn.location.pathname.indexOf('/api') !== 0) {
      // not an API method, call the app stack normally
      return conn.call(app);
    }
    // API method, call the proxy app stack
    return conn.call(apiProxy);
  };
});

app.get('/', function (conn) { /*...*/ });
```

The simulated API server that receives proxy requests is, to no one's surprise, another Mach server. It exposes two regular JSON routes, shown in Listing 10-52: one to fetch a tallied list of votes and another to submit a single vote.

Listing 10-52. API Server's Routes

```
// example-014/api.js
var votes = require('./votes');
// ...

app.get('/api/vote', function (conn) {
  var tallies = {};
  var voteCount = votes.length;
  votes.forEach(function (vote) {
    var tally = tallies[vote] || {
      count: 0,
      percent: 0.0
    };
    tally.count += 1;
    tally.percent = Number((tally.count / voteCount * 100).toFixed(2));
```

```
    tallies[vote] = tally;
    return tallies;
  });
  return conn.json(200, tallies);
});

app.post('/api/vote', function (conn) {
  console.log(conn.params);
  var vote = conn.params.vote || '';
  if (!vote) {
    return conn.json(400, {err: 'Empty vote submitted.'});
  }
  votes.push(vote);
  return conn.json(201, {count: 1});
});

mach.serve(app, 8090);
```

■ **Note**   To run example-014, both web.js (or web2.js) and api.js must be launched with Node.js. The web server will listen for HTTP requests on port 8080, and the API server will listen on port 8090.

The web server renders an HTML page as the user interface for a small voting application. Though it is common knowledge that "you don't vote for kings," the peasantry is still fond of popularity contests and this web application indulges them. Figure 10-10 shows the rendered page at http://localhost:8080.

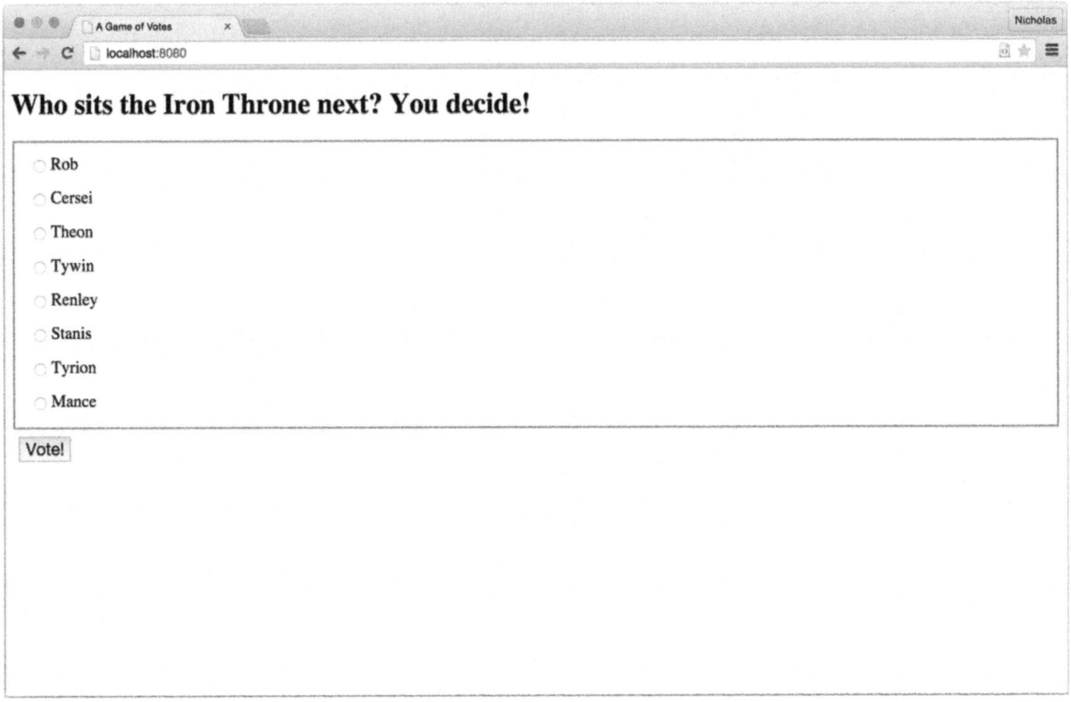

Figure 10-10. *Voting for a new monarch*

When the form is submitted, an event handler finds the checked option value and sends a request to the web server with the vote data. The sendVote() method in Listing 10-53 makes an AJAX request to POST /api/data *on the web server,* which is then proxied to the API server where the vote is recorded.

Once the submission is complete, the getTallies() function in Listing 10-53 queries the web server at GET /api/vote to fetch the vote tallies. Again, this request is proxied and the JSON data is returned to the client.

Listing 10-53. Submitting a Vote

```
// example-014/index.html
var formPoll = document.querySelector('#poll');
// ...

function sendVote(vote) {
  function serializeVote(conn) {
    conn.request.setHeader('Content-Type', 'application/json');
    conn.request.content = JSON.stringify({
      vote: vote
    });
  }
  return mach.post('/api/vote', serializeVote);
}

function getTallies() {
  return mach.get('/api/vote').then(function (conn) {
    return JSON.parse(conn.responseText);
  });
}

formPoll.addEventListener('submit', function (e) {
  // ...
  var vote = checkbox.value;
  sendVote(vote).then(function () {
    // ...
    return getTallies().then(function (tallies) {
      // show tally data...
    });
  }).catch(function (error) {
    showError(error.err || error.message || 'The night is dark and full of errors.');
  });
});
```

The web page displays the proxied tally data, shown in Figure 10-11, once the response has been received and parsed.

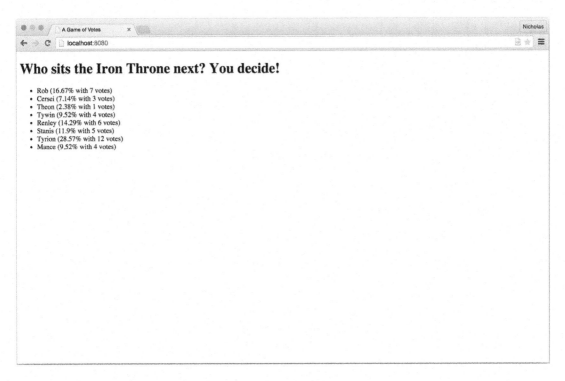

Figure 10-11. *Tallies are displayed when a vote is submitted*

If errors occur during a proxied request—for example, if the API server is offline—they will be returned to the client as HTTP request errors. Because these errors will be infrastructure related and not application related, it may be wise to handle them in a custom middleware wrapper and deliver more meaningful errors instead.

Summary

While Mach certainly isn't the only, or even the most popular, Node.js web server available, it has a strong simplicity and terse API that make it flexible. Its core architecture ensures that its common components are available everywhere while its environment-specific components are loaded as extensions.

A suite of common middleware that plugs into a promise-based API makes request and response chains easy to tap and manipulate. Custom middleware is simple to write when more functionality is required.

Request and response messages build on Node's native streams by parsing request queries and bodies on-demand, and delivering response content to clients in chunks. This ensures that the lowest possible memory and processing overhead are used during HTTP operations. Request and response content may also be piped, converted to buffers for in-memory manipulation, parsed by various format handlers, and converted to strings with varied encodings.

Beyond Mach's role as an HTTP server, it can fulfill several other important HTTP-related roles:

- Rewriting request URLs

- Mapping requests to virtual hosts

- Acting as an HTTP proxy

- Sending HTTP client requests

Mach's fresh ideas are worthy additions to the Node.js web server pantheon.

CHAPTER 11

Mongoose

The human mind gets used to strangeness very quickly if [strangeness] does not exhibit interesting behavior.

—Dan Simmons

MongoDB is a popular cross-platform document database, often lumped into the "NoSQL" classification with other nonrelational data stores such as CouchDB, Cassandra, RavenDB, and so forth. It is a popular choice for data storage among Node.js developers because its "records" are stored as plain JSON objects, and its query interface and stored functions are written in plain JavaScript.

Storing, accessing, and manipulating data in MongoDB is not terribly complex, but Node.js libraries such as Mongoose can help application developers map MongoDB documents onto application objects that have definite schemas, validations, and behavior—all concepts that are not (by design) parts of MongoDB. Mongoose implements the query interface native to MongoDB, but also gives developers a composable, fluent interface that simplifies portions of the query API.

Though MongoDB is not the direct subject of this chapter, it is necessary to establish a few basic concepts about how MongoDB works before delving into Mongoose. If you're familiar MongoDB already, feel free to skip the next section.

Basic MongoDB Concepts

A relational database server hosts database schemas (sometimes just called databases), which encapsulate related entities like tables, views, stored procedures, functions, etc. Database tables in turn contain tuples (also known as rows or records). A tuple is composed of a number of fields, each containing a value of a predetermined data type. The tuple is one-dimensional, and its definition (the data types its fields can hold) is determined at the table level. All tuples within a table, then, share the same structure, though their individual field values may differ. The names and data types of a tuple's fields are referred to as the tuple's schema.

MongoDB has a superficially similar data hierarchy, as shown in Table 11-1.

Table 11-1. *Understanding MongoDB by Analogy to Relational Database Systems*

RDBMS	MongoDB
Server	Server
Schema	Database
Table	Collection
Tuple	Document
Field	Property

Table 11-2 defines the key terms that describe Mongoose components and how they relate to each other. The code in Listing 11-1 shows how these terms are appear in code. This chapter will cover each in detail but because many of them are closely related, you might wish to refer back to this section as the chapter progresses.

Table 11-2. *Mongoose Terms and Definitions*

Term	Definition
Schema	Defines the data types, constraints, defaults, validations, and so forth for the properties of a document instance; enforced at the application level
Model	Constructor function that creates or fetches document instances
Document	Instance object created or fetched by a Mongoose model; will have Mongoose-specific properties and methods as well as data properties
JSON object	Plain JavaScript object that contains only the data properties from a document

Listing 11-1. Mongoose Terms and Definitions in Code

```
// albumSchema is a schema
var albumSchema = mongoose.Schema({/*...*/});

// Album is a model
var Album = mongoose.model('Album', albumSchema);

// Album is a model
Album.findById(/*...*/, function (err, album) {
  // album is a document
  console.log(album);
});

// Album is a model
Album.findById(/*...*/)
  .lean(true)
  .exec(function (err, album) {
    // album is a JSON object (because of `lean(true)`)
    console.log(album);
  });
```

```
// Album is a model
Album.findById(/*...*/)
  .exec(function (err, album) {
    // album is a document
    // toObject() returns a JSON object
    console.log(album.toObject());
  });
```

Unlike RDBMS tuples, MongoDB documents are *not* one-dimensional. They are complete JSON objects that may contain other objects or arrays. In fact, documents within the same collection need not even have the same properties, because MongoDB collections are actually schemaless. A MongoDB collection can hold document objects of any shape or size (within MongoDB's storage limits). In practice, though, collections tend to hold documents of similar "shape," though some may have optional properties, or may contain properties that represent some arbitrary data. But in general, applications usually assume that data exists in particular "shapes," so although MongoDB does not enforce document schemas, applications often do.

By default, MongoDB documents are automatically assigned a surrogate primary key called _id. This key has a special type (MongoDB's ObjectId type) and is used as MongoDB's primary collection index. MongoDB can use a different field as a primary key if directed. Additional fields can be added to secondary indexes within a collection, either as simple or compound keys.

MongoDB does not support the notion of foreign keys, a strong feature of RDBMS databases. Instead, MongoDB relies on the power of nested documents to store data associations. Consider the classic trinity of all RDBMS examples: customer, postal address, and shopping cart order. In an RDBMS system, there would likely be foreign keys from the postal address to the customer (to identify residency), and from the order to one or more postal addresses (to identify shipping and billing addresses). In a MongoDB customer document, however, it would be sufficient to simply store the postal address as a nested object in the customer document *as well as* the order document. Consider Listing 11-2.

Listing 11-2. Duplication Sometimes Acceptable in MongoDB

```
// customer
{
  "_id": 1001,
  "name": "...",
  "postalAddress" {
    "street": "...",
    "city": "...",
    "state": "...",
    "zip": "..."
  }
}

// order
{
  "_id": 2001,
  "customer": 1001,
  "items": [
    {"sku": 3001, "qty": 2}
  ],
```

```
"shippingAddress" {
    "street": "...",
    "city": "...",
    "state": "...",
    "zip": "..."
  }
}
```

There are any number of reasons why this "violation" of referential integrity might be acceptable from a business point of view:

- Perhaps orders are never altered. If there is a mistake in an order—for example, the shipping address is wrong—the entire order gets re-created to offset the faulty order. The correct shipping address gets added to the new order.

- If a customer changes a postal address, old orders won't be updated with the new address, so there's no data integrity issue at stake.

- Maybe changing a postal address always happens within the customer domain, never in the order domain.

- Perhaps a customer can override a shipping address with a "temporary" address (shipping a gift) that should *not* be added to the customer record.

- If different postal metrics are derived from orders than from customers (e.g., a C-level executive wants to know how many orders were shipped to Missouri last month regardless of who actually *lives* in Missouri this month), that data is already segregated.

- Maybe disk space is cheap and the velocity gained by not enforcing referential integrity outweighs any potential cost.

While foreign keys and referential integrity are critical to RDBMS databases, strong MongoDB document design can often render the issue moot.

Finally, though MongoDB's query API may look a bit daunting to SQL practitioners, it quickly becomes obvious that, for the most part, looking for data involves the same concepts: selecting (find), filtering (where), applying compound conditions (and, or, in), aggregating (group), paging (skip, limit), and so on. How queries are composed and executed differs mostly in syntax.

A Simple Mongoose Example

Mongoose is a library for Node.js applications. To develop with Mongoose (and follow the examples in this chapter), you need to install Node.js and MongoDB on your platform of choice. The default installation procedure and configuration for both should be sufficient to run this chapter's example code.

■ **Note**   This chapter assumes that you are familiar with Node.js applications and modules, and that you know how to install them with npm. A working knowledge of MongoDB will be very helpful, but it is not required, since interaction with MongoDB will mostly occur through Mongoose in the chapter examples. Some examples will demonstrate how to query MongoDB directly to verify the results of Mongoose operations.

This section demonstrates basic Mongoose concepts that will be explored in detail later in this chapter. This example involves three steps:

1. Create a basic Mongoose schema that reflects the structured data in a JSON file.

2. Read the JSON file and import the data into MongoDB with a Mongoose model.

3. Run a basic web server that will use a Mongoose model to fetch data from MongoDB and deliver it to a web browser.

The first line of each listing that follows will show the file path in which the example code may be found. Subsequent examples will indicate whether a particular example file should be executed with Node.js in a terminal.

Creating a Mongoose Schema for JSON Data

Mongoose documents represent the domain data in an application. For this chapter's example application, a JSON file of music albums defines the initial set of data to be added to MongoDB. Listing 11-3 shows the structure of example-001/albums.json: an array of album objects, each containing information about the composer, title, publication year, track list, and so forth.

Listing 11-3. Album JSON Data File

```
// example-001/albums.json
[
  {
    "composer": "Kerry Muzzey",
    "title": "Renaissance",
    "price": 4.95,
    "releaseDate": "2014-01-13T06:00:00.000Z",
    "inPublication": true,
    "genre": ["Classical", "Trailer Music", "Soundtrack"],
    "tracks": [
      {
        "title": "The Looking Glass",
        "duration": {
          "m": 3,
          "s": 20
        }
      }
      //additional tracks...
    ]
  }
  //additional albums...
]
```

Mongoose is an object data mapper (ODM), so at the heart of Mongoose data access are model functions that can be used to query the MongoDB collections they represent. A Mongoose model must have a name by which it can be referred, and a schema that enforces the shape of the data it will access and manipulate. The code in Listing 11-4 creates an album schema that closely matches the JSON data in example-001/albums. json. Schemas will be covered in detail later, but it should be apparent that a schema defines the properties and their data types for a given Mongoose model. Finally, a model function is created by pairing a name ("Album") with a schema. This model function is assigned to module.exports in the example-001/album-model.js file so that it can be imported into other modules as needed in a Node.js application.

■ **Tip** A Mongoose schema defines the data structure for a model. The model function provides the query interface for working with stored document data. A model must have a name and a schema.

Listing 11-4. Mongoose Album Schema and Model

```
// example-001/album-model.js
'use strict';
var mongoose = require('mongoose');

var albumSchema = mongoose.Schema({
  composer: String,
  title: String,
  price: Number,
  releaseDate: Date,
  inPublication: Boolean,
  genre: [String],
  tracks: [
    {
      title: String,
      duration: {
        m: Number,
        s: Number
      }
    }
  ]
});

var Album = mongoose.model('Album', albumSchema);

module.exports = Album;
```

Importing Data with Mongoose

Now that the Album schema and model are defined, a Node.js script can read the data from albums.json and use the Album model to create documents in MongoDB. The import script needs to do three things:

1. Connect to a running MongoDB server with Mongoose

2. Read and parse the contents of the albums.json file.

3. Use the Album model to create documents in MongoDB.

Mongoose connects to MongoDB with a URI that identifies the protocol, server, and database that Mongoose will use. In Listing 11-5 the URI simply points to the local MongoDB instance: mongodb://localhost/music. Mongoose will proactively create the database if it does not already exist on the MongoDB instance, so there is no need to do so manually. If the MongoDB connection fails, Mongoose will raise an error event, and if it succeeds, Mongoose will raise an open event. Listing 11-5 demonstrates how both events are handled with callback functions. Once the open event is emitted, the albums.json file is read and parsed, and the array of albums is passed to the Album.create() method of the Album model. This creates the album documents in MongoDB, which may then be queried with the Album model later.

Listing 11-5. Importing Album Data with Mongoose

```
// example-001/import-albums.js
'use strict';
var mongoose = require('mongoose');
var Album = require('./album-model');
var file2json = require('./file2json');
var fs = require('fs');
var path = require('path');

// connect to the "music" database on localhost;
// the database will be automatically created
// if it does not exist
mongoose.connect('mongodb://localhost/music');
var db = mongoose.connection;

db.on('error', function (err) {
  console.error(err);
  process.exit(1);
});

db.once('open', function importAlbums() {
  var albumsFile = path.join(__dirname, 'albums.json');
  file2json(albumsFile, 'utf8', function (err, albums) {
    if (err) {
      console.error(err);
      return process.exit(1);
    }

    console.log('creating %d albums', albums.length);

    // use the model to create albums in bulk;
    // the collection will be automatically created
    // if it does not exist
    Album.create(albums, function (err) {
      if (err) {
        console.error(err);
        return process.exit(1);
      }
      process.exit(0);
    });
  });
});
```

Before running the script, MongoDB needs to be running locally. Some MongoDB installations will configure MongoDB to start automatically, but others leave that decision to users. To determine if MongoDB is running, simply execute the mongo command in your terminal. You should see output similar to Listing 11-6 if MongoDB is running. You may kill the process at any time by pressing Ctrl+c.

Listing 11-6. MongoDB Terminal Client, mongo

```
$ mongo
MongoDB shell version: 2.6.7
connecting to: test
>
```

If you receive an error, start the MongoDB server manually by executing mongod -f followed by the location of the default MongoDB configuration file. The location of this file varies by system, so you may need to consult the MongoDB installation documentation. On OS X systems with a Homebrew MongoDB installation, for example, the configuration file may be found at /usr/local/etc/mongod.conf. Listing 11-7 shows how to start the daemon manually with this configuration file path.

Listing 11-7. Starting mongod Manually.

```
$ mongod -f /usr/local/etc/mongod.conf
```

Once the mongod server has been started, you can run the example-001/import-albums.js script with Node.js. Listing 11-8 shows the output that will be displayed when the script has imported documents into MongoDB.

Listing 11-8. Running the Import Script

```
example-001$ node import-albums.js
creating 3 albums
```

In Listing 11-9 the mongo terminal client is launched, followed by a series of commands (after each > prompt) to verify that the music database and albums collection have been created. The show dbs command displays all databases hosted by the running MongoDB instance. To see the collections in a database, first switch to that database context by issuing the use <db> command, where <db> is the name of the database you are targeting. Next, execute show collections to see a list of collections owned by the database—in this case, albums and system.indexes (a collection that MongoDB manages).

Listing 11-9. Verifying Album Data Has Been Added to MongoDB

```
$ mongo
MongoDB shell version: 2.6.7
connecting to: test
> show dbs
admin      (empty)
local      0.078GB
music      0.078GB
> use music
switched to db music
> show collections
albums
system.indexes
>
```

With the music database selected, you can issue a few basic queries to see the album data added during the import. Within a database context, the database collections are accessed through the db object. Collections exist as properties of the db object, and operations performed against collections are methods on each collection object, respectively. To see the number of records within the albums collection, for example, the db.albums.count() method can be invoked on the collection, as shown in Listing 11-10. Likewise, to query album records, the db.albums.find() method can be used with criteria ("where" clause) and projection ("select" clause) arguments to control what data is returned.

Listing 11-10. Querying Album Data in the albums Collection

```
> db.albums.count()
3
> db.albums.find({}, {composer: 1})
{ "_id" : ObjectId("54c537ca46a13e0f4cebda82"), "composer" : "Kerry Muzzey" }
{ "_id" : ObjectId("54c537ca46a13e0f4cebda88"), "composer" : "Audiomachine" }
{ "_id" : ObjectId("54c537ca46a13e0f4cebdaa3"), "composer" : "Jessica Curry" }
```

Because the criteria argument (the first object passed to db.albums.find()) is empty in Listing 11-10, all records are returned. The projection object, however, specifies a single property to be returned by the query: composer. All other properties are excluded except for _id, which is returned by default and will always be included unless the projection parameter specifies otherwise.

Querying Data with Mongoose

Once the album data has been loaded into MongoDB, you can use the same model from Listing 11-4 to query that data.

The code in Listing 11-11 uses the Node.js http module to create a rudimentary web server that can receive HTTP requests and return JSON data in response. In this example the web server returns the same response for *any* URL query (to keep things simple). When a request is received, the Album Mongoose model is used to query MongoDB for album documents. Its find() function is invoked with a criteria argument, a projection argument, and a callback. With the exception of the callback, this syntax is identical to the db.albums.find() method used in Listing 11-10 to examine album documents.

Listing 11-11. Querying MongoDB with Mongoose

```
// example-001/http-server.js
'use strict';
var mongoose = require('mongoose');
var Album = require('./album-model');
var http = require('http');
var url = require('url');

/*
 * The http server will handle requests and responses
 */
var server = http.createServer(function (req, res) {
  Album.find({}, {composer: 1}, function (err, albums) {
    var statusCode = err ? 500 : 200;
    var payload = err ? err : albums;
    res.writeHead(statusCode, {'Content-Type': 'application/json'});
    res.write(JSON.stringify(payload, null, '  '));
    res.end();
  });
});
```

```
/*
 * Connect to the MongoDB instance and report
 * errors if any occur.
 */
mongoose.connect('mongodb://localhost/music');
var db = mongoose.connection;

db.on('error', function (err) {
  console.error(err);
  process.exit(1);
});

db.once('open', function () {
  /*
   * The MongoDB connection is open, start
   * listening for HTTP requests.
   */
  server.listen(8080);
  console.log('listening on port 8080');
});
```

In Listing 11-12, the web server is launched from the example-001 directory with the command node http-server.js. Pressing Ctrl+c will stop the server.

Listing 11-12. Running the HTTP Server

```
example-001$ node http-server.js
listening on port 8080
```

The album data fetched from MongoDB may now be viewed in a web browser by navigating to http://localhost:8080, or by issuing the curl terminal command as shown in Listing 11-13.

Listing 11-13. Sending a curl Request to the HTTP Server

```
$ curl -v http://localhost:8080/
* Hostname was NOT found in DNS cache
*    Trying 127.0.0.1...
* Connected to localhost (127.0.0.1) port 8080 (#0)
> GET / HTTP/1.1
> User-Agent: curl/7.37.1
> Host: localhost:8080
> Accept: */*
>
< HTTP/1.1 200 OK
< Content-Type: application/json
< Date: Thu, 29 Jan 2015 01:20:09 GMT
< Connection: keep-alive
< Transfer-Encoding: chunked
<
[
```

```
{
  "_id": "54c7020c342ee81670b261ef",
  "composer": "Kerry Muzzey"
},
{
  "_id": "54c7020c342ee81670b261f5",
  "composer": "Audiomachine"
},
{
  "_id": "54c7020c342ee81670b26210",
  "composer": "Jessica Curry"
}
```

The rest of this chapter will build on this Mongoose schema, model, and album data stored in the MongoDB database.

Working with Schemas

Mongoose schemas are simple objects that describe the structure of and data types in a MongoDB document. While MongoDB itself is schemaless, Mongoose enforces schemas for documents at the application level. Schemas are defined by invoking the Mongoose module's Schema() function, passing it an object hash where the keys represent document properties and the values represent the data type for each property. The return value is an object of type Schema with additional helper properties and functions for expanding or augmenting the schema's definition.

Data Types

For scalar properties, Mongoose uses the native JavaScript data types String, Boolean, Number, and Date, shown in Listing 11-14.

Listing 11-14. Primitive Types in a Mongoose Schema

```
// example-001/album-model.js
var albumSchema = mongoose.Schema({
  composer: String,
  title: String,
  price: Number,
  releaseDate: Date,
  inPublication: Boolean
  // other properties...
});
```

Properties that are object literals or arrays use the literal notation for each type ({} and []). Nested object literals are written inline, using the same Mongoose schema types for their own properties. Array types contain only one element, which defines the type of object that will occupy the array. This type can be any valid Mongoose data type, including an object literal defined inline as the first element of the array. In Listing 11-15, genre is declared as an array of strings while tracks is declared as an array of object literals.

Listing 11-15. Complex Types in a Mongoose Schema

```
// example-001/album-model.js
var albumSchema = mongoose.Schema({
  // ...other properties
  genre: [String],
  tracks: [
    {
      title: String,
      duration: {
        m: Number,
        s: Number
      }
    }
  ]
});
```

Mongoose itself provides two special object types: `ObjectId` and `Mixed`.

When a document is created in MongoDB, it is assigned an `_id` property that serves as a unique identifier for the record. This property uses MongoDB's own `ObjectId` data type. Mongoose exposes this type via `mongoose.Schema.Types.ObjectId`. This type is rarely used directly. When querying a document by ID, for example, the string representation of the identifier is typically used.

■ **Note**   When a schema property holds arbitrary data (remember, MongoDB is schemaless), it may be declared with the type `mongoose.Schema.Types.Mixed`. If a property is marked as `Mixed`, Mongoose will not track changes made against it. When Mongoose persists a document, it creates a query internally that only adds or updates properties that have changed, and since a `Mixed` property is not tracked, the application must inform Mongoose when it has changed. Documents created by Mongoose models expose a `markModified(path)` method that will force Mongoose to consider the property identified by the `path` argument as dirty.

Setting a Mongoose schema property to an empty object literal (one with no properties) will cause Mongoose to treat it as `Mixed`.

Finally, because Mongoose is a Node.js library, it takes advantage of Node's `Buffer` type to store large blocks of binary data such as image, audio, or video assets. Because binary data can be quite large, many applications store URL references to binary assets located on a content delivery network such as Amazon's Simple Storage Service (S3) instead of storing binaries in a data store such as MongoDB. Use cases differ across applications, however, and Mongoose schemas are flexible enough to support either approach.

Nested Schemas

Mongoose schemas may be nested; that is, a schema may reference another schema as a property type. This can be particularly useful if larger schemas share common custom data types, such as customer and order schemas sharing a postal address data type. In Listing 11-16 the album track schema is declared independent of the album schema, and gets assigned as the data type for the `albumSchema.tracks` property.

Listing 11-16. Nested Mongoose Schemas

```
// breaking apart schemas...
var trackSchema = mongoose.Schema({
  title: String,
  duration: {
    m: Number,
    s: Number
  }
});

var albumSchema = mongoose.Schema({
  // ...
  tracks: [trackSchema]
});
```

Default Property Values

Adding sensible default values to schema properties instructs Mongoose to fill in missing data when a document is created. This is useful for document properties that aren't optional but typically hold some known value.

In Listing 11-17 the m and s properties (minute and second) of the album schema default to zero because it is entirely possible that a track would be less than one minute long, or be exactly *X* minutes and zero seconds. The releaseDate property in the album schema also has a default value: the function Date. now. When a default value is a function, Mongoose will invoke the function, cast its return value to the type of the property, and then assign that value to the property.

Listing 11-17. Default Property Values

```
// adding default property values...
var trackSchema = mongoose.Schema({
  // ...
  duration: {
    m: {type: Number, default: 0},
    s: {type: Number, default: 0}
  }
});

var albumSchema = mongoose.Schema({
  // ...
  price: {type: Number, default: 0.0},
  releaseDate: {type: Date, default: Date.now},
  // ...
});
```

Adding a default to a property requires that the type assignment look a bit different. Notice that m: Number has become m: {type: Number, default: 0}. Normally, assigning an object hash to a property would cause the property to have a Mixed or object type, but the presence of the type property in the object literal short-circuits that process and tells Mongoose that the other key/value pairs in the hash are property settings.

Required Properties

The required attribute may be used on the type definition of nonoptional properties. When a document is saved, any missing property that the document schema requires will raise a validation error, which will be passed to the save operation's callback. Album composers, album titles, track titles, and even track duration objects are all required in Listing 11-18.

Listing 11-18. Required Properties

```
// adding required attributes
var trackSchema = mongoose.Schema({
  title: {type: String, required: true},
  duration: {
    required: true,
    type: {
      m: {type: Number, default: 0},
      s: {type: Number, default: 0}
    }
  }
});

var albumSchema = mongoose.Schema({
  composer: {type: String, required: true},
  title: {type: String, required: true},
  // ...
});
```

If a string is used in place of a boolean value for a required attribute, the string will be used as the error message if a validation error is raised, as shown in Listing 11-19. (Document validation will be covered shortly.)

Listing 11-19. Custom Error Message for a Required Property

```
var trackSchema = mongoose.Schema({
  title: {type: String, required: 'Missing track title!'},
  // ...
});
```

Secondary Indexes

Mongoose documents automatically acquire an indexed _id property when saved to MongoDB. Secondary indexes can be added to a schema, however, to enhance performance when querying against other fields.

MongoDB supports both simple (single field) and compound (multifield) indexes. In Listing 11-20 the following indexes are added to the track and album schemas:

- Track title (simple)

- Album composer (simple)

- Album title (simple)

- Album title + album composer (compound)

- Album genre (simple)

Listing 11-20. Adding Secondary Indexes to Schemas

```
// adding secondary indexes...
var trackSchema = mongoose.Schema({
  title: {type: String, required: true, index: true},
  // ...
});

var albumSchema = mongoose.Schema({
  composer: {type: String, required: true, index: true},
  title: {type: String, required: true, index: true},
  // ...
  genre: {type: [String], index: true},
  // ...
});

albumSchema.index({composer: 1, title: 1});
```

Simple indexes are added at the property level by appending an index field to a property type declaration and setting it to true. Compound indexes, on the other hand, must be defined for the schema as a whole using the Schema.index() method. The object passed to index() contains property names that correspond to the schema properties to be indexed, and a numeric value that may be either 1 or -1.

MongoDB sorts indexes in either ascending or descending order. Compound indexes are defined with a numeric value instead of a boolean value (like simple indexes) to indicate the order in which each field should be indexed. For simple indexes, the order doesn't matter because MongoDB can search either way. But for compound indexes, the order is very important because it limits the kind of sort operations MongoDB can perform when a query uses a compound index. The MongoDB documentation covers compound indexing strategies in depth.

In Listing 11-20 a compound index for composer and title is added to the album schema in addition to simple indexes for both fields. It is entirely likely that a user will search for an album by composer, title, or both.

Schema Validation

Mongoose will enforce schema validation rules when documents are persisted. A validation rule is a function defined for a particular schema property that evaluates the property's value and returns a boolean value to indicate validity. Listing 11-21 demonstrates how to attach a property validator to a schema object.

Listing 11-21. Validating Schema Properties

```
// adding schema validation...
var trackSchema = mongoose.Schema({/*...*/});

var albumSchema = mongoose.Schema({
  // ...
  tracks: [trackSchema]
});

albumSchema.path('tracks').validate(function (tracks) {
  return tracks.length > 0;
}, 'Album has no tracks.');
```

The schema's path() method returns an instance of SchemaType, an object that encapsulates the definition of a schema's property—in this case, the tracks property, which is an array of track objects for the album. The SchemaType.validate() method attaches a validation function to the schema's property. The first argument is the actual validation function, which receives, as its only argument, the value to be validated. The second argument to validate() is the message that will be used if a validation error is raised.

When an album document is saved, this function will be executed as part of the Mongoose validation process, evaluating the tracks property to ensure that the album has at least one track.

Validation rules may also be attached to schema properties as part of the property definition. The tracks definition in Listing 11-22 includes the validate property. The value of this property is a two-element array (a tuple) where the validation function is element 0 and the error message is element 1.

Listing 11-22. Declaring Property Validators Inline

```
function validateTrackLength (tracks) {
  return tracks.length > 0;
}

var albumSchema = mongoose.Schema({
  // ...
  tracks: {
    type: [trackSchema],
    validate: [validateTrackLength, 'Album has no tracks.']
  }
});
```

While the Mongoose validation process is itself asynchronous, simple validation functions, like those in Listing 11-22, are synchronous. For most cases synchronous validation is perfectly acceptable, but for other cases asynchronous validators might be required. An asynchronous validation function accepts a second argument—a callback called respond (by convention)—that will be invoked when the asynchronous validation has completed. A true or false value is passed to respond to indicate successful or failed validation, respectively. Listing 11-23 shows how the validation function for album tracks could be made asynchronous.

Listing 11-23. Asynchronous Property Validators

```
albumSchema.path('tracks').validate(function (tracks, respond) {
  process.nextTick(function () {
    respond(tracks.length > 0);
  });
}, 'Album has no tracks.');
```

To see the validation function at work, the tracks for each album in example-002/albums.json can be removed so that the JSON data resembles Listing 11-24.

Listing 11-24. Albums Without Tracks

```
// example-002/albums.json
[
  {
    "composer": "Kerry Muzzey",
    "title": "Renaissance",
    "price": 4.95,
    "releaseDate": "2014-01-13T06:00:00.000Z",
```

```
    "inPublication": true,
    "genre": ["Classical", "Trailer Music", "Soundtrack"],
    "tracks": []
  },
  {
    "composer": "Audiomachine",
    "title": "Tree of Life",
    "price": 9.49,
    "releaseDate": "2013-07-16T05:00:00.000Z",
    "inPublication": true,
    "genre": ["Classical", "Trailer Music"],
    "tracks": []
  },
  {
    "composer": "Jessica Curry",
    "title": "Dear Esther",
    "price": 6.99,
    "releaseDate": "2012-02-14T06:00:00.000Z",
    "inPublication": true,
    "genre": ["Classical", "Video Game Soundtrack"],
    "tracks": []
  }
]
```

Validation occurs whenever documents are persisted; that is, whenever Model.create() is called, or the save() method is called on a document instance. If validation fails, an error is passed as the first argument to a callback for each of these methods. (Documents will be discussed in detail later.)

If the import process is run again, the validator will trigger in example-002/import-albums.js when Album.create() is called to create new Mongoose documents from the incomplete JSON data. The console output in Listing 11-25 shows the serialized ValidationError that is raised, and the ValidatorError for the tracks property present in its errors collection.

Listing 11-25. Console Output when Schema Validation Fails

```
example-002$ node import-albums.js
creating 3 albums
{ [ValidationError: Validation failed]
  message: 'Validation failed',
  name: 'ValidationError',
  errors:
   { tracks:
      { [ValidatorError: Album has no tracks.]
        message: 'Album has no tracks.',
        name: 'ValidatorError',
        path: 'tracks',
        type: 'user defined',
        value: [] } } }
```

After breaking apart the album and track schemas and adding default property values, required attributes, secondary indexes, and validation, the album schema has changed quite a bit from the simple schema in example-001. Listing 11-26 shows the more robust version.

313

Listing 11-26. More Robust Album Schema

```
// example-002/album.js
'use strict';
var mongoose = require('mongoose');

var trackSchema = mongoose.Schema({
  title: {type: String, required: true, index: true},
  duration: {
    required: true,
    type: {
      m: {type: Number, default: 0},
      s: {type: Number, default: 0}
    }
  }
});

var albumSchema = mongoose.Schema({
  composer: {type: String, required: true, index: true},
  title: {type: String, required: true, index: true},
  price: {type: Number, default: 0.0},
  releaseDate: {type: Date, default: Date.now},
  inPublication: Boolean,
  genre: {type: [String], index: true},
  tracks: [trackSchema]
});

albumSchema.index({composer: 1, title: 1});

albumSchema.path('tracks').validate(function (tracks) {
  return tracks.length > 0;
}, 'Album has no tracks.');

var Album = mongoose.model('Album', albumSchema);

module.exports = Album;
```

Schema References

Though MongoDB is a relationless data store, relationships between documents in collections can be created through informal references that act as foreign keys. The integrity enforcement and resolution of these foreign keys to objects is left entirely to the application, of course. Mongoose builds these informal relationships through population references—links between schemas that enable automatic eager loading (and manual lazy loading) of document graphs. To expand on the music application example, it is very likely that users will create their own personal album libraries. Because album documents can be large, it might be best to avoid duplicating album data in each library document. Instead, references will be created from library documents to individual albums, a kind of many-to-many relationship. When libraries are loaded by Mongoose, these references can be resolved so that full library object graphs are returned populated with album documents.

To keep things simple, a single library is defined in example-003/library.json. This library, shown in Listing 11-27, references albums by composer and title. Each album will need to be dereferenced to a document ID in a corresponding MongoDB album document when the data is imported.

Listing 11-27. Library JSON Data

```
// example-003/library.json
{
  "owner": "Nicholas Cloud",
  "albums": [
    {
      "composer": "Kerry Muzzey",
      "title": "Renaissance"
    },
    {
      "composer": "Audiomachine",
      "title": "Tree of Life"
    },
    {
      "composer": "Jessica Curry",
      "title": "Dear Esther"
    }
  ]
}
```

The library import script is similar to the album import script, as shown in Listing 11-28, but it performs one additional important step. After the library.json file is read and turned into a plain JavaScript object, the album data is resolved to the actual album document objects imported in example-001/import-albums.js.

Listing 11-28. Importing Library Data into MongoDB

```
// example-003/import-library.js
'use strict';
var mongoose = require('mongoose');
var Album = require('./album-model');
var Library = require('./library-model');
var file2json = require('./file2json');
var fs = require('fs');
var path = require('path');

function handleError(err) {
  console.error(err);
  process.exit(1);
}

function resolveAlbums(libraryJSON, cb) {
  /*
   * [3] use a compound $or criteria to look up multiple
   * album documents
   */
```

```
  var albumCriteria = {
    $or: libraryJSON.albums
  };

  Album.find(albumCriteria, cb);
}

mongoose.connect('mongodb://localhost/music');
var db = mongoose.connection;
db.on('error', handleError);
db.once('open', function importLibrary () {

  /*
   * [1] read the library.json file data and convert it to
   * a normal JS object
   */
  var libraryFile = path.join(__dirname, 'library.json');
  file2json(libraryFile, 'utf8', function (err, libraryJSON) {
    if (err) return handleError(err);

    /*
     * [2] look up album documents that match each composer/title
     * in the library JSON data
     */
    resolveAlbums(libraryJSON, function (err, albumDocuments) {
      if (err) return handleError(err);

      console.log('creating library');

      /*
       * [4] assign the album documents to the library object
       */
      libraryJSON.albums = albumDocuments;

      /*
       * [5] then create a library document from the JSON data and
       * save the document
       */
      var libraryDocument = new Library(libraryJSON);

      libraryDocument.save(function (err) {
        if (err) return handleError(err);
        process.exit(0);
      });
    });

  });
});
```

Each step in the import flow is annotated in Listing 11-28, but several steps involve concepts that have not yet been introduced.

In step [3] a compound $or criteria object is created to filter MongoDB album documents by composer and title. The $or criteria property is covered later in the chapter, but for now it is sufficient to understand that MongoDB will examine all documents in the albums collection and determine if the document matches *any* of the composer/title pairs in the $or array, shown in Listing 11-29. Since all three albums previously imported match at least one of the pairs in this criteria, they will all be returned as results.

Listing 11-29. Library Import $or Criteria

```
{ $or:
  [ { composer: 'Kerry Muzzey', title: 'Renaissance' },
    { composer: 'Audiomachine', title: 'Tree of Life' },
    { composer: 'Jessica Curry', title: 'Dear Esther' } ] }
```

In step [4] the found album documents are assigned to the libraryJSON.albums property, replacing the existing array of composer/title data. When the library document is saved, Mongoose will enforce the library schema in Listing 11-30. Unlike previous property descriptions, the albums property is a reference property that will hold an array of ObjectIds as defined by the type attribute. The ref attribute tells Mongoose that this field can also be populated with album documents during a query (if specified), or when a library document is saved.

Listing 11-30. Library Schema

```
// example-003/library-model.js
'use strict';
var mongoose = require('mongoose');

var librarySchema = mongoose.Schema({
  owner: String,
  albums: [{type: mongoose.Schema.Types.ObjectId, ref: 'Album'}]
});

var Library = mongoose.model('Library', librarySchema);

module.exports = Library;
```

Mongoose documents may all be cast to their ObjectIds. Mongoose is smart enough to perform this cast automatically, so adding album documents to the albums property will pass the schema check. Alternatively, the import script could pluck the _id property from each album document and place it into the albums array instead. The result would be identical.

Finally, in step [5] an individual document instance is created by invoking the Library constructor and passing in the raw JSON data to assign to each document property. Documents may also be created with no constructor argument, assigning data to each property on the instance imperatively, but using the constructor argument shorthand is common. After the document has been created, its save() method is invoked with a callback that is passed an error if the persistence process fails. This differs from the album import script in which multiple album documents were created in MongoDB at once by using the model's static create() function. Listing 11-31 demonstrates the difference.

Listing 11-31. Creating a Single Document and Multiple Documents

```
// create a single document
var libraryDocument = new Library(plainJSONLibrary);
libraryDocument.save(function (err) {...});

// create multiple documents at once
Albums.create(arrayOfJSONAlbums, function (err) {...});
```

In Listing 11-32, the library import script is run exactly as the album import script was run.

Listing 11-32. Running the Library Import Script

```
example-003$ node import-library.js
creating library
```

Once the import has completed, the library data may be verified with the mongo terminal client. The output in Listing 11-33 reveals that Mongoose did indeed satisfy the library schema by casting each album object to its identifier. (The next section, *Working with Models and Documents*, will examine how schema reference properties can be used to eagerly load referenced documents.)

Listing 11-33. Verifying the Library Import in MongoDB

```
example-003$ mongo
MongoDB shell version: 2.6.7
connecting to: test

> use music
switched to db music

> db.libraries.find()
{ "_id" : ObjectId("54ed1dfdb11e8ae7252af342"), "owner" : "Nicholas Cloud", "albums" :
[ ObjectId("54ed1dcb6fb525ba25529bd1"), ObjectId("54ed1dcb6fb525ba25529bd7"),
ObjectId("54ed1dcb6fb525ba25529bf2") ], "__v" : 0 }
```

Schema Middleware

Mongoose raises events on a schema object whenever particular MongoDB documents are validated, saved, or removed from a document collection. Events are raised *before* and *after* each one of these operations. Subscriptions to these events are assigned with a schema's pre() and post() methods, respectively. A subscription is simply a function, or *middleware* that receives arguments related to each event. Post-event middleware simply observes the document after the event is complete, but pre-event middleware may actually interrupt the document life cycle before an event is completely processed.

In Listing 11-34, a duration object has been added to the library schema, identical to the duration object in each album track. This object, however, will hold the computed total length of the library as a whole. A pre-event middleware function is attached to the library schema for the save event. Before the library is saved, this function will iterate over each album and each track to sum the lengths of all tracks, then assign the calculated values to properties on the duration object. The middleware function receives a single argument, the callback function next(). When the duration summation has completed, next() is invoked to trigger any additional middleware functions attached to the schema.

Listing 11-34. Pre-save Middleware

```
// example-004/library-model.js
'use strict';
var mongoose = require('mongoose');

var librarySchema = mongoose.Schema({
  owner: String,
  albums: [{type: mongoose.Schema.Types.ObjectId, ref: 'Album'}],
  duration: {
    h: {type: Number, default: 0},
    m: {type: Number, default: 0}
  }
});

librarySchema.pre('save', function (next) {
  var hours = 0, mins = 0;
  /*
   * iterate over all albums and add hours
   * and minutes
   */
  this.albums.forEach(function (album) {
    album.tracks.forEach(function (track) {
      hours += track.duration.h;
      mins += track.duration.m;
    });
  });
  /*
   * divide total mins by 60 seconds and
   * add that to hours, then assign remaining
   * minutes back to mins
   */
  hours += (mins / 60);
  mins = (mins % 60);
  this.duration = {h: hours, m: mins};
  next();
});

var Library = mongoose.model('Library', librarySchema);

module.exports = Library;
```

Pre-event middleware can execute in a synchronous or asynchronous manner. The code in Listing 11-34 is synchronous, which means that other middleware functions will be scheduled only after the duration summation has been completed. To change this behavior and schedule them all immediately, one after the next, the schema's pre() method is called with an additional boolean argument that flags the handler function as asynchronous middleware.

The middleware function itself also receives an additional parameter, the done() function callback shown in Listing 11-35. In synchronous middleware, control is passed to the next middleware function when a previous middleware function has finished and invoked next(). This is still the case with asynchronous middleware, but the done() function must also be invoked when the asynchronous operation has finished during a future event loop turn. The order of execution in Listing 11-35 is

1. Schedule the duration summation process for the next event loop pass.

2. Invoke next() to pass control to the next piece of middleware.

3. At some future point in time, signal that this middleware operation is complete by invoking done().

Listing 11-35. Asynchronous Pre-save Middleware

```
// example-005/library-model.js
// ...
librarySchema.pre('save', true, function (next, done) {

  var hours = 0, mins = 0;
  process.nextTick(function () {              // #1
    /*
     * iterate over all albums and add hours
     * and minutes
     */
    this.albums.forEach(function (album) {
      album.tracks.forEach(function (track) {
        hours += track.duration.h;
        mins += track.duration.m;
      });
    });
    /*
     * divide total mins by 60 seconds and
     * add that to hours, then assign remaining
     * minutes back to mins
     */
    hours += (mins / 60);
    mins = (mins % 60);
    this.duration = {h: hours, m: mins};
    done();                                    // #3
  });

  next();                                      // #2
});

var Library = mongoose.model('Library', librarySchema);

module.exports = Library;
```

If an error is raised in a synchronous, pre-event middleware function, it should be passed as the only argument to next(). Errors raised during asynchronous functions, however, should be passed to done() instead. Any error passed to these callbacks will cause the operation that triggered the event to fail, and will be delivered to the final operation callback (for example, the callback passed to a document's save() method).

Post-event middleware functions receive no control flow arguments, but instead receive a copy of the document as it stands after the event's operation has completed.

Working with Models and Documents

A Mongoose model is a constructor function that creates document instances. These instances conform to a Mongoose schema and expose a collection of methods for document persistence. Models are associated with MongoDB collections. In fact, when a Mongoose document is saved, the collection to which it corresponds will be created if it does not already exist. By convention, models are named in the singular form of the noun they represent (e.g., Album), but collections are named in the plural form (e.g., albums).

A model constructor function is created by invoking mongoose.model() with a model name and a model schema. All documents created with this constructor function, either directly in user code or indirectly when Mongoose executes queries and returns document instances, will conform to the model's schema. Listing 11-36 shows the code responsible for creating the Album constructor function used by the import scripts to create album documents in MongoDB.

Listing 11-36. Album Model

```
// example-006/album-model.js

//...schema definition...

var Album = mongoose.model('Album', albumSchema);

module.exports = Album;
```

When a Mongoose model is registered with the mongoose.model() function, Mongoose can then resolve that model by name when referenced in relationship properties. This technique was used earlier to create a reference between the library schema and the Album model, as shown in Listing 11-37.

Listing 11-37. Library Schema References Album Model

```
// example-006/library-model.js

// ...
var librarySchema = mongoose.Schema({
  // ...
  albums: [{type: mongoose.Schema.Types.ObjectId, ref: 'Album'}],
  // ...
});
```

New documents can be created with a model constructor function, or fetched from a MongoDB data store with model query methods. Each document can save or remove itself from a MongoDB collection. This is very similar to the ActiveRecord data access pattern commonly used in RDBMS libraries. In Listing 11-38, a new album document instance is created with the Album constructor function. Album data is assigned to each property (with the appropriate data types) defined by the album schema. Finally, the save() method is called on the document, and its callback is invoked when the associated document has been created in MongoDB.

Listing 11-38. Creating and Saving a New Document Instance

```
// example-006/add-album-instance.js
'use strict';
var mongoose = require('mongoose');
var Album = require('./album-model');
```

```
function handleError(err) {
  console.error(err);
  process.exit(1);
}

mongoose.connect('mongodb://localhost/music');
var db = mongoose.connection;
db.on('error', handleError);
db.once('open', function addAlbumInstance() {

  var album = new Album();
  album.composer = 'nervous_testpilot';
  album.title = 'Frozen Synapse';
  album.price =  8.99;
  album.releaseDate = new Date(2012, 8, 6);
  album.inPublication = true;
  album.genre = ['Dance', 'DJ/Electronica', 'Soundtrack'];
  album.tracks = [
    {
      title: 'Welcome to Markov Geist',
      duration: {m: 1, s: 14}
    },
    // ...additional tracks...
  ];

  album.save(function (err) {
    if (err) return handleError(err);
    console.log('album saved', album);
    process.exit(0);
  });
});
```

The script output shows the document data after the album has been saved:

```
example-006$ node add-album-instance.js
album saved { __v: 0,
  inPublication: true,
  title: 'Frozen Synapse',
  composer: 'nervous_testpilot',
  _id: 54f117e4a27cc5375e156c6d... }
```

MongoDB can be queried to verify that the document was, in fact, created in the albums collection, as shown in Listing 11-39.

Listing 11-39. Verifying the Mongoose Document Has Been Created in MongoDB

```
example-006$ mongo
MongoDB shell version: 2.6.7
connecting to: test
> use music
switched to db music
> db.albums.find({composer: 'nervous_testpilot'}, {_id: 1, composer: 1, title: 1})
{ "_id" : ObjectId("54f117e4a27cc5375e156c6d"), "title" : "Frozen Synapse",
"composer" : "nervous_testpilot" }
```

Document instance properties may also be set by passing an object hash directly to the model constructor. This can be particularly useful when document data already exists in a plain JavaScript object, such as a deserialized JSON web request body, or JSON data parsed from a flat file. Listing 11-40 adapts the previous example to load the new album data from a JSON file, then uses the Album model constructor to create a document from the new JSON data. Since the JSON data conforms to the album schema (or, in the case of the releaseDate date string, can be converted directly to the property type Date), the album instance will be persisted without errors.

Listing 11-40. Alternative Way to Create a Document with Property Data

```
// example-007/add-album-instance-alt.js
'use strict';
var mongoose = require('mongoose');
var Album = require('./album-model');
var file2json = require('./file2json');
var path = require('path');

function handleError(err) {
  console.error(err);
  process.exit(1);
}

mongoose.connect('mongodb://localhost/music');
var db = mongoose.connection;
db.on('error', handleError);
db.once('open', function addAlbumInstance() {

  var albumFile = path.join(__dirname, 'album.json');
  file2json(albumFile, 'utf8', function (err, albumJSON) {
    var album = new Album(albumJSON);
    album.save(function (err) {
      if (err) return handleError(err);
      console.log('album saved', album);
      process.exit(0);
    });
  });

});
```

Document Instance Methods

Documents are more than just data: they may also include custom behavior. When document instances are created, Mongoose creates a prototype chain with copies of functions defined on the schema object's methods property. Document methods defined in this way may access particular document instances with the this keyword.

Listing 11-41 shows two instance methods defined on the album schema: one to find the next album track given the previous track's title, and another that will find similar albums based on shared genres. The findSimilar() method uses query syntax that will be covered later in the section Working with Queries, but for now you simply need to know that it effectively finds albums that have genres that overlap with the instance album and that do not share the same _id as the instance album (so the instance itself is excluded from the list).

Listing 11-41. Defining Document Instance Methods in a Schema

```
// example-008/album-model.js

// ...
var albumSchema = mongoose.Schema({/*...*/});

albumSchema.methods.nextTrack = function (previousTrackTitle) {
  var i = 0, len = this.tracks.length;
  for (i; i < len; i += 1) {
    if (this.tracks[i].title !== previousTrackTitle) {
      continue;
    }
    // return the next track, or, if this is the last track,
    // return the first track
    return this.tracks[i + 1] || this.tracks[0];
  }
  throw new Error('unable to find track ' + previousTrackTitle);
};

albumSchema.methods.findSimilar = function (cb) {
  var criteria = {
    _id: {$ne: this._id},
    genre: {$in: this.genre}
  };
  this.model('Album').find(criteria)
    .exec(cb);
};

var Album = mongoose.model('Album', albumSchema);

module.exports = Album;
```

The script in Listing 11-42 loads the album titled *Renaissance,* then calls `album.nextTrack()` to determine which track follows "Fall from Grace." Then it calls `album.findSimilar()` to load albums related to *Renaissance* and prints their titles and genres to the terminal. The output reveals that there is, indeed, overlapping genres for each album, and that the instance album itself is not included in the results.

Listing 11-42. Using Document Instance Methods

```
// example-008/index01.js
'use strict';
var mongoose = require('mongoose');
var Album = require('./album-model');

function handleError(err) {
  console.error(err);
  process.exit(1);
}
```

```
mongoose.connect('mongodb://localhost/music');
var db = mongoose.connection;
db.on('error', handleError);
db.once('open', function () {
  Album.findOne({title: 'Renaissance'})
    .exec(function (err, album) {
      if (err) return handleError(err);

      var nextTrack = album.nextTrack('Fall from Grace');
      console.log('next track:', nextTrack.title);

      album.findSimilar(function (err, albums) {
        if (err) return handleError(err);
        console.log('this album:', album.title, album.genre);
        albums.forEach(function (album) {
          console.log('similar album:', album.title, album.genre);
        });
        process.exit(0);
      });
    });
});
```

```
example-008$ node index01.js
next track: Fall from Grace (Choir Version)
this album: Renaissance ["Classical","Trailer Music","Soundtrack"]
similar album: Tree of Life ["Classical","Trailer Music"]
similar album: Dear Esther ["Classical","Video Game Soundtrack"]
similar album: Frozen Synapse ["Dance","Electronica","Soundtrack"]
```

Document Virtuals

Like instance methods, virtual getter and setter *properties* can be added to documents via the schema. These virtual properties act like normal data properties but are not persisted when the document is saved. They are useful for computing and returning values based on document data, or for parsing data that contains, or can be converted to, values for other document properties.

A virtual getter and setter have been added to the album schema in Listing 11-43 that define a property, composerInverse, that will get the inversed version of a composer's name ("last, first") and set the composer's name correctly ("first last") given an inverse form.

Listing 11-43. Virtual Document Properties

```
// example-08/album-model.js

var albumSchema = mongoose.Schema({/*...*/});

// ...
albumSchema.virtual('composerInverse').get(function () {
  var parts = this.composer.split(' '); //first last
  if (parts.length === 1) {
    return this.composer;
  }
```

```
  return [parts[1], parts[0]].join(', '); //last, first
});

albumSchema.virtual('composerInverse').set(function (inverse) {
  var parts = inverse.split(', '); //last, first
  if (parts.length === 1) {
    this.composer = inverse;
  }
  this.composer = [parts[1], parts[0]].join(' '); //first last
});
// ...
```

The string argument passed to the Schema.virtual() method defines the document path where the property will reside once a document instance is created. Document virtuals may be assigned to subdocuments and nested objects as well by specifying the full path starting at the root document. For example, if the value of the composer property was an object with firstName and lastName properties, the virtual might live at composer.inverse instead.

The script and subsequent output in Listing 11-44 shows the composerInverse property in action.

Listing 11-44. Getting and Setting a Virtual Property

```
// example-008/index02.js
'use strict';
var mongoose = require('mongoose');
var Album = require('./album-model');

function handleError(err) {
  console.error(err);
  process.exit(1);
}

mongoose.connect('mongodb://localhost/music');
var db = mongoose.connection;
db.on('error', handleError);
db.once('open', function () {
  Album.find({}).exec(function (err, albums) {
    if (err) return handleError(err);

    albums.forEach(function (album) {
      console.log('album.composer:', album.composer);
      var inverse = album.composerInverse;
      console.log('album.composerInverse:', inverse);
      album.composerInverse = inverse;
      console.log('album.composer:', album.composer);
      console.log(/*newline*/);
    });

    process.exit(0);
  });
});
```

```
example-008$ node index02.js
album.composer: Kerry Muzzey
album.composerInverse: Muzzey, Kerry
album.composer: Kerry Muzzey

album.composer: Audiomachine
album.composerInverse: Audiomachine
album.composer:  Audiomachine

album.composer: Jessica Curry
album.composerInverse: Curry, Jessica
album.composer: Jessica Curry

album.composer: nervous_testpilot
album.composerInverse: nervous_testpilot
album.composer:  nervous_testpilot
```

Static Model Methods

Static methods may also be added to models (not document instances), and are commonly used to encapsulate complicated criteria construction when querying against a collection. The inPriceRange() method in Listing 11-45 is attached to the album schema's statics property. It receives two numeric arguments that represent the lower and upper bounds of a price range, and finds albums that are priced within that range, inclusively.

Listing 11-45. Adding a Static Method to a Model

```
// example-009/album-model.js

var albumSchema = mongoose.Schema({/*...*/});

// ...
albumSchema.statics.inPriceRange = function (lower, upper, cb) {
  var criteria = {
    price: {$gte: lower, $lte: upper}
  };
  this.find(criteria)
    .exec(cb);
};
// ...
```

When the album model is later created from the schema, any method on statics will be bound to the model. While the value of this in instance methods is the document itself, the value of the this keyword in static methods is the model constructor function (e.g., Album). Any function that can be called on the model, such as find() and create(), may be accessed in a static method.

The script in Listing 11-46 receives two prices as command-line arguments and then finds albums within the range of those prices. The inPriceRange() method is called on the Album model, just as any other static method. Encapsulating queries in this manner can be a good way to maintain separate concerns, as query logic is isolated to models and won't pollute other portions of the application.

Listing 11-46. Using Static Model Methods// example-009/index.js

```
'use strict';
var mongoose = require('mongoose');
var Album = require('./album-model');

var lower = Number(process.argv[2] || 0);
var upper = Number(process.argv[3] || lower + 1);

console.log('finding albums between $%s and $%s', lower.toFixed(2), upper.toFixed(2));

function handleError(err) {
  console.error(err);
  process.exit(1);
}

mongoose.connect('mongodb://localhost/music');
var db = mongoose.connection;
db.on('error', handleError);
db.once('open', function () {
  Album.inPriceRange(lower, upper, function (err, albums) {
    if (err) return handleError(err);
    console.log('found albums:', albums.length);
    albums.forEach(function (album) {
      console.log(album.title, '$' + album.price.toFixed(2));
    });
    process.exit(0);
  });
});
```

```
example-009$ node index.js 5.00 10.00
finding albums between $5.00 and $10.00
found albums: 3
Tree of Life $9.49
Dear Esther $6.99
Frozen Synapse $8.99

example-009$ node index.js 9.00 10.00
finding albums between $9.00 and $10.00
found albums: 1
Tree of Life $9.49

example-009$ node index.js 20.00
finding albums between $20.00 and $21.00
found albums: 0
```

■ **Note** The query examples in the next section do not use static model methods for encapsulation. This is done to simplify each example, though in a real maintainable application, it might be considered bad practice.

Working with Queries

Mongoose queries are plain objects composed of zero or more properties that specify the parameters of the query. (An empty query object matches everything.) Properties on these criteria objects share MongoDB's native query syntax. Models expose several different query methods that use criteria objects in order to filter and return Mongoose documents.

For the following examples a web server provides access to MongoDB data via Mongoose models. To start the web server, ensure that your MongoDB instance is running and then execute the command in Listing 11-47 in each example directory. (A comment at the top of each code example reveals which directory it lives in.) The script output will inform you that the web server is running on port 8080. All interactions with the web server will be demonstrated with the cURL terminal utility available for most platforms, though each example could be run with any standard HTTP client.

Listing 11-47. Starting the Web Server in Example 10

```
example-XYZ$ node index.js
listening on port 8080
```

Model.find()

Basic CRUD operations may be conveniently mapped to corresponding Mongoose model functions with very little effort. The route in Listing 11-48, for example, is a general route that uses Album.find() to locate album documents that contain properties matching those in the criteria object. The criteria object gets composer and title parameters from the URL query string if they have been sent as part of the request. If one or both of these parameters are set on the criteria object, Mongoose will return only documents that have matching properties (similar to a where clause in traditional SQL). If no parameters are sent, the criteria object will remain empty and Mongoose will find *all* album documents.

Listing 11-48. Finding Albums That Match a Given Criteria

```
// example-010/album-routes.js

/**
 * GET /album(?composer={string}&title={string})
 * @param req
 * @param cb
 */
routes.GET['^\/album(?:\\?.+)?$'] = function (req, cb) {
  cb = httpd.asJSON(cb);
  var criteria = {};
  if (req.query.composer) {
    criteria.composer = req.query.composer;
  }
  if (req.query.title) {
    criteria.title = req.query.title;
  }
```

```
Album.find(criteria)
  .sort({composer: 1, title: 1})
  .lean(true)
  .exec(function (err, albums) {
    if (err) return cb(500, err);
    cb(200, albums);
  });
};
```

The `Album.find()` method will return a Mongoose Query object that exposes additional methods for manipulating the results of the find operation.

■ **Note** Model methods can be invoked in several ways. The first, shown in Listing 11-48, returns a `Query` object with a fluent interface that allows query options to be chained together until the `Query.exec()` method is called. The second method avoids the `Query` object altogether. If a callback is passed as the last argument to a model's query method (e.g., `find({}, function () {...})`) the underlying query will be executed immediately and the error or result passed to the callback. For simple queries, the second method is more terse.

The first Query directive is `Query.sort()`, which accepts an object that uses MongoDB's sorting notation. The properties in this object tell MongoDB which properties in the document should be used for sorts, and in which direction each sort should be ordered (1 for ascending, -1 for descending). When the results in Listing 11-48 are fetched, they will be ordered first by composer, then by album title.

After `Query.sort()`, the `Query.lean()` method is invoked to instruct Mongoose to deliver plain JSON objects instead of Mongoose documents as results. By default, Mongoose will always fetch documents, which carry Mongoose-specific properties and methods for validating, persisting, and otherwise managing document objects. Since this route (and most routes in this file) simply serialize results and return them to the client, it is preferable to fetch them as Plain Old JavaScript Objects (or JSON objects) populated only with data.

Once a query has been prepared, its `exec()` method is passed a callback to receive either an error or data from the `Album.find()` operation. The results will be an array of album objects that match whatever criteria (if any) was used to perform the query.

Several `curl` commands are shown in Listing 11-49 with various query string parameters. In each case the output is a serialized JSON array delivered from the web API.

■ **Note** The following examples use MongoDB identifiers that were generated on my computer. These identifiers will differ on your computer. You may use the `mongo` terminal client to discover the identifiers assigned to your MongoDB documents, as demonstrated in previous examples.

Listing 11-49. Using `curl` to Find Albums with Various Criteria

```
example-010$ curl -X GET http://localhost:8080/album?composer=Kerry%20Muzzey
[{"_id":"54ed1dcb6fb525ba25529bd1","composer":"Kerry Muzzey","title":"Renaissance"... ]

example-010$ curl -X GET http://localhost:8080/album?title=Dear%20Esther
[{"_id":"54ed1dcb6fb525ba25529bf2","composer":"Jessica Curry","title":"Dear Esther"... ]
```

```
example-010$ curl -X GET
"http://localhost:8080/album?composer=Audiomachine&title=Tree%20of%20Life"
[{"_id":"54ed1dcb6fb525ba25529bd7","composer":"Audiomachine","title":"Tree of Life"... ]
```

Model.findById()

While `Album.find()` will always fetch an array of documents (even if its criteria specifies a unique identifier), `Album.findById()` will only find a single document that matches a given identifier, if any exist. The route in Listing 11-50 fetches a single album by `albumID`—a parameter passed as the last URL segment instead of the query string. The `lean()` method is again invoked on the returned `Query` to eliminate the unnecessary properties and methods in a full Mongoose document instance.

Listing 11-50. Finding a Single Album That Matches a Given Criteria

```
// example-010/album-routes.js

/**
 * GET /album/{id}
 * @param req
 * @param cb
 */
routes.GET['^\/album\/([a-z0-9]+)$'] = function (req, cb) {
  cb = httpd.asJSON(cb);
  var albumID = req.params[0];
  Album.findById(albumID)
    .lean(true)
    .exec(function (err, album) {
      if (err) return cb(500, err);
      cb(200, album);
    });
};
```

```
example-010$ curl -X GET http://localhost:8080/album/54f3a4df056601726f867685
{"_id":"54f3a4df056601726f867685","composer":"nervous_testpilot","title":"Frozen Synapse"... }
```

Earlier an additional album was created by the import script `example-007/add-album-instance-alt.js`, in which a deserialized JSON object was passed to the `Album` constructor to create an album instance. Listing 11-51 demonstrates the same process within an HTTP POST route. The body of the request is serialized album data that is first converted to a JSON object, then passed to the `Album` model constructor. Once the document instance has been created, the `save()` method validates the data (with rules defined in the album schema) and creates the new MongoDB document.

Listing 11-51. Creating a New Album Document

```
// example-010/album-routes.js

/**
 * POST /album
 * @param req
 * @param cb
 */
```

```
routes.POST['^\/album$'] = function (req, cb) {
  console.log(req.body);
  cb = httpd.asJSON(cb);
  var albumJSON = req.body;
  var album = new Album(albumJSON);
  album.save(function (err) {
    if (err) return cb(500, err);
    cb(201, album.toObject());
  });
};
```

If validation fails, or if the album otherwise cannot be created, an error will be passed to the final callback and delivered to the client as an HTTP 500 Internal Server Error. If the album document is created, the data is passed back to the client as serialized JSON. Unlike previous routes where Query.lean() was used to ensure that only data is serialized, the album document returns its own data in JSON format when its toObject() method is called. This is the manual equivalent of the process that lean() performs in a query chain.

The curl request in Listing 11-52 reads the content of example-010/new-album.json and sets it as the request body. The Content-Type informs the web server to deserialize the payload accordingly.

Listing 11-52. Creating a New Album with a curl Request

```
example-010$ curl -X POST http://localhost:8080/album \
> -d @new-album.json \
> -H "Content-Type: application/json"
{"_id":"54f66ed2fa4af12b43fee49b","composer":"Aphelion","title":"Memento"... }
```

The album data in example-010/new-album.json lacks a releaseDate property, a condition that did not cause the schema validation to fail on import because releaseDate is not required. Indeed, releaseDate defaults to Date.now, and if queried with the mongo client, will be exactly that. Unfortunately, the album was not, in fact, released today, so it is necessary to create another route to update the newly minted album document.

Model.findByIdAndUpdate()

An album instance may be updated in a number of ways. The Album.findById() method could fetch the document, its properties could be set with updated data, then it could be saved back to the data store. Or the Album.findByIdAndUpdate() method could be used to do all of that at once and return the newly updated album document, the exact approach taken in Listing 11-53.

Listing 11-53. Finding and Updating an Album by ID

```
// example-010/album-routes.js
/**
 * PUT /album/{id}
 * @param req
 * @param cb
 */
routes.PUT['^\/album\/([a-z0-9]+)$'] = function (req, cb) {
  cb = httpd.asJSON(cb);
  var albumID = req.params[0];
  var updatedFields = req.body;
```

```
Album.findByIdAndUpdate(albumID, updatedFields)
  .lean(true)
  .exec(function (err, album) {
    if (err) return cb(500, err);
    cb(200, album);
  });
};
```

Like Listing 11-51, a serialized JSON object is sent in the body of an HTTP request. This request is a PUT request, however, and includes the album identifier in the URL. The only data sent in the request body are the properties to be updated. It is unnecessary to send the full document across the wire because Mongoose will apply the deltas appropriately. Once the request body is deserialized, the album ID and updated fields are passed to findByIdAndUpdate(). If the update operation succeeds, the updated document will be passed to the final query callback, assuming no errors occur.

The curl command in Listing 11-54 creates a PUT request with a simple JSON payload that specifies a new value for releaseDate. When the request finishes, the printed response shows the updated album data.

Listing 11-54. Finding and Updating an Album by ID with curl

```
example-010$ curl -X PUT http://localhost:8080/album/54f66ed2fa4af12b43fee49b \
> -d '{"releaseDate": "2013-08-15T05:00:00.000Z"}' \
> -H "Content-Type: application/json"
{"_id":"54f66ed2fa4af12b43fee49b"..."releaseDate":"2013-08-15T05:00:00.000Z"... }
```

Model.findByIdAndRemove()

To remove a document from MongoDB, the DELETE route uses the Album.findByIdAndRemove() method to look up the MongoDB document and then remove it from the albums collection. The removed album is passed to the final callback in Listing 11-55 if the operation is successful.

Listing 11-55. Finding and Removing an Album by ID

```
// example-010/album-routes.js

/**
 * DELETE /album/{id}
 * @param req
 * @param cb
 */
routes.DELETE['^\/album\/([a-z0-9]+)$'] = function (req, cb) {
  cb = httpd.asJSON(cb);
  var albumID = req.params[0];
  Album.findByIdAndRemove(albumID)
    .lean(true)
    .exec(function (err, album) {
      if (err) return cb(500, err);
      cb(200, album);
    });
};

example-010$ curl -X DELETE http://localhost:8080/album/54f3aa9447429f44763f2603
{"_id":"54f66ed2fa4af12b43fee49b","composer":"Aphelion","title":"Memento"... }
```

A document instance also has a remove() method that can be invoked much like its save() method. In Listing 11-56 an album instance is fetched by ID. Query.lean() is *not* called this time because it is the document, not its plain JSON representation, that will possess a remove() method. Once the instance is fetched, remove() is called with a callback that will receive an error on failure, or a copy of the removed document instance if successful.

Listing 11-56. Removing a Document Instance

```
Album.findById(albumID)
  .exec(function (err, albumInstance) {
    albumInstance.remove(function (err, removedAlbum) {
      // album has been removed
    });
  });
```

Model.count()

Another useful model method is count(), which receives the same type of criteria objects as the find*() methods, but returns a simple record count instead of full objects. The HTTP route in Listing 11-57 uses the same query parameters as the general album search and returns the result count in the HTTP response.

Listing 11-57. Counting Albums That Match Criteria

```
// example-011/album-routes.js

/**
 * GET /album/count(?composer={string}&title={string})
 * @param req
 * @param cb
 */
routes.GET['^\/album\/count(?:\\?.+)?$'] = function (req, cb) {
  cb = httpd.asJSON(cb);
  var criteria = {};
  if (req.query.composer) {
    criteria.composer = req.query.composer;
  }
  if (req.query.title) {
    criteria.title = req.query.title;
  }
  Album.count(criteria)
    .exec(function (err, count) {
      if (err) return cb(500, err);
      cb(200, count);
    });
};

example-011$ curl -X GET http://localhost:8080/album/count
4

example-011$ curl -X GET http://localhost:8080/album/count?composer=Jessica%20Curry
1
```

Query.Populate()

Earlier, in Listing 11-28, a script was used to add a music library to MongoDB. The library schema defined an array property, albums, that contained references to album documents, show in Listing 11-58.

Listing 11-58. Album References in the Library Schema

```
var librarySchema = mongoose.Schema({
  // ...
  albums: [{type: mongoose.Schema.Types.ObjectId, ref: 'Album'}],
  // ...
});
```

Mongoose documents with foreign references can be fetched with or without resolving those references to other document objects. The route in Listing 11-59 fetches a library by ID, then calls the Query.populate() method to eagerly fetch the associated albums for the library. Mongoose is smart enough to know that, even though albums is technically an array, the objects it contains actually refer to other album documents.

Listing 11-59. Populating Albums with a Library Model

```
// example-011/library-routes.js

/**
 * GET /library/(id)
 * @param req
 * @param cb
 */
routes.GET['^\/library\/([a-z0-9]+)$'] = function (req, cb) {
  cb = httpd.asJSON(cb);
  var libraryID = req.params[0];
  Library.findById(libraryID)
    .populate('albums')
    .lean(true)
    .exec(function (err, library) {
      if (err) return cb(500, err);
      if (!library) return cb(404, {
        message: 'no library found for ID ' + libraryID
      });
      cb(200, library);
    });
}
```

Figure 11-1 shows a formatted version of the HTTP response. Each album in the albums collection has been fully dereferenced. Because Query.lean() was also called in the query chain, Mongoose converted the library *and* album data into plain JSON objects.

```
▼ {
    _id: "54ed249312c06b3726d3abcd",
    owner: "Nicholas Cloud",
    albums: ▼ [
        ▼ {
            _id: "54ed1dcb6fb525ba25529bd1",
            composer: "Kerry Muzzey",
            title: "Renaissance",
            price: 4.95,
            releaseDate: "2014-01-13T06:00:00.000Z",
            inPublication: true,
            tracks: ▸ [ {title: "The Looking Glass", _id: "54ed1dcb6fb525ba25529bd6", duration: {m: 3,…],
            genre: ▸ ["Classical", "Trailer Music", "Soundtrack"],
            __v: 0
        },
        ▸ {_id: "54ed1dcb6fb525ba25529bd7", composer: "Audiomachine", title: "Tree of Life",…},
        ▸ {_id: "54ed1dcb6fb525ba25529bf2", composer: "Jessica Curry", title: "Dear Esther",…}
    ],
    __v: 0
}
```

Figure 11-1. Library population results

Finding Documents with Query Operators

At this point the album and library routes consist of basic CRUD operations (create, read, update, and delete) that form the basis of many web APIs, but more could be done to make the API robust. MongoDB supports a number of helpful query operators that serve to filter data in specific ways.

The $lt and $gt Operators

The $lt and $gt operators can be used to find documents with values that are less than ($lt) or greater than ($gt) some value. The route in Listing 11-60 allows clients to search for albums that have been released on, before, or after a specific date that is passed to the route as a query parameter.

Listing 11-60. Finding Albums by Release Date

```
// example-011/album-routes.js

/**
 * GET /album/released/MM-DD-YYYY
 * GET /album/released/MM-DD-YYYY/before
 * GET /album/released/MM-DD-YYYY/after
 * @param req
 * @param cb
 */
```

```
routes.GET['^\/album\/released\/([\\d]{2}-[\\d]{2}-[\\d]{4})(?:\/(before|after))?$'] =
function (req, cb) {
  cb = httpd.asJSON(cb);
  var date = req.params[0];
  var when = req.params[1];

  var criteria = {releaseDate: {}};
  if (when === 'before') {
    criteria.releaseDate.$lt = new Date(date);
  } else if (when === 'after') {
    criteria.releaseDate.$gt = new Date(date);
  } else {
    when = null;
    criteria.releaseDate = new Date(date);
  }

  Album.find(criteria)
    .select('composer title releaseDate')
    .lean(true)
    .exec(function (err, albums) {
      if (err) return cb(500, err);
      if (albums.length === 0) {
        return cb(404, {
          message: 'no albums ' + (when || 'on') + ' release date ' + date
        });
      }
      cb(200, albums);
    });
};
```

To find albums released *on* a specific date, a normal criteria object is used to map the date value to the releaseDate property:

```
{releaseDate: new Date(...)}
```

If searching for albums before or after the date, however, the criteria object uses the $lt or $gt operator, respectively:

```
{releaseDate: {$lt: new Date(...)} }
```

```
// or
```

```
{releaseDate: {$gt: new Date(...)} }
```

To find albums that were released before, and up to, a specific date, the $lte ("less than or equal") operator could be used. Likewise, the $gte operator would find albums released from a specific date onward. To find all albums that were released on any date *but* the date provided, the $ne ("not equal") operator would filter accordingly. Its inverse, $eq, if used alone is functionally equivalent to setting the releaseDate value on the criteria object directly.

To keep the response small, the Query.select() method is invoked before the query is executed. This method limits the properties returned from each result object. In this case, the query selects only the composer, title, and releaseDate properties, all included in a space-separated string. All other properties are ignored.

Listing 11-61 shows the filtered JSON data returned for each kind of release date query.

Listing 11-61. Using `curl` to Find Albums by Release Date

```
example-011$ curl -X GET http://localhost:8080/album/released/01-01-2013
{"message":"no albums on release date 01-01-2013"}

example-011$ curl -X GET http://localhost:8080/album/released/01-01-2013/before
[{"_id":"54ed1dcb6fb525ba25529bf2","composer":"Jessica Curry","title":"Dear
Esther","releaseDate":"2012-02-14T06:00:00.000Z"},{"_id":"54f3a4df056601726f867685",
"composer":"nervous_testpilot","title":"Frozen Synapse","releaseDate":"2012-09-
06T05:00:00.000Z"}]

example-011$ curl -X GET http://localhost:8080/album/released/01-01-2013/after
[{"_id":"54ed1dcb6fb525ba25529bd1","composer":"Kerry Muzzey","title":"Renaissance",
"releaseDate":"2014-01-13T06:00:00.000Z"},{"_id":"54ed1dcb6fb525ba25529bd7","composer":
"Audiomachine","title":"Tree of Life","releaseDate":"2013-07-16T05:00:00.000Z"}]
```

Notice that, even though the `Query.select()` filter did *not* specify the _id property for inclusion, it is still present in each response. To omit this property, a negation needs to be added to the select string. Prefixing the _id property with a minus sign will prevent it from being selected:

```
Album.find(...)
  .select('-_id composer title releaseDate')
  // ...
```

■ **Note**   The _id property is the only property that may be specified for exclusion when an inclusive select (one that specifies the properties to be fetched) is performed. Otherwise, excluded and included properties *may not be mixed.* A query is either selecting only specific properties or excluding only specific properties, but not both. If any property in a `Query.select()` string is negated (except for _id), *all* specified properties must be negated or an error will be raised.

The $in and $nin Operators

It is often helpful to select documents with property values that match some subset of possibilities. The $in operator (and its inverse, $nin) tests a document property value against each element in an array. The document fulfills the criteria if its property matches at least one of the elements in the array. To find albums from two composers, for example, the criteria object in Listing 11-62 might be used.

Listing 11-62. Using the $in Query Operator to Filter by Composer

```
{composer: {$in: ['Kerry Muzzey', 'Jessica Curry']}}
```

The $nin operator does the exact opposite: it will match only if the property value is *not* included in the specified set.

Both $in and $nin work for properties with scalar values (like strings, numbers, dates, etc.), but they can also be used to search within collections. The web route in Listing 11-63 accepts a music genre as a URL parameter and returns related genres in the HTTP response.

Listing 11-63. Using the $in Query Operator to Filter by Genre

```
// example-011/album-routes.js

/**
 * GET /album/genre/(genre)/related
 * @param req
 * @param cb
 */
routes.GET['^\/album\/genre\/([a-zA-Z]+)/related$'] = function (req, cb) {
  cb = httpd.asJSON(cb);
  var principalGenre = req.params[0];
  var criteria = {
    genre: {$in: [principalGenre]}
  };
  Album.find(criteria)
    .lean(true)
    .select('-_id genre')
    .exec(function (err, albums) {
      if (err) return cb(500, err);
      var relatedGenres = [];
      albums.forEach(function (album) {
        album.genre.forEach(function (albumGenre) {
          // don't include the principal genre
          if (albumGenre === principalGenre) return;
          // ensure duplicates are ignored
          if (relatedGenres.indexOf(albumGenre) < 0) {
            relatedGenres.push(albumGenre);
          }
        });
      });
      cb(200, {genre: principalGenre, related: relatedGenres});
    });
};
```

```
example-011$ curl -X GET http://localhost:8080/album/genre/Dance/related
{"genre":"Dance","related":["Electronica","Soundtrack"]}
```

To determine what constitutes a "related" genre, the criteria object selects albums that have the principal genre as an element in each document's genre array. It then compiles a list of all other genres that have been assigned to albums in the result set and returns that list to the client. Though Album.genre is an array, MongoDB knows to traverse it for values that match the elements in the $in operator. The Query. select() method excludes the _id property and includes only the genre property, since it alone contains the data in which this route is interested.

The $in operator is useful for finding elements in arrays of scalar values, but a different approach is needed when searching arrays of complex objects. Each subdocument in Album.tracks has its own properties and values, for example. To search for albums with tracks that meet some criteria, properties for tracks can be referenced with their full property paths, starting from the album itself. In Listing 11-64, albums will be fetched that posses any track with a `title` property that matches the value for `tracks.title` in the criteria object.

Listing 11-64. Using a Subdocument Path in a Criteria Object

```
// example-012/album-routes.js
/**
 * GET /album(?composer={string}&title={string}&track={string})
 * @param req
 * @param cb
 */
routes.GET['^\/album(?:\\?.+)?$'] = function (req, cb) {
  cb = httpd.asJSON(cb);
  var criteria = {};
  // ...
  if (req.query.track) {
    criteria['tracks.title'] = req.query.track;
  }
  // ...
  Album.find(criteria)
    .lean(true)
    .exec(function (err, albums) {
      if (err) return cb(500, err);
      cb(200, albums);
    });
};
```

```
example-012$ curl -X GET http://localhost:8080/album?track=The%20Looking%20Glass
[{"_id":"54ed1dcb6fb525ba25529bd1","composer":"Kerry Muzzey","title":"Renaissance"... }
```

The $and and $or Operators

Simple criteria objects can query a property by using normal object notation. For example, to find an album that is in publication, the simple criteria object in Listing 11-65 would be sufficient.

Listing 11-65. Simple Criteria Object

```
Album.find({inPublication: true}, function (err, albums) {/*...*/});
```

This approach is insufficient for complicated, compound queries, however, such as the pseudo-query in Listing 11-66.

Listing 11-66. Painful Pseudo-Query

```
(select albums that
  (
    (are in publication and were released within the last two years) or
    (are categorized as classical and priced between $9 and $10)
  )
)
```

Fortunately, the $and and $or operators can be used to construct a criteria object that will produce the desired set of albums. Both operators accept an array of criteria objects that may contain simple queries, or complex queries that *also* contain $and, $or, or any other valid query operators. The $and operator performs a logical AND operation using each criteria object in its array, selecting only documents that match *all* specified criteria. In contrast, the $or operator performs a logical OR operation, selecting documents that match *any* of its criteria.

In Listing 11-67, the album recommendations route composes a criteria object that uses *both* compound operators. Note that whereas the keys in simple criteria objects are property names, in compound criteria objects the keys are the compound operators followed by arrays of simple and/or complex criteria objects.

Listing 11-67. Using $and and $or to Find Album Recommendations

```
// example-012/album-routes.js
/**
 * GET /album/recommended
 * @param req
 * @param cb
 */
routes.GET['^\/album\/recommended$'] = function (req, cb) {
  cb = httpd.asJSON(cb);
  var nowMS = Date.now();
  var twoYearsMS = (365 * 24 * 60 * 60 * 1000 * 2);
  var twoYearsAgo = new Date(nowMS - twoYearsMS);

  var criteria = {
    $or: [
      // match all of these conditions...
      { $and: [{inPublication: true}, {releaseDate: {$gt: twoYearsAgo}}] },
      // OR
      // match all of these conditions...
      { $and: [{genre: {$in: ['Classical']}}, {price: {$gte: 5, $lte: 10}}] }
    ]
  };

  Album.find(criteria)
    .lean(true)
    .select('-_id -tracks')
    .exec(function (err, albums) {
      if (err) return cb(500, err);
      cb(200, albums);
    });
};

example-012$ curl -X GET http://localhost:8080/album/recommended
[{"composer":"Kerry Muzzey","title":"Renaissance","price":4.95... },
 {"composer":"Audiomachine","title":"Tree of Life","price":9.49... },
 {"composer":"Jessica Curry","title":"Dear Esther","price":6.99... }]
```

The $regex Operator

Often, searching for documents that match a precise text field query yields suboptimal results. Regular expressions can be used to broaden these searches so that documents are selected with fields that *resemble* a particular query parameter. In SQL-based languages, the like operator can be used for this purpose, but MongoDB favors regular expressions. The $regex operator adds a regular expression to a criteria object property, selecting documents that match the regular expression and excluding those that do not. It is often paired with the $options operator which may contain any valid regular expression flag such as i (case-insensitive). The route in Listing 11-68 accepts a query parameter, owner, which is converted to a regular expression and applied against the owner property of every library document.

Listing 11-68. Finding a Library with a Regular Expression

```
// example-012/library-routes.js
/**
 * GET /library?
 * @param req
 * @param cb
 */
routes.GET['^\/library(?:\\?.+)?$'] = function (req, cb) {
  cb = httpd.asJSON(cb);
  var criteria = {};
  if (req.query.owner) {
    criteria.owner = {
      $regex: '^.*' + req.query.owner + '.*$',
      $options: 'i'
    }
  } else {
    return cb(404, {message: 'please specify an owner'});
  }
  Library.find(criteria)
    .populate('albums')
    .exec(function (err, libraries) {
      if (err) return cb(500, err);
      cb(200, libraries);
    });
};
```

The criteria object specifies the property against which the regular expression will be applied, and an object that includes both the expression (the $regex property) and any options to apply while matching (the $options property). In Listing 11-69 the curl command uses the owner cloud is as a query string parameter. Since the regular expression in Listing 11-68 above surrounds the query parameter with the regular expression wildcard .*, and since the regular expression options specify the case-insensitive option i, the route will return the only library in MongoDB, owned by Nicholas Cloud. Listing 11-69 shows the curl command and HTTP response output.

Listing 11-69. Finding a Library by Owner with cURL

```
curl -X GET http://localhost:8080/library?owner=cloud
[{"_id":"54ed249312c06b3726d3abcd","owner":"Nicholas Cloud"... ]
```

Advanced Query Operators

There are many more MongoDB operators that may be used in Mongoose queries, and while an in-depth analysis of each warrants many more pages, Table 11-3 provides a high-level overview of additional advanced query operators.

Table 11-3. *Additional Advanced Query Operators*

Operator	Description
$not, $nor	Negative logical operators that combine query clauses and select documents that match accordingly
$exists	Selects documents where the specified property exists (remember, MongoDB documents are technically schemaless)
$type	Selects documents where the specified property is of a given type
$mod	Selects documents where a modulo operator on a specified field returns a specified result (e.g., select all albums where the price is divisible evenly by 3.00)
$all	Selects documents with an array property that contains all specified elements
$size	Selects documents with an array property of a given size
$elemMatch	Selects documents where a subdocument in an array matches more than one condition

Summary

MongoDB is schemaless and extremely flexible by design, but application developers often add constraints on data in application code to enforce business rules, ensure data integrity, conform to existing application abstractions, or achieve any number of other goals. Mongoose recognizes and embraces this reality, and rests snugly between application code and the data store.

Mongoose schemas add constraints to otherwise free-form data. They define the shape and validity of the data to be stored, enforce constraints, create relationships between documents, and expose the document life cycle via middleware.

Models provide a full but extensible query interface. Criteria objects that conform to MongoDB query syntax are used to find specific data. Chainable query methods give developers control over the property selection, reference population, and whether full documents or plain JSON objects are retrieved. Custom static methods that encapsulate complicated criteria objects and more involved queries can be added to models to keep application concerns properly segregated.

Finally, Mongoose documents can be extended with custom instance methods that contain domain logic, and custom getters and setters that aid in computed property manipulation.

CHAPTER 12

■ ■ ■

Knex and Bookshelf

The report of my death was an exaggeration.

—Samuel Langhorne Clemens (Mark Twain)

In this chapter, we will explore two libraries that work together to ease many of the difficulties that Node.js developers often encounter when working with relational databases. The first, Knex, provides a flexible and consistent interface for interacting with several well-known SQL platforms such as MySQL and PostgreSQL. The second, Bookshelf, builds on this foundation by providing developers with a powerful object-relational mapping (ORM) library that simplifies the process of modeling the entities that comprise an application's data structure, along with the various relationships that exist between them. Readers who are familiar with Backbone.js and its emphasis on structuring data within Models and Collections will quickly find themselves at home with Bookshelf, as the library follows many of the same patterns and provides many of the same APIs.

In this chapter, you will learn how to do the following:

- Create SQL queries with the Knex query builder

- Create complex database interactions without resorting to nested callback functions, with the help of promises

- Ensure the integrity of your application's data through the use of transactions

- Manage changes to your database's schema with the help of Knex migration scripts

- Bootstrap your database with sample data using Knex seed scripts

- Define one-to-one, one-to-many, and many-to-many relationships between Bookshelf models

- Use eager loading to efficiently retrieve complex object graphs based on Bookshelf relationships

---

■ **Note**   Most of the examples in this chapter make heavy use of the promise-based and Underscore-inspired APIs that both Bookshelf and Knex provide. As a result, readers who are unfamiliar with either of these concepts are encouraged to first read Chapter 17, which covers Q, and 19, which covers Underscore and Lo-Dash.

Knex

Knex provides a database abstraction layer (DBAL) for MySQL, PostgreSQL, MariaDB, and SQLite3, a unified interface through which developers can interact with each of these Structured Query Language (SQL) databases without having to concern themselves with minor variations in syntax and response format that exist between each platform. Applications backed by such relational databases can benefit from a number of Knex features, including these:

- A promise-based interface that allows for cleaner control of asynchronous processes

- A stream interface for efficiently piping data through an application as needed

- Unified interfaces through which queries and schemas for each supported platform can be created

- Transaction support

In addition to the library itself, Knex also provides a command-line utility with which developers can do the following:

- Create, implement, and (when necessary) revert database migrations, scripted schema changes that can then be committed with an application's source code

- Create database "seed" scripts, a consistent method by which an application's database can be populated with sample data for local development and testing

Each of these subjects will be covered in more detail throughout this chapter.

Installing the Command-Line Utility

Before going any further, you should ensure that you have installed the command-line utility provided by Knex. Available as an npm package, the installation process is shown in Listing 12-1.

Listing 12-1. Installing the knex Command-Line Utility via npm

```
$ npm install -g knex$ knex --version
Knex CLI version: 0.7.3
```

Adding Knex to Your Project

In addition to installing the knex command-line utility, you will also need to add the knex npm module as a local dependency within each project in which you intend to use it, along with a supported database library, as shown in Listing 12-2.

Listing 12-2. Installing Knex and a Supported Database Library As a Local Project Dependency via npm

```
$ npm install knex --save
# Supported database libraries include (be sure to --save):
$ npm install mysql
$ npm install mariasql
$ npm install pg
$ npm install sqlite3
```

■ **Note**   SQLite implements a self-contained, serverless database within a single file on your disk and requires no additional tools. If you don't have access to a database server such as MySQL at the moment, the sqlite3 library will provide you with a quick and easy way to begin experimenting with Knex without requiring additional setup. *The examples referenced throughout this chapter will use this library.*

Configuring Knex

With your dependencies now in place, all that remains is to initialize Knex within your project. Listing 12-3 shows what that process looks like if you happen to be using MySQL, PostgreSQL, or MariaDB, while Listing 12-4 shows how to initialize Knex for use with SQLite3.

Listing 12-3. Initializing Knex for Use with MySQL, PostgreSQL, or MariaDB (Substitute mysql for pg or mariasql As Needed)

```
var knex = require('knex')({
    'client': 'mysql',
    'connection': {
        'host': '127.0.0.1',
        'user': 'user',
        'password': 'password',
        'database': 'database'
    },
    'debug': false // Set this to true to enable debugging for all queries
});
```

Listing 12-4. Initializing Knex for Use with SQLite3

```
// example-sqlite-starter/lib/db.js

var knex = require('knex')({
    'client': 'sqlite3',
    'connection': {
        'filename': 'db.sqlite'
    }
});
```

As you can see, the configuration settings required for SQLite3 are quite a bit simpler than those required for other, more full-featured solutions. Instead of providing connection settings, we simply provide the name of a file (db.sqlite) in which SQLite will store its data.

The SQL Query Builder

The primary focus of Knex is on providing developers with a unified interface through which they can interact with multiple, SQL-based databases without having to worry about minor variations in syntax and response format that exist between each of them. To that end, Knex provides a number of methods, most of which fall into one of two categories: query builder methods and interface methods.

Query Builder Methods

Query builder methods are those that aid developers in the creation of SQL queries. Examples of such methods include select(), from(), where(), limit(), and groupBy(). At last count, Knex provides more than 40 such methods, with which platform-agnostic queries can be created. Listing 12-5 shows a simple SQL query, along with an example demonstrating how such a query can be created using Knex.

Listing 12-5. Example Demonstrating the Creation of a Simple SQL Query Using Knex

```
// example-sqlite-starter/example1.js
// SELECT id, name, postal_code FROM cities;knex.select('id', 'name', 'postal_code').
from('cities');
```

While the example shown in Listing 12-5 demonstrates the basic method by which SQL queries can be created with Knex, it does little to convey the true value of the library. That value should start to become more apparent as we take a look at the various interface methods that Knex provides. It is with these methods that we can begin to submit our queries and process their resulting data.

Interface Methods

Knex provides a number of interface methods that allow us to submit and process our queries in several convenient ways. In this section, we'll take a look at two of the most useful approaches that are available to us.

Promises

The event-driven nature of JavaScript makes it well suited for efficiently handling complex, asynchronous tasks. Traditionally, JavaScript developers have managed asynchronous control flow through the use of callback functions, as shown in Listing 12-6.

Listing 12-6. Simple Callback Function

```
var request = require('request');
request({
    'url': 'http://mysite.com',
    'method': 'GET'
}, function(err, response) {
    if (err) throw new Error(err);
    console.log(response);
});
```

Callback functions allow us to defer the execution of a particular sequence of code until the appropriate time. Such functions are easy to understand and implement. Unfortunately, they are also very difficult to manage as applications grow in complexity. Imagine a scenario in which additional asynchronous processes must run after the initial response is received in Listing 12-6. To do so would require the use of additional, nested callback functions. As additional asynchronous steps are added to this code, we begin to experience what many developers refer to as "callback hell" or the "pyramid of doom," terms that describe the unmaintainable mass of spaghetti code that frequently results from such an approach.

Fortunately, JavaScript promises provide developers with a convenient solution to this problem—a solution that Knex makes extensive use of through its promise-based interface for submitting and processing queries. Listing 12-7 shows this API in action.

Listing 12-7. Demonstration of the Promise-Based API Provided by Knex

```
// example-sqlite-starter/example2.js

knex.pluck('id').from('cities').where('state_id', '=', 1)
    .then(function(cityIds) {
        return knex.select('id', 'first_name', 'last_name').from('users')
        .whereIn('city_id', cityIds);
    })
    .then(function(users) {
        return [
            users,
            knex.select('*').from('bookmarks').whereIn('user_id', _.pluck(users, 'id'))
        ];
    })
    .spread(function(users, bookmarks) {
        _.each(users, function(user) {
            user.bookmarks = _.filter(bookmarks, function(bookmark) {
                return bookmark.user_id = user.id;
            });
        });
        console.log(JSON.stringify(users, null, 4));
    })
    .catch(function(err) {
        console.log(err);
    });
```

In this example, three queries are submitted in succession:

1. Cities within a particular state are selected.

2. Users who live within the returned cities are selected.

3. Bookmarks for each of the returned users are selected.

After our final query has returned, we then attach each bookmark to the appropriate user and display the result, which you can see in Listing 12-8.

Listing 12-8. Data Logged to the Console As a Result of the Code in Listing 12-7

```
[
    {
        "id": 1,
        "first_name": "Steve",
        "last_name": "Taylor",
        "bookmarks": [
            {
                "id": 1,
                "url": "http://reddit.com",
                "label": "Reddit",
                "user_id": 1,
                "created_at": "2015-03-12 12:09:35"
            },
```

```
    {
        "id": 2,
        "url": "http://www.theverge.com",
        "label": "The Verge",
        "user_id": 1,
        "created_at": "2015-03-12 12:09:35"
    }
  ]
  }
]
```

Thanks to the promise-based interface provided by Knex, at no point does our code ever reach beyond one level of indentation, thereby ensuring that our application remains easy to follow. More importantly, should an error occur at any point during this process, it would be conveniently caught and handled by our final catch statement.

■ **Note**   JavaScript promises are a powerful tool for writing complex, asynchronous code in a manner that is easy to follow and maintain. If you are unfamiliar with this concept, you are encouraged to skip to Chapter 17 and read about the Q promise library for more in-depth information on this subject.

Streams

One of the biggest benefits to writing applications with Node.js is the platform's ability to execute I/O-intensive procedures in a very efficient manner. Unlike synchronous languages such as PHP, Python, or Ruby, Node.js is capable of handling thousands of simultaneous connections within a single thread, allowing developers to write applications capable of meeting enormous demands, while using minimal resources. Node.js provides several important tools for accomplishing this feat, one of the most important of which is streams.

Before we take a look at streams, let's examine another example of a traditional JavaScript callback function, as shown in Listing 12-9.

Listing 12-9. JavaScript Callback Function That Accepts the Contents of a Loaded File

```
var fs = require('fs');
fs.readFile('data.txt', 'utf8', function(err, data) {
    if (err) throw new Error(err);
    console.log(data);
});
```

In this example, we use the readFile() method of the native fs library available within Node.js to read the contents of a file. Once that data is loaded into memory (in its entirety), it is then passed to our callback function for further processing. This approach is simple and easily understood. However, it's not very efficient, as our application must first load the entire contents of the file into memory before passing it back to us. This isn't a terrible problem for smaller files, but larger files may begin to cause issues, depending on the resources available to the server that happens to be running this application.

Node.js streams resolve this issue by piping data through one or more functions in multiple, smaller chunks. By doing so, streams allow developers to avoid dedicating large portions of a server's available resources for any single request. The example shown in Listing 12-10 accomplishes the same goal of our previous example, without loading the contents of the entire file into memory all at once.

Listing 12-10. Pair of Node.js Streams Working Together to Efficiently Load and Display
the Contents of a File

```
// example-read-file-stream/index.js

var fs = require('fs');
var Writable = require('stream').Writable;
var stream = fs.createReadStream('data.txt');
var out = Writable();
out._write = function(chunk, enc, next) {
    console.log(chunk.toString());
    next();
};
stream.pipe(out);
```

Streams are a relatively underutilized feature of Node.js, which is unfortunate, as they happen to be
one of the more powerful aspects of the platform. Fortunately, Knex provides a streaming interface for
consuming query results that allows us to take advantage of these benefits, as shown in Listing 12-11.

Listing 12-11. Processing the Results of a Query via the Streaming Interface Provided by Knex

```
var Writable = require('stream').Writable;
var ws = Writable();
ws._write = function(chunk, enc, next) {
    console.dir(chunk);
    next();
};
var stream = knex.select('*').from('users').stream();
stream.pipe(ws);
```

In this example, the results of our query on the users table (which could be quite large for some
applications) are streamed in smaller chunks to our writable stream, instead of being passed along in their
entirety. This approach can also be paired with the library's promise interface to create a more robust
implementation, as shown in Listing 12-12.

Listing 12-12. Combining the Streaming and Promise-Based Interfaces Provided by Knex for Better
Error Handling

```
var Writable = require('stream').Writable;
var ws = Writable();
ws._write = function(chunk, enc, next) {
    console.dir(chunk);
    next();
};
knex.select('*').from('users').stream(function(stream) {
    stream.pipe(ws);
}).then(function() {
    console.log('Done.');
}).catch(function(err) {
    console.log(err);
});
```

In this example, we combine the power of the streaming and promise-based interfaces provided by Knex. When a callback function is passed to the library's `stream()` method, that callback function receives the generated promise as opposed to being returned directly. Instead, a promise is returned, which is resolved once the stream is complete.

■ **Note**   The streaming interface provided by Knex is compatible with MySQL, PostgreSQL, and MariaDB databases. SQLite3 is not currently supported.

Transactions

One of the biggest benefits to using ACID-compliant, relational databases lies in their ability to group multiple queries into a single unit of work (i.e., a "transaction") that will either succeed or fail as a whole. In other words, should a single query within the transaction fail, any changes that may have occurred as a result of previously run queries within the transaction would be reverted.

By way of an example, consider a financial transaction that occurs at your bank. Suppose you wanted to send $25 to your cousin on her birthday. Those funds would first have to be withdrawn from your account and then inserted into your cousin's account. Imagine a scenario in which the application enabling that exchange of funds were to crash for any number of reasons (e.g., a faulty line of code or a larger system failure) after those funds were removed from your account, but before they were inserted into your cousin's account. Without the safety net provided by transactions, those funds would have essentially vanished into thin air. Transactions allow developers to ensure that such processes only ever happen in full—never leaving data in an inconsistent state.

■ **Note**   The acronym ACID (Atomicity, Consistency, Isolation, Durability) refers to a set of properties that describe database transactions. Atomicity refers to the fact that such transactions can either succeed in their entirety or fail as a whole. Such transactions are said to be "atomic."

Previous examples within this chapter have demonstrated the process of creating and submitting database queries with Knex. Before we continue, let's review another example that does not take advantage of transactions. Afterward, we'll update this example to take advantage of the peace of mind that transactions provide.

In the example shown in Listing 12-13, a moveFunds() function is declared that, when called, uses the knex object to move the specified amount of funds from one account to another. This function returns a promise that is either resolved or rejected once this process completes, depending on the success or failure of the call. A glaring error exists here—can you spot it?

Listing 12-13. moveFunds() Function Demonstrating the Process of Moving Funds from One Account to Another Without the Security of Transactions

```
// example-financial/bad.js

/**
 * Moves the specified amount of funds from sourceAccountID to destAccountID
 */
var moveFunds = function(sourceAccountID, destAccountID, amount) {
```

```
    return knex.select('funds').from('accounts')
        .where('id', sourceAccountID)
        .first(function(result) {
            if (!result) {
                throw new Error('Unable to locate funds for source account');
            }
            if (result.funds < amount) {
                throw new Error('Not enough funds are available in account');
            }
            return knex('accounts').where('id', sourceAccountID).update({
                    'funds': result.funds - amount
            });
    }).then(function() {
            return knex.select('funds').from('accounts')
                .where('id', destAccountID);
    }).first(function(result) {
            if (!result) {
                throw new Error('Unable to locate funds for destination account');
            }
            return knex('accounts').where('id', destAccountID).update({
                    'funds': result.funds + amount
                });
    });
};

/* Move $25 from account 1 to account 2. */
moveFunds(1, 2, 25).then(function(result) {
    console.log('Transaction succeeded.', result);
}).catch(function(err) {
    console.log('Transaction failed!', err);
});
```

In this example, the following steps are required to accomplish the goal of moving funds from a source account to a destination account:

1. The total funds currently available within the source account are determined.

2. If insufficient funds are available to complete the process, an error is thrown.

3. The funds to be transferred are deducted from the source account.

4. The total funds currently available within the destination account are determined.

5. If the destination account cannot be found, an error is thrown.

6. The funds to be transferred are added to the destination account.

If you haven't spotted the mistake already, a glaring problem presents itself at step 5. In the event that the destination account cannot be found, an error is thrown, but at this point the funds to be moved have already been deducted from the source account! We could attempt to solve this problem in a number of ways. We could catch the error within our code and then credit the funds back to the source account, but this would still not account for unforeseen errors that could arise due to network problems or in the event that our application server were to lose power and completely crash in the middle of this process.

It is at this point that the power of database transactions starts to become evident. In Listing 12-14, our moveFunds() function is refactored to wrap this entire procedure into a single, "atomic" transaction that will either succeed or fail as a whole. Note the creation of the trx object, from which our transaction-aware queries are built.

Listing 12-14. Transaction-Aware Implementation of Listing 12-13

```
// example-financial/index.js

/**
 * Moves the specified amount of funds from sourceAccountID to destAccountID
 */
var moveFunds = function(sourceAccountID, destAccountID, amount) {

    return knex.transaction(function(trx) {

        return trx.first('funds')
            .from('accounts')
            .where('id', sourceAccountID)
            .then(function(result) {
                if (!result) {
                    throw new Error('Unable to locate funds for source account');
                }
                if (result.funds < amount) {
                    throw new Error('Not enough funds are available in account');
                }
                return trx('accounts').where('id', sourceAccountID)
                    .update({
                        'funds': result.funds - amount
                    });
            })
            .then(function() {
                return trx.first('funds')
                    .from('accounts')
                    .where('id', destAccountID);
            })
            .then(function(result) {
                if (!result) {
                    throw new Error('Unable to locate funds for destination account');
                }
                return trx('accounts').where('id', destAccountID)
                    .update({
                        'funds': result.funds + amount
                    });
            });

    });

};
```

```
/* Move $25 from account 1 to account 2. */
displayAccounts()
    .then(function() {
        return moveFunds(1, 2, 25);
    }).then(function() {
        console.log('Transaction succeeded.');
    }).catch(function(err) {
        console.log('Transaction failed!', err);
    });
```

As you can see, the transaction-aware example shown in Listing 12-14 largely resembles that shown in Listing 12-13, but it does differ in one important way. Instead of creating our query by calling builder methods directly on the knex object, we first initiate a transaction by calling knex.transaction(). The callback function that we provide is then passed a "transaction-aware" stand-in (trx) from which we then begin to create our series of queries. From this point forward, any queries that we create from the trx object will either succeed or fail as a whole. The knex.transaction() method returns a promise that will be resolved or rejected once the transaction as a whole is complete, allowing us to easily integrate this transaction into an even larger series of promise-based actions.

Migration Scripts

Just as an application's source code is destined to change over time, so too is the structure of the information that it stores. As such changes are made, it is important that they be implemented in a way that can be repeated, shared, rolled back when necessary, and tracked over time. Database migration scripts provide developers with a convenient pattern for accomplishing this goal.

A Knex migration script is composed of two functions, up and down, as shown in Listing 12-15. The script's up function is responsible for modifying a database's structure in some desired way (e.g., creating a table, adding a column), while its down function is responsible for restoring the database's structure to its previous state.

Listing 12-15. Knex Migration Script with *up* Function Creating a New Table and *down* Function Dropping the Table

```
// example-sqlite-starter/migrations/20150311082640_states.js

exports.up = function(knex, Promise) {
    return knex.schema.createTable('states', function(table) {
        table.increments().unsigned().primary().notNullable();
        table.string('name').notNullable();
        table.timestamp('created_at').defaultTo(knex.fn.now()).notNullable();
    });
};

exports.down = function(knex, Promise) {
    return knex.schema.dropTable('states');
};
```

Configuring Your Project for Migrations

The Knex command-line utility provides developers with simple tools for creating and managing migration scripts. To get started, you'll first need to create a special configuration file by running the following command within the root folder of your project:

```
$ knex init
```

After running this command, a file (knexfile.js) will be created with contents similar to those shown in Listing 12-16. You should alter the contents of this file as needed. Whenever a Knex migration script is run, Knex will determine its connection settings based on the contents of this file and the value of the NODE_ENVIRONMENT environment variable.

■ **Note**   On OS X and Linux, environment variables are set from the terminal by running export ENVIRONMENT_VARIABLE=value. The command to be used within the Windows command line is set ENVIRONMENT_VARIABLE=value.

Listing 12-16. knexfile.js

```
// example-sqlite-starter/knexfile.js

module.exports = {

    'development': {
        'client': 'sqlite3',
            'connection': {
                'filename': './db.sqlite'
        }
        },
        'seeds': {
            'directory': './seeds'
        }
    },
    'staging': {
        'client': 'postgresql',
            'connection': {
                'database': 'my_db',
            'user': 'username',
            'password': 'password'
        },
        'pool': {
            'min': 2,
            'max': 10
            }
        }
    }
};
```

Creating Your First Migration

With our Knex configuration file now in place, we can move forward with the creation of our first migration script. The command for doing so is shown here:

```
$ knex migrate:make users_table
```

When creating your own migrations, substitute the `users_table` portion of the command with a term that describes the change your migration implements. After running this command, Knex will create a migration script for you that resembles the one shown in Listing 12-17.

Listing 12-17. New Knex Migration Script

```
exports.up = function(knex, Promise) {
};

exports.down = function(knex, Promise) {
};
```

After creating your first migration script, your project's file structure should resemble that shown in Listing 12-18.

Listing 12-18. Excerpt of Project's File Structure After Creating First Migration

```
.
├── knexfile.js
└── migrations
    └── 20141203074309_users_table.js
```

■ **Note** Knex migration scripts are stored in a `migrations` folder at the root level of a project. If this directory does not exist, Knex will create it for you. Knex automatically prepends a timestamp to the file name of migration scripts, as shown in Listing 12-18. This ensures that a project's migrations are always sorted by the order in which they were created.

It is now up to us to modify the up and down functions within our newly created migration script. Let's take a look at two alternative approaches.

Defining Schema Updates with Schema Builder Methods

In addition to providing methods for constructing queries, Knex also provides methods for defining a database's underlying structure (schema). With the help of these "schema builder" methods, developers can create platform-agnostic blueprints that describe the various tables, columns, indexes, and relationships that make up a database. These blueprints can then be applied to any supported platform to generate the desired database. The migration script shown in Listing 12-15 shows the Knex schema builder in action, while Listing 12-19 shows the query generated by the script's up method.

Listing 12-19. SQL Query Generated Through Use of Schema Builder Methods, As Shown in Listing 12-15

```
// example-raw-migration/migrations/20150312083058_states.js

CREATE TABLE states (
  id integer PRIMARY KEY AUTOINCREMENT NOT NULL,
  name varchar(255) NOT NULL,
  created_at datetime NOT NULL DEFAULT(CURRENT_TIMESTAMP)
);
```

Schema builder methods are useful, in that they allow developers to easily define schemas in a way that can be applied to each of the platforms supported by Knex. They also require a minimal amount of knowledge regarding raw SQL queries, making it possible for developers with little experience working directly with SQL databases to get up and running quickly. That said, schema builder methods are also limiting. To provide a generic interface for defining database schemas that work across multiple platforms, Knex must make certain decisions for you—a fact that you may not be comfortable with. Developers with more experience working directly with SQL databases may wish to bypass the schema builder methods entirely, opting instead to craft their own SQL queries. This is easily accomplished, as we are about to see.

Defining Schema Updates with Raw SQL Queries

In Listing 12-20, we see a Knex migration script that creates a new users table through the use of raw SQL queries. This is accomplished through the use of the knex.schema.raw() method. When called, this method returns a promise that will be either resolved or rejected, depending on the success or failure of the query that it receives.

Listing 12-20. Knex Migration Script Defined with Raw SQL Queries

```
// example-raw-migration/migrations/20150312083058_states.js

var multiline = require('multiline');

exports.up = function(knex, Promise) {

    var sql = multiline.stripIndent(function() {/*
        CREATE TABLE states (
            id integer PRIMARY KEY AUTOINCREMENT NOT NULL,
            name varchar(255) NOT NULL,
            created_at datetime NOT NULL DEFAULT(CURRENT_TIMESTAMP)
        );
    */});
    return knex.schema.raw(sql);

};

exports.down = function(knex, Promise) {
    return knex.schema.raw('DROP TABLE states;');
};
```

■ **Note**   The example shown in Listing 12-20 makes use of an additional library that is unrelated to Knex: multiline. The multiline library is quite useful because it allows us to define large chunks of text that span multiple lines without requiring that each line end with a continuation character.

Running Knex Migrations

With our newly created migration script now defined and ready for use, our only remaining task is to run the migration, bringing our database up to date with our desired changes. The command for doing so is shown here:

```
$ knex migrate:latest
```

This command will instruct Knex to run all available migration scripts that have not yet been run, in the order in which they were created. Once complete, our database will have been brought fully up to date with our desired changes. If you're curious as to how Knex keeps track of which migrations have and have not been run, the answer lies in the knex_migrations table that Knex automatically creates for itself (see Figure 12-1). Within this table, Knex maintains a running list of which migrations have been implemented. The name of this table can be changed by modifying the configuration file we created via the knex init command.

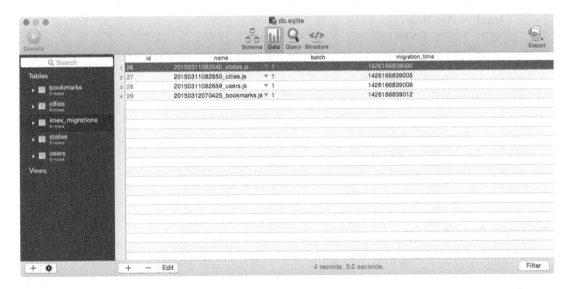

Figure 12-1. *The knex_migrations table used by Knex to track which migration scripts have already been applied to your database*

Reverting Knex Migrations

The act of running Knex migration scripts is not a one-way street. They can also be undone, which is particularly important during development. The command for doing so is as follows:

```
$ knex migrate:rollback
```

This command will instruct Knex to revert all migration scripts that were run as a result of the most recent execution of knex migrate:latest. To verify the status of your database in regard to your migration scripts, you can run the following command to determine your database's current migration version:

```
$ knex migrate:currentVersion
```

Seed Scripts

In the previous section, you learned how Knex migration scripts can empower you to script changes to a database's structure—scripts that can be shared with others, reverted when necessary, and tracked within version control. Knex seed scripts serve a similar purpose, but with a focus on data rather than structure. Seed scripts provide a consistent way in which to specify how a newly created database can be filled with sample data, to get a new development environment up and running. Listing 12-21 shows the contents of a seed script included with one of this chapter's example projects.

Listing 12-21. Simple Knex Seed Script That Removes All Existing Records from the states Table and Inserts Two New Ones

```
// example-sqlite-starter/seeds/01-states.js

exports.seed = function(knex, Promise) {

    return Promise.join(
        knex('states').del(),
        knex('states').insert([
            {
                'id': 1,
                'name': 'Georgia'
            },
            {
                'id': 2,
                'name': 'Tennessee'
            }
        ]);
    );
};
```

Creating Seed Scripts

You can instruct Knex to create a new seed script using the following command:

```
$ knex seed:make users
```

By default, Knex saves newly created seed scripts to the seeds folder at the root path of your project. You can customize this folder by modifying the contents of the your project's knexfile.js configuration file (see Listing 12-16).

Running Seed Scripts

After creating seed scripts for your application, you can populate your database with them by running this command:

```
$ knex seed:run
```

> ■ **Note**   Seed scripts are always run in alphabetical order. If the order in which your seeds are run is important, take care to name them appropriately to ensure they run in the desired order.

Bookshelf

Bookshelf builds on the foundation laid by Knex to provide a flexible ORM library that simplifies the process of creating classes ("models") to represent the various objects that make up an application. This section explores the various ways in which developers can use Bookshelf to accomplish the following:

- Create classes ("models") to represent the various tables used within an application's database

- Extend models with custom behavior unique to the needs of their application

- Define complex relationships between models (one-to-one, one-to-many, many-to-many)

- Easily navigate through the various relationships that exist between models without resorting to complex SQL queries, with the help of "eager loading"

Developers who are familiar with Backbone will quickly find themselves at home with Bookshelf, as it follows many of the same patterns and implements many of the same APIs. You could easily describe Bookshelf as "Backbone for the server," and you wouldn't be far off base.

What Is an Object-Relational Mapper?

Relational databases store information as a series of rows within one or more tables, each table having one or more columns that describe the various attributes of the records they contain—just as you might go about structuring information within a spreadsheet. In most applications, separate tables are created to represent each type of available entity (e.g., "Account", "User", "Comment"). The various relationships that exist between each of these entities are then defined through the use of "foreign key" columns, as shown in Figure 12-2.

accounts			
id	**name**	**created_at**	**updated_at**
Integer	String	Timestamp	Timestamp

users						
id	**account_id**	**first_name**	**last_name**	**email**	**created_at**	**updated_at**
Integer	Integer	String	String	String	Timestamp	Timestamp

Figure 12-2. *Here, the relationship between users and accounts (an account has one or more users, users belong to accounts) is described via the* account_id *foreign key column within the* users *table.*

This approach to storing information is powerful and serves as the predominant method by which applications store data, for many good reasons (all of which extend well beyond the scope of this book). Unfortunately, this approach is also at odds with the object-oriented approach with which most applications tend to view data.

Object-relational mapping (ORM) tools such as Bookshelf allow developers to interact with the flat tables of information stored within relational databases as a series of interconnected objects, with which they can interact and navigate through to achieve some desired goal. In effect, ORM libraries provide developers with a "virtual object database" that allows them to more easily interact with the flat records contained within relational database tables.

Creating Your First Bookshelf Model

A Bookshelf model can be thought of as a class that, when instantiated, represents a record within a database. In their simplest form, Bookshelf models serve as data containers, providing built-in functionality for getting and setting attribute (i.e., column) values and for creating, updating, and destroying records. As we'll soon see, however, Bookshelf models become much more useful when we extend them with our own custom methods and define the relationships that exist between them.

Bookshelf models are defined via the bookshelf.Model.extend() method, as shown in Listing 12-22. In this simple example, a User model is defined whose records will be persisted to our database's users table.

Listing 12-22. Simple Bookshelf Model That Represents an Application's Users

```
// example-bookshelf1/lib/user.js

var knex = require('./db');
var bookshelf = require('bookshelf')(knex);

var User = bookshelf.Model.extend({
    'tableName': 'users',
    'idAttribute': 'id' // The primary key for our table. Defaults to: 'id'
});

module.exports = User;
```

Creating New Instances

In Listing 12-23, a new instance of the User model is created, modified, and then saved to the database.

Listing 12-23. Saving a New Instance of User to the Database

```
// example-bookshelf1/create.js

var User = require('./lib/user');
var user = new User();

user.set({
    'first_name': 'Steve',
    'last_name': 'Taylor',
    'email': 'steve.taylor@mydomain.com'
});
```

```
// Individual attributes can also be set as shown below
// user.set('first_name', 'Steve');

user.save().then(function(user) {
    // user has been saved
    console.log('User saved', user.toJSON());
    /*
    {
      first_name: 'Steve',
      last_name: 'Taylor',
      email: 'steve.taylor@mydomain.com',
      id: 1
    }
    */
});
```

Bookshelf provides a convenient forge() method that allows us to simplify this example just a bit, as shown in Listing 12-24. This method does nothing more than create and return a new instance of User behind the scenes for us, allowing us to forego the use of the new keyword.

Listing 12-24. Creating a New Instance of the User Model via the forge() Method

```
// example-bookshelf1/forge.js

User.forge({
    'id': 1,
    'first_name': 'John'
}).fetch().then(function(user) {

    /* An object containing every attribute / value for
    this model can be retrieved via the 'toJSON' method. */
    console.log(user.toJSON());
});
```

Fetching Instances

Instances of the User model can be retrieved in a similar manner. In Listing 12-25, a new instance of User is created with a value of 1 for its id attribute. When fetch() is called, Bookshelf will use any attributes set on the model to build the query used to fetch the desired record. In this example, the query used will be

```
SELECT * FROM users WHERE 'id' = 1;
```

Listing 12-25. Retrieving an Instance of the User Model from the Database

```
// example-bookshelf1/fetch.js

User.where({
    'id': 1
}).fetch().then(function(user) {
    // Individual attributes get be retrieved with the get method
    // console.log('first_name', user.get('first_name'));
    console.log(user.toJSON());
});
```

363

Destroying Instances

Just as model instances can be saved, they can also be deleted via the destroy() method, as shown in Listing 12-26.

Listing 12-26. Deleting an Instance of the User Model

```
// example-bookshelf1/destroy.js

User.where({
    'id': 1
}).fetch().then(function(user) {
    return user.destroy();
}).then(function() {
    console.log('User destroyed.');
});
```

In this example, destroy is called as an instance method on user. We could, however, instruct Bookshelf to simply seek out and destroy the record without first fetching the instance ourselves, as shown in Listing 12-27.

Listing 12-27. Instructing Bookshelf to Destroy the Specified Record

```
User.where({
    'id': 1
}).destroy().then(function() {
    console.log('User destroyed.');
});
```

Fetching Multiple Models (Collections)

In addition to retrieving a single instance of our model via the fetch() method, we can also retrieve multiple instances via the fetchAll() method, as shown in Listing 12-28.

Listing 12-28. Fetching All Instances of User with a Value of John for first_name

```
// example-bookshelf1/fetch-collection.js

User.where({
    'last_name': 'Doe'
}).fetchAll().then(function(users) {
    console.log(JSON.stringify(users.toJSON(), null, 4));
    /*
    [{
        "id": 3,
        "first_name": "John",
        "last_name": "Doe",
        "email": "john.doe@mydomain.com"
    },
```

```
    {
        "id": 4,
        "first_name": "Jane",
        "last_name": "Doe",
        "email": "jane.doe@mydomain.com"
    }]
    */
});
```

In this example, our call to fetchAll() returns a promise that resolves to a collection of multiple users. This collection provides a number of built-in methods specifically designed for interacting with multiple models. Given Bookshelf's strong focus on following Backbone patterns, most of the same methods available within Backbone collections are also available here. Listing 12-29 demonstrates a few common use cases.

Listing 12-29. Commonly Used Bookshelf Collection Methods

```
/* Iterate through a collection */
users.each(function(user, index) {
    console.log(user, index);
});

/* Create an array composed of models matching more specific criteria */
users = users.filter(function(user, index) {
    if (user.get('last_name') === 'Smith') return true;
});

/* A simpler method for filtering models, when a function call is not needed */
users = users.where({
    'last_name': 'Smith'
});

/* Return the first entry matching the specified criteria */
var johnSmith = users.find(function(user) {
    if (user.get('last_name') === 'Smith') return true;
});

/* Returns an array containing the first name of every user */
var firstNames = users.pluck('first_name');
```

Extending with Custom Behavior

In their simplest state, Bookshelf models do little more than serve as containers for records within a database, providing built-in methods for reading and writing attribute values and performing save or destroy operations. While this is useful, Bookshelf models begin to reach their full potential only when we begin to extend them with their own unique behavior as befitting the needs of our application.

An example of such behavior is demonstrated in Listing 12-30. Here, we update the User model seen in previous examples to include a sendEmail() method. Doing so allows us to abstract away the complexity involved with sending e-mail to registered users of our application.

Listing 12-30. Extending the User Model with a Method for Sending Outbound E-mails from Our Application

```
var Promise = require('bluebird');
var Handlebars = require('handlebars');

var User = bookshelf.Model.extend({
    'tableName': 'users',
    /**
     * Sends an e-mail to the user. Requires an `options` object
     * with values for `subject` and `message`. These values will be
     * compiled as Handlebars templates, passed this user's attributes,
     * and the result(s) will be used to generate the outgoing message.
     */
    'sendEmail': function(options) {
        var self = this;
        return Promise.resolve().then(function() {
                var subject = Handlebars.compile(options.subject)(self.toJSON());
                var message = Handlebars.compile(options.message)(self.toJSON());
            // Use your e-mail library of choice here, along with the
            // appropriate connection settings.      });
    }
});

User.where({
    'id': 1
}).fetch().then(function(user) {
    return user.sendEmail({
        'subject': 'Welcome, {{first_name}}',
        'message': 'We are happy to have you on board, {{first_name}} {{last_name}}.'
    });
});
```

In addition to those methods inherited from Backbone, Bookshelf collections also provide several methods of their own. Listing 12-31 demonstrates the use of the invokeThen() method, allowing us to easily invoke methods on each of the models contained within the collection.

Listing 12-31. Invoking an Imagined sendEmail() Method on Each Model Contained Within a Collection

```
// example-bookshelf1/invoke-then.js

User.where({
    'last_name': 'Doe'
}).fetchAll().then(function(users) {
    return users.invokeThen('sendEmail', {
        'subject': 'Congratulations on having such a great name, {{first_name}}.',
        'message': '{{first_name}} really is a great name. Seriously - way to go.'
    });
}).then(function(users) {
    console.log('%s users were complimented on their name.', users.length);
});
```

The invokeThen() method demonstrated in this example returns a promise of its own, which will be resolved only after all the calls to sendEmail() on our collection's models have themselves been resolved. This pattern also provides us with a convenient method for interacting with multiple models simultaneously.

Performing Validation

Those familiar with Backbone will find Bookshelf's event system quite familiar. In regard to validation, of particular interest are the saving and destroying events emitted by Bookshelf. By tapping into these events, Bookshelf models can be customized with unique behavior to either allow or deny these actions, based on some desired criteria. Listing 12-32 shows an example in which users with an e-mail address containing the string "hotmail.com" are prevented from being saved to the database.

Listing 12-32. Demonstration of Bookshelf's Event System, Which Allows for Implementation of Custom Validation Rules

```
// example-bookshelf1/lib/user.js

var User = bookshelf.Model.extend({
    'tableName': 'users',
    'initialize': function() {
        this.on('saving', this._validateSave);
    },
    '_validateSave': function() {
        var self = this;
        return Promise.resolve().then(function() {
            if (self.get('email').indexOf('hotmail.com') >= 0) {
                throw new Error('Hotmail email addresses are not allowed.');
            }
        });
    }
});
```

To prevent calls to save or destroy from succeeding, simply tap into the model's saving or destroying events, passing a reference to your own custom validation functions. If an error is thrown, the call will be prevented. Asynchronous validation is also possible through the use of promises. In Listing 12-33, a custom validation function returns a promise that is ultimately rejected.

Listing 12-33. Custom Validation Function That Returns a Promise

```
// example-bookshelf1/validation.js

User.forge({
    'first_name': 'Jane',
    'last_name': 'Doe',
    'email': 'jane.doe@hotmail.com'
}).save().then(function() {
    console.log('Saved.');
}).catch(function(err) {
    /* Our call to `save` will result in an error, due to this user's
    hotmail.com e-mail address. */
    console.log(err);
});
```

Customizing the Export Process

Previous examples have shown the use of the toJSON() method, which (by default) returns an object containing every available attribute/value for the model on which it is called (or for every available model, if called on a collection). Should you wish to customize the data returned by this method, you can do so by overriding the toJSON() method, as shown in Listing 12-34.

Listing 12-34. Customizing the Data Returned by Our Model's toJSON() Method

```
var User = bookshelf.Model.extend({
    'tableName': 'users',
    'toJSON': function() {
        var data = bookshelf.Model.prototype.toJSON.call(this);
        data.middle_name = 'Danger';
     return data;
    }
});
```

Within this example's overridden toJSON() method, we first call the prototype's toJSON() method, giving us the data that this method would have originally returned, had it not been overwritten. We then strip out the data we wish to hide, add some additional information of our own, and return it.

A common scenario in which this pattern is often seen involves the use of a User model, within which sensitive password information is held. Modifying the model's toJSON() method to automatically strip out such information, as shown in Listing 12-34, helps to prevent this information from unintentionally leaking out over an API request.

Defining Class Properties

Bookshelf's extend() method, which we've seen in previous examples, accepts two parameters:

- An object of instance properties to be inherited by created instances of the model

- An object of class properties to be assigned directly to the model

Previous examples within this chapter have demonstrated the process of assigning instance properties via extend(), but we have yet to look at an example demonstrating the use of class properties. Listing 12-35 shows class properties in action.

Listing 12-35. Defining the getRecent() Class Method on the User Model

```
// example-bookshelf1/lib/user.js

var User = bookshelf.Model.extend({
    'tableName': 'users'
}, {

    /**
     * Returns a collection containing users who have signed in
     * within the last 24 hours.
     */
    'getRecent': function() {
        return User.where('last_signin', '>=', knex.raw("date('now', '-1 day')")).fetch();
        }

});
```

368

```
// example-bookshelf1/static.js

User.getRecent().then(function(users) {
    console.log('%s users have signed in within the past 24 hours.', users.length);
    console.log(JSON.stringify(users.toJSON(), null, 4));
});
```

Class-level properties provide a convenient location in which we can define various helper methods related to the model in question. In this contrived example, the getRecent() method returns a promise that resolves to a collection containing every user who has signed in within the last 24 hours.

Extending with Subclasses

Bookshelf's extend() method correctly sets up the prototype chain. As a result, in addition to creating models that inherit directly from Bookshelf's Model class, developers can also create models that inherit from each other, as shown in Listing 12-36.

Listing 12-36. Creating a Base Model That Extends Directly from Bookshelf's Model Class, from Which Other Models Can Also Extend

```
// example-bookshelf-extend/lib/base.js

/**
 * This model serves as a base from which all other models
 * within our application extend.
 *
 * @class Base
 */
var Base = bookshelf.Model.extend({
    'initialize': function() {
        this._initEventBroadcasts();
    },
    'foo': function() {
        console.log('bar', this.toJSON());
    }
});

// example-bookshelf-extend/lib/user.js

/**
 * @class User
 */
var User = Base.extend({
    'tableName': 'users'
});
```

```
// example-bookshelf-extend/index.js

var User = require('./lib/user');
User.where({
    'id': 1
}).fetch().then(function(user) {
    user.foo();
});
```

Having the ability to create models that extend across multiple levels of inheritance provides some useful opportunities. Most of the applications in which we use Bookshelf follow the lead shown in Listing 12-36, in which a Base model is created from which all other models within the application extend. By following this pattern, we can easily add core functionality to all models within our application simply by modifying our Base class. In Listing 12-36, the User model (along with every other model that extends from Base) will inherit the Base model's foo() method.

Relationships

ORM libraries such as Bookshelf provide convenient, object-oriented patterns for interacting with data stored in flat, relational database tables. With Bookshelf's help, we can specify the relationships that exist between our application's models. For example, an account may have many users, or a user may have many bookmarks. Once these relationships have been defined, Bookshelf models open up new methods that allow us to more easily navigate through these relationships.

The table shown in Table 12-1 list some of the more commonly used relationships.

Table 12-1. *Commonly Used Bookshelf Relationships*

Association	Relationship Type	Example
One-to-one	hasOne	A User has a Profile
One-to-one	belongsTo	A Profile has a User
One-to-many	hasMany	An Account has many Users
One-to-many	belongsTo	A User belongs to an Account
Many-to-many	belongsToMany	A Book has one or more Authors

In the following sections, you will discover the differences between these relationships, how they are defined, and how they can best be put to use within an application.

One-to-One

A one-to-one association is the simplest form available. As its name suggests, a one-to-one association specifies that a given model is associated with exactly one other model. That association can take the form of a hasOne relationship or a belongsTo relationship, based on the direction in which the association is traversed.

The database schema behind the example that we will soon see is shown in Figure 12-3. In this example, the profiles table has a user_id foreign key column with which it is related to the users table.

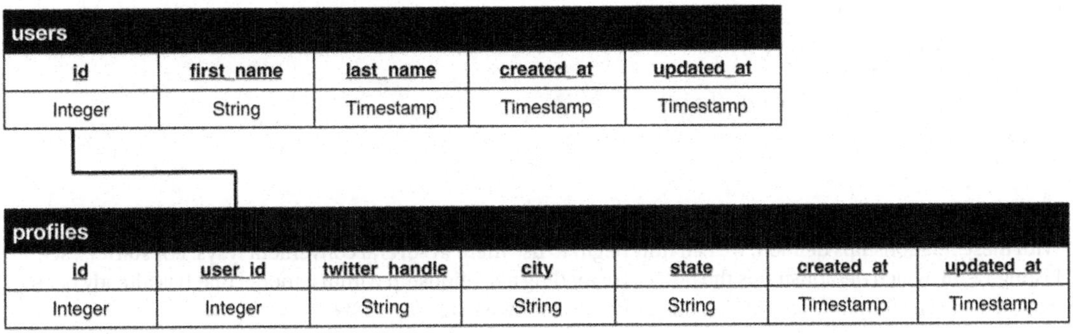

users				
id	**first_name**	**last_name**	**created_at**	**updated_at**
Integer	String	Timestamp	Timestamp	Timestamp

profiles						
id	**user_id**	**twitter_handle**	**city**	**state**	**created_at**	**updated_at**
Integer	Integer	String	String	String	Timestamp	Timestamp

Figure 12-3. *The database schema behind our one-to-one relationships*

hasOne and belongsTo

A hasOne relationship specifies that a model "has one" of another model, while the belongsTo relationship specifies just the opposite, that it is owned by or "belongs to" another model. In other words, a belongsTo relationship serves as the inverse of the hasOne relationship. The process by which these relationships are defined with Bookshelf is shown in Listing 12-37.

Listing 12-37. Defining the hasOne and belongsTo Bookshelf Relationships

```
// example-bookshelf-relationships1/lib/user.js

/**
 * @class User
 *
 * A User has one Profile
 */
var User = bookshelf.Model.extend({
    'tableName': 'users',
    /**
     * Bookshelf relationships are defined as model instance
     * methods. Here, we create a 'profile' method that will
     * allow us to access this user's profile. This method
     * could have been named anything, but in this case -
     * 'profile' makes the most sense.
     */
    'profile': function() {
        return this.hasOne(Profile);
    }
});

// example-bookshelf-relationships1/lib/profile.js

/**
 * @class Profile
 *
 * A Profile belongs to one User
 */
```

```
var Profile = bookshelf.Model.extend({
    'tableName': 'profiles',
    'user': function() {
        return this.belongsTo(User);
    }
});
```

Bookshelf relationships are defined through the use of special instance methods, as shown in Listing 12-37. With these relationships defined, we can now begin to use them in several convenient ways. For starters, see Listing 12-38, which demonstrates the process of loading a relationship within a model that has already been instantiated. The output from running this example is shown in Listing 12-39.

Listing 12-38. Loading a Relationship on a Model That Has Already Been Instantiated

```
// example-bookshelf-relationships1/index.js

User.where({
    'id': 1
}).fetch().then(function(user) {
    return user.load('profile');
}).then(function(user) {
    console.log(JSON.stringify(user.toJSON(), null, 4));
});
```

Listing 12-39. The Resulting Output from Listing 12-38

```
{
    "id": 1,
    "first_name": "Steve",
    "last_name": "Taylor",
    "created_at": "2014-10-02"
    "profile": {
    "id": 1,
    "user_id": 1,
    "twitter_handle": "staylor",
    "city": "Portland",
    "state": "OR",
    "created_at": "2014-10-02"
    }
}
```

In Listing 12-38, an instance of the User model is retrieved. When fetched, the default behavior of a Bookshelf model is to retrieve only information about itself, not about its related models. As a result, in this example we must first load the model's related Profile via the load() method, which returns a promise that is resolved once the related model has been fetched. Afterward, we can reference this user's profile via the user's related instance method.

Bookshelf relationships become even more useful when we begin to look at the manner in which they can be "eagerly loaded," as shown in Listing 12-40. In this example, we fetch an instance of the User model *as well as* its related Profile. We can do so by passing the fetch() method an object of options in which we specify one or more relationships that we are also interested in. The returned promise resolves to an instance of User that already has its profile relationship populated.

Listing 12-40. Using "Eager Loading" to Fetch Our User, and Its Related Profile, with a Single Call

```
// example-bookshelf-relationships1/eager.js

User.where({
    'id': 1
}).fetch({
    'withRelated': ['profile']
}).then(function(user) {
    console.log(JSON.stringify(user.toJSON(), null, 4));
});
```

One-to-Many

The one-to-many association forms the basis for the most commonly encountered relationships. This association builds on the simple one-to-one association we just saw, allowing us to instead associate one model with many other models. These relationships can take the form of a hasMany or a belongsTo relationship, as we will soon see.

The database schema behind the examples we are about to review is shown in Figure 12-4. In this example, the users table has an account_id foreign key column with which it is related to the accounts table.

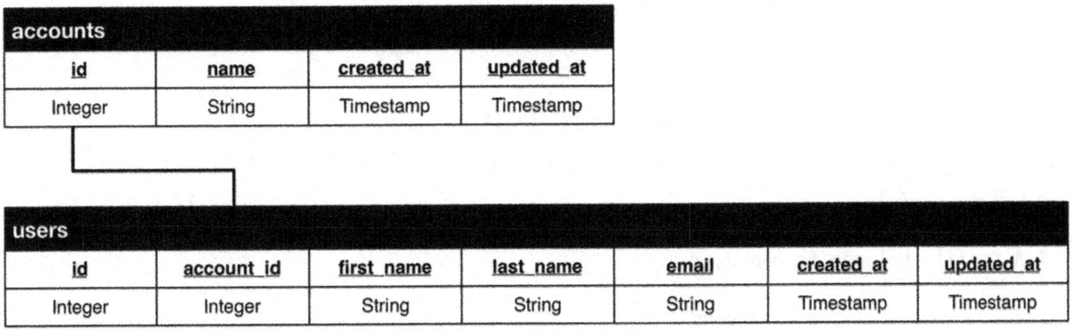

Figure 12-4. *The database schema behind our one-to-many relationships*

hasMany and belongsTo

A hasMany relationship specifies that a model may have multiple (or none at all) of a particular model. The belongsTo relationship, which we have already seen in previous examples, is also applicable in one-to-many associations. The process by which these relationships are defined with Bookshelf is shown in Listing 12-41. Listing 12-42 demonstrates their usage.

Listing 12-41. Defining the hasMany and belongsTo Bookshelf Relationships

```
// example-bookshelf-relationships2/lib/account.js

/**
 * @class Account
 *
 * An Account has one or more instances of User
 */
```

```
var Account = bookshelf.Model.extend({
    'tableName': 'accounts',
    'users': function() {
        return this.hasMany(User);
    }
});


// example-bookshelf-relationships2/lib/user.js

/**
 * @class User
 *
 * A User belongs to an Account
 * A User has one Profile
 */
User = bookshelf.Model.extend({
    'tableName': 'users',
    'account': function() {
        return this.belongsTo(Account);
        },
        'profile': function() {
            return this.hasOne(Profile);
        }
});


// example-bookshelf-relationships2/lib/profile.js

/**
 * @class Profile
 *
 * A Profile belongs to one User
 */
Profile = bookshelf.Model.extend({
    'tableName': 'profiles',
    'user': function() {
        return this.belongsTo(User);
    }
});
```

Listing 12-42. Loading an Instance of the Account Model, Along with All of Its Related Users

```
// example-bookshelf-relationships2/index.js

Account.where({
    'id': 1
}).fetch({
    'withRelated': ['users']
}).then(function(account) {
    console.log(JSON.stringify(account.toJSON(), null, 4));
});
```

```
{
    "id": 1,
    "name": "Acme Company",
    "created_at": "2014-10-02",
    "users": [
        {
            "id": 1,
            "account_id": 1,
            "first_name": "Steve",
            "last_name": "Taylor",
            "email": "steve.taylor@mydomain.com",
            "created_at": "2014-10-02"
        },
        {
            "id": 2,
            "account_id": 1,
            "first_name": "Sally",
            "last_name": "Smith",
            "email": "sally.smith@mydomain.com",
            "created_at": "2014-10-02"
        }
    ]
}
```

In Listing 12-42, we see another example of Bookshelf's "eager loading" functionality, with which we can fetch a model *as well as* any of its related models that we also happen to be interested in. The concept of "eager loading" becomes even more interesting when we discover that we can also load nested relationships—those that exist deeper within the object(s) we wish to fetch. Only when we begin to utilize Bookshelf's eager loading functionality can we begin to appreciate the "virtual object database" that it and similar ORM tools provide. The example shown in Listing 12-43 should help to clarify this concept.

Listing 12-43. Eagerly Loading an Account, All of Its Users, and the Profile for Each User

```
// example-bookshelf-relationships2/nested-eager.js

Account.where({
    'id': 1
}).fetch({
    'withRelated': ['users', 'users.profile']
}).then(function(account) {
    console.log(JSON.stringify(account.toJSON(), null, 4));
});

/*
{
    "id": 1,
    "name": "Acme Company",
    "created_at": "2014-10-02",
    "users": [
```

```
    {
        "id": 1,
            "account_id": 1,
            "first_name": "John",
            "last_name": "Doe",
            "email": "john.doe@domain.site",
            "created_at": "2014-10-02",
            "profile": {
                "id": 1,
                "user_id": 1,
                "twitter_handle": "john.doe",
                "city": "Portland",
                "state": "OR",
                "created_at": "2014-10-02"
            }
    },
    {
        "id": 2,
            "account_id": 1,
            "first_name": "Sarah",
            "last_name": "Smith",
            "email": "sarah.smith@domain.site",
            "created_at": "2014-10-02",
            "profile": {
                "id": 2,
                "user_id": 2,
                "twitter_handle": "sarah.smith",
                "city": "Asheville",
                "state": "NC",
                "created_at": "2014-10-02"
            }
        }
    ]
}
*/
```

Many-to-Many

Many-to-many associations differ from the one-to-one and one-to-many associations this chapter has already covered, in that they allow one record to be associated with one or more records of a different type, *and vice versa*. To help clarify this point, see Figure 12-5, which illustrates a commonly cited example involving authors and books.

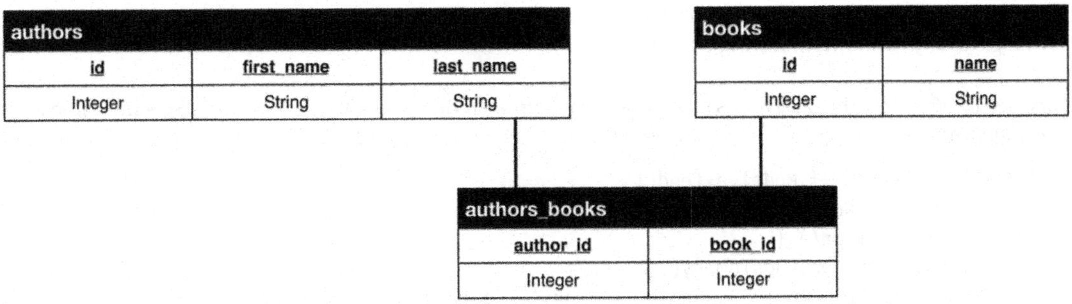

authors		
id	first_name	last_name
Integer	String	String

books	
id	name
Integer	String

authors_books	
author_id	book_id
Integer	Integer

Figure 12-5. *A many-to-many association made possible through the use of a third join table. In this example, an author can write multiple books, and a book can have multiple authors*

A single foreign key column, as seen in previous examples (see Figure 12-5), would not suffice here. In order to model this relationship, a third join table (authors_books) is required, in which multiple relationships for any given record can be stored.

belongsToMany

The database schema shown in Figure 12-5 can be modeled with Bookshelf via the belongsToMany relationship, as shown in Listing 12-44.

Listing 12-44. Modeling a belongsToMany Relationship with Bookshelf

```
// example-bookshelf-relationships3/lib/author.js

var Author = bookshelf.Model.extend({
    'tableName': 'authors',
    'books': function() {
        return this.belongsToMany(require('./book'));
    }
});

// example-bookshelf-relationships3/lib/book.js

var Book = bookshelf.Model.extend({
    'tableName': 'books',
    'authors': function() {
        return this.belongsToMany(require('./author'));
    }
});
```

It is important to note that when using the belongsToMany relationship, Bookshelf will automatically make a few assumptions regarding your database schema, unless specifically told otherwise. Bookshelf will assume the following:

- That a third join table exists, which derives its name from that of the two related tables, separated by an underscore, and ordered alphabetically. In this example: authors_books.

- That the column names used within your join table are derived from the singular versions of the two related tables, followed by _id. In this example: author_id and book_id.

377

If you prefer to follow a different naming convention, you can do so by modifying the call to this.belongsToMany as shown in Listing 12-45.

Listing 12-45. Modeling a belongsToMany Relationship with Bookshelf, While Providing Specific Table and Column Names

```
var Author = bookshelf.Model.extend({
    'tableName': 'authors',
    'books': function() {
        return this.belongsToMany(
            require('./book'), 'authors_books', 'author_id', 'book_id');
    }
});

var Book = bookshelf.Model.extend({
    'tableName': 'books',
    'authors': function() {
        var Author = require('../author');
        return this.belongsToMany(Author, 'authors_books', 'book_id', 'author_id');
    }
});
```

The process of using this relationship is shown in Listing 12-46.

Listing 12-46. Example Usage (and Resulting Output) of Code from Listing 12-45

```
// example-bookshelf-relationships3/index.js

Book.fetchAll({
    'withRelated': ['authors']
}).then(function(books) {
    console.log(JSON.stringify(books.toJSON(), null, 4));
});

/*
[
    {
        id: 1,
        name: 'Pro JavaScript Frameworks for Modern Web Development',
        authors: [{
            id: 1,
            first_name: 'Tim',
            last_name: 'Ambler',
            _pivot_book_id: 1,
            _pivot_author_id: 1
        }, {
            id: 2,
            first_name: 'Nicholas',
            last_name: 'Cloud',
```

```
        _pivot_book_id: 1,
        _pivot_author_id: 2
    }]
}
]
*/
```

Summary

If you were to quickly survey the database landscape over the past several years, it would be easy to walk away with the impression that so-called "NoSQL" storage platforms have largely supplanted the old guard of relational databases such as MySQL and PostgreSQL, but nothing could be further from the truth. Much like Mark Twain's prematurely reported death in 1897, the death of the relational database is also an exaggeration.

Relational databases offer a number of compelling features, the vast majority of which lie far outside the scope of this chapter. Many wonderful books are available that devote themselves entirely to this subject, and we encourage you to read a few of them before making critical decisions regarding how and where a project stores its information. That said, a key feature to look for in such systems (and one which was covered earlier in the chapter) is support for transactions: the process by which multiple queries can be grouped into a single unit of work that will either succeed or fail as a whole. The examples involving a financial exchange that we looked at in Listing 12-13 and Listing 12-14 demonstrated the important role this concept has in mission-critical applications.

The platform-agnostic API provided by Knex, combined with its promise-based interface, transaction support, and migration manager, provides developers with a convenient tool for interacting with relational databases. When paired with its sister application, Bookshelf, an ORM that is instantly familiar to those with prior Backbone experience, a powerful combination is formed that simplifies the process of working with complex data.

Related Resources

- Knex: http://knexjs.org

- Bookshelf: http://bookshelfjs.org

- Backbone.js: http://backbonejs.org

- Underscore.js: http://underscorejs.org

- MySQL: www.mysql.com

- PostgreSQL: www.postgresql.com

- MariaDB: http://mariadb.org

- SQLite: www.sqlite.org

- Multiline: https://github.com/sindresorhus/multiline

CHAPTER 13

Faye

The problem with quotes on the Internet is you can never be sure they're authentic.

—Abraham Lincoln

Web-based applications have grown increasingly sophisticated in recent years, thanks in large part to the widespread adoption of modern web development technologies such as HTML5, WebSockets, and newly standardized JavaScript APIs (e.g., Geolocation, Web Storage, and Web Audio). Functionality that was once the exclusive domain of traditional desktop applications has found a new home in the browser, allowing web developers to create applications that weren't even possible just a few short years ago.

However, as web browsers have continued to mature, the fundamental protocol of the Web, HTTP, has begun to show signs of age. The simple "request-response" pattern of communication that it implements, in which a client (e.g., a web browser) requests a resource from a server and receives a response in return, no longer addresses the real-time nature of the problems that many of today's most innovative web applications seek to solve. Applications that deal with rapidly changing data (e.g., multiplayer games, social networking sites, and chat rooms) have a strong need to perform what is often referred to as "data push"—the ability to initiate communication from the server to the client.

Just as web browsers have matured, so too have the expectations of the people who use them. Web applications that provide their users with information only when asked for it will quickly find themselves sidelined by more proactive alternatives that go out of their way to *notify* users when events of interest to them occur.

In this chapter, we will be exploring Faye, a library for Node.js and the browser that provides developers with a robust toolset for building applications that rely on near real-time communication. Topics covered include

- HTTP, Bayeux, and WebSockets
- Communicating through Faye via publish-subscribe (PubSub) channels
- Developing Faye extensions
- Managing security

HTTP, Bayeux, and WebSockets

HTTP is referred to as a "request-response" protocol because it allows a client to request a resource from a server and to receive a response in return. The protocol is also described as "stateless," in that each of these message pairs operates independently of the others; no "state" (i.e., memory) is maintained across requests. This concept is illustrated in Figure 13-1.

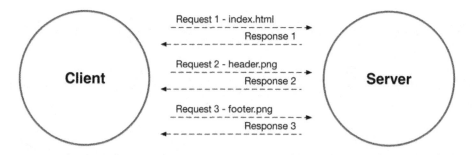

***Figure 13-1.** HTTP is a stateless, request-response protocol*

HTTP's greatest strength, the intuitive pattern of communication that it enables, has allowed the Web to grow into the runaway success that it is today. Unfortunately, the protocol's simpleness also comes with a high cost, in that it is woefully inadequate at addressing the bidirectional, asynchronous nature of event-driven messaging.

By way of an example, imagine a scenario in which multiple users are participating in a chat room (see Figure 13-2). Each user needs to be notified as soon as other members post new messages, but the request-response nature of HTTP fails to address how such events originating at the server level are to be communicated to clients, as shown in Figure 13-3.

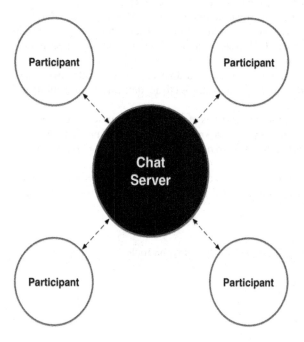

***Figure 13-2.** An event-driven messaging platform, in which users must be notified as soon as new messages are posted by fellow participants*

Figure 13-3. *HTTP does not allow a server to initiate communication with a client in this manner*

WebSockets

Unlike HTTP, the WebSocket Protocol was purposefully designed to allow browsers to establish a *full-duplex* (bidirectional), long-lived TCP connection with a remote server (see Figure 13-4). The protocol was standardized in 2011 (RFC 6455) and now enjoys widespread support among recent versions of most popular web browsers. As a result, supporting browsers can now communicate with servers in a truly asynchronous fashion (assuming those servers are configured to support such connections). A simple example that demonstrates the usage of the WebSocket API is shown in Listing 13-1.

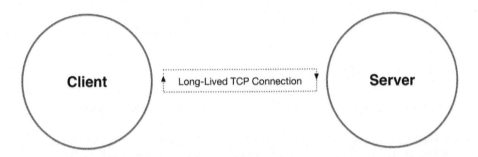

Figure 13-4. *The WebSocket Protocol allows clients to establish a long-lived connection with a remote server, with which messages may be passed in both directions*

Listing 13-1. Simple Example Demonstrating the Use of the WebSocket API Within the Browser

```
var connection = new WebSocket('ws://domain.com/app');

// The connection has been established
connection.onopen = function() {
    connection.send('Hello, world.');
};

// A message has been received from the server
connection.onmessage = function(e) {
    console.log('Incoming message', e);
};
```

With the introduction of the WebSocket Protocol, a new and exciting chapter for the Web was opened, a chapter in which *real-time* messaging is possible. It is important to bear in mind, however, that the protocol does have its limitations—limitations that aren't necessarily obvious at first glance. These limitations will be discussed in greater detail in the following section on the Bayeux protocol.

The Bayeux Protocol

Long before the arrival of widespread browser support for WebSockets, developers at the Dojo Foundation worked together to tackle the problem of implementing asynchronous, event-driven messaging over HTTP. The result was an innovative solution known as the Bayeux protocol that still has important implications to this day.

Bayeux enables low-latency, event-driven messaging over standard HTTP requests through the use of a technique known as "long-polling." Using this approach, a client submits an HTTP request to a remote server, which then hangs on to that request indefinitely instead of immediately returning a response (as would occur in a standard HTTP transaction). As the server maintains this open connection, it waits to be notified of any messages that need to be forwarded to the client. When a message arrives, the server forwards the message to the client and closes the connection. Afterward, the client immediately establishes another long-polling connection to the server, at which point the process repeats itself (see Figure 13-5).

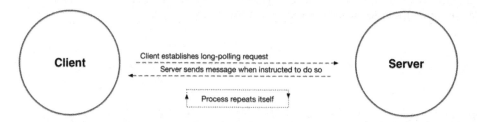

Figure 13-5. *Asynchronous messaging over HTTP, made possible by Bayeux's use of long-polling*

Now that WebSockets enjoy widespread support, you may be wondering why this chapter bothers to discuss a seemingly outdated concept such as the Bayeux protocol. As it turns out, Bayeux isn't nearly as outdated as you might initially think. As wonderful as WebSockets are, they still have their limitations—limitations that Bayeux happens to be particularly adept at resolving.

Network Challenges

Although recent versions of most popular web browsers now include support for WebSockets, a successful connection between the client and the server is not always guaranteed. The long-lived connections that the WebSocket Protocol was designed to enable differ significantly from the short-lived, "request-response" connections that the Web was originally built on, and in order for these connections to function properly, the various networks and proxy servers that forward information between a client and a server must be properly configured. It's not unheard of for improperly configured proxy servers to block such connections entirely or to drop them without warning when they go unused for any significant amount of time.

Bayeux, the protocol on which the topic of this chapter, Faye, relies, was designed from the beginning to be very forward thinking. Although Bayeux was originally designed to bring asynchronous messaging to the Web via long-polling HTTP connections, the protocol also includes support for "upgrading" those connections to more efficient, modern standards when possible (see Figure 13-6). As a result of this behavior, Bayeux-based servers are capable of bringing asynchronous messaging to the Web even when browser or network limitations attempt to get in the way.

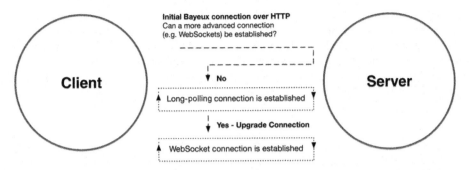

Figure 13-6. *Bayeux connections are established via HTTP and upgraded when possible*

Legacy Browser Support

As previously stated, WebSockets now enjoy widespread support among the *latest versions* of all major browsers. Depending on the needs of your application, you may need to provide support for browsers that don't conform to the latest standards. The Bayeux protocol's reliance on standard HTTP connections (which are upgraded, when possible) allows you to do exactly that.

Dropped Connections and Missed Messages

The WebSocket Protocol provides no built-in support for detecting what (if any) messages might have been lost in the event of a service interruption. Bayeux-based servers, on the other hand, are capable of hanging on to messages in the event of a service interruption. The servers can then forward these messages once the client is able to successfully reestablish their connection, preventing important messages from being lost in the process.

A Focus on Channels Rather Than Sockets

The WebSocket API provides developers with a simple, clearly defined interface for establishing socket connections between a client and a server and for sending messages between them (as discussed in the following section). It does not, however, provide any higher-level abstractions for managing those interactions. Faye takes an alternative approach, choosing instead to present users with an interface for interacting via publish-subscribe (PubSub) channels, while completely hiding the inner workings of the network layer that it operates on top of. As a result, Faye has the ability to transparently support a number of different connection schemes, without requiring any changes at the application layer.

Getting Started with Faye

Faye consists of two distinct libraries: one for the server (Node.js) and one for the browser. Before we continue, let's take a look at the basic steps that are involved in installing and configuring Faye at the server level.

The following example demonstrates the installation of Faye from the command line via npm within an existing Node.js project:

```
$ npm install faye --save
```

Faye works in conjunction with Node's built-in `http` and `https` modules to create a port capable of accepting connections. This process is demonstrated in Listing 13-2. In this example, a web server is created that serves static files from our project's `public` folder. A new instance of Faye is then created and attached to this server, allowing clients to connect to the web server and Faye on the same port.

Listing 13-2. Initializing Faye Within Node.js

```
// faye-starter/lib/server.js

var faye = require('faye');
var http = require('http');
var express = require('express');
var app = express();
var server = http.createServer(app);

// Creating a new instance of Faye
var bayeux = new faye.NodeAdapter({
    'mount': '/faye' // The path at which Faye can be reached
});

// Attaching Faye to the web server instance we have already created
bayeux.attach(server);

// Serving static files out of our project's `/public` folder
app.use('/', express.static(__dirname + '/../public'));

// Our web server and Faye are both reachable at port 7000
server.listen(7000);
```

Now that our server is ready to accept connections, we can move on to configuring Faye within the browser (see Listing 13-3). We first create a script tag that loads Faye's client-side library (`client.js`), which is available under the mount path that we specified in Listing 13-2. Next, we create a new client and configure it to connect to that mount path.

Listing 13-3. Configuring Faye Within the Browser

```
// faye-starter/public/index.html

<!DOCTYPE html>
<html lang="en">
<head>
    <meta charset="utf-8">
    <meta http-equiv="X-UA-Compatible" content="IE=edge">
    <meta name="viewport" content="width=device-width, initial-scale=1">
    <title>Faye - Starter Example</title>
</head>
<body>
```

```
<script src="http://localhost:7000/faye/client.js"></script>
<script>
var client = new Faye.Client('http://localhost:7000/faye');
</script>
```

```
</body>
</html>
```

PubSub Messaging

Instead of presenting developers with an API for interacting directly with socket connections, Faye emphasizes the use of publish-subscribe (PubSub) topic channels. To see this process in action, revisit Listing 13-2 (the example in which we configured our server) and append the code shown in Listing 13-4. With the addition of this code, we instruct our server to publish a random number to the /numbers channel every two seconds.

Listing 13-4. Publishing a Message to the /numbers Channel Every Two Seconds

```
// faye-starter/lib/server.js

setInterval(function() {
    // Pass a topic channel, along with a payload of data
    bayeux.getClient().publish('/numbers', {
        'number': Math.floor((Math.random() * 100) + 1)
    });
}, 2000);
```

Now revisit the example shown in Listing 13-3, in which we configured Faye for use within the browser. Listing 13-5 shows an updated version of this example in which we subscribe to the /numbers channel. As messages are received, their content is appended to the DOM. Note also that when we create this subscription, we receive an object with a cancel() method that allows us to unsubscribe from this channel at any time. Before you continue, take a few minutes to see this example in action by running npm start within the faye-starter folder.

Listing 13-5. Listening for Messages on the /numbers Channel from Within the Browser

```
// faye-starter/public/index.html

<!DOCTYPE html>
<html lang="en">
<head>
    <meta charset="utf-8">
    <meta http-equiv="X-UA-Compatible" content="IE=edge">
    <meta name="viewport" content="width=device-width, initial-scale=1">
    <title>Faye - Starter Example</title>
</head>
<body>
```

```
<a href="#" id="cancelbt">Cancel Subscription to `/numbers` channel</a>

<ul id="container"></ul>

<script src="http://localhost:7000/faye/client.js"></script>
<script src="/bower_components/jquery/dist/jquery.js"></script>

<script>
var client = new Faye.Client('http://localhost:7000/faye');

var subscription = client.subscribe('/numbers', function(data) {
    console.log('Incoming message on the `/numbers` channel', data);
    $('#container').append('<li>' + data.number + '</li>');
});

$('#cancelbt').one('click', function() {
    console.log('Canceling subscription to `/numbers` channel');
    subscription.cancel();
});
</script>

</body>
</html>
```

In Listing 13-4, we saw a demonstration of how messages can be published at the server level. The process by which clients can publish their own messages works in almost the exact same way. The example shown in Listing 13-6 demonstrates the sending of a Hello, world message to the /foo channel from a browser-based client.

Listing 13-6. Publishing a Message from the Browser

```
client.publish('/foo', {
    'text': 'Hello, world.'
}).then(function() {
    // Message was received by server
});
```

Wildcard Channels

In addition to having the ability to subscribe to messages on a specific channel, Faye clients can also subscribe to multiple channels by passing a wildcard pattern to the subscribe() method, as shown in Listing 13-7.

Listing 13-7. Using Wildcard Syntax to Subscribe to Multiple Channels Matching a Specified Pattern

```
/**
 * Subscribes the client to a single channel segment. Messages received
 * on any channel that exists directly beneath `/foo` will be logged.
 */
client.subscribe('/foo/*', function(message) {
    console.log('Message received', message);
});
```

```
/**
 * Subscribes the client to *all* channel segments beneath `/foo`.
 */
client.subscribe('/foo/**', function(message) {
    console.log('Message received', message);
});
```

Faye's support for wildcard channels presents several interesting possibilities, including the creation of namespaced topic channels devoted to a specific user (or group of users). For example, consider an application that organizes its users in a manner similar to that shown in Figure 13-7.

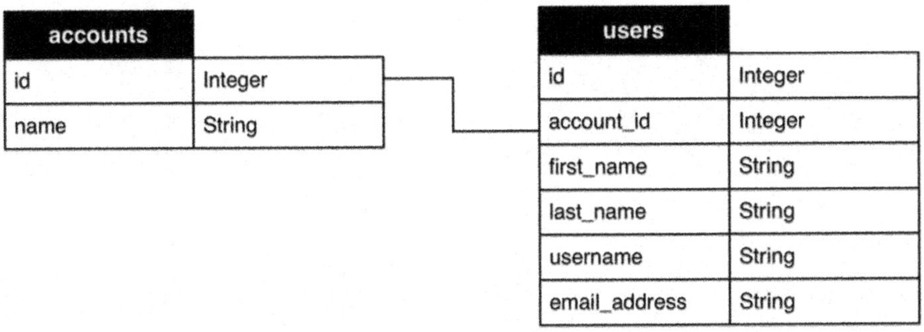

accounts	
id	Integer
name	String

users	
id	Integer
account_id	Integer
first_name	String
last_name	String
username	String
email_address	String

Figure 13-7. An application in which multiple users are grouped under a parent account

In this application, every user belongs to a parent account (which can have multiple users). Given this structure, it is easy to imagine a scenario in which we might want to publish a message to a specific user, or to all users within a particular account. With the help of wildcard subscriptions and namespaced channels, we can easily accomplish this goal.

The faye-security project that is included with this chapter (see Figure 13-8) builds on several previously covered topics (AngularJS, Knex, and Bookshelf) to create an application that allows registered users to sign in and test out various aspects of Faye's functionality—including the use of wildcard subscriptions and namespaced channels.

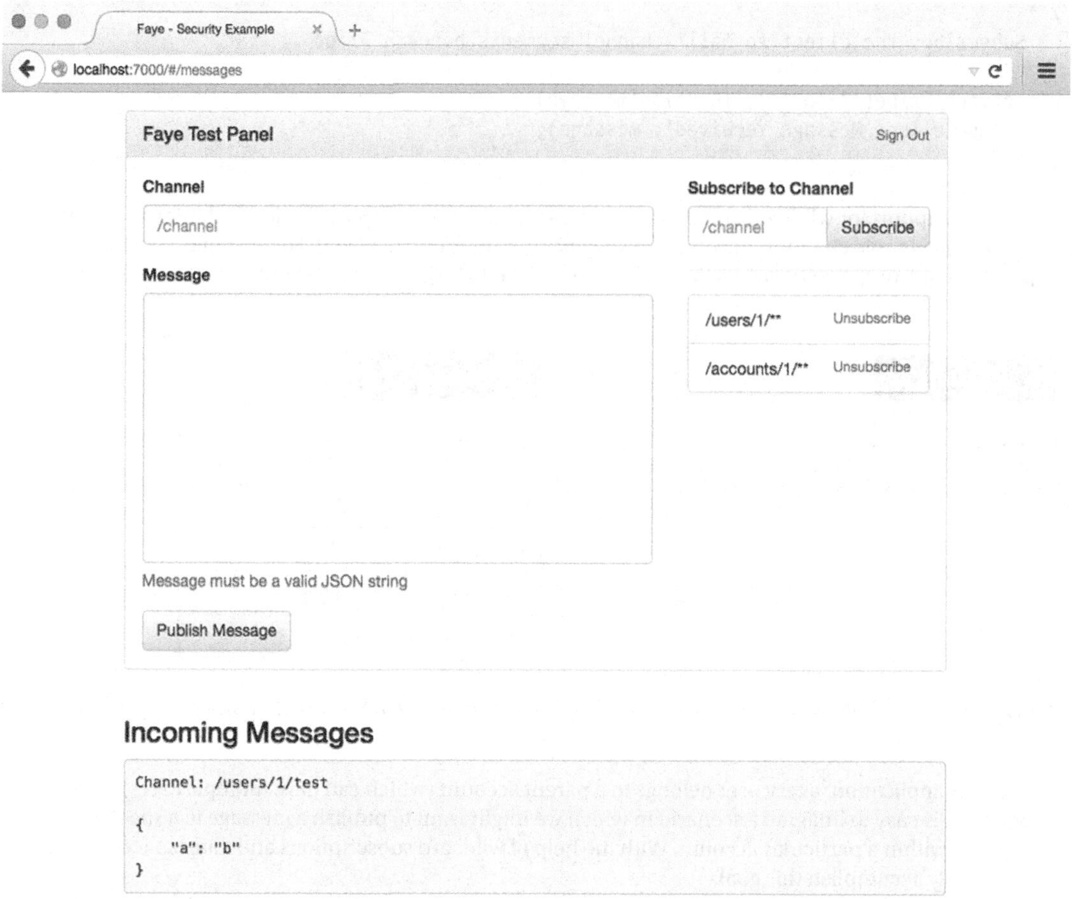

Figure 13-8. After signing in, users are presented with a view that allows them to manage channel subscriptions and to publish messages

When this application's sign-in form is submitted, a request to the server is made that verifies the username and password that the user provided. If this request is successful, the server returns an object that contains information about the authorized user, including a token that will be used to authenticate all future requests. An excerpt from the /login route's Angular controller (which is responsible for making this request) is shown in Listing 13-8.

Listing 13-8. A Token is Returned After a Successful Login Attempt

```
// faye-security/public/app.js (excerpt)

$scope.login = function() {
    if (!$scope.loginForm.$valid) return;
    $http.post('/api/auth', $scope.model)
    .then(function(result) {
```

```
        $.cookie('token', result.data.token, { 'path': '/' });
        $location.path('/messages');
    })
    .catch(function(err) {
        alert('Unable to sign in. Please try again.');
    });
};
```

Among other things, the controller for the /messages route will automatically create two wildcard subscriptions for the user, as shown in Listing 13-9.

Listing 13-9. Angular Controller for the /messages Route Creates Two Subscriptions Using Faye's Wildcard Syntax

```
// faye-security/public/app.js (excerpt)

// Subscribe to channels pertaining to the user's account
faye.client.subscribe('/accounts/' + me.account_id + '/**');
// Subscribe to channels pertaining directly to the user
faye.client.subscribe('/users/' + me.id + '/**');
```

These subscriptions will allow us to publish messages to everyone within this user's account (as well as to the user directly) by directing those messages to channels that are prefixed appropriately. Listing 13-10 shows this process in action.

Listing 13-10. A Message is Published to Each Available Account Every Ten Seconds by the Server

```
// faye-security/lib/server.js (excerpt)

setInterval(function() {
    db.models.Account.where({}).fetchAll().then(function(accounts) {
        accounts.forEach(function(account) {
            bayeux.getClient().publish(_.sprintf('/accounts/%s/random', account.id), {
                'account': account.toJSON()
            });
        });
    });
}, 10000);
```

Implementing Security with Extensions

By default, Faye places no restrictions on clients in regard to which channels they are allowed to interact with. This can be problematic, for obvious reasons: without additional safeguards, nothing would prevent a user from interacting with channels that are intended for other users. Fortunately, we can easily put those safeguards in place with the help of Faye's support for extensions.

Faye provides a simple API for creating extensions that can intercept and (optionally) modify messages as they move between the client and the server. Such extensions can be created both on the server and within the browser. The process is identical, regardless of where they are created. Listing 13-11 shows a simple example of a Faye extension.

Listing 13-11. Simple Faye Extension That Logs All Incoming and Outgoing Messages to the Console

```
client.addExtension({
    'incoming': function(message, callback) {
        console.log('Incoming message', message);
        callback(message);
    },
    'outgoing': function(message, callback) {
        console.log('Outgoing message', message);
        callback(message);
    }
});
```

Now that we have seen what a simple Faye extension looks like, let's apply this concept to the sample web application that is included with this chapter. Refer back to Listing 13-9 and take note of the fact that after a user signs in, a token that allows us to authorize subsequent requests is stored as a cookie within the user's browser. Now refer to Listing 13-12, which shows how the application integrates this information into a Faye extension.

Listing 13-12. A Faye Extension Is Created That Automatically Appends the User's Token to All Outgoing Messages

```
// faye-security/public/app.js (excerpt)

client.addExtension({
    'outgoing': function(message, callback) {
        message.ext = message.ext || {};
        message.ext.token = $.cookie('token');
        callback(message);
    }
});
```

With the Faye extension shown in Listing 13-12 in place, all outgoing messages, *including subscription requests*, will automatically have the user's token appended to them. We can use this fact to our advantage by creating a corresponding extension on the server, as shown in Listing 13-13.

Listing 13-13. Server-side Faye Extension That Rejects Subscription Requests to Secure Channels when the Appropriate Credentials Are Not Provided

```
// faye-security/lib/faye-extensions/auth.js

var db = require('../db');

module.exports = function(bayeux) {

    bayeux.addExtension({

        'incoming': function(message, callback) {
            if (message.channel !== '/meta/subscribe') return callback(message);
            var token = message.ext && message.ext.token;
            var segments = message.subscription.split('/');
```

```
        switch (segments[1]) {
            case 'accounts':
                db.models.User.where({
                    'token': token,
                    'account_id': segments[2]
                }).fetch({
                    'require': true
                }).then(function(user) {
                    return callback(message);
                }).catch(function(err) {
                    message.error = 'Permission denied.';
                    return callback(message);
                });
            break;
            case 'users':
                db.models.User.where({
                    'token': token,
                    'id': segments[2]
                }).fetch({
                    'require': true
                }).then(function(user) {
                    return callback(message);
                }).catch(function() {
                    message.error = 'Permission denied.';
                    return callback(message);
                });
            break;
            default:
                return callback(message);
            break
        }
    }

});

};
```

When the server receives a message on the /meta/subscribe channel, the extension shown in
Listing 13-13 checks to see if the specified channel falls under one of our secure namespaces (/accounts or
/users). If it does, the extension checks for the presence of a token and uses that information to look up the
corresponding user from the database. If a match is found, the message is allowed to continue on its way.
Otherwise, the subscription is rejected as a result of the error property being assigned to the message.

Summary

In this chapter, you became familiar with a number of concepts that allow you to implement near real-time
communication within browser-based applications. You successfully installed and configured Faye both
on the server and within the browser. You discovered how Faye facilitates the passing of messages between
clients through the use of publish-subscribe topic channels. You then took that concept a step further through
the use of namespaced channels and wildcard subscriptions. You also learned how to extend Faye, allowing
you to monitor, modify, and (optionally) reject messages as they pass between clients and the server.

In our experience, the best approach for implementing asynchronous, event-driven communication on the Web involves a plan that takes advantage of WebSockets, has fallback solutions in place, and provides a convenient layer of abstraction on top that doesn't force you to think about the network layer. Faye aligns with these needs quite well by combining the speed and efficiency of WebSockets with the stability of the Bayeux protocol to create a rock-solid approach to implementing asynchronous, event-driven communication on the Web.

Related Resources

- Faye: `http://faye.jcoglan.com/`

- The Dojo Foundation: `http://dojofoundation.org/`

- The Bayeux Protocol: `http://svn.cometd.org/trunk/bayeux/bayeux.html`

CHAPTER 14

Q

I'm an idea-man. Hard work isn't my forte.

—Q, *Star Trek: Voyager*

JavaScript is an asynchronous language. Developers can instruct the JavaScript runtime, whether in the browser or on the server, to "schedule" code to be run at a future point in time. This feature is often used to delay the start of a CPU-intensive or long-running operation, giving an application time to finish its current tasks before moving on to more labor-intensive ones. This feature is so powerful that traditionally synchronous languages like Java, C#, PHP, and Ruby have followed suit and adopted it. Some languages, like C#, have implemented the asynchronous execution model as a language feature (via the async and await keywords); other languages, like PHP, support asynchronicity with external libraries like React (not to be confused with FaceBoook's JavaScript library, React). In either case, asynchronous code and synchronous code are bound to meet.

Q, a JavaScript library that encapsulates asynchronous behavior behind an interface that reads very much like synchronous code, is the topic of this chapter. Q produces *promises*, specialized objects that may be chained together to eliminate nested callbacks, propogate values and errors, and generally manage flow control in asynchronous code. Before plumbing the depths of Q, however, it is worthwhile to take a small detour and examine why asynchronous code can be difficult to write and manage.

Timing Is Everything

Synchronous code is fairly simple to read because the computer executes one statement at a time. Return values that are generated by synchronous code (for example, by a method invocation) are available to calling code immediately after they are returned. Languages with structured exception handling features provide try/catch/finally blocks that can be used to anticipate and deal with errors when they arise, so that trivial (or recoverable) errors don't prove fatal to an application. But structured exception handling only works with synchronous code; it behaves like a goto statement that causes code to "jump" to some other point in the application and resume statement execution at that point.

Asynchronous code behaves a bit differently. In JavaScript, asynchronous code is scheduled to run at a future point in time (sometimes *right after* the currently executing code). This breaks the synchronous model because future code will only run after the current stack unwinds. Return values and errors that are created in asynchronous code, then, must also be handled in the future, when that code actually runs.

Many languages (JavaScript included) solve this problem with *callbacks*, functions that are passed as arguments to asynchronous code that will be invoked once that code has run to handle errors and deal with "return values." The Node.js runtime, which relies heavily on JavaScript's scheduling capabilities, even specifies a standard signature for all callback functions so that asynchronous errors are handled and propagated correctly.

Unfortunately, nested asynchronous code can quickly become complex. Consider the example in Listing 14-1.

Listing 14-1. Asynchronous Node.js Example

```
// example-001/index.js
'use strict';
var fs = require('fs');
var path = require('path');
var playerStats = require('./player-stats');

function getPlayerStats(gamesFilePath, playerID, cb) {
  // fs.readFile() is asynchronous
  fs.readFile(gamesFilePath, {encoding: 'utf8'}, function (err, content) {
    if (err) {
      return cb(err);
    }

    var games = JSON.parse(content);
    var playerGames = games.filter(function (game) {
      return game.player === playerID;
    });

    // playerStats.calcBest() is asynchronous
    playerStats.calcBest(playerGames, function (err, bestStats) {
      if (err) {
        return cb(err);
      }
      // playerStats.calcAvg() is asynchronous
      playerStats.calcAvg(playerGames, function (err, avgStats) {
        if (err) {
          return cb(err);
        }
        cb(null, {best: bestStats, avg: avgStats});
      });
    });
  });
}

var gamesFilePath = path.join(__dirname, 'games.json');
getPlayerStats(gamesFilePath, 42, function (err, stats) {
  if (err) {
    console.error(err);
    return process.exit(1);
  }
  console.log('best:', stats.best);
  console.log('avg: ', stats.avg)
});
```

In this example, JavaScript code is scheduled four times:

1. The declaration and invocation of `getPlayerStats()`

2. The invocation of `fs.readFile()`

3. The invocation of `playerStats.calcBest()`

4. The invocation of `playerStats.calcAvg()`

It is easy to imagine that `playerStats` might be an external service that is slow to respond to inquiries. But if this code was synchronous, as in Listing 14-2, everything would be scheduled once. Each function and method would be invoked in order, all grouped in a `try/catch` block to deal with any synchronous errors, and stats would be written to the console as received.

Listing 14-2. Synchronous Node.js Example

```
// example-002/index.js
'use strict';
var fs = require('fs');
var path = require('path');
var playerStats = require('./player-stats');

try {
    var gamesFilePath = path.join(__dirname, 'games.json');
    // fs.readFileSync() is synchronous
    var content = fs.readFileSync(gamesFilePath, {encoding: 'utf8'});
    var games = JSON.parse(content);
    var playerGames = games.filter(function (game) {
      return game.player === 42;
    });
    // playerStats.calcBestSync() is synchronous
    console.log('best:', playerStats.calcBestSync(playerGames));
    // playerStats.calcAvgSync() is synchronous
    console.log('avg :', playerStats.calcAvgSync(playerGames));
} catch (e) {
    console.error(e);
    process.exit(1);
}
```

This synchronous example is much easier to follow though every statement blocks the flow of execution until finished. Asynchronous callback-driven code, while alleviating this drawback, still has a number of significant problems.

First, there is no real canonical standard to which callback signatures must adhere. The Node.js convention is the most widely adopted, but module authors can (and do) create APIs that do not honor this standard. Often this happens when a JavaScript module wraps or emulates an existing, non-JavaScript API. The module author might make a decision to mimic the callback signature pattern of that API over the Node.js convention for familiarity.

Second, callbacks propagate errors manually. Each callback must inspect the `err` object and determine what to do with it or forward it to another callback that will do the same. A lot of boilerplate error-checking code tends to be the result. In synchronous code, exceptions are propagated up the stack automatically until handled by a `catch` block.

It is also easy to miss or improperly handle *synchronous errors* that occur in asynchronous code. In Listing 14-3, a `try/catch` block wraps the synchronous `JSON.parse` call, then propagates either the parsed JavaScript object when successful, or the caught exception when parsing fails.

Listing 14-3. Improperly Invoking a Callback Within a try/catch Block

```
// example-003/improper-async-error-handling.js
'use strict';
var fs = require('fs');
var path = require('path');

function readJSONFile(filePath, cb) {
  fs.readFile(filePath, function (err, buffer) {
    try {
      var json = JSON.parse(buffer.toString());
      cb(null, json);
    } catch (e) {
      console.log('where did this error come from?', e.message);
      cb(e);
    }
  });
}

var gamesFilePath = path.join(__dirname, 'games.json');
readJSONFile(gamesFilePath, function (err, json) {
  if (err) {
    return console.error('parsing json did not succeed :(');
  }
  console.log('parsing json was successful :)');
  throw new Error('should never happen, right?');
});
```

Assume that the games.json file exists and has valid JSON data. In this example the callback will be invoked within the try block, after the data has been parsed. But notice what happens when an exception is thrown *within the callback*. This exception will unwind the stack back *into the* try *block* and cause the catch block to trap the exception, invoking the callback *a second time* with the very same error the callback generated. This will likely have unintended consequences. The appropriate way to handle this error, as demonstrated in Listing 14-4, is to avoid invoking the callback in the try/catch block altogether.

Listing 14-4. Improperly Invoking a Callback Within a try/catch Block

```
// example-003/proper-async-error-handling.js
'use strict';
var fs = require('fs');
var path = require('path');

function readJSONFile(filePath, cb) {
  fs.readFile(filePath, function (err, buffer) {
    var json, err;
    try {
      json = JSON.parse(buffer.toString());
    } catch (e) {
      err = e;
    }
```

```
    if (err) {
      console.log('where did this error come from?', e.message);
      return cb(err);
    }
    cb(null, json);
  });
}

var gamesFilePath = path.join(__dirname, 'games.json');
readJSONFile(gamesFilePath, function (err, json) {
  if (err) {
    return console.error('parsing json did not succeed :(');
  }
  console.log('parsing json was successful :)');
  throw new Error('should never happen, right?');
});
```

Finally, nesting callbacks is a double-edged sword. On the one hand, each callback has access to data in its own closure and the closures encompassing it; on the other hand, nesting quickly leads to convoluted and tightly coupled code. The true flow of a program can become obscured, producing an unmaintainable ecosystem conducive to bugs.

Promises vs. Callbacks

To mitigate the challenges created by asynchronous callbacks, a number of proposals and specifications were drawn up by members of the JavaScript community, culminating in the Promises/A+ specification. This specification, and the others from which it draws, defines a way to encapsulate asynchronous operations within a special object called a "promise" that may be combined with other promises to create a kind of asynchronous chain through which values and errors can be propagated and dealt with as necessary.

A promise, as defined by the Promises/A+ spec, represents its asynchronous operation with three states: pending, fulfilled, and rejected. If we think of this in callback terms, it would correspond to Listing 14-5.

Listing 14-5. Callback Equivalents to Promise States

```
// invoking the function means the operation is "pending"
asyncFunction(function asyncCallback (err, asyncData) {
  if (err) {
    // if an error occurred the operation is "rejected"
  }
  // otherwise the operation is "fulfilled"
});
```

A promise is also called a "thenable" because it has a then() method that accepts two optional callbacks: the first to be invoked if the promise's asynchronous operation is fulfilled, and the second to be invoked if the operation is rejected. The full signature is displayed in Listing 14-6.

Listing 14-6. Thenable Method Signature

```
/**
 * @param {Function} [onFulfilled]
 * @param {Function} [onRejected]
 * @returns {Promise}
 */
promise.then(onFulfilled, onRejected)
```

But wait! Isn't the whole point of promises to eliminate callbacks? No, the point of promises is to streamline the process of chaining asynchronous operations together, a process that usually leads developers down the path of *nested* callbacks. Notice that a promise's then() method actually returns a promise, too. This promise will also be either fulfilled or rejected *according to what happens in the original promise's callbacks*. By taking advantage of this feature, the player stats code can be rewritten in Listing 14-7 to nearly eliminate nesting.

Listing 14-7. Promises Reduce Nesting

```
// example-004/index.js
'use strict';
var fs = require('fs');
var path = require('path');
var playerStats = require('./player-stats');
var Q = require('q');

function getPlayerStats(gamesFilePath, playerID, cb) {
  // load() returns a promise
  playerStats.load(gamesFilePath, playerID)
    .then(function (games) {
      // Q.all() returns a promise
      return Q.all([
        // calcBest() returns a promise
        playerStats.calcBest(games),
        // calcAvg() returns a promise
        playerStats.calcAvg(games)
      ]);
    })
    .done(function (allStats) {
      cb(null, {best: allStats[0], avg: allStats[1]});
    }, function (err) {
      cb(err);
    });
}

var gamesFilePath = path.join(__dirname, 'games.json');
getPlayerStats(gamesFilePath, 42, function (err, stats) {
  if (err) {
    console.error(err);
    return process.exit(1);
  }
  console.log('best:', stats.best);
  console.log('avg: ', stats.avg)
});
```

In Listing 14-7, only the final done() invocation receives resolution and rejection callbacks; all other invocations only receive a resolution callback (the functions from the playerStats module). Thenables that are called in succession are called promise *chains*. What happens if one of those intermediate then() invocations generates an error? Unlike the asynchronous callback model, promises will automatically propagate an error through the promise chain until it is handled (like structured exception handling). There are specific rules and use cases that can change this behavior, but in general it works exactly as one would expect.

Other interesting aspects of this example will be explained later (like how the return values of fulfillment and rejection callbacks can affect a promise chain). It should be immediately evident, however, that promises can reduce callback nesting and automate error propagation, two of the chief problems that arise from asynchronous JavaScript code.

The Promise of Q

Q is an open source JavaScript library that implements the Promises/A+ specification, but it is hardly the only one available to developers. Several other libraries, like when.js and Bluebird, offer thenables as well, a fact that is important to note because a stated goal of the spec is to provide "an interoperable base which all Promises/A+ conformant promise implementations can be depended on to provide." This means that *any* promise library that conforms to the specification may be used with any other library that does the same. Developers aren't forced to choose among a series of competing candidates. Most promise libraries offer auxiliary functionality that complements the core thenable interface. Developers are free to choose and mix promise libraries that solve different problems as needed. (Unfortunately, libraries that don't conform to the Promises/A+ spec, like jQuery.Deferred, will not integrate this way.)

Q is the subject of this chapter for a few strong reasons:

- It conforms to the Promises/A+ spec.
- It was written by Kris Kowal, a contributor to the spec.
- It enjoys wide adoption and support in the JavaScript community (client- and server-side).
- AngularJS, a popular browser framework backed by Google, borrows heavily from Q.

The rest of this chapter will examine Q's implementation in light of the case made for promises over asynchronous, callback-driven code.

Deferreds and Promises

While the Promises/A+ specification defines how a thenable object behaves, it does not explicitly state how an asynchronous operation should trigger the callbacks provided to a thenable. It only defines the rules for representing the state of an asynchronous operation in a promise, and how values and errors are propagated through promise chains. In practice, many promise libraries use an object called a *deferred* to manipulate the state of a promise. Deferreds are usually created first, wired up to handle the resolution of an asynchronous operation, then generate a promise to be used by calling code later. Listing 14-8 demonstrates how to create a deferred and return its promise.

Listing 14-8. Creating a Deferred

```
var Q = require('q');

function asyncFunc() {
  // create a deferred
  var d = Q.defer();

  // perform some async operation and
  // manipulate the *deferred*

  // return the deferred's promise
  return d.promise;
}

// the function returns a thenable!
asyncFunc().then(function () {
  // success :)
}, function () {
  // error :(
});
```

In Listing 14-8 Q.defer() is invoked to create a deferred object which will be used to manipulate the state of the promise in the future, when asynchronous code is actually run (more on this in a bit). The important thing here is that the deferred owns a promise—one that is returned from asyncFunc(), and to which callbacks may be attached by calling its then() method. The actual invocation of asyncFunc() and the subscriptions to the state changes for the returned promise are all scheduled together. However asyncFunc() chooses to resolve or reject its deferred (and thereby change the state of the promise returned) is entirely up to the developer.

Listing 14-9 is a simple implementation of the calcAvg() function from the fictitious playerStats module mentioned earlier. Using a reduce operation to sum a series of numbers and then divide by the series length (yielding the average) is a synchronous operation. To make it asynchronous, the code is wrapped in the Node.js function process.nextTick(), which schedules the code to run on the next iteration of the event loop. (The same could be accomplished with setTimeout() or setImmediate().) If the calculation is successful, the promise is put into a resolved state with d.resolve(), which accepts some value to be passed to any resolution callbacks attached to the promise. Likewise, if an error arises (for example, the length of the games array is zero, generating a divide-by-zero error), the promise is placed into a rejected state with d.reject().

Listing 14-9. Using a Deferred in the calcAvg() Implementation

```
// example-004/player-stats.js
var Q = require('q');

module.exports = {

  // load: function (gamesFilePath, playerID) {...}

  // calcBest: function (games) {...},
```

```
  calcAvg: function (games) {
    var stats = {
      totalRounds: 0,
      avgRoundsWon: 0,
      avgRoundsLost: 0
    };

    var deferred = Q.defer();

    process.nextTick(function () {
      if (games.length === 0) {
        deferred.reject(new Error('no games'));
        return;
      }

      var wins = 0, losses = 0;
      games.forEach(function (game) {
        if (game.rounds === 0) return;
        stats.totalRounds += game.rounds;
        wins += game.won;
        losses += game.lost;
      });

      stats.avgRoundsWon = (wins / stats.totalRounds * 100)
        .toFixed(2) + '%';
      stats.avgRoundsLost = (losses / stats.totalRounds * 100)
        .toFixed(2) + '%';

      deferred.resolve(stats);
    });

    return deferred.promise;
  }
};
```

Listing 14-10 demonstrates how deferreds and promises can also be used to wrap asynchronous, callback-driven APIs.

Listing 14-10. Using a Deferred to Wrap an Asynchronous, Callback-Driven API

```
// example-005/callbackdb/database.js
'use strict';

module.exports = {
  customer: {
    // requires a callback
    find: function (criteria, cb) {
      cb(null, {
        id: criteria.id,
        name: 'Nicholas Cloud'
      });
    }
  }
};
```

```
// example-005/callbackdb/find-customer-callback.js
var Q = require('q'),
  db = require('./database');

function loadCustomer(customerID) {
  var d = Q.defer();

  // db.customer.find() is asynchronous
  db.customer.find({id: customerID}, function (err, customer) {
    if (err) {
      return d.reject(err);
    }
    d.resolve(customer);
  });

  return d.promise;
}

loadCustomer(1001).then(function (customer) {
  console.log('found', customer.id, customer.name);
}, function (err) {
  console.error(err);
});
```

This model of wrapping asynchronous code is so common, in fact, that Q provides a number of convenience methods to reduce the burden of writing boilerplate code. Q's deferred objects have a makeNodeResolver() method that, when invoked, creates a dummy callback that can be passed to any standard asynchronous callback-based function. When this callback is invoked, however, it simply changes the state of the deferred with the appropriate value or error, whichever happened to be passed to the callback. Listing 14-11 shows how a resolver can replace the need for a manually written callback.

Listing 14-11. Making a Node Resolver Callback

```
// example-005/callbackdb/database.js
'use strict';

module.exports = {
  customer: {
    // requires a callback
    find: function (criteria, cb) {
      cb(null, {
        id: criteria.id,
        name: 'Nicholas Cloud'
      });
    }
  }
};

// example-005/callbackdb/find-customer-makenoderesolver.js
var Q = require('q'),
  db = require('./database');
```

```
function loadCustomer(customerID) {
  var d = Q.defer();

  // db.customer.find() is asynchronous
  var deferredCallback = d.makeNodeResolver();
  db.customer.find({id: customerID}, deferredCallback);

  return d.promise;
}

loadCustomer(2001).then(function (customer) {
  console.log('found', customer.id, customer.name);
}, function (err) {
  console.error(err);
});
```

In this case the client code calling loadCustomer() expects a promise, but the database API expects a callback, so makeNodeResolver() naturally fits. If the *inverse* is true—if the client code expected to pass a callback to the loadCustomer() function but the database actually returned a promise—invoking the nodeify() method on the *database's promise* would invoke the callback appropriately. The promise in Listing 14-12 is tapped in precisely this manner.

Listing 14-12. Passing a Traditional Asynchronous Callback to a Promise with nodeify()

```
// example-005/promisedb/database.js
'use strict';
var Q = require('q');

module.exports = {
  customer: {
    // returns a promise; does not use callbacks
    find: function (criteria) {
      return Q({
        id: criteria.id,
        name: 'Nicholas Cloud'
      });
    }
  }
};

// example-005/promisedb/find-customer-nodeify.js
var Q = require('q'),
  db = require('./database');

function loadCustomer(customerID, cb) {

  // db.customer.find() returns a promise
  db.customer.find({id: customerID})
    .nodeify(cb);
```

```
  /* equivalent to:
   *
   * db.customer.find({id: customerID}).then(function (customer) {
   *   cb(null, customer);
   * }, function (err) {
   *   cb(err);
   * });
   */
}

loadCustomer(3001, function (err, customer) {
  if (err) {
    return console.err(err);
  }
  console.log('found', customer.id, customer.name);
});
```

Values and Errors

Resolving *deferreds* with simple values or errors usually meets most needs, but there are a number of promise resolution rules defined by the Promises/A+ spec—and Q's implementation—that give a developer further control over promise state.

Resolving Deferreds with Promised Values

The behavior of deferreds can change depending on what "value" is passed to their resolve() methods. If the value is a normal object or primitive, it will be passed to the resolution callback attached to the deferred's promise as is. If the "value" is *another promise*, as in Listing 14-13, the state of the second promise will be essentially "forwarded" to the appropriate callbacks of the first: if the second promise becomes resolved, the resolution callback of the first will receive its value; if it becomes rejected, the rejection callback of the first will receive its error.

Listing 14-13. Resolving a Deferred with a Promise

```
// example-006/index.js
'use strict';

var Q = require('q'),
  airport = require('./airport'),
  reservation = require('./reservation');

function findAvailableSeats(departingFlights) {
  var d = Q.defer();
  process.nextTick(function () {
    var availableSeats = [];
    departingFlights.forEach(function (flight) {
      var openFlightSeats = reservation.findOpenSeats(flight);
      availableSeats = availableSeats.concat(openFlightSeats);
    });
```

```
    // resolve the deferred with an object value
    if (availableSeats.length) {
      d.resolve(availableSeats);
    } else {
      d.reject(new Error('sorry, no seats available'));
    }
  });
  return d.promise;
}

function lookupFlights(fromAirport, toAirport, departingAt) {
  var d = Q.defer();
  process.nextTick(function () {
    var departingFlights = airport.findFlights(
      fromAirport, toAirport, departingAt
    );
    // resolve the deferred with another promise
    d.resolve(findAvailableSeats(departingFlights));
  });
  return d.promise;
}

lookupFlights('STL', 'DFW', '2015-01-10').then(function (seats) {
  console.log('available seats:', seats);
}, function (err) {
  console.error('sorry:', err);
});
```

Because the first deferred ultimately depends on the resolution or rejection of the second promise, it will remain in a pending state for as long as the second promise is pending as well. Once the second promise is resolved or rejected, the deferred will follow suit, invoking the appropriate callback.

Forwarding Values, Errors, and Promises in Callbacks

Once a resolution or rejection callback receives a value or error, several things can happen. If the end of the promise chain has been reached (or if there is no other chained promises), usually the client code will do something with the value or log the error.

Because thenables always return another promise when then() is invoked, however, it is possible to use resolution and rejection callbacks to manipulate values and errors and then forward them to the new promise, to be handled by later callbacks.

Manipulating a value is easy enough. Simply alter or transform the value passed to the resolution callback and return it. In Listing 14-14 an array is manipulated in the resolution callback for a database promise, and then returned once the values are appropriately filtered.

Listing 14-14. Returning a Value in a Resolution Callback

```
// example-007/index.js
'use strict';
var db = require('./database');
```

```
function findPalindromeNames() {
  // db.customers.find() returns a promise
  return db.customer.find().then(function (customers) {
    // return a filtered array that will be forwarded
    // to the next resolution callback
    return customers.filter(function (customer) {
      // filter customers with palindrome names
      var name = customer.name.toLowerCase();
      var eman = name.split('').reverse().join('');
      return name === eman;
    }).map(function (customer) {
      // return only customer names
      return customer.name;
    });
  });
}

findPalindromeNames().then(function (names) {
  console.log(names);
});
```

Resolution callbacks can also forward errors to promises down the chain. If they do, then the next rejection callback will be invoked with the returned error. In Listing 14-15, if a user submits too many guesses (for some fictional contest), an error is created and thrown inside a thenable's resolution callback. This error will be propagated to the next rejection callback in the promise chain.

Listing 14-15. Throwing an Error in a Resolution Callback

```
// example-008/index.js
'use strict';
var db = require('./database');
var MaxGuessError = require('./max-guess-error');

var MAX_GUESSES = 5;

function submitGuess(userID, guess) {
  // db.user.find() returns a promise
  return db.user.find({id: userID}).then(function (user) {
    if (user.guesses.length === MAX_GUESSES) {
      throw new MaxGuessError(MAX_GUESSES);
    }
    // otherwise update the user...
  });
}

submitGuess(1001, 'Professor Plum').then(function () {
  // won't get called if there is an error
  console.log('guess submitted');
}, function (maxGuessError) {
  // oops, an error occurred!
  console.error('invalid guess');
  console.error(maxGuessError.toString());
});
```

Recall that, in a traditional asynchronous callback model, thrown exceptions must be manually handled and accounted for (which means that unpredictable exceptions will often slip past scrutiny). Q handles this automatically; any exception thrown in a thenable callback will be caught and propagated appropriately, even though all thenable callbacks are executed asynchronously.

Rejection callbacks follow similar rules, but with a mental twist. They do not receive values; instead, they receive errors, so a developer might reasonably expect that returning an error from a rejection callback would trigger the next rejection callback further down the promise chain. But that is incorrect. In Listing 14-16, the last promise in the chain will be resolved, not rejected, even though an error is returned from the rejection callback inside submitGuess().

Listing 14-16. Returning an Error in a Rejection Callback

```
// example-009/index.js
'use strict';
var db = require('./database');
var NotFoundError = require('./not-found-error');

function submitGuess(userID, guess) {
  // db.user.find() returns a promise
  return db.user.find({id: userID}).then(function (user) {
    /*
     * database generates an error so this promise
     * won't be resolved
     */
  }, function (err) {
    var notFoundError = new NotFoundError(userID);
    notFoundError.innerError = err;
    return notFoundError;
  });
}

submitGuess(1001, 'Colonel Mustard').then(function (value) {
  /*
   * oops, this promise was resolved, and
   * value === notFoundError!
   */
  console.log('guess submitted');
  console.log(value);
}, function (notFoundError) {
  /*
   * you expect this promise to get rejected...
   * but you are wrong
   */
  console.error('an error occurred');
  console.error(notFoundError);
});
```

This seems counterintuitive. If an error is returned from a rejection callback one might reasonably expect it to propagate, but that isn't what happens. On second glance, however, this begins to make sense, because it allows developers to handle errors that do *not* need to be propagated and still gracefully resolve the promise chain by returning some value.

If the code in Listing 14-16 is modified to queue guesses when the database becomes unavailable, it makes sense to resolve the promise chain even when an error is generated, as demonstrated in Listing 14-17.

Listing 14-17. Muffling an Error in a Rejection Callback

```
// example-010/index.js
'use strict';
var db = require('./database');
var guessQueue = require('./guess-queue');

function submitGuess(userID, guess) {
  // db.user.find() returns a promise
  return db.user.find({id: userID}).then(function (user) {
    /*
     * database generates an error so this promise
     * won't be resolved
     */
  }, function (err) {
    console.error(err);
    /*
     * database is probably offline, queue for future
     * processing
     */
    return guessQueue.enqueue(userID, guess);
  });
}

submitGuess(1001, 'Miss Scarlett').then(function (value) {
  /*
   * guess is queued when the database connection
   * fails, so the error is suppressed
   */
  console.log('guess submitted');
}, function (notFoundError) {
  console.error('an error occurred');
  console.error(notFoundError);
});
```

Like resolution callbacks, errors must be *thrown* in rejection callbacks in order to properly set the next promise's state to rejected, as demonstrated in Listing 14-18.

Listing 14-18. Throwing an Error in a Rejection Callback

```
// example-011/index.js
'use strict';
var db = require('./database');
var NotFoundError = require('./not-found-error');

function submitGuess(userID, guess) {
  // db.user.find() returns a promise
  return db.user.find({id: userID}).then(function (user) {
    /*
     * database generates an error so this promise
     * won't be resolved
     */
```

```
  }, function (err) {
    /*
     * error is *thrown*, not returned
     */
    var notFoundError = new NotFoundError(userID);
    notFoundError.innerError = err;
    throw notFoundError;
  });
}

submitGuess(1001, 'Mrs. Peacock').then(function (value) {
  /*
   * since error was thrown within the promise
   * the promise will not be resolved
   */
}, function (notFoundError) {
  /*
   * the promise is rejected, as expected!
   */
  console.error('an error occurred');
  console.error(notFoundError);
});
```

Just as deferreds can be resolved with other promises, so too can thenable callbacks return promises that, when resolved or rejected, will affect the state of the callback chain. Promises may be returned from both resolution and rejection callbacks. In Listing 14-19, a second promise is returned if the database call is successful, otherwise an exception is thrown.

Listing 14-19. Returning Another Promise in a Resolution Callback

```
// example-012/index.js
'use strict';
var db = require('./database');
var MaxGuessError = require('./max-guess-error');

var MAX_GUESSES = 5;

function submitGuess(userID, guess) {
  // db.user.find() returns a promise
  return db.user.find({id: userID}).then(function (user) {
    if (user.guesses.length === MAX_GUESSES) {
      throw new MaxGuessError(MAX_GUESSES);
    }
    // otherwise update the user
    user.guesses.push(guess);
    return db.user.update(user);
  });
}
```

```
submitGuess(1001, 'Professor Plum').then(function () {
  /*
   * should be called with the database has
   * finished updating the user
   */
  console.log('guess submitted');
}, function (maxGuessError) {
  console.error('invalid guess');
  console.error(maxGuessError.toString());
});
```

Turning Simple Values into Promises

Q can turn any value *into* a promise, simply by invoking Q as a function with the value as its only argument. Listing 14-20 wraps a simple string that will be used as the value passed to the next resolution handler in the promise chain.

Listing 14-20. Turning a Value into a Promise

```
// example-013/index.js
'use strict';
var Q = require('q');

Q('khan!').then(function (value) {
  console.log(value); //khan!
});
```

This may seem trivial but it can be a convenient way to wrap existing, synchronous code with actual return values into a promise-based API. You can invoke Q without a value, which will create an empty promise in a resolved state.

Invoking Q with a promise from another library will also wrap that promise in Q's interface as well. This can be very helpful when a developer wishes to use Q's promise methods like nodeify() when dealing with another promise library that has no equivalent.

Reporting Progress

Sometimes asynchronous operations take a long period to complete. During this time it can be helpful to give some indication of progress to client code, whether as a simple meter (e.g., percentage complete) or to deliver bits of data as they are made available (e.g., events raised by EventEmitter). Q augments the Promises/A+ spec by adding a third callback parameter to then(), shown in Listing 14-21, which can be used to capture progress events as they occur.

Listing 14-21. Q's Thenable Method Signature

```
/**
 * @param {Function} [onFulfilled]
 * @param {Function} [onRejected]
 * @param {Function} [onProgress]
 * @returns {Promise}
 */
promise.then(onFulfilled, onRejected, onProgress)
```

While the Promises/A+ specification does not establish a pattern for progress notification, Q still conforms because its thenables all still support the prescribed then() method signature.

Just as the fulfillment and rejection callbacks are invoked when a deferred is fulfilled or rejected, so too, the progress callback is invoked when a deferred's notify() method is called. This method accepts a single argument, which is then passed to the progress callback. In Listing 14-22, a long-running asynchronous operation keeps track of how many attempts it makes to do some work (perhaps call an API that is frequently unresponsive). Each time an attempt is made, a counter is incremented and its value is passed to the notify() method. The progress callback receives this data immediately. Once the deferred has been resolved, the promise chain is finished and the final done() callback is invoked.

Listing 14-22. Notifying the Deferred's Promise

```
<!-- example-014/index.html -->
<form>
  <p>The UI thread should respond to text field input, even though many DOM elements are
being added.</p>
  <input type="text" placeholder="type something here" />
</form>
<div id="output"></div>

<script>
  (function () {
    var Q = window.Q;
    var output = document.querySelector('#output');

    function writeOutput(msg) {
      var pre = document.createElement('pre');
      pre.innerHTML = msg;
      output.insertBefore(pre, output.firstChild);
    }

    function longAsync() {
      var d = Q.defer();

      var attempts = 0;

      var handle = setInterval(function () {
        // each time the scheduled code runs,
        // send a notification with the attempt
        // number
        attempts += 1;
        d.notify(attempts);
        if (attempts === 1200) {
          clearInterval(handle);
          return d.resolve();
        }
      }, 0);

      return d.promise;
    }
```

```
    // not using the rejection callback, only the
    // resolution and progress callbacks
    longAsync().then(function () {
      writeOutput('(done)');
    }, null, function (attempts) {
      writeOutput('notification: ' + attempts);
    });
  }());
</script>
```

It is important to note that, while any resolution or rejection callbacks attached to a thenable will be invoked according to what has already happened in a promise chain, only those progress callbacks that are attached prior to a notification event will actually receive an update. Consider the code in Listing 14-23 and the resulting console output in Listing 14-24.

Listing 14-23. Notifying a Deferred's Promise Before Progress Callback Is Added

```
// example-015/index.js
'use strict';
var Q = require('q');

function brokenPromise() {
  var d = Q.defer();
  process.nextTick(function () {
    console.log('scheduled first');
    d.notify('notifying');
    d.resolve('resolving');
    console.log('logging');
  });
  return d.promise;
}

var promise = brokenPromise();

process.nextTick(function () {
  console.log('scheduled second');
  promise.then(function (value) {
    console.log(value);
  }, null, function (progress) {
    console.log(progress);
  });
});
```

In Listing 14-23, a deferred is created, then notified and resolved asynchronously. The callbacks are attached to then() only *after* the deferred's methods have been invoked. The console output in Listing 14-24 reflects what happens when the code is run as a Node.js script.

Listing 14-24. Console Output Without Notification

```
$ node index.js
scheduled first
logging
scheduled second
resolving
```

The logging statement is displayed before notifying or resolving, as there are no callbacks attached to the deferred's promise when the scheduled code in the function brokenPromise() is actually run. After brokenPromise() is invoked, more code is scheduled to attach a resolution callback and a progress callback to the promise. When the scheduled code runs, the progress callback is completely ignored, yet the resolution callback receives its value. Why? Because the progress callback was added in code scheduled *after* the deferred's notify() method was called. Resolutions and rejections are, according to the Promises/A+ spec, guaranteed to propagate when new callbacks are added to a thenable, but Q treats notifications as "real-time" events that only propagate to callbacks attached at the time of notification.

Everything Ends

To further mimic synchronous code conventions, Q provides both catch() and finally() methods that parallel their respective counterparts in synchronous, structured exception handling.

The catch() method is really an alias for then(null, onRejection). Like then(), catch() will not halt the promise chain, but it does allow developers to deal with errors at arbitrary points in the promise chain. The code in Listing 14-25 uses catch() to intercept a potential HTTP failure. Because catch() itself returns a promise, its callback can return any value (or throw another error) to be handled later in the promise chain.

Listing 14-25. Catching Errors in a Promise Chain

```
// example-016/index.js
'use strict';
var Q = require('q');
var api = require('./api');
var InvalidTeamError = require('./invalid-team-error');

function loadTeamRoster(teamID) {
  // api.get() returns a promise
  return api.get('/team/' + teamID + '/roster')
    .catch(function (err) {
      /*
       * throw a meaningful exception rather than
       * propagate an HTTP error
       */
      if (err.statusCode === 404) {
        throw new InvalidTeamError(teamID);
      }
    });
}
```

```
loadTeamRoster(123).then(function (roster) {
  console.log(roster);
}).catch(function (err) {
  console.error(err.message);
});
```

The finally() method behaves like then() with one caveat: it may not alter any value or error it receives, though it may return an entirely new promise to be propagated along the promise chain. If it returns nothing, the original value or error it received will be passed along instead.

The real purpose of the finally() method mirrors the purpose of the finally portion of a try/catch block. It allows code to clean up resources before the thread of execution proceeds. Listing 14-26 shows how a database connection might be closed using a finally() block. Regardless of whether the connection or update succeeds, the code in the finally() callback will always run, cleaning up the database handle if it remains open.

Listing 14-26. Cleaning Up Resources in a Promise Chain

```
// example-017/index.js
'use strict';
var Q = require('q');
var db = require('./database');

var user = {
  id: 1001,
  name: 'Nicholas Cloud',
  occupation: 'Code Monkey'
};

db.connect().then(function (conn) {
  return conn.user.update(user)
    .finally(function () {
      if (conn.isOpen) {
        conn.close();
      }
    });
});
```

When finally() is called, it does not actually terminate the promise chain. But there will likely be places in code where you will wish to do so, to handle a final value or error in a series of asynchronous operations when no further handlers will be added. This can be accomplished in a number of ways. The obvious way to terminate a chain is to simply discontinue it by ignoring a final promise created by then(). Unfortunately, that promise may have already been rejected by upstream code in the promise chain. This means that Q will hold onto any error generated in the promise chain that is *not* handled in case a future rejection callback is added. If a promise chain is "terminated" without a rejection callback, as in Listing 14-27, the error is never reported—it evaporates into the ether—and the resolution callback will never be executed.

Listing 14-27. Improperly Terminating a Promise Chain

```
// example-018/index01.js
'use strict';
var Q = require('q');

function crankyFunction() {
  var d = Q.defer();
  process.nextTick(function () {
    d.reject(new Error('get off my lawn!'));
  });
  return d.promise;
}

// no rejection callback to display the error
crankyFunction().then(function (value) {
  console.log('never resolved');
});
```

To counter this, promises created by Q also have a done() method, which does not return a promise and throws any unhandled error in a future turn of the event loop to be addressed by other means. This method is demonstrated in Listing 14-28.

Listing 14-28. Terminating a Promise Chain with done()

```
// example-018/index02.js
crankyFunction().done(function (value) {
  //...
});
```

Even though a rejection callback is not supplied, the JavaScript context will still terminate because an unhandled error was automatically thrown by Q's done() method. The console output in Listing 14-29 shows what happens if crankyFunction()'s promise chain is terminated by a done() method.

Listing 14-29. Unhandled Error Thrown by done()

```
$ node index02.js
/.../node_modules/q/q.js:126
                    throw e;
                    ^
Error: get off my lawn!
    at /.../code/q/example-018/index02.js:7:14
    at process._tickCallback (node.js:419:13)
    at Function.Module.runMain (module.js:499:11)
    at startup (node.js:119:16)
    at node.js:906:3
```

Flow Control with Q

Promise chains are a fantastic way to flatten asynchronous, callback-based APIs. They also simulate, in their own way, the structured exception handling pattern developers become familiar with in synchronous code. These features simplify flow control in promise-based code, but a bit of creativity can be used to leverage promises for the following more complex flows in which a number of asynchronous operations can be "grouped" and treated as a whole:

- *Sequential flow*: Independent asynchronous operations are scheduled and executed, one at a time, each starting after the preceding completes.

- *Parallel flow*: Independent, asynchronous operations are all scheduled at once and aggregate all results.

- *Pipeline flow*: Dependent, asynchronous operations are executed, one at a time, each depending on the values created in a preceding operation.

In each type of flow, the rejection of *one* operation triggers the failure of the flow in general. The sequential flow is concerned with side effects and not values (meaning it doesn't actually fetch or create data that will be used later), though it could be adapted to aggregate fetched data if necessary. The parallel flow aggregates data from a number of different asynchronous operations and delivers its results when all are complete. The pipeline flow passes some data through a series of operations, so at least one operation will fetch or create data, and there will be some value to handle at the end of the flow.

Sequential Flow

The functions in Listing 14-30 represent a series of steps common to web applications. They change a user's password. Each is highly simplified, of course, but the three basic steps must be completed sequentially:

1. Change the actual password.

2. Notify the user (probably via e-mail) that their password has been changed.

3. Because our company is a Good Corporate Citizen, it forwards the password on to the National Security Agency (NSA).

Listing 14-30. Functions Executed in a Sequential Flow

```
// example-019/index.js
function changePassword(cb) {
  process.nextTick(function () {
    console.log('changing password...');
    cb(null);
  });
}

function notifyUser(cb) {
  process.nextTick(function () {
    console.log('notifying user...');
    var randomFail = Date.now() % 2 === 0;
    cb(randomFail ? new Error('fail!') : null);
  });
}
```

```
function sendToNSA(cb) {
  process.nextTick(function () {
    console.log('sending to NSA...');
    cb(null);
  });
}
```

Each operation's function is asynchronous and conforms to the standard Node.js callback pattern. The changePassword() and sendToNSA() functions will always succeed in the example in Listing 14-30, but to make things interesting, the notifyUser() function sometimes succeeds and other times fails based on a calculated value.

To orchestrate these three operations in a sequential promise flow, they are first added to an array of "steps" in the appropriate execution order. An "empty" promise (lastPromise) is created by invoking Q without any parameters; it will be the first resolved promise in the sequential promise chain.

In Listing 14-31, the code iterates over the array of steps to encapsulate each step in a promise. For each iteration, it invokes the then() method on lastPromise and assigns the result—a newly minted promise—back to the lastPromise variable. (This builds a promise chain within a loop.)

Inside each resolution callback, the code transforms the current "step" (one of the functions defined in Listing 14-30) into a promise by passing it to Q.denodeify(). The same could be accomplished manually by setting up a deferred and using deferred.makeNodeResolver(), as demonstrated earlier in Listing 14-11, but Q.denodeify() streamlines this process. The result is a promise that can be returned from the resolution callback as the next step in the promise chain.

Listing 14-31. Orchestrating a Sequential Flow with Promises

```
// example-019/index.js
var Q = require('q');

var steps = [changePassword, notifyUser, sendToNSA];
var lastPromise = Q();
steps.forEach(function (step) {
  lastPromise = lastPromise.then(function () {
    /*
     * denodeify and invoke each function step
     * to return a promise
     */
    return Q.denodeify(step)();
  });
});

lastPromise.done(function () {
  console.log('all done');
}, function (err) {
  console.error(err);
});
```

Finally, resolution and rejection callbacks are attached to the *last* promise created by the loop.

When the next scheduled loop executes, the first step will begin. When it resolves, the next promise in the chain will be invoked, and so on, until the end of the sequential flow is reached. If an error occurs at any point in the chain, it will immediately cause the final rejection callback to be invoked. (There are no intermediate rejection callbacks; a sequential flow should fail when any one step fails.) If all steps resolve, the final resolution callback will output the console message: all done.

Parallel Flow

Applications will often fetch data from a variety of sources, then send it to some client as a unified whole. In Listing 14-32, user data and a list of US states are both fetched at the same time, perhaps for a web page on which a user may change his or her mailing address.

Listing 14-32. Functions Executed in a Parallel Flow

```
// example-20/index01.js
function getUser(id, cb) {
  process.nextTick(function () {
    cb(null, {id: id, name: 'nick'});
  });
}

function getUSStates(cb) {
  process.nextTick(function () {
    cb(null, ['MO', 'IL' /*, etc.*/]);
  });
}
```

Because these two asynchronous functions have nothing to do with each other, it makes sense that they should be scheduled at the same time (instead of one waiting for the other to finish). Q's utility function all() accepts an array of promises to be scheduled all at once, but since the functions in Listing 14-32 are not yet promises, they must be converted with one of Q's function call methods. Because the functions conform to the Node.js callback signature, the code in Listing 14-33 passes each function to Q.nfcall() (node-function-call), which will wrap each in promises, using deferreds to supply the appropriate callbacks. Because the getUser() function accepts a single data parameter, the user ID must be passed as the *second* argument to Q.nfcall() when the getUser() promise is created. Q will bind the user ID as the first parameter to the getUser() function when it is invoked internally.

Q's all() function itself returns a promise, which will be resolved with an array of values. The ordinal position of each value in the array will correspond to the ordinal sequence in which the promises were ordered in the array passed to Q.all(). In this case, user data will occupy index 0, while the US states array will occupy index 1.

If an error occurs in any of the promises, the rejection callback on the aggregate promise will be invoked.

Listing 14-33. Orchestrating a Parallel Flow with Promises

```
// example-20/index01.js
var Q = require('q');

Q.all([
  Q.nfcall(getUser, 123),
  Q.nfcall(getUSStates)
]).then(function (results) {
  console.log('user:', results[0]);
  console.log('states:', results[1]);
}, function (err) {
  console.error('ERR', err);
});
```

Because accessing values in an array is ungainly, a promise may be continued with the spread() method, which operates identically to then(), except that it "explodes" the results array into actual individual arguments, as shown in Listing 14-34.

Listing 14-34. Spreading Results

```
// example-20/index02.js
var Q = require('q');

Q.all([
  Q.nfcall(getUser, 123),
  Q.nfcall(getUSStates)
]).spread(function (user, states) {
  console.log('user:', user);
  console.log('states:', states);
}, function (err) {
  console.error('ERR', err);
});
```

Q also provides a companion function, `Q.allSettled()`, which behaves like `Q.all()` with a few key differences. First, it will *always* invoke the resolution callback of the aggregate promise. Second, each value will be an object with a `state` property, which will report the actual state of the promise that created the value, and one of the following properties that depend on the value of `state`:

- `value`, which will contain the data created by the promise *if it resolved*

- `reason`, which will contain any error created *if the promise was rejected*

The choice between using `Q.all()` or `Q.allSettled()` will depend on the nature of the application code, but either may be used to create a parallel flow.

Pipeline Flow

Pipeline flows are useful when a set of data needs to be transformed according to some sequential rule set. The difference between a pipeline and the sequential flow covered earlier is that each step in a pipeline passes data to the next, whereas the sequential flow is concerned primarily with creating a linear series of side effects.

The pipeline functions in Listing 14-35 represent a simplified filtering system, perhaps for a recruiting agency looking to place talent with clients. The `loadCandidates()` function will "fetch" a list of possible candidates, and the other functions will be responsible for whittling down the selection based on some criteria. Notice that `filterBySkill()` and `groupByStates()` are actually factory functions. They accept some configuration parameters (the skill and states desired), then return a function that accepts a Node.js callback to be used in the pipeline.

Listing 14-35. Functions Executed in a Pipeline Flow

```
// example-021/index.js
function loadCandidates(cb) {
  console.log('loadCandidates', arguments);
  process.nextTick(function () {
    var candidates = [
      {name: 'Nick', skills: ['JavaScript', 'PHP'], state: 'MO'},
      {name: 'Tim', skills: ['JavaScript', 'PHP'], state: 'TN'}
    ];
    cb(null, candidates);
  });
}
```

```
function filterBySkill(skill) {
  return function (candidates, cb) {
    console.log('filterBySkill', arguments);
    candidates = candidates.filter(function (c) {
      return c.skills.indexOf(skill) >= 0;
    });
    cb(null, candidates);
  };
}

function groupByStates(states) {
  var grouped = {};
  states.forEach(function (state) {
    grouped[state] = [];
  });
  return function (candidates, cb) {
    console.log('groupByStates', arguments);
    process.nextTick(function () {
      candidates.forEach(function (c) {
        if (grouped.hasOwnProperty(c.state)) {
          grouped[c.state].push(c);
        }
      });
      cb(null, grouped);
    });
  };
}
```

The loadCandidates() function is added to the steps array directly, but the filterBySkill() and groupByStates() functions are invoked with their initialization values.

Like the serial and parallel flows, the pipeline flow uses promise chaining to coordinate the execution sequence. In Listing 14-36, however, the result created by each step—the value passed to the resolution callback for each promise—is placed into an array and passed as an argument to the *next* promise in the sequence. In the parallel flow example, Q.nfcall() was used to invoke each step; in this example, Q.nfapply() (node-function-apply) is used. Each call mimics its native JavaScript counterpart (Function.prototype.call() and Function.prototype.apply()), which is why an array is used to pass the result to each step instead of passing the result as a direct argument. This is necessary because the first step in the pipeline, loadCandidates(), accepts *no* arguments (other than the callback). Passing an empty array to Q.nfapply() ensures the function is called properly.

Listing 14-36. Orchestrating a Pipeline Flow with Promises

```
// example-021/index.js
var Q = require('q');

var steps = [
  loadCandidates,
  filterBySkill('JavaScript'),
  groupByStates(['MO', 'IL'])
];
```

```
var lastPromise = Q();
steps.forEach(function (step) {
  lastPromise = lastPromise.then(function (result) {
    var args = [];
    if (result !== undefined) {
      args.push(result);
    }
    return Q.nfapply(step, args);
  });
});

lastPromise.done(function (grouped) {
  console.log('grouped:', grouped);
}, function (err) {
  console.error(err);
});
```

When the pipeline has finished, the last value passed to the last asynchronous callback will be the value passed to the done() resolution callback. Should any asynchronous operation generate an error, the rejection callback will be invoked instead.

A single value is passed to each callback for each asynchronous function in Listing 14-35. It is possible to pass *more* than one value to these callbacks, even though the Promises/A+ specification stipulates that only *one* value may be passed as a resolution parameter. Q mitigates this discrepancy by packaging up all values passed to an asynchronous function callback into an array, which it then passes to the promise's resolution callback. This array would then need to be passed to Q.nfapply(), as it contains all the data to be used as arguments to the next function step.

Summary

Callbacks are standard mechanisms to deal with asynchronous code. They provide a control flow mechanism for developers to "continue" execution *after* a future turn of the event loop. But callbacks can quickly become nested, convoluted, and hard to manage.

Using a promise library like Q to encapsulate asynchronous operations, to "flatten" code, can dramatically improve a code base. Q's ability to automatically propagate values and errors, to chain callbacks in an asynchronous manner, report progress during long-running asynchronous operations, and deal with unhandled errors at the end of a promise chain makes it a powerful tool in any developer's toolbox.

Q can be used to manage trivial, linear program flows, but with a bit of creativity can also be adapted to more complex flows. This chapter examined the sequential, parallel, and pipeline flows, but Q's utility methods give developers an extra measure of flexibility when orchestrating other flows as well.

Related Resources

- Q: https://github.com/kriskowal/q

- Promises/A+ spec: https://promisesaplus.com/

CHAPTER 15

Async.js

Always something new, always something I didn't expect, and sometimes it isn't horrible.

—Robert Jordan

Coordinating software flow can be cumbersome, especially when asynchronous operations finish at different times. Chapter 16 demonstrated how promises can be used to address this problem. This chapter discusses Async.js, a callback-driven JavaScript library that provides a suite of powerful functions to manage asynchronous collection manipulation and control flow.

Chapter 16 covered three common flows in which asynchronous code can be problematic: sequential flow, parallel flow, and pipeline flow. To address these flows with promises, Chapter 16 showed how to adapt each callback-oriented task with Q's helper methods so that each could be wrapped conveniently within a promise. The Async.js library *embraces* the callback-driven approach to asynchronous programming, however, but in such a way that many of the downsides presented by callback-driven code (such as nested callbacks) are avoided.

Many of the Async.js control flow functions follow a similar pattern:

1. The first argument to each control flow function is typically an array of functions to be executed as tasks. Task function signatures will vary a bit based on the exact Async.js control flow function used, but they will always receive a Node.js-style callback as a last argument.

2. The last argument to each control flow function is a final callback function to be executed when all tasks are complete. The final control flow function also receives a Node.js-style callback and may or may not receive additional arguments as well.

Note A Node.js-style callback is simply a callback function that always expects an error as its first argument. When the callback is invoked, either an error object is passed as its only argument, or `null` is passed in for the error value and any further values are passed in as additional arguments.

Listing 15-1 shows how this pattern is typically applied.

Listing 15-1. Flow Control Function Pattern

```
var tasks = [
  function (/*0..n args, */ cb) {/*...*/},
  function (/*0..n args, */ cb) {/*...*/},
  function (/*0..n args, */ cb) {/*...*/}
];

function finalCallback (err, result) {/*...*/};

async.someFlowControlFunction(tasks, finalCallback);
```

The rest of the chapter will examine a number of control flow functions, and how they vary, if at all, from this general pattern. Since all flows organize tasks and handle errors and values in a similar way, it becomes easier to understand each by contrast.

■ **Note**   The meaning of *async* in Async.js relates to organizing asynchronous operations. The library itself does not *guarantee* that task functions execute asynchronously. If a developer uses Async.js with synchronous functions, each will be executed synchronously. There is one semi-exception to this rule. The `async.memoize()` function (which has nothing to do with control flow) makes a function cacheable, so that subsequent invocations won't actually *run* the function but will return a cached result instead. Async.js forces each subsequent invocation to be asynchronous because *it assumes that the original function was itself asynchronous.*

Sequential Flow

A sequential flow is one in which a series of steps must be executed in order. A step may not start until a preceding step finishes (except for the first step), and if any step fails, the flow fails as a whole. The functions in Listing 15-2 are the steps for changing a fictitious user's password, the same scenario used to introduce sequential flows in Chapter 16. These steps are slightly different, however.

First, each is wrapped in a factory function that takes some initial data and returns a callback-based function to be used as a step in the sequential flow.

Second, the first step (the task wrapped in the `changePassword()` function) actually passes new credentials to its callback as an operation result. Steps in a sequential flow are not required to generate results, but if a step does pass a result to its callback, it has no bearing on the other steps in the sequence. If some (or all) steps rely on results from previous steps, a pipeline flow is needed. (Pipelines are discussed later in the chapter.)

Listing 15-2. Sequential Steps

```
// example-001/async-series.js
'use strict';
var async = require('async');
var userService = require('./user-service');
var emailService = require('./email-service');
var nothingToSeeHere = require('./nothing-to-see-here');
```

```
function changePassword(email, password) {
  return function (cb) {
    process.nextTick(function () {
      userService.changePassword(email, password, function (err, hash) {
        // new credentials returned as results
        cb(null, {email: email, passwordHash: hash});
      });
    });
  };
}

function notifyUser(email) {
  return function (cb) {
    process.nextTick(function () {
      // the email service invokes the callback with
      // no result
      emailService.notifyPasswordChanged(email, cb);
    });
  };
}

function sendToNSA(email, password) {
  return function (cb) {
    process.nextTick(function () {
      // the nothingToSeeHere service invokes the
      // callback with no result
      nothingToSeeHere.snoop(email, password, cb);
    });
  }
}
```

In Listing 15-3, each factory function is executed with its initial data, returning task functions that are added to a steps array. This array becomes the first argument to async.series(), followed by a final callback that receives any error generated during the execution of the series, or an array of results populated by each step in the series. If any results are generated, they are stored according to the order of their corresponding steps in the steps array. For example, the result from changePassword() will be the first element in the results array because changePassword() was invoked as the first task.

Listing 15-3. Sequential Flow

```
// example-001/async-series.js
var email = 'user@domain.com';
var password = 'foo!1';

var steps = [
  //returns function(cb)
  changePassword(email, password),
  //returns function(cb)
  notifyUser(email),
  //returns function(cb)
  sendToNSA(email, password)
];
```

```
async.series(steps, function (err, results) {
  if (err) {
    return console.error(err);
  }
  console.log('new credentials:', results[0]);
});
```

Because these steps are asynchronous, they can't be invoked one at a time in the same way that synchronous functions can be called. But Async.js tracks the executing of each step internally, invoking the next step only when the previous step's callback has been invoked, thus creating a sequential flow. If any step in the sequential flow passes an error to its callback, the series will be aborted and the final series callback will be invoked with that error. When an error is raised the results value will be undefined.

The factory functions used in this chapter are convenient ways to pass initial data to each step, but they but not necessary. The factories could be eliminated in favor of JavaScript's native function binding facilities, as in Listing 15-4, but the code becomes more difficult to read when the steps are actually added to the array. For simple scenarios in which no initial data or bindings are necessary, anonymous task functions may be declared directly within the steps array. (It is always a good idea to name your functions and declare them in a way that promotes readability and maintainability, however.)

Listing 15-4. Series Steps with Argument Binding

```
function changePassword(email, password, cb) {/*...*/}

function notifyUser(email, cb) {/*...*/}

function sendToNSA(email, password, cb) {/*...*/}

var steps = [
  changePassword.bind(null, email, password),
  notifyUser.bind(null, email),
  sendToNSA.bind(null, email, password)
];
```

For the rest of this chapter we'll be using factory functions instead of bind(), but developers are free to choose whatever approach feels most natural to them.

Parallel Flow

Sometimes it is helpful to run independent tasks in parallel and then aggregate results after all tasks are finished. JavaScript is an asynchronous language, so it has no true parallelism, but scheduling long, nonblocking operations in succession will release the event loop to handle other operations (like UI updates in a browser environment, or handling additional requests in a server environment). Multiple asynchronous tasks can be scheduled in one turn of the event loop, but there is no way to predict at which future turn each task will complete. This makes it difficult to collect the results from each task and return them to calling code. Fortunately, the async.parallel() function gives developers the means to do just that.

Listing 15-5 shows two functions that wrap jQuery GET requests. The first fetches user data for a given userID, and the second fetches a list of U.S. states. It is easy to imagine that these functions may be part of a user's profile page on which the user would be able to update personal information such as phone numbers, postal addresses, and so forth. When the page loads, it makes sense to fetch this information all at once. These are two different API calls, though, so even if they are scheduled simultaneously, the results need to be handled at some future point in time.

Listing 15-5. Parallel Steps

```
// example-002/views/async-parallel.html
function getUser(userID) {
  return function (cb) {
    $.get('/user/' + userID).then(function (user) {
      cb(null, user);
    }).fail(cb);
  };
}

function getUSStates(cb) {
  $.get('/us-states').then(function (states) {
    cb(null, states);
  }).fail(cb);
}
```

In Listing 15-6, Async.js is imported into a fictitious web page with a standard `<script>` tag. Tasks are scheduled using the `async.parallel()` function, which, like `async.series()`, accepts an array of task functions to be executed and a final callback function that will receive an error or the aggregated results. Parallel tasks are simply functions that accept a single callback argument that should be invoked once the asynchronous operation within a task function is completed. All callbacks conform to the Node.js callback convention.

The `getUser()` function in Listing 15-6 is a factory that accepts a `userID` argument and returns a function that accepts a conventional Node.js-style callback. Because `getUSStates()` has no actual arguments it need not be wrapped in a factory function but is used directly instead.

Both functions fetch data with jQuery's AJAX API. AJAX promises pass data from successful AJAX calls to any callback passed to the promise's `then()` method, whereas errors are passed to any callbacks passed to the promise's `fail()` method. Because the signature of a `fail()` callback accepts a single error argument, the callback passed to each task from Async.js can also be used as the callback to `fail()`.

Listing 15-6. Parallel Flow

```
<!-- example-002/views/async-parallel.html -->
<h1>User Profile</h1>
<form>
  <fieldset>
    <div>
      <label>First Name</label>
      <input type="text" id="first-name" />
    </div>
    <div>
      <label>US States</label>
      <select id="us-states"></select>
    </div>
  </fieldset>
</form>

<script>
(function (async, $) {
```

```
function getUser(userID) {
  return function (cb) {
    $.get('/user/' + userID).then(function (user) {
      cb(null, user);
    }).fail(cb);
  };
}

function getUSStates(cb) {
  $.get('/us-states').then(function (states) {
    cb(null, states);
  }).fail(cb);
}

var userID = 1001;

async.parallel([
  getUser(userID),
  getUSStates
], function (err, results) {
  if (err) {
    return alert(err.message);
  }
  var user = results[0],
    states = results[1];
  $('#first-name').val(user.firstName);
  // ...
  $('#us-states').append(states.map(function (state) {
    return $('<option></option>')
      .html(state)
      .attr('value', state);
  }));
});

}(window.async, window.jQuery));
</script>
```

The Async.js library will iterate over each task in the tasks array, scheduling them one after the other. As each task completes, its data is stored, and once all tasks have finished, the final callback passed to async.parallel() is invoked.

Results are sorted according to the order of tasks passed to async.parallel(), *not* the order in which tasks are actually resolved. If an error occurs in any parallel task, that error will be passed to the final callback, all unfinished parallel tasks will be ignored once they complete, and the results argument in the final callback will be undefined.

Pipeline Flow

When tasks in a series each depends on a value from a preceding task, a pipeline flow (or waterfall) is needed. Listing 15-7 represents tasks for a fictitious corporate rewards program in which a user's age is calculated (based on date of birth), and if the user's age meets certain thresholds, the user is awarded a cash prize.

Each function receives some input and then passes some output to its callback. The output of each function becomes the input for the next function in the series.

1. The getUser() factory function accepts a **userID** and returns another function that, when invoked, looks up a **user** record. It passes the **user** record to its callback.

2. The calcAge() function accepts a **user** argument and invokes its callback with the calculated **age** of the user.

3. The reward() function accepts a numeric **age** argument and invokes its callback with the selected **reward** if the **age** meets certain thresholds.

Listing 15-7. Waterfall (Pipeline) Steps

```
// example-003/callback-waterfall
'use strict';
var db = require('./database');

function getUser(userID, cb) {
  process.nextTick(function () {
    // pass cb directly to find because
    // it has the same signature:
    // (err, user)
    db.users.find({id: userID}, cb);
  });
}

function calcAge(user, cb) {
  process.nextTick(function () {
    var now = Date.now(),
      then = user.birthDate.getTime();
    var age = (now - then) / (1000 * 60 * 60 * 24 * 365);
    cb(null, Math.round(age));
  });
}

function reward(age, cb) {
  process.nextTick(function () {
    switch (age) {
      case 25: return cb(null, '$100');
      case 35: return cb(null, '$150');
      case 45: return cb(null, '$200');
      default: return cb(null, '$0');
    }
  });
}
```

This pipeline would be rather hideous and difficult to maintain if organized with nested callbacks. If additional steps are ever added to the reward program, the code will need to be teased apart and restructured to accommodate new steps in the pipeline flow. Trapping errors and propagating them through callbacks also happens manually. The example code in Listing 15-8 shows how these tasks would be run *without* Async.js.

Listing 15-8. A Waterfall of Nested Callbacks

```
// example-003/callback-waterfall
function showReward(userID, cb) {
  getUser(userID, function (err, user) {
    if (err) {
      return cb(err);
    }
    calcAge(user, function (err, age) {
      if (err) {
        return cb(err);
      }
      reward(age, cb);
    });
  })
}

showReward(123, function (err, reward) {
  if (err) {
    return console.error(err);
  }
  console.log(reward);
});
```

Fortunately Async.js makes it relatively painless to organize a pipeline flow that is both maintainable and handles errors gracefully. The code in Listing 15-9 uses async.waterfall() to organize the series of tasks to be executed, then provides a final callback to capture any error raised by pipeline tasks or to receive the final reward value if no errors occurr.

Listing 15-9. Waterfall (Pipeline) Flow

```
// example-003/async-waterfall.js
'use strict';
var async = require('async');
var db = require('./database');

function getUser(userID) {
  // using a factory function to pass in
  // the userID argument and return another
  // function that will match the callback
  // signature that async.waterfall expects
  return function (cb) {
    process.nextTick(function () {
      // pass cb directly to find because
      // it has the same signature:
      // (err, user)
      db.users.find({id: userID}, cb);
    });
  };
}
```

```
// the calcAge and reward functions
// do not change

async.waterfall([
  getUser(1000),
  calcAge,
  reward
], function (err, reward) {
  if (err) {
    return console.error(err);
  }
  console.log('reward:', reward);
});
```

Like async.series() and async.parallel(), an error passed to a callback in *any* waterfall task will immediately halt the pipeline and invoke the final callback with the error.

Reusing a Pipeline

Pipelines are so helpful for processing data that async.seq() will take a series of functions, just like async. waterfall(), and combine them into a single, reusable pipeline function that can be called multiple times. This could be done manually, of course, by using a closure to wrap async.waterfall(), but async.seq() is a convenience function that saves developers the trouble.

Listing 15-10 shows a series of functions used to process a make-believe cellular phone bill. The createBill() function accepts a calling plan and creates a bill object with both the plan and the normal monthly rate. carrierFee() appends a chunk of change to this amount just because the phone company can. The prorate() function then determines if some amount is to be credited to the user (if the user started a new plan in the middle of a billing cycle, for example). And finally, govtExtortion() appends a calculated tax onto the bill before it is delivered.

Listing 15-10. Sequence (Pipeline) Steps

```
// example-004/async-seq.js
'use strict';
var async = require('async');
var dateUtil = require('./date-util');

function createBill(plan, cb) {
  process.nextTick(function () {
    var bill = {
      plan: plan,
      total: plan.billAmt
    };
    cb(null, bill);
  });
}

function carrierFee(bill, cb) {
  process.nextTick(function () {
    bill.total += 10;
    cb(null, bill);
  });
}
```

```
function prorate(bill, cb) {
  if (!bill.plan.isNew) {
    return cb(null, bill);
  }
  process.nextTick(function () {
    bill.plan.isNew = false;
    var days = dateUtil().daysInMonth();
    var amtPerDay = bill.plan.billAmt / days;
    var prorateAmt = ((bill.plan.billDay - 1) * amtPerDay);
    bill.total -= prorateAmt;
    cb(null, bill);
  });
}

function govtExtortion(bill, cb) {
  process.nextTick(function () {
    bill.total = bill.total * 1.08;
    cb(null, bill);
  });
}
```

Creating a pipeline with async.seq() is very similar to using async.waterfall(), as shown in Listing 15-11. The primary difference is that async.seq() does not invoke the steps immediately but returns a pipeline() function that will be used to run the tasks later. The pipeline() function accepts the initial arguments that will be passed to the *first* step, eliminating the need for factory functions or binding values to the first step when the pipeline is defined. Also, unlike most other async functions, async.seq() is variadic (accepts a varying number of arguments). It does not accept an array of tasks like async.waterfall(), but instead accepts each task function as an argument.

In Listing 15-11 the pipeline() function is created and then invoked with two parameters: a plan object, which will be passed to createBill(), and a final callback to receive either an error or a final bill object for the user.

Listing 15-11. Sequence (Pipeline) Flow

```
// example-004/async-seq.js
var pipeline = async.seq(
  createBill,
  carrierFee,
  prorate,
  govtExtortion
);

var plan = {
  type: 'Lots of Cell Minutes Plan!+',
  isNew: true,
  billDay: 15,
  billAmt: 100
};
```

```
pipeline(plan, function (err, bill) {
  if (err) {
    return console.error(err);
  }
  //bill = govtExtortion(prorate(carrierFee(createBill(plan))))
  console.log('$', bill.total.toFixed(2));
});
```

Loop Flow

Flows that repeat until some condition is met are called *loops*. Async.js has several looping functions that help coordinate the asynchronous code to be executed and the conditions to be tested within them.

Looping While Some Condition Remains True

The first two functions, async.whilst() and async.doWhilst(), parallel the well-known while and do/while looping constructs in many programming languages. Each loop runs *while* some condition evaluates to true. Once the condition evaluates to false, the loops halt.

The async.whilst() and async.doWhilst() functions are nearly identical, except that async.whilst() performs the condition evaluation before any code in the loop is run, whereas async.doWhilst() executes one iteration of the loop *before* performing evaluating the condition. Looping code in async.doWhilst() is guaranteed to run at least once, whereas looping code in async.whilst() may not run at all if the initial condition is false.

Listing 15-12 shows async.whilst() being used to call an API ten times to get a random "winner" for some contest. Before the loop runs, an array of names is examined to determine if ten winners have already been selected. This process is repeated until the array has a length of ten. If an error occurs during one of the API calls within the loop, the async.whilst() flow is terminated and the final callback is invoked with the error; otherwise the final callback will be invoked once the loop condition evaluates to false.

Listing 15-12. Looping While Some Condition Remains True

```
<!-- example-005/views/async-whilst.html -->
<h1>Winners!</h1>
<ul id="winners"></ul>

<script>
(function (async, $) {

  function pickWinners(howMany, cb) {
    var winners = [];

    async.whilst(
      // condition test:
      // continue looping until we have enough winners
      function () { return winners.length < howMany; },
      // looping code
      function (cb) {
        $.get('/employee/random').done(function (employee) {
          var winner = employee.firstName + ' ' + employee.lastName;
```

435

```
              // avoid potential duplicates
              if (winners.indexOf(winner) < 0) {
                winners.push(winner);
              }
              cb(null);
            }).fail(function (err) {
              cb(err);
            });
        },
        // final callback
        function (err) {
          // if there is an error just ignore it
          // and pass back an empty array, otherwise
          // pass the winners
          cb(null, err ? [] : winners);
        }
      );
    }

    pickWinners(3, function (err, winners) {
      $('ul#winners').append(winners.map(function (winner) {
        return $('<li></li>').html(winner);
      }));
    });

}(window.async, window.jQuery));
</script>
```

The code in Listing 15-13 shows an abbreviated modification of the async.whilst() loop using async.doWhilst() instead. Notice that the order of arguments has changed. The looping function is now the first argument to async.doWhilst() and the condition test is the second. This structurally mirrors do/while loop syntax.

Listing 15-13. Looping Once and Then Continuing While Some Condition Remains True

```
<!-- example-005/views/async-dowhilst.html -->
<h1>Winners!</h1>
<ul id="winners"></ul>

<script>
(function (async, $) {

  function pickWinners(howMany, cb) {
    var winners = [];

    async.doWhilst(
      // looping code
      function (cb) {
        $.get('/employee/random').done(function (employee) {
          var winner = employee.firstName + ' ' + employee.lastName;
          // avoid potential duplicates
```

```
          if (winners.indexOf(winner) < 0) {
            winners.push(winner);
          }
          cb(null);
        }).fail(function (err) {
          cb(err);
        });
      },
      // condition test is now the second function
      // argument
      function () { return winners.length < howMany; },
      // final callback
      function (err) {
        // if there is an error just ignore it
        // and pass back an empty array, otherwise
        // pass the winners
        cb(null, err ? [] : winners);
      }
    );
  }

  pickWinners(3, function (err, winners) {
    $('ul#winners').append(winners.map(function (winner) {
      return $('<li></li>').html(winner);
    }));
  });

}(window.async, window.jQuery));
</script>
```

Looping Until Some Condition Becomes False

Closely related to the async.whilst() and async.doWhilst() functions are the async.until() and async.doUntil() functions, which follow similar execution patterns but, instead of performing a loop when some condition is *true*, perform loops until some condition tests *false*.

The code in Listing 15-14 shows how a simple HTTP heartbeat can be created in the browser to test an API endpoint for availability. The Heartbeat() constructor function creates a loop with async.until() that will execute repeatedly until the value of the _isStopped property is set to true. Heartbeat() exposes a stop() method that, when invoked sometime after the object is created, will prevent the loop from continuing. Each turn of the loop makes an HTTP request to the server, and if the request succeeds, the loop sets the isAvailable property to true; if it fails, isAvailable is set to false. To create a delay between iterations of the loop, a setTimeout() function wraps the callback invocation within the loop, scheduling future iterations of the loop to run at a later time (every three seconds in this example).

Listing 15-14. Looping Until Some Condition Becomes False

```html
<!-- example-006/views/async-until.html -->
<section id="output"></section>

<script>
(function (async, $) {

  var output = document.querySelector('#output');

  function write() {
    var pre = document.createElement('pre');
    pre.innerHTML = Array.prototype.join.call(arguments, ' ');
    output.appendChild(pre);
  }

  function Heartbeat(url, interval) {
    var self = this;
    this.isAvailable = false;
    this.isStopped = false;
    this.writeStatus = function () {
      write(
        '> heartbeat [isAvailable: %s, isStopped: %s]'
          .replace('%s', self.isAvailable)
          .replace('%s', self.isStopped)
      );
    };

    async.until(
      // test condition
      function () { return self.isStopped; },
      // loop
      function (cb) {
        $.get(url).then(function () {
          self.isAvailable = true;
        }).fail(function () {
          self.isAvailable = false;
        }).always(function () {
          self.writeStatus();
          // delay the next loop by scheduling
          // the callback invocation in the
          // future
          setTimeout(function () {
            cb(null);
          }, interval);
        });
      },
```

```
      // final callback
      function (/*err*/) {
        self.isAvailable = false;
        self.writeStatus();
      }
    );
  }

  Heartbeat.prototype.stop = function () {
    this.isStopped = true;
  };

  var heartbeat = new Heartbeat('/heartbeat', 3000);

  setTimeout(function () {
    // 10 seconds later
    heartbeat.stop();
  }, 10000);

}(window.async, window.jQuery));
</script>
```

The async.doUntil() function behaves like async.doWhilst(): it runs the loop first before evaluating the test condition. Its signature also swaps the order of the test condition function and the looping function.

Retry Loops

A common use case for loops is the *retry loop*, where a task is attempted up to a given number of times. If the task fails but hasn't met the retry limit, it is executed again. If the retry limit is met, the task is aborted. The async.retry() function simplifies this process by handling the retry logic for developers. Setting up a loop is as simple as specifying a retry limit, a task to execute, and a final callback that will handle errors or receive a result.

Listing 15-15 demonstrates a simple API call for reserving a seat at some concert or movie. The available seats are listed in an array, most preferable to least preferable. The execution limit is the length of the array. Each time the task runs, it shifts the array, removing the first (most preferable) seat from the collection. If the reservation fails, it continues this process until there are no more seats left.

Listing 15-15. Retry Loop

```
<!-- example-007/views/async-retry -->
<section id="output"></section>

<script>
(function (async, $) {

  var output = document.querySelector('#output');

  function write() {
    var pre = document.createElement('pre');
    pre.innerHTML = Array.prototype.join.call(arguments, ' ');
    output.appendChild(pre);
  }
```

```
function reserve(name, availableSeats) {
  console.log(availableSeats);
  return function (cb) {
    var request = {
      name: name,
      seat: availableSeats.shift()
    };
    write('posting reservation', JSON.stringify(request));
    $.post('/reservation', request)
      .done(function (confirmation) {
        write('confirmation', JSON.stringify(confirmation));
        cb(null, confirmation);
      }).fail(function (err) {
        cb(err);
      });
  };
}

var name = 'Nicholas';
var availableSeats = ['15A', '22B', '13J', '32K'];

async.retry(
  availableSeats.length,
  reserve(name, availableSeats),
  function (err, confirmation) {
    if (err) {
      return console.error(err);
    }
    console.log('seat reserved:', confirmation);
  }
);
}(window.async, window.jQuery));
</script>
```

Each time the task is run it invokes its callback. If the task succeeds and passes a value to the callback, the final async.retry() callback is invoked with that value (in this case, confirmation). If an error occurs, the loop is repeated until it reaches the loop limit. The last error is passed to the final callback; previous errors are lost unless accumulated manually. Listing 15-16 demonstrates a potential way to accomplish this by collecting errors in an array, then passing the array itself as the err argument to the callback. If the retry loop fails, the final callback's error will be an array of every error generated during each turn of the loop.

Listing 15-16. Accumulating Errors in a Retry Loop

```
function reserve(name, availableSeats) {
  var errors = [];
  return function (cb) {
    // ...
    $.post('/reservation', body)
      .done(function (confirmation) {
        cb(null, confirmation);
```

```
  }).fail(function (err) {
    errors.push(err);
    cb(errors);
  });
};
}
```

Infinite Loops

Infinite loops are bad news in synchronous programming because they arrest the CPU and prevent any other code from executing. But asynchronous infinite loops don't suffer from this downside because, like all other code, they are scheduled for future turns of the event loop by the JavaScript scheduler. Other code that needs to be run can "butt in" and request to be scheduled.

An infinite loop can be scheduled with async.forever(). This function takes a task function as its first argument and a final callback as its second. The task will continue to run indefinitely unless it passes an error to its callback. Scheduling asynchronous operations back to back using setTimeout() with a wait duration of 0 or setImmediate() can create near nonresponsive code in a loop, so it is best to pad each asynchronous task with a longer wait duration, at least in the hundreds of milliseconds.

The loop in Listing 15-17 makes an HTTP GET request during each turn of the infinite loop, loading stock information for the user's dashboard. Each time the GET request succeeds the stock information is updated and the loop waits for three seconds before executing again. If an error occurs during the loop, the final callback is invoked with the error and the loop is terminated.

Listing 15-17. Infinite Loop

```
<!-- example-008/views/async-forever.html -->
<ul id="stocks"></ul>

<script>
(function (async, $) {
  $stockList = $('ul#stocks');

  async.forever(function (cb) {
    $.get('/dashboard/stocks')
      .done(function (stocks) {
        // refresh the stock list with new stock
        // information
        $stockList.empty();
        $stockList.append(stocks.map(function (stock) {
          return $('<li></li>').html(stock.symbol + ' $' + stock.price);
        }));
        // wait three seconds before continuing
        setTimeout(function () {
          cb(null);
        }, 3000);
      }).fail(cb);
  }, function (err) {
    console.error(err.responseText);
    })
}(window.async, window.jQuery));
</script>
```

Batch Flow

The last type of control flow this chapter covers is batching. Batches are created by partitioning some data into chunks, and then operating on each chunk one at a time. Batches have some threshold that defines how much data can be put into a chunk. Data added to a batch flow after work has commenced on a chunk is queued until work is complete, then gets processed in a new chunk.

Asynchronous Queue

An asynchronous queue is one way to process items in a batch flow. A queue can be created by calling `async.queue()` with two parameters. The first is a task function that will be executed for each data item that will be added to the queue. The second is a number that represents *the maximum number of task workers that the queue will schedule concurrently* to process data. In Listing 15-18 a queue is created to make HTTP requests for any URL added to the queue. The result of each HTTP request will be added to the `results` hash when each request has been completed. The maximum number of HTTP requests that can be running at any one time is three. If additional URLs are added to the queue while three requests are in progress, they will be held for future processing. As workers are released (when requests complete) they will be assigned to queued URLs as needed. There will never be more than three HTTP requests in progress at a given time.

Listing 15-18. Using Queue for Sequential Batches

```
// example-009/index.js
'use strict';
var async = require('async');
var http = require('http');

var MAX_WORKERS = 3;
var results = {};

var queue = async.queue(function (url, cb) {
  results[url] = '';
  http.get(url, function (res) {
    results[url] = res.statusCode + ' Content-Type: ' + res.headers['content-type'];
    cb(null);
  }).on('error', function (err) {
    cb(err);
    });
}, MAX_WORKERS);

var urls = [ // 9 urls
  'http://www.appendto.com',
  'http://www.nodejs.org',
  'http://www.npmjs.org',
  'http://www.nicholascloud.com',
  'http://www.devlink.net',
  'http://javascriptweekly.com',
  'http://nodeweekly.com',
  'http://www.reddit.com/r/javascript',
  'http://www.reddit.com/r/node'
];
```

```
urls.forEach(function (url) {
  queue.push(url, function (err) {
    if (err) {
      return console.error(err);
    }
    console.log('done processing', url);
  });
});
```

The queue will emit a number of events at certain points in its life cycle. Functions may be assigned to corresponding event properties on the queue object to handle these events. These event handlers are optional; the queue will operate correctly with or without them.

The first time the queue has reached the maximum number of active workers, it will invoke any function assigned to queue.saturated. When the queue is handling all items and no other items are queued, it will call any function assigned to queue.empty. Finally, when all workers have completed and the queue is empty, any function assigned to queue.drain will be called. The functions in Listing 15-19 handle each of these raised events.

Listing 15-19. Queue Events

```
// example-009/index.js
queue.saturated = function () {
  console.log('queue is saturated at ' + queue.length());
};

queue.empty = function () {
  console.log('queue is empty; last task being handled');
};

queue.drain = function () {
  console.log('queue is drained; no more tasks to handle');
  Object.keys(results).forEach(function (url) {
    console.log(url, results[url]);
  });
  process.exit(0);
};
```

■ **Note** The empty and drained events differ subtly. When empty is triggered, workers may still be active though no items remain in the queue. When drained is triggered, all workers have ceased and the queue is completely empty.

Asynchronous Cargo

The async.cargo() function is similar to async.queue() in that it queues up items to be processed by some task function. They differ, however, in how the work load is divided. async.queue() runs multiple *workers* up to a maximum concurrency limit—its saturation point. async.cargo() runs a single worker at a time, but splits up the queued items to be processed into payloads of a predetermined size. When the worker is executed, it will be given one payload. When it has completed, it will be given another, until all payloads

443

have been processed. The saturation point for cargo, then, is when a *full* payload is ready to be processed. Any items added to the cargo after the worker has started will be grouped into the next payload to be processed.

A cargo is created by supplying the task function as the first argument to async.cargo() and a maximum payload size as the second. The task function will receive an array of data (with a length up to the maximum payload size) to be processed and a callback to be invoked once the operation is complete.

The code in Listing 15-20 shows how async.cargo() can be used to package a series of database updates into a fictitious transaction, one payload at a time. The task function iterates over the "update" objects supplied to it, converting each into an UPDATE query in some imaginary relational data store. Once all the queries have been added to a transaction, the transaction is committed and the callback is invoked.

Listing 15-20. Using Cargo for Parallel Batches

```
// example-010/index-01.js
'use strict';
var async = require('async');
var db = require('db');

var MAX_PAYLOAD_SIZE = 4;
var UPDATE_QUERY = "UPDATE CUSTOMER SET ? = '?' WHERE id = ?;";

var cargo = async.cargo(function (updates, cb) {
  db.begin(function (trx) {
    updates.forEach(function (update) {
      var query = UPDATE_QUERY.replace('?', update.field)
        .replace('?', update.value)
        .replace('?', update.id);
      trx.add(query);
    });
    trx.commit(cb);
    });
}, MAX_PAYLOAD_SIZE);

var customerUpdates = [ // 9 updates to be processed in payloads of 4
  {id: 1000, field: 'firstName', value: 'Sterling'},
  {id: 1001, field: 'phoneNumber', value: '222-333-4444'},
  {id: 1002, field: 'email', value: 'archer@goodisis.com'},
  {id: 1003, field: 'dob', value: '01/22/1973'},
  {id: 1004, field: 'city', value: 'New York'},
  {id: 1005, field: 'occupation', value: 'Professional Troll'},
  {id: 1006, field: 'twitter', value: '@2cool4school'},
  {id: 1007, field: 'ssn', value: '111-22-3333'},
  {id: 1008, field: 'email', value: 'urmom@internet.com'},
  {id: 1009, field: 'pref', value: 'rememberme=false&colorscheme=dark'}
];

customerUpdates.forEach(function (update) {
  cargo.push(update, function () {
    console.log('done processing', update.id);
  });
});
```

The cargo object has the same event properties as the queue object, shown in Listing 15-21. The main difference is that the cargo's saturation limit is reached once a maximum number of payload items has been added, at which point the worker will commence.

Optional function handlers may be assigned to event properties as needed.

Listing 15-21. Cargo Events

```
// example-010/index-01.js
cargo.saturated = function () {
  console.log('cargo is saturated at ' + cargo.length());
};

cargo.empty = function () {
  console.log('cargo is empty; worker needs tasks');
};

cargo.drain = function () {
  console.log('cargo is drained; no more tasks to handle');
};
```

■ **Note** Both async.queue() and async.cargo() schedule the task function to run in the next immediate tick of the event loop. If items are added to a queue or cargo *synchronously*, one after the other, then the thresholds of each will be applied as expected; the queue will throttle the maximum number of workers, and the cargo will divide the maximum number of items to be processed. If items are added to each *asynchronously*, however—if items are added *after* the next immediate turn of the event loop—the task functions may be invoked at less than their maximum capacities.

The code in Listing 15-22 pulls each update out of the customerUpdates array and pushes it to the cargo, then schedules the next push to happen 500 milliseconds later, in a future turn of the event loop. Because cargo schedules its task immediately, the UPDATE query will run with one—maybe two—updates each time, depending on how long it takes for a task to finish and for the next task to be scheduled.

Listing 15-22. Adding Items to Cargo Asynchronously

```
// example-010/index-02.js
(function addUpdateAsync() {
  if (!customerUpdates.length) return;
  console.log('adding update');
  var update = customerUpdates.shift();
  cargo.push(update, function () {
    console.log('done processing', update.id);
  });
  setTimeout(addUpdateAsync, 500);
}());
```

To guarantee that the maximum thresholds are met for both queue and cargo, push items to each *synchronously*.

Summary

This chapter has covered a number of common synchronous control flows and demonstrated how Async.js can be used to adapt these patterns for asynchronous code. Table 15-1 shows each flow and the corresponding Async.js functions that were covered.

Table 15-1. *Flows and Corresponding Async.js Functions*

Flow	Async.js Function(s)
Sequential	`async.series()`
Parallel	`async.parallel()`
Pipeline	`async.waterfall()`, `async.seq()`
Loop	`async.whilst()`/`async.doWhilst()`, `async.until()`/`async.doUntil()`
	`async.retry()`, `async.forever()`
Batch	`async.queue()`, `async.cargo()`

Sequential and parallel flows allow developers to execute multiple independent tasks, then aggregate results as needed. Pipeline flows can be used to chain tasks together, where the output of each task becomes the input of a succeeding task. To repeat asynchronous tasks a given number of times, or according to some condition, looping flows may be used. Finally, batching flows are available to divide data into chunks to be processed asynchronously, one batch after the next.

By cleverly organizing asynchronous function tasks, coordinating the results of each task, and delivering errors and/or task results to a final callback, Async.js helps developers avoid nested callbacks and brings traditional synchronous control flow operations into the asynchronous world of JavaScript.

CHAPTER 16

■ ■ ■

Underscore and Lodash

You must be the kind of [person] who can get things done. But to get things done, you must love the doing, not the secondary consequences.

—Ayn Rand

JavaScript is a pragmatic utility language, useful in no small part because of its simple APIs and sparse type system. It is an easy language to learn and master because its surface area is so small. And while this characteristic lends itself nicely to productivity, sadly it means that JavaScript types have historically lacked advanced features that would make the language stronger, such as functional iteration constructs native to collections and hashes.

To fill this gap, Jeremy Ashkenas created a library in 2009 called Underscore.js, a collection of over 100 functions used to manipulate, filter, and transform hashes and collections. Many of these functions, such as `map()` and `reduce()`, embody concepts common to functional languages. Others, like `isArguments()` and `isUndefined()` are specific to JavaScript.

As the presence of Underscore became ubiquities in many web applications, two exciting things happened. First, the ECMAScript 5 specification was published in the same year. It features a number of Underscore-like methods on native JavaScript objects such as `Array.prototype.map()`, `Array.prototype. reduce()`, and `Array.isArray()`. While ECMAScript 5 (and to a lesser degree ECMAScript 6 and 7) expands the APIs of several key types, it only includes a fraction of the functionality that Underscore.js provides.

Second, Underscore was forked into a new project called Lodash with the goal of dramatically improving the performance and expanding its API. Since Lodash implements all of Underscore's functions while adding its own, Underscore is a subset of Lodash. All of the corresponding ECMAScript spec functions are part of Lodash as well. The table in Listing 16-1 shows Underscore and Lodash functions mapped to their native ECMAScript counterparts.

Table 16-1. *Underscore and Lodash Functions Compared to Current (and Proposed) Native JavaScript Implementations*

ECMAScript 5	Underscore/Lodash
Array.prototype.every()	all()/every()
Array.prototype.filter()	select()/filter()
Array.prototype.forEach()	each()/forEach()
Array.isArray()	isArray()
Object.keys()	keys()
Array.prototype.map()	map()
Array.prototype.reduce()	inject()/foldl()/reduce()
Array.prototype.reduceRight()	foldr()/reduceRight()
Array.prototype.some()	some()
ECMAScript 6	**Underscore/Lodash**
Array.prototype.find()	find()
Array.prototype.findIndex()	findIndex()
Array.prototype.keys()	keys()
ECMAScript 7	**Underscore/Lodash**
Array.prototype.contains()	include()/contains()

Because Underscore and Lodash share an API Lodash can be used as a drop-in replacement for Underscore. The inverse isn't necessarily the case, however, because of the extra functionality that Lodash supplies. For example, while both Underscore and Lodash have a clone() method, only Lodash implements a cloneDeep() method. Often developers choose Lodash over Underscore because of these extra features, but the performance benefit is tangible as well. According to a function-by-function performance benchmark, Lodash is 35% faster on average than Underscore. It achieves this performance gain by favoring simple loops over native delegation for functions like forEach(), map(), reduce(), and so forth.

This chapter focuses mostly on features of Underscore and Lodash *that are not already (or are scheduled to be) implemented in JavaScript* (the functions in Listing 16-1 and Listing 16-2). Mozilla's excellent documentation covers each of the native functions, and the Underscore and Lodash API documentation covers each of their implementations as well.

But Underscore and Lodash offer a great deal more than just a few handy functions for objects and collections, several of which will be explored in this chapter.

■ **Note**   For brevity, the remainder of this chapter simply refers to Underscore, but understand that, unless otherwise noted, Underscore and Lodash are interchangeable.

Installation and Usage

Underscore may be directly imported as a library in the web browser or any server-side JavaScript environment, such as Node.js. It has no external dependencies.

You can download the Underscore.js script directly from the Underscore website (http://underscorejs.org) or install it with a package manager like npm, Bower, or Component.

In the browser, you can include Underscore directly as a script, or load it with an AMD- or CommonJS-compatible module loader (such as RequireJS or Browserify). In Node.js the package is simply required as a CommonJS module.

Accessing the Underscore object (on which its utility functions live) depends on how the library is loaded. When Underscore is loaded in the browser with a `script` tag, the library will attach itself to `window._`. For variables created by module loaders in any environment, it is convention to assign the actual underscore character to the module, as shown in Listing 16-1.

Listing 16-1. Loading the Underscore Library in a Node.js Module

```
// example-001/index.js
'use strict';
var _ = require('underscore');

console.log(_.VERSION);
// 1.8.2
```

All Underscore functions live on the `_` ("underscore") object. Because Underscore is a utility library, it holds no state other than a handful of settings (but we'll cover more on that later in the chapter). All functions are *idempotent*, which means passing a value to any function multiple times will yield the same result each time. Once the Underscore object is loaded, it may be used immediately.

Underscore's utility functions operate mostly on collections (arrays and array-like objects, such as arguments), object literals, and functions. Underscore is most commonly used to filter and transform data. Many Underscore functions complement each other and can work together to create powerful combinations. Because this can be so useful, Underscore has built-in support for function chains that create terse pipelines that apply multiple transformations to data at once.

Aggregation and Indexing

Pieces of data in a collection often share similar schemas, yet have an identifying attribute that makes each unique. It can be helpful to distinguish these two types of relationships in a set of data—commonality and individuality—in order to quickly filter and work with a subset of objects that matches aggregation criteria.

Underscore has a number of functions that perform these tasks, but three specific functions can be tremendously beneficial when working with collections: `countBy()`, `groupBy()`, and `indexBy()`.

countBy()

Counting objects that share some characteristic is a common way to generalize data. Given a collection of URLs, one can imagine some analytic process that determines how many URLs belong to specific top-level domains (e.g., .com, .org, .edu, etc.). Underscore's `countBy()` function is an ideal candidate for this task. It invokes a callback on each element in an array to determines which category the element fits into (in this example, which top-level domain the URL occupies). The callback returns some string value that represents this category. The final result is an object with keys that represent all categories returned from the callback, and numeric counts representing the number of elements that fall into each category. Listing 16-2 shows a primitive implementation that yields an object with a count of two .org domains and one .com domain.

Listing 16-2. Counting Elements by Some Criteria

```
// example-002/index.js
'use strict';
var _ = require('underscore');

var urls = [
  'http://underscorejs.org',
  'http://lodash.com',
  'http://ecmascript.org'
];

var counts = _.countBy(urls, function byTLD(url) {
  if (url.indexOf('.com') >= 0) {
    return '.com';
  }
  if (url.indexOf('.org') >= 0) {
    return '.org';
  }
  return '?';
});

console.log(counts);
// { '.org': 2, '.com': 1 }
```

If the items in a collection are objects with properties, and the values for a specific property represent the data to be counted, an iterator function is not required. The name of the property to be tested may be used as a substitute. Note that in Listing 16-3 the keys in the final result will be the *values* for the property examined on each object.

Listing 16-3. Counting Elements by Some Property

```
// example-003/index.js
'use strict';
var _ = require('underscore');

var urls = [
  {scheme: 'http', host: 'underscorejs', domain: '.org'},
  {scheme: 'http', host: 'lodash', domain: '.com'},
  {scheme: 'http', host: 'ecmascript', domain: '.org'},
];

var counts = _.countBy(urls, 'domain');

console.log(counts);
// { '.org': 2, '.com': 1 }
```

If one or more objects in the collection lack the property to be tested, the final result object will contain an undefined key paired with the number of those objects as well.

groupBy()

Underscore's groupBy() function is similar to countBy(), but instead of reducing results to numeric counts, groupBy() places elements into categorized collections in the result object. The URL objects in Listing 16-4 are each placed into collections for each corresponding top-level domain.

Listing 16-4. Grouping Elements by Some Property

```
// example-004/index.js
'use strict';
var _ = require('underscore');

var urls = [
  {scheme: 'http', host: 'underscorejs', domain: '.org'},
  {scheme: 'http', host: 'lodash', domain: '.com'},
  {scheme: 'http', host: 'ecmascript', domain: '.org'},
];

var grouped = _.groupBy(urls, 'domain');

console.log(grouped);

/*
{
  '.org': [
    { scheme: 'http', host: 'underscorejs', domain: '.org' },
    { scheme: 'http', host: 'ecmascript', domain: '.org' }
  ],
  '.com': [
    { scheme: 'http', host: 'lodash', domain: '.com' }
  ]
}
*/
```

■ **Note**   The groupBy() function may also use an iterator function as its second argument (instead of a property name) if a greater degree of control is required to categorize elements.

It is worth mentioning that counts may easily be derived from grouped objects by simply querying the length of each grouped array. It may be advantageous, depending on application context, to prefer grouping over counting. Listing 16-5 shows how to get the count for a single set of grouped data, as well as a function for creating an object of counts from groupBy() results.

Listing 16-5. Deriving Counts from Grouped Objects

```
// example-005/index.js
'use strict';
var _ = require('underscore');

var urls = [
  {scheme: 'http', host: 'underscorejs', domain: '.org'},
  {scheme: 'http', host: 'lodash', domain: '.com'},
  {scheme: 'http', host: 'ecmascript', domain: '.org'},
];

var grouped = _.groupBy(urls, 'domain');
var dotOrgCount = grouped['.org'].length;
console.log(dotOrgCount);
// 2

function toCounts(grouped) {
  var counts = {};
  for (var key in grouped) {
    if (grouped.hasOwnProperty(key)) {
      counts[key] = grouped[key].length;
    }
  }
  return counts;
}

console.log(toCounts(grouped));
// { '.org': 2, '.com': 1 }
```

indexBy()

It can also be useful to identify differences amoung data in a collection, especially if those differences can serve as unique identifiers. Fishing a single object out of a collection by a known identifier is a pretty common scenario. Done manually, this would require looping over each element in the collection (perhaps with a while or for loop) and returning the first that possesses a matching unique identifier.

Imagine an airline website on which a customer selects departure and destination airports. The user chooses each airport via drop-down menus and is then shown additional data about each airport. This additional data is loaded from airport objects in an array. The values chosen in each drop-down menu are the unique airport codes, which are then used by the application to find the full, detailed airport objects.

Fortunately, the developer who created this application used Underscore's indexBy() function to create an index object from the airports array, shown in Listing 16-6.

Listing 16-6. Indexing Objects by Property

```
// example-006/index.js
'use strict';
var _ = require('underscore');

var airports = [
  {code: 'STL', city: 'St Louis', timeZone: '-6:00'},
  {code: 'SEA', city: 'Seattle', timeZone: '-8:00'},
  {code: 'JFK', city: 'New York', timeZone: '-5:00'}
];

var selected = 'SEA';

var indexed = _.indexBy(airports, 'code');
console.log(indexed);
/*
{
  STL: {code: 'STL', city: 'St Louis', timeZone: '-6:00'},
  SEA: {code: 'SEA', city: 'Seattle', timeZone: '-8:00'},
  JFK: {code: 'JFK', city: 'New York', timeZone: '-5:00'}
}
*/

var timeZone = indexed[selected].timeZone;
console.log(timeZone);
// -8:00
```

The indexBy() function behaves a bit like groupBy(), except that each object has a unique value for the indexed property, so the final result is an object whose keys (which must be unique) are the values of each object for a specified property, and whose values are the objects that posses each property. In Listing 16-6 the keys for the indexed object are each airport code, and the values are the corresponding airport objects.

Keeping an indexed object with relatively stable reference data in memory is a fundamental caching practice. It incurs a one-time performance penalty (the indexing process) to avoid multiple iteration penalties (having to traverse the array each time an object is needed).

Being Choosy

Developers often extract wanted data, or omit unwanted data, from collections and objects. This might be done for legibility (when data will be shown to a user), for performance (when data is to be sent over a network connection), for privacy (when data returned from an object or module's API should be sparse), or for some other purpose.

Selecting Data from Collections

Underscore has a number of utility functions that select one or more elements from a collection of objects based on some criteria. In some circumstances this criteria may be a function that evaluates each element and returns true or false (whether the element "passes" the criteria test). In other circumstances the criteria may be a bit of data that will be compared to each element (or a part of each element) for equality, the success or failure of which determines whether the element "matches" the criteria used.

filter()

The filter() function uses the criteria function approach. Given an array of elements and a function, filter() applies the function to each element and returns an array consisting only of elements that passed the criteria test. In Listing 16-7 an array of playing cards is filtered so that only spades are returned.

Listing 16-7. Filtering an Array with a Criteria Function

```
// example-007/index.js
'use strict';
var _ = require('underscore');

var cards = [
  {suite: 'Spades', denomination: 'King'},
  {suite: 'Hearts', denomination: '10'},
  {suite: 'Clubs', denomination: 'Ace'},
  {suite: 'Spades', denomination: 'Ace'},
];

var filtered = _.filter(cards, function (card) {
  return card.suite === 'Spades';
});

console.log(filtered);
/*
[
  { suite: 'Spades', denomination: 'King' },
  { suite: 'Spades', denomination: 'Ace' }
]
*/
```

where()

The where() function is similar to filter() but uses the comparison criteria approach instead. Its first argument is an array of objects, but its second argument is a criteria object whose keys and values will be compared to the keys and values of each element in the array. If an element contains all the keys and corresponding values in the criteria object (using strict equality), the element will be included in the array returned by where().

In Listing 16-8, a set of board game objects is filtered by an object that specifies a minimum player count and play time. *Pandemic* is excluded because it does not match the playTime value of the criteria object, though it does match the minPlayer value.

Listing 16-8. Filtering an Array by Criteria Comparison

```
// example-008/index.js
'use strict';
var _ = require('underscore');

var boardGames = [
  {title: 'Ticket to Ride', minPlayers: 2, playTime: 45},
  {title: 'Pandemic', minPlayers: 2, playTime: 60},
  {title: 'Munchkin Deluxe', minPlayers: 2, playTime: 45}
];
```

```
var filtered = _.where(boardGames, {
  minPlayers: 2,
  playTime: 45
});

console.log(filtered);
/*
[
  { title: 'Ticket to Ride', minPlayers: 2, playTime: 45 },
  { title: 'Munchkin Deluxe', minPlayers: 2, playTime: 45 }
]
*/
```

find() and findWhere()

The filter() and where() functions always return collections. If no object passes the criteria test each returns an empty set. A developer could use these functions to find an individual object within a set (e.g., by some unique identifier), but would then have to fish that object from the result array by using index zero. Fortunately, Underscore provides find() and findWhere() functions that complement filter() and where(). They each return the *first* object to pass the criteria check or return undefined if no objects in the set pass. In Listing 16-9 a collection is searched twice for specific entries. Note that even though multiple items would fulfill the {what: 'Dagger'} criteria object passed to findWhere(), only the first match in the collection is returned.

Listing 16-9. Finding a Single Item in a Collection

```
// example-009/index.js
'use strict';
var _ = require('underscore');

var guesses = [
  {who: 'Mrs. Peacock', where: 'Lounge', what: 'Revolver'},
  {who: 'Professor Plum', where: 'Study', what: 'Dagger'},
  {who: 'Miss Scarlet', where: 'Ballroom', what: 'Candlestick'},
  {who: 'Reverend Green', where: 'Conservatory', what: 'Dagger'}
];

var result = _.find(guesses, function (guess) {
  return guess.where === 'Ballroom';
});

console.log(result);
// { who: 'Miss Scarlet', where: 'Ballroom', what: 'Candlestick' }

result = _.findWhere(guesses, {what: 'Dagger'});

console.log(result);
// { who: 'Professor Plum', where: 'Study', what: 'Dagger' }
```

Selecting Data from Objects

The Underscore functions covered up to this point all filter larger collections into focused, smaller ones (or even a single object) when a portion of data is unnecessary to the application. Objects are also collections of data, indexed by string keys instead of ordered numbers; and like arrays, filtering data in individual objects can be quite useful.

pluck()

A developer could get a property's value from each object in a collection by looping over each element and capturing the desired property value in an array, or by using Array.prototype.map() (or Underscore's equivalent, map()). But a faster, more convenient option is to use Underscore's pluck() function, which takes an array as its first argument and the name of the property to lift from each element as its second. The pluck() function is used in Listing 16-10 to extract the numbers that landed face-up from a roll of three dice. These values are then summed (with Array.prototype.reduce()) to determine the total value of the roll.

Listing 16-10. Plucking Properties from Objects in a Collection

```
// example-010/index.js
'use strict';
var _ = require('underscore');

var diceRoll = [
  {sides: 6, up: 3},
  {sides: 6, up: 1},
  {sides: 6, up: 5}
];

var allUps = _.pluck(diceRoll, 'up');

console.log(allUps);
// [ 3, 1, 5 ]

var total = allUps.reduce(function (prev, next) {
  return prev + next;
}, 0);

console.log(total);
// 9
```

While pluck() is quite useful for selecting individual properties from objects, it only operates on collections and is not very useful for dealing with individual objects.

values()

The ECMAScript 5 specification introduced the keys() function on the Object constructor, a handy utility for turning the keys of any object literal into an array of strings. Underscore has a corresponding keys() implementation but *also* has a values() function that, sadly, has no counterpart in native JavaScript. The values() function is used to extract all property values from an object, and is arguably most *valu*able (dad joke) for objects that hold a collection of "constants," or serve as an enumeration would in another language. Listing 16-11 demonstrates how this extraction takes place.

Listing 16-11. Extracting Values from an Object Literal

```
// example-011/index.js
'use strict';
var _ = require('underscore');

var BOARD_TILES = {
  IND_AVE: 'Indiana Avenue',
  BOARDWALK: 'Boardwalk',
  MARV_GARD: 'Marvin Gardens',
  PK_PLACE: 'Park Place'
};

var propertyNames = _.values(BOARD_TILES);

console.log(propertyNames);
// [ 'Indiana Avenue', 'Boardwalk', 'Marvin Gardens', 'Park Place' ]
```

Reference data (e.g., a hash of US state abbreviations and names) is often retrieved and cached all at once. This data will typically be dereferenced by key so that some particular value can be extracted, but sometimes it is useful to work with all values regardless of key, as the Underscore template in Listing 16-12 demonstrates. (Underscore templates will be discussed later in this chapter, but Listing 16-12 should give you enough to grasp basic usage.) Each value in the BOARD_TILES hash (the tile name) is rendered as a list item in an unordered list. The keys are inconsequential; only the values matter, a perfect scenario for the values() function.

Listing 16-12. Extracting Values from an Object Literal

```
<!-- example-011/index.html -->

<div id="output"></div>

<script id="tiles-template" type="text/x-template">
<ul class="properties">
  <% _.each(_.values(tiles), function (property) { %>
  <li><%- property %></li>
  <% }); %>
</ul>
</script>

<script>
(function (_) {
  var template = document.querySelector('#tiles-template').innerHTML;
  var bindTemplate = _.template(template);
  var BOARD_TILES = {
    IND_AVE: 'Indiana Avenue',
    BOARDWALK: 'Boardwalk',
    MARV_GARD: 'Marvin Gardens',
    PK_PLACE: 'Park Place'
  };
  var markup = bindTemplate({tiles: BOARD_TILES});
  document.querySelector('#output').innerHTML = markup;
}(window._));
</script>
```

pick()

Finally, to whittle an object down to a subset of its keys and values, developers can use Underscore's pick() function. When passing in a target object and one or more property names, pick() will return another object composed solely of those properties (and their values) from the target. In Listing 16-13 the name and numPlayers properties are extracted from a larger hash of board game details with pick().

Listing 16-13. Picking Properties from an Object Literal

```
// example-012/index.js
'use strict';
var _ = require('underscore');

var boardGame = {
  name: 'Settlers of Catan',
  designer: 'Klaus Teuber',
  numPlayers: [3, 4],
  yearPublished: 1995,
  ages: '10+',
  playTime: '90min',
  subdomain: ['Family', 'Strategy'],
  category: ['Civilization', 'Negotiation'],
  website: 'http://www.catan.com'
};

var picked = _.pick(boardGame, 'name', 'numPlayers');

console.log(picked);
/*
{
  name: 'Settlers of Catan',
  numPlayers: [ 3, 4 ]
}
*/
```

omit()

The inverse of pick() is omit(), which returns an object composed of all properties *except* the ones specified. The properties designer, numPlayers, yearPublished, ages, and playTime are all eliminated from the result object created by omit() in Listing 16-14.

Listing 16-14. Omitting Properties from an Object Literal

```
// example-013/index.js
'use strict';
var _ = require('underscore');

var boardGame = {
  name: 'Settlers of Catan',
  designer: 'Klaus Teuber',
  numPlayers: [3, 4],
```

```
  yearPublished: 1995,
  ages: '10+',
  playTime: '90min',
  subdomain: ['Family', 'Strategy'],
  category: ['Civilization', 'Negotiation'],
  website: 'http://www.catan.com'
};

var omitted = _.omit(boardGame, 'designer', 'numPlayers',
  'yearPublished', 'ages', 'playTime');

console.log(omitted);
/*
{
  name: 'Settlers of Catan',
  subdomain: [ 'Family', 'Strategy' ],
  category: [ 'Civilization', 'Negotiation' ],
  website: 'http://www.catan.com'
}
*/
```

In addition to property names, both pick() and omit() accept a predicate that will evaluate each property and value instead. If the predicate returns true, the property will be included in the resulting object; if it returns false, the property will be excluded. The predicate for pick() in listing 16-15 will only add properties to the result object for values that are arrays; in this case, the properties numPlayers, subdomain, and category.

Listing 16-15. Picking Properties from an Object Literal with a Predicate Function

```
// example-014/index.js
'use strict';
var _ = require('underscore');

var boardGame = {
  name: 'Settlers of Catan',
  designer: 'Klaus Teuber',
  numPlayers: [3, 4],
  yearPublished: 1995,
  ages: '10+',
  playTime: '90min',
  subdomain: ['Family', 'Strategy'],
  category: ['Civilization', 'Negotiation'],
  website: 'http://www.catan.com'
};

var picked = _.pick(boardGame, function (value, key, object) {
  return Array.isArray(value);
});
```

```
console.log(picked);
/*
{
  numPlayers: [ 3, 4 ],
  subdomain: [ 'Family', 'Strategy' ],
  category: [ 'Civilization', 'Negotiation' ]
}
*/
```

Chaining

Underscore contains a number of utility functions that are frequently used together to create transformation pipelines for data. To begin a chain, an object or collection is passed to Underscore's chain() function. This returns a chain wrapper on which many Underscore functions may be called in a fluent manner, each compounding the effects of the preceding function call.

Listing 16-16 shows an array of coffee shops and the hours during which each is open. The whatIsOpen() function accepts a numeric hour and a period ('AM' or 'PM'). These are then used to evaluate the coffee shops in the collection and return the names of the coffee shops that are open during that time.

Listing 16-16. Chaining Functions on a Collection

```
// example-015/index.js
'use strict';
var _ = require('lodash');

/*
Note that lodash, not underscore, is used for
this example. The cloneDeep() function below
is unique to lodash.
*/

var coffeeShops = [
  {name: 'Crooked Tree', hours: [6, 22]},
  {name: 'Picasso\'s Coffee House', hours: [6, 24]},
  {name: 'Sump Coffee', hours: [9, 16]}
];

function whatIsOpen(hour, period) {
  return _.chain(coffeeShops)
    .cloneDeep()                            // #1
    .map(function to12HourFormat (shop) {   // #2
      shop.hours = _.map(shop.hours, function (hour) {
        return (hour > 12 ? hour - 12 : hour);
      }
      return shop;
    })
    .filter(function filterByHour (shop) { // #3
      if (period === 'AM') {
        return shop.hours[0] <= hour;
      }
```

```
    if (period === 'PM') {
      return shop.hours[1] >= hour;
    }
    return false;
  })
  .map(function toShopName (shop) {        // #4
    return shop.name;
  })
  .value();                                // #5
}

console.log(whatIsOpen(8, 'AM'));
// [ 'Crooked Tree', 'Picasso\'s Coffee House' ]

console.log(whatIsOpen(11, 'PM'));
// [ 'Picasso\'s Coffee House' ]
```

After chain() wraps the coffeeShops array in a fluent API, the following functions are called to manipulate and filter the collection until the desired data has been produced.

1. cloneDeep() recursively clones the array and all objects and their properties. In step 2 the array data is actually modified, so the array is cloned to preserve its original state.

2. map(function to12HourFormat() {/*...*/}) iterates over each item in the cloned array and replaces the second 24-hour number in the hours array with its 12-hour equivalent.

3. filter(function filterByHour() {/*...*/}) iterates over each modified coffee shop and evaluates its hours based on the period ('AM' or 'PM') specified: the first element for the opening hour and the second for the closing hour. The function returns true or false to indicate whether the coffee shop should be retained or dropped from the results.

4. map(function toShopName() {/*...*/}) returns the name of each remaining coffee shop in the collection. The result is an array of strings that will be passed to any subsequent steps in the chain.

5. Finally, value() is called to terminate the chain and return the final result: the array of names of coffee shops that are open during the hour and period provided to whatIsOpen() (or an empty array if none match the criteria).

This may seem like a lot to grasp, but Underscore chains can be reduced to a few simple principles that are easy to remember:

- Chains can be created with any initial value, though *object* and *array* are the most typical starting points.

- Any Underscore function that operates on a value is available as a chained function.

- The return value of a chained function becomes the input value of the next function in the chain.

- The first argument of a chained function is always the value on which it operates. For example, Underscore's map() function normally accepts two arguments, a collection and a callback, but when invoked as a chained function, it only accepts a callback. This pattern holds for all chained functions.

- Always invoke the value() function to terminate a chain and retrieve its final, manipulated value. If a chain does not return a value, this is unnecessary.

Chaining functions for a collection or object might seem natural and obvious, but Underscore also has a number of functions that work on primitives. Listing 16-17 shows how a chain can wrap the number 100 to eventually generate the lyrics to "99 Bottles of Beer."

Listing 16-17. Chaining Functions on a Primitive

```
// example-016/index.js
'use strict';
var _ = require('underscore');

_.chain(100)
  .times(function makeLyrics (number) {
    if (number === 0) {
      return '';
    }
    return [
      number + ' bottles of beer on the wall!',
      number + ' bottles of beer!',
      'Take one down, pass it around!',
      (number - 1) + ' bottles of beer on the wall!',
      '♫ ♪ ♫ ♪ ♫ ♪ ♫ ♪ ♫ ♪ ♫',
    ].join('\n');
  })
  .tap(function orderLyrics (lyrics) {
    // reverse the array so the song is in order
    lyrics.reverse();
  })
  .map(function makeLoud (lyric) {
    return lyric.toUpperCase();
  })
  .forEach(function printLyrics (lyric) {
    console.log(lyric);
  });
```

The times() function takes a number as its first argument and a callback to be invoked for each decremented value of that number. In this example, the callback makeLyrics() will be invoked starting with the number 99 (not 100) and ending with the number 0, for 100 total iterations. For each invocation, one refrain of "99 Bottles" is returned. This creates an array of strings, which is then passed to the next function in the chain.

Because the final chained function forEach() creates side effects instead of returning a value, there is no need to terminate the chain by calling value(). Instead, Listing 16-18 shows the results that are printed to the console.

Listing 16-18. The Song to Ruin All Road Trips

```
99 BOTTLES OF BEER ON THE WALL!
99 BOTTLES OF BEER!
TAKE ONE DOWN, PASS IT AROUND!
98 BOTTLES OF BEER ON THE WALL!
♫ ♪ ♫ ♪ ♫ ♪ ♫ ♪ ♫ ♪ ♫
98 BOTTLES OF BEER ON THE WALL!
98 BOTTLES OF BEER!
TAKE ONE DOWN, PASS IT AROUND!
97 BOTTLES OF BEER ON THE WALL!
♫ ♪ ♫ ♪ ♫ ♪ ♫ ♪ ♫ ♪ ♫
          ...
```

Function Timing

Functions execute when they are scheduled on JavaScript's internal event loop. Native functions like `setTimeout()`, `setInterval()`, and Node's `setImmediate()` give developers a degree of control over when these functions run—which turn of the event loop will handle their invocations. Underscore augments these primitives with a number of control functions that add flexibility to function scheduling.

defer()

Underscore's `defer()` function mimics the behavior of `setImmediate()` in a Node.js environment; which is to say, `defer()` schedules a function to execute on the next immediate turn of the event loop. This is equivalent to using `setTimeout()` with a delay of 0. Since `setImmediate()` is not a JavaScript standard function, using Underscore's `defer()` in both browser and server environments can provide a greater degree of consistency than poly-filling `setImmediate()` in the browser.

The example code in Listing 16-19 demonstrates the value of `defer()` in a user interface. It loads a large data set of playing card information for the popular card game *Dominion*, then populates an HTML table with card details.

While the data is fetched from the server and then processed, the user sees the message, "Please be patient while cards are loading!" Once the GET request has completed, the `processCards()` handler begins to process almost 200 cards in blocks of 10. For each block (except the first), the handler *defers* processing, which has two beneficial effects. First, it allows the UI time to paint the previous 10 processed rows in the table, and second, it allows the user to scroll in between window paints. Because the block size is so small, the scroll speed is relatively normal for the user. If `processCards()` attempted to render all table rows at once, the UI would freeze until all DOM elements had been added to the table.

Listing 16-19. Deferring a Function

```
<!-- example-017/views/defer.html -->
<p id="wait-msg">Please be patient while cards are loading!</p>
<table id="cards">
  <thead>
    <tr>
      <th>Name</th>
      <th>Expansion</th>
      <th>Cost</th>
```

```
    <th>Benefit</th>
    <th>Description</th>
  </tr>
</thead>
<tbody></tbody>
</table>

<script>
$(function () {
  var $waitMsg = $('#wait-msg');
  var $cards = $('#cards tbody');

  function processCards(cards) {
    var BLOCK_SIZE = 10;

    // process the first chunk of 10 cards
    (function processBlock() {
      if (!cards.length) {
        $waitMsg.addClass('hidden');
        return;
      }

      // take the first 10 cards from the array;
      // splice() will reduce the length of the array
      // by 10 each time
      var block = cards.splice(0, BLOCK_SIZE);

      _.forEach(block, function (card) {
        var $tr = $('<tr></tr>');
        $tr.append($('<td></td>').html(card.name));
        $tr.append($('<td></td>').html(card.expansion));
        $tr.append($('<td></td>').html(card.cost));
        $tr.append($('<td></td>').html(card.benefits.join(', ')));
        $tr.append($('<td></td>').html(card.description));
        $cards.append($tr);
      });

      // defer the next block of 10 cards to
      // allow the user to scroll and the UI to
      // refresh
      _.defer(processBlock);
    }());

  }

  // kick off the process by loading the data set
  $.get('/cards').then(processCards);
}());
</script>
```

debounce()

"Debouncing" is the practice of ignoring duplicate invocations, requests, messages, and so forth in a system for some period of time. In JavaScript, debouncing a function can be very helpful if a developer anticipates that duplicate, identical function calls may be made in quick succession. A common scenario for a debounced function, for example, is preventing a form's submit handler from being called more than once when a user accidentally clicks a Submit button multiple times on a web page.

A custom debounce implementation would require a developer to track the invocations of a function over a short period of time (perhaps only hundreds of milliseconds) using setTimeout() and clearTimeout() for each duplicate invocation. Fortunately, Underscore provides a debounce() function that handles this plumbing for developers, as demonstrated in Listing 16-20.

Listing 16-20. Debouncing a Function

```
<!-- example-018/debounce.html -->
<button id="submit">Quickly Click Me Many Times!</button>
<script>
(function () {
  var onClick = _.debounce(function (e) {
    alert('click handled!');
  }, 300);

  document.getElementById('submit')
    .addEventListener('click', onClick);
}());
</script>
```

In Listing 16-20 an onClick() function is created by invoking debounce(). The first argument to debounce() is the function that will actually be run once all duplicate invocations have stopped. The second argument is a duration, in milliseconds, that must elapse between invocations for the callback to finally be triggered. For example, if a user clicks the #submit button once, and then clicks it again within the 300-millisecond time span, the first invocation is ignored and the wait timer is restarted. Once the wait period has timed out, the debounce() callback will be invoked, alerting the user that the click has been handled.

■ **Note** Each time a debounced function is invoked, its internal timer is reset. The specified time span represents the minimum time that must pass between the last invocation and its preceding invocation (if any) before the callback function executes.

In Figure 16-1, a debounced function with a timeout of 300ms is called three times. After the first call at point A, 250ms elapse, at which point another call happens at point B and the wait timer is reset. The interval between B and the next call, C, is shorter: 100ms. Again, the wait timer resets. At point C a third call is made, after which the wait duration of 300ms is met. At point D the debounced function's callback is invoked.

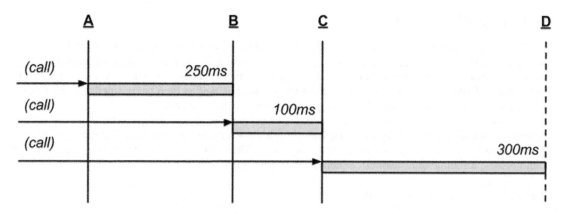

Figure 16-1. *A debounced function invoked multiple times*

The debounced function's callback will receive any arguments passed to the debounce() function itself. For example, in Listing 16-20, jQuery's event object e is forwarded to the debounced function's callback. While each invocation may pass different arguments, it is important to realize that *only the arguments passed during the last invocation within the wait period* will actually be forwarded to the callback. The debounce() function receives an optional third, immediate parameter which may be true or false. Setting this parameter to true will invoke the callback for the *first* invocation instead, ignoring all subsequent duplicates for the wait period. If the arguments passed to the debounced function vary, capturing the first parameters passed instead of the last might be strategically beneficial.

throttle()

Underscore's throttle() function is similar to debounce(). It ignores subsequent invocations of a function for a specified period of time, but does *not* reset its internal timer with each function call. It effectively ensures that only one invocation happens *during* a specified period, whereas debounce() guarantees that only one invocation will happen sometime *after* the last invocation of a debounced function. Throttling a function can be particularly useful if a function is likely to be called many times with the same arguments, or when the granularity of the arguments is such that it is not useful to account for every invocation of the function.

The in-memory JavaScript message bus, postal.js, is a useful library for routing messages through an application. Some application modules send messages at a frequency that might not be useful for humnan consumption, so any function that displays these messages to a user might be a good candidate for throttling.

The code in Listing 16-21 demonstrates a simplified version of this scenario. Don't worry about understanding the postal.js API entirely—it is sufficient to understand that postal.publish() will place a message onto the bus, and postal.subscribe() will invoke a callback when that message is received. In this example a message is published once every 100ms. The callback attached to the subscription, however, is throttled at 500ms. So, with a little padding for timing inconsistencies (the JavaScript event loop timer has low precision), the UI will display roughly 20 or 21 updates even though 100 updates have been placed on the message bus (roughly 1 in 5 messages will be displayed).

Listing 16-21. Using a Throttled Function to Control Status Updates

```html
<!-- example-019/throttle.html -->
<section id="friends"></section>

<script>
$(function () {

  var $friends = $('#friends');

  function onStatusUpdate(data) {
    var text = data.name + ' is ' + data.status;
    $friends.append($('<p></p>').html(text));
  }

  /*
   * subscribing to status updates from friends
   * with a throttled callback that will only
   * fire *once* every 500ms
   */
  postal.subscribe({
    channel: 'friends',
    topic: 'status.update',
    callback: _.throttle(onStatusUpdate, 500)
  });

}());
</script>

<script>
  $(function () {
    var i = 1;
    var interval = null;

    /*
     * publishing a status update from a
     * friend every 100ms
     */
    function sendMessage() {
      if (i === 100) {
        return clearInterval(interval);
      }
      i += 1;
      postal.publish({
        channel: 'friends',
        topic: 'status.update',
```

```
      data: {
        name: 'Jim',
        status: 'slinging code'
      }
    });
  }

  setInterval(sendMessage, 100);
}());
</script>
```

Figure 16-2 illustrates how `throttle()` differs from `defer()`. Once a throttled function is invoked at point A, it will ignore all further invocations (at points B and C) until its wait duration has passed—in this case, 300ms. Once elapsed, the next call at point D will invoke the throttled function.

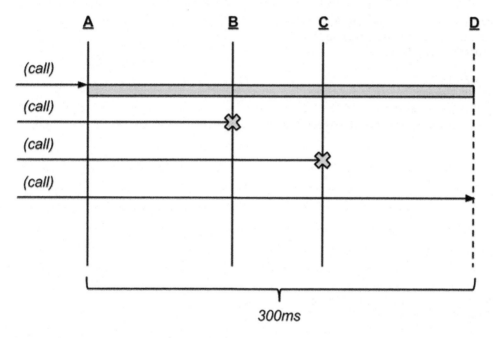

Figure 16-2. *A throttled function invoked multiple times*

Templates

Underscore offers a micro-templating system that compiles a template string (typically HTML) into a function. When this function is invoked with some data, it uses the template string's binding expressions to populate the template, returning a new HTML string. Developers who have used templating tools like Mustache or Handlebars will be familiar with this process. Unlike these more robust templating libraries, however, Underscore's templates have a much smaller feature set and no real template extension points. Underscore can be a strong choice as a template library when the templates in an application are fairly trivial and you have no desire or need to incur the overhead of a template-specific library in an application.

Template systems usually begin with some markup, and Underscore is no exception. Data binding expressions are added to a template with "gator tags" (so named because the opening and closing elements, <% and %>, look kind of like alligators). Listing 16-22 shows a simple block of HTML that will later be bound to an object literal containing two properties, title and synopsis.

Listing 16-22. Template with "Gator Tags"

```
<h1><%- title %></h1>
<p class="synopsis"><%- synopsis %></p>
```

Gator tags come in three varieties. The tags used in Listing 16-22 generate safe HTML output by escaping any HTML tag sequences. If the movie synopsis contained an HTML tag such as <strong>, it would be converted to <strong>. In contrast, the gator tag <%= may be used to output unescaped strings with HTML markup in-tact. The third gator tag is the JavaScript evaluation tag, and it simply begins with <% (more on this tag will be covered in a bit). All gator tags share the same closing tag, %>.

To turn the HTML in Listing 16-22 into a populated template the HTML string is first compiled by passing it to Underscore's template() function. A reusable binding function is returned. When a data object is passed to this binding function, any properties that match the binding expressions in the original template string will be substituted in the final, computed output. Under the hood Underscore uses JavaScript's with keyword to magically bring these properties into the template's scope. Listing 16-23 demonstrates how to bind a simple template string to a data object, and shows the HTML that is produced as a result.

Listing 16-23. Binding an Underscore Template

```
<!-- example-020/index.html -->
<div id="output"></div>

<script>
(function (_) {
  var markup =
    '<h1><%- title %></h1>' +
    '<p class="synopsis"><%- synopsis %></p>';

  // compile the string into a function
  var compiledTemplate = _.template(markup);

  // invoke the function with data to
  // get the rendered string
  var rendered = compiledTemplate({
    title: 'Sunshine',
    synopsis: 'A team of scientists are sent to re-ignite a dying sun.'
  });

  document.querySelector('#output').innerHTML = rendered;

}(window._));
</script>
<div id="output">
  <h1>Sunshine</h1>
  <p class="synopsis">A team of scientists are sent to re-ignite a dying sun.</p>
</div>
```

Once a template string is compiled to a function it may be invoked any number of times with different data to produce different rendered markup. It is common for applications to compile template strings into functions during page load (or during application startup, if Node.js is the runtime environment), then call each as needed during the lifetime of the application. If template strings do not change, there is no need to recompile them.

Loops and Other Arbitrary JavaScript in Templates

Many templating libraries include shorthand tags for common templating chores like iterating over a collection. To keep its templating system thin, Underscore forgoes syntactical sugar and, instead, allows developers to write template loops in plain, valid JavaScript.

In Listing 16-24 an unordered list of actors is created by using Underscore's each() function within the template. There are two important things to note here. First, plain JavaScript is evaluated within gator tag code blocks. These blocks are created by using gator tags *without* a hyphen symbol in the opening tag (e.g., <% %> instead of <%- %>). Second, the each() loop is split in the middle, where valid templating markup is used to render the actor variable, created by the loop itself, in a list item element. Finally, the loop is terminated by a closing brace, parenthesis, and semicolon, as if it were a normal JavaScript loop.

Listing 16-24. Looping in a Template

```
<!-- example-021/index.html -->
<div id="output"></div>

<script>
(function (_) {
  var markup =
    '<h1><%- title %></h1>' +
    '<p class="synopsis"><%- synopsis %></p>' +
    '<ul>' +
    '<% _.each(actors, function (actor) { %>' +
    ' <li><%- actor %></li>' +
    '<% }); %>' +
    '</ul>';

  // compile the string into a function
  var compiledTemplate = _.template(markup);

  // invoke the function with data to
  // get the rendered string
  var rendered = compiledTemplate({
    title: 'Sunshine',
    synopsis: 'A team of scientists are sent to re-ignite a dying sun.',
    actors: ['Cillian Murphy', 'Hiroyuki Sanada', 'Chris Evans']
  });

  document.querySelector('#output').innerHTML = rendered;
```

```
}(window._));
</script>
<div id="output">
  <h1>Sunshine</h1>
  <p class="synopsis">A team of scientists are sent to re-ignite a dying sun.</p>
  <ul>
    <li>Cillian Murphy</li>
    <li>Hiroyuki Sanada</li>
    <li>Chris Evans</li>
  </ul>
</div>
```

JavaScript evaluation tags can also be used to execute arbitrary JavaScript code. The template in Listing 16-25 calculates a rating percentage for the movie based on X out of Y stars awarded to it by critics. The template uses Underscore's internal print() function to render the result of the calculation in the template output, an alternative to gator tag interpolation that is sometimes used in more complex expressions.

Listing 16-25. Arbitrary JavaScript Within a Template

```
<!-- example-022/index.html -->
<div id="output"></div>

<script>
(function (_) {
  var markup =
    '<p>' +
    '<%- voted %> out of <%- total %> stars!' +
    ' (<% print((voted / total * 100).toFixed(0)) %>%)' +
    '</p>';

  var compiledTemplate = _.template(markup);

  var rendered = compiledTemplate({
    voted: 4, total: 5
  });

  document.querySelector('#output').innerHTML = rendered;

}(window._));
</script>
<div id="output">
  <p>4 out of 5 stars! (80%)</p>
</div>
```

■ **Note**   Generally it is bad practice to perform calculations in a template (the application's "view"). Instead, the actual calculated value should be part of the data passed to the compiled template function. Listing 16-25 should be considered for demonstration purposes only.

Living Without Gator Tags

Gator tags can be a bit unruly in nontrivial templates. Fortunately, Underscore allows developers to change the syntax of template tags with regular expressions. Setting the `templateSettings` property on the Underscore object to a hash of key/value settings alters the behavior of Underscore for the lifetime of your page (or Node.js process), and affects all rendered templates.

Listing 16-26 shows how to change Underscore's gator tag syntax into a more terse Mustache/Handlebars syntax. In this case, the three different types of tags (evaluation, interpolation, and escaped interpolation) are each assigned a regular expression on the global settings object.

Listing 16-26. Changing Template Syntax

```
<!-- example-023/index.html -->
<div id="output"></div>

<script>
(function (_) {
  _.templateSettings = {
    // arbitrary JavaScript code blocks: {{ }}
    evaluate: /\{\{(.+?)\}\}/g,
    // unsafe string interpolation: {{= }}
    interpolate: /\{\{=(.+?)\}\}/g,
    // escaped string interpolation: {{- }}
    escape: /\{\{-(.+?)\}\}/g
  };

  var markup =
    '<h1>{{- title }}</h1>' +
    '<p class="synopsis">{{- synopsis }}</p>' +
    '<ul>' +
    '{{ _.each(actors, function (actor) { }}' +
    '  <li>{{- actor }}</li>' +
    '{{ }); }}' +
    '</ul>';

  var compiledTemplate = _.template(markup);

  var rendered = compiledTemplate({
    title: 'Sunshine',
    synopsis: 'A team of scientists are sent to re-ignite a dying sun.',
    actors: ['Cillian Murphy', 'Hiroyuki Sanada', 'Chris Evans']
  });

  document.querySelector('#output').innerHTML = rendered;

}(window._));
</script>
```

Any markup compiled by the template system must now support the specified Mustache syntax. Templates that still contain gator tags will not be rendered correctly.

Table 16-2 is a convenient reference for matching template settings to syntax and the regular expressions that enable each syntax.

Table 16-2. *Global Template Settings*

Setting	Template Syntax	Regular Expression
evaluate	{{ ... }}	/{{(.+?)}}/g
interpolate	{{= ... }}	/{{=(.+?)}}/g
escape	{{- ... }}	/{{-(.+?)}}/g

Accessing the Data Object Within a Template

As mentioned, Underscore uses JavaScript's with keyword to evaluate a data object's properties in a template's scope as "first class" variables. But the object itself may also be referenced through the obj property in the template. To modify a previous example, in Listing 16-27 the template tests for the data property obj.percent in an if/else block before attempting to calculate a percentage. If the percent property exists on the data object, it is rendered; otherwise the calculated value is rendered.

Listing 16-27. The "obj" Variable

```
<!-- example-024/index.html -->
<div id="output"></div>

<script>
(function (_) {
  var markup =
    '<%- voted %> out of <%- total %> stars!' +
    '<% if (obj.percent) { %>' +
    ' (<%- obj.percent %>%)' +
    '<% } else { %>' +
    ' (<% print((voted / total * 100).toFixed(0)) %>%)' +
    '<% } %>';

  var compiledTemplate = _.template(markup);

  var rendered = compiledTemplate({
    voted: 4, total: 5, percent: 80.2
  });

  document.querySelector('#output').innerHTML = rendered;

}(window._));
</script>
```

As a micro-optimization (and perhaps a security feature), the scoped object can be given a name so that the with keyword is avoided altogether. This makes the templating function run slightly faster, but also requires that *all* properties in the template be referenced as properties of the named data object. To specify a name for the data object, an options object may be passed to Underscore's template() function when compiling the template. This object's variable property will assign the data object's variable name, which may then be referred to in the template. Listing 16-28 shows this setting in action.

Listing 16-28. Setting the Data Object's Variable Name

```
<!-- example-025/index.html -->
<div id="output"></div>

<script>
(function (_) {
  var markup =
    '<%- movie.voted %> out of <%- movie.total %> stars!' +
    '<% if (movie.percent) { %>' +
    ' (<%- movie.percent %>%)' +
    '<% } else { %>' +
    ' (<% print((movie.voted / movie.total * 100).toFixed(0)) %>%)' +
    '<% } %>';

  var settings = {variable: 'movie'};
  // settings is the *third* parameter
  var compiledTemplate = _.template(markup, null, settings);

  var rendered = compiledTemplate({
    voted: 4, total: 5, percent: 80.1
  });

  document.querySelector('#output').innerHTML = rendered;

}(window._));
</script>
```

■ **Note**   The `variable` property may be set in Underscore's global settings. However, giving variables good and relevant names is important, so it makes more sense to name a variable according to its context. Instead of defining some generic variable like `data` or `item`, the examples in this section use the variable name `movie` and apply it by passing a settings object to `template()` when the movie template is compiled.

Default Template Data

While not part of its templating system, Underscore's `defaults()` function can be used to ensure that a template always has default data. This will prevent binding failures in the event that a data object is missing one or more referenced properties. The first parameter to the `defaults()` function is an object with potentially missing properties. Any following arguments may be objects with properties set to default values, which will fill in any missing properties on the first object. The return value is an object that represents the "merged" properties of all arguments. Listing 16-29 shows this effect on a `data` object that is missing its `synopsis` property. When the `data` and `DEFAULTS` objects are passed to the `defaults()` function, the returned object contains the title from `data` and the synopsis from `DEFAULTS`.

Listing 16-29. Default Template Values

```
<!-- example-026/index.html -->
<div id="output"></div>

<script>
(function (_) {
  var markup =
    '<h1><%- title %></h1>' +
    '<p class="synopsis"><%- synopsis %></p>';

  // compile the string into a function
  var compiledTemplate = _.template(markup);

  var DEFAULTS = {
    title: 'A Great Film',
    synopsis: 'An epic hero defeats and evil villain and saves the world!'
  };

  var data = {
    title: 'Lord of the Rings'
  };

  // fill in any missing data values with defaults
  var merged = _.defaults(data, DEFAULTS);

  var rendered = compiledTemplate(merged);

  document.querySelector('#output').innerHTML = rendered;

}(window._));
</script>
```

If multiple default objects are passed to defaults(), they are evaluated from first to last. Once a missing property is found on a default object, it will be ignored on any following default objects.

Summary

Modern and future implementations of ECMAScript have given developers a great many utility functions on primitive types like String, Array, Object, and Function. Unfortunately, the world moves faster than specifications come to fruition so libraries like Underscore and Lodash occupy the intersection of developer needs and language maturity.

With over 100 utility functions and a micro-templating system, Underscore enables developers to manipulate, transform, and render data in objects and collections. Underscore can be used in browser and server environments and has no dependencies. It can be added to a web page with a simple `script` tag or imported as an AMD or CommonJS module. Popular package managers like Bower, npm, component, and NuGet can all download prebuilt Underscore packages for a developer's platform of choice.

Underscore's strong feature set and ubiquitous availability make it an ideal and unobtrusive Swiss Army knife for JavaScript projects.

Related Resources

- Underscore: `http://underscorejs.org/`
- Loadash: `https://lodash.com/`

Index

K

■ V, W, X

■ Y, Z

Get the eBook for only $5!

Why limit yourself?

Now you can take the weightless companion with you wherever you go and access your content on your PC, phone, tablet, or reader.

Since you've purchased this print book, we're happy to offer you the eBook in all 3 formats for just $5.

Convenient and fully searchable, the PDF version enables you to easily find and copy code—or perform examples by quickly toggling between instructions and applications. The MOBI format is ideal for your Kindle, while the ePUB can be utilized on a variety of mobile devices.

To learn more, go to www.apress.com/companion or contact support@apress.com.

CPSIA information can be obtained
at www.ICGtesting.com
Printed in the USA
LVOW05s1611020317

525955LV00006B/103/P

9 781484 206638